GOLDEN GLORY

GOLDEN GLORY

The History of Central City Basketball

TOM WALLACE

Acclaim Press
MORLEY, MISSOURI

AP™
Acclaim Press
— *Your Next Great Book* —
P.O. Box 238
Morley, MO 63767
(573) 472-9800
www.acclaimpress.com

Book Design: Devon Burroughs
Cover Design: M. Frene Melton
Cover photo: Greg Lamb

Library of Congress Control Number: 2014922909
ISBN-13: 978-1-938905-92-6
ISBN-10: 1-938905-92-X

First Printing 2015
Printed in the United States of America
10 9 8 7 6 5 4 3 2 1

This publication was produced using available information.
The publisher regrets it cannot assume responsibility for errors or omissions.

Contents

Dedication

This book is dedicated to all the former Golden Tide players, coaches and team managers who stood in dozens of dank, stinking dressing rooms and spoke the words "all for one and one for all."

T. W.

Acknowledgments

Researching and writing this book about Central City High School's basketball history was a true labor of love. OK, there were times when it was all labor, but even then, what always kept me going was the understanding that this was *my* school, and to give anything less than total effort was not acceptable.

Golden Tide basketball was the best, so it deserved nothing but the best.

Although a book such as this might have only a single author, there are dozens of people whose contributions made it possible. While space limits me from naming them all, there are a few that I have to acknowledge for the help and guidance they provided.

First, thanks to Freddie Mayes and Nancy Williams for getting this project off the ground. Their support was invaluable. And thanks to fellow scribe Gary West for mentioning me for this gig.

Mark Stone and Richard Deavers gave me access to old *Times-Argus* articles and photos, along with their vast knowledge of Golden Tide history. They also caught miscues on my part, and they pointed out some things I missed. Their help made this a better and more accurate book.

Jowanna Bandy allowed me to go through old *Leader-News* archives, which proved to be very helpful. A big thank-you goes out to Coni Wallace and Janet Harris at the Greenville Library, where I spent hours and hours doing research. They were always helpful and generous.

Grant Sparks, Mary and Jackie Day, Ralph Dillihay, Corky Withrow, Marion Tinsley, Jack Simpson, Billy Mason, Ted Curtis, Jackie Bowen and the late Bob Lawton are responsible for many of the photographs found in this book.

John Roll, Julie Hansen and my old coach Ralph Evitts helped identify players from other schools. Thanks to them for their assistance.

Thanks to Billy Wynn Hicks for getting me some great information about the 1944-45 team that advanced to the championship game of the state tournament.

Deborah Bonner got me information about her father, W.C. Mobberly, for which I am extremely grateful. W.C. is the greatest unsung hero in Golden Tide history.

Finally, I want to thank all the former players who took the time to share their memories and stories with me. The list is too long to name them all, so I'll simply say, "thanks, guys. It's greatly appreciated."

One final note: Sadly, many of the individuals quoted in this book are no longer living. But rather than insinuate myself in the book with such attributions as "my uncle Bob told me" or "as told to the author," I opted to treat those individuals as if they are still with us. That seemed to me to be the proper thing to do, for in essence they are alive, and will always live within these pages. They are the true authors of this magnificent story.

Tom Wallace

Introduction

Legend has it that in Central City's old gym, when seats wrapped around the upper level, some of which were located behind the baskets, a certain elderly lady would remove her heavy winter coat and then drape it across the backboard, where it remained throughout the game. No one dared ask her to remove it, and she never felt the need to do so.

Another legend holds that a Central City player once launched a long shot, one that bounced high in the air, an attempt destined to be an almost-certain miss until a helpful fan intervened by reaching over, grabbing the ball and directing it through the basket. Score two points for the Golden Tide. In the heat of battle you take points any way you can get them.

Are these stories fact or fiction? Real or imagined? Myth or gospel? More than likely, the answer to those questions can be found somewhere in the middle.

Fortunately for all of us, mythology is a large enough tent to accommodate absolute truth, supreme fiction and whatever else lies in between. And as with all wonderful stories, they simultaneously belong to the teller and the listener. If they do tend to slide toward the fiction side of the fence—and more times than not they probably do—the storyteller will not be held accountable for bearing false witness. Perjury does not exist in mythology.

Oftentimes it is impossible to know what is real and what is imagined. Fact can bleed into fiction and fiction into fact. The line between the two is easily blurred. If you have any doubts, then ponder these next three examples and ask yourself if they are truth or fiction.

During games the feisty and always-nervous Delmas Gish had a habit of chewing wadded-up pieces of colored paper ripped from a small notepad he kept in his coat pocket. He popped those things like a kid eating M&M's. When the game was over, dozens and dozens of BB-like multi-colored balls of paper lay on the floor beneath his feet. It was once remarked that if the old coach ever had an ulcer, it would most certainly be the color of a rainbow.

Or what about the rabid Central City fan who always sat by the front entrance, intently watching the action while rocking his body back and forth with ever-increasing intensity, waiting until the moment when the Tide gained possession of the ball, at which time he would dig into his coat pocket and rub the rabbit's foot he counted on to bring about a positive outcome for his beloved team? Good luck charms come in all forms; apparently, some can even be furry.

Our final example is one that clearly illustrates the point that what is actually true can at the same time be of questionable veracity. A Central City fan whose first name was Preston, when entering the gym, quietly said the word "Press" to the ticket seller, at which time Preston would be permitted entrance into the arena free of charge, the duped ticket seller believing that our sly Golden Tide fan was a member of the media there to cover the game. Not quite a lie, since most people did in fact call him Press, but not exactly true either.

Tell those three stories, all of which are true, and you are likely to be met by disbelievers who will be quick to dismiss them as little more than tall tales handed down from generation to generation by followers of Golden Tide basketball. That's OK. Nowhere is it written that those disbelievers are required to accept any part of Central City's mythology as fact. After all, our stories are not their stories.

But here is one indisputable fact, an absolute truth that no one can challenge or deny: When Central City High School closed its doors in 1990, it had won more basketball games than any school in the Commonwealth of Kentucky, and it had the second-most wins of any school in the United States.

Overall, the Golden Tide's record was 1,578 wins against only 588 losses. That computes to a winning percentage of 72.9. There were 17 trips to the state tournament, 17 30-win seasons (still the most of any school in Kentucky) and 51 20-win seasons.

(It should also be noted that Central City's win total likely would be higher had won-loss records from the very earliest years of the school's existence not been lost to time.)

Those are impressive results for a small coal-mining community whose high school rarely had more than 50 students in a graduating class. Some classes had far fewer than 50 students, meaning the pool for potential basketball talent wasn't all that large. Yet, year after year, decade after decade, there were enough talented players to keep Central City basketball among the state's elite programs. This long line of succession didn't happen by accident; developing potential basketball players was part of the culture. Most young boys growing up in Central City idolized the Golden Tide players while dreaming of one day following in their heroes' footsteps.

This is how traditions are born, and how they continue to thrive.

Central City's story isn't all that different from countless other communities within the Commonwealth. In those towns, both small and large, where church and school are the primary gathering places, the exploits of high school sports teams were all-important. Fans lived and died with the outcome of each and every game. A big victory lifted a town's spirit, filling it with a sense of pride and accomplishment, while a tough loss left the locals feeling down and grumpy.

As for the players, they were treated like Roman soldiers, admired by the old and idolized by the young. Years came and went but the special bond between players and fans endured. Today's hero would become tomorrow's legend, just as the quiet fourth-grader with dreams of wearing the black and gold might very well become the next superstar.

What, then, makes Central City's story different? Why is it special? Well, there are several key answers to both questions, beginning, of course, with those 1,578 victories. When you have more wins than any other school in the state, it makes you special. Sports are all about numbers, and numbers don't lie. If you're good, you don't need to brag—the numbers will make your case for you. Conversely, if you stink, numbers leave you nowhere to hide. In this case the numbers are clearly on Central City's side.

Here is another key reason why Central City was so successful on the basketball court—consistency at the top. From 1925 until the doors closed in 1990, only six men occupied the head coach's chair. Contrast that with Greenville and Graham, both of whom had 21 coaches during the same time span, or Muhlenberg Central, which had 12 coaches despite not coming into existence until 1950. Such an extreme degree of coaching chaos will inevitably make it difficult to achieve any level of sustained excellence. Lack of continuity usually sounds the death knell for any athletic program.

This continuity is really remarkable, and the role it played in Central City's success cannot be overstated. Players throughout the system, from first grade to the 12th, knew who their coach would be, what to expect, how to play and how to behave. There was no revolving door. The men who coached at Central City didn't use the position as a means to secure a job elsewhere, perhaps at a larger school willing to hand out a bigger paycheck. No, Golden Tide coaches were definitely in it for the long haul.

Equally remarkable was the transition from one coach to the next. It was always smooth and seamless. There was no debate, no backbiting, no turmoil. Some might even argue that the transitions were orchestrated, an argument that is very likely true. When George Taylor decided to step down, he handed the reins to Delmas Gish, a Central City alumnus. Gish, in turn, gave the job to one of his former players, Jackie Day, who, when he gave up coaching, handed the job to his assistant, Wayne Divine. When Divine left to become principal after one season, the job went to his assistant, Bill Loney. When Loney's tenure ended, the job went to Tony Hopper, another ex-Golden Tide player.

Rarely has the changing of the guard anywhere been handled more gracefully than it was in regards to the Central City coaching position. It was a model of professionalism.

Those six men coached throughout a time span that covers 65 years and were responsible for all but 42 of those 1,578 victories. Therein lies much of the reason for the success, the sustained excellence, that ultimately sets Central City apart from all but a small handful of other outstanding programs.

Early Beginnings

Virtually all successful sports teams, those that have maintained long-term excellence, have essentially been the child of a single father. What would the New York Yankees have become had Babe Ruth not showed up? Or the University of Kentucky without Adolph Rupp, Western Kentucky without Ed Diddle or UCLA without John Wooden? How many World Series rings, NCAA championships or conference titles would those teams have won had such legendary figures not arrived on the scene? No doubt, none of them would have been nearly so successful.

Central City's story is no different. The school's basketball success, sustained excellence, tradition and pride can all be traced back to one man—George Taylor. There is simply no debating the fact that he is the father of Central City basketball. Before Taylor showed up, Central City was just another small school with an average basketball team. Better than some, but certainly nothing special. What the basketball program lacked in the years before Taylor took over was steadiness, continuity and leadership. It was a ship without a captain.

That all changed when Taylor took the job in 1925. Within a few short years, under his stern tutelage, Central City soon became a force to be taken seriously. As the victories piled up, as the championships were won, so began the great tradition that is Central City basketball. Taylor had no way of knowing it at the time, but he was laying the foundation for what became a basketball dynasty. Of perhaps even more importance, he was also giving the small town of Central City its primary identity and its single greatest source of pride.

Although it's hard to imagine, there was basketball at Central City High School prior to Taylor landing on these shores. The first team dates back to 1909-10, when members of the team constructed their own outdoor court and baskets at Armstrong's Blacksmith Shop. At the time, the new building, which later became the elementary school, was being constructed on Morehead Street. While the building was under construction, classes were held on the second floor of the Sam Danner store at the corner of Second and Morehead streets. Players on this very first Central City team included Tom Hayes, C.C. Dank, Carl Moulden, Bryant Lawton, Earl Muir, Lee Moore and Fuqua Bennett.

The first indoor court was in the Fortney Building on Center Street, a location that was later home to Wolfe Motor Service. The building had two stories, and the gym was on the second floor. Members of the team served as janitors for the main school building, raking in a combined $30 per month, which they used to pay rent for use of the gym.

The 1911-12 squad was the first to play against an out-of-city opponent, facing off against Beaver Dam. This group included Bryant Lawton, Bernes Frost, Lee Moore, Paul Frost, Joe Yonts, Fuqua Bennett and Frank West.

John Riley Kirk was the first paid coach. He also served as principal and teacher.

(Sadly, that team's won-loss record, along with records for the following nine seasons, have all been lost. It wouldn't be until the 1921-22 season that consistent records were kept.)

Basketball, in those days, was still in its infancy, having been invented less than a quarter-century earlier by Dr. James Naismith. Initially, the sport wasn't taken very seriously. Administrators and school officials viewed the sport as a means of keeping athletes busy (meaning away from possible mischief) and in good physical condition during the months between the end of football season in the fall and the start of baseball season in the spring. In the eyes of many, basketball was regarded more as an activity than a real sport.

In some states, however, basketball was quick to catch on. Kentucky happened to be one of those states. With each passing year, more and more schools picked up the sport and began to take it seriously. Still, there was a lot of chaos, confusion and an overall lack of organization. What was needed was a single governing body, one that would establish certain standards for all schools to adhere to, while at the same time putting in play a state-wide tournament system that would crown district, regional and state champions. That need was met when the Kentucky High School Athletic Association was organized in 1917.

The Golden Tide's basketball fortunes, prior to Taylor taking over, were actually quite good. In 1921-22, the first year records were kept, the Tide, coached by Tim Meinschein, had a 13-3 record. The next season, again under Meinschein, the Tide went 8-2.

In the next two seasons, 1923-24 and 1924-25, the Tide won 21 games and lost 12. There was a different coach in each of those seasons, the first team led by R.H. Carlson, the second by Arthur G. Bacon. Overall, then, for those four seasons, Central City's record was 42-17. That computes to a 71.2 winning percentage. Not shabby by any standards.

It was Meinschein's first team that gave Central City its initial taste of post-season success. That team beat Whitesville 22-18 to capture the district title, then whipped Livermore 20-5 before falling to Owensboro 75-16.

Ironically, Taylor, the man who put Central City basketball on the map, got off to a rather shaky start. His first team ended the season with a dismal 6-11 record. In every way, it was an inglorious beginning for a coach who ended his career with an 81-percent winning percentage (438-105), took eight teams to the Sweet 16, including one stretch of five years in a row, had six teams that won 30 or more games in a season and captured the district title an incredible 14 times during his 17-year tenure.

(In fairness to Taylor, who took over the coaching duties after the season was already in progress, he inherited some of those 11 losses. Although he accepted 6-11 as his first-year record, not all of those losses were his.)

That first year at the helm proved to be the lone hiccup on this coaching legend's resume, marking the only time a Taylor-coached team ended the season with a losing mark. In the next season, he turned things around with ferocious force, guiding his team to a 20-5 record. And that would only prove to be the beginning. Never again would one of Taylor's teams fail to win at least 20 games in a season. What Taylor did in a brief span of time was to unleash a black and gold clad basketball force that wiped out the enemy with startling regularity.

Heroes and Debates

"All for one and one for all."

Throughout the years, Central City players uttered those seven words prior to leaving the locker room and during every huddle. We might do well to call it the Golden Tide prayer. Certainly, this was the mantra all players believed in. Why? Because it was nothing less than a verbalization of brotherhood. What it meant was that your teammates had your back and would be there to pick you up when you were struggling.

Of course, the success of any sports team ultimately rests upon the shoulders of those who play the game. They are the warriors who step onto the court to confront and battle the enemy. Victory is achieved through their sweat, effort, determination and willingness to sacrifice personal glory for the good of the team, a code that was instilled in every player who put on the Central City uniform.

"All for one and one for all" meant everything or it meant nothing. To those who wore the black and gold they were sacred words.

Few teams in any sport have had more outstanding players than Central City. From George Taylor's time on the bench thru to the days when Tony Hopper occupied the coach's chair, Golden Tide fans were blessed to see a long line of terrific players. While a handful of players were genuinely great talents, there were hundreds more who, by getting the absolute maximum out of their individual abilities, managed to achieve positive results.

In the world of sports, arguments will forever continue as to whether this player was superior to that player, or whether one team was better than another team. One Golden Tide fan might pick his all-time starting five, while another person might pick a totally different five. Friendly debate is a big part of the fun for sports fans.

OK, we can all agree that Corky Withrow is Central City's (and Muhlenberg County's) all-time greatest player. No sane person is going to challenge that assertion. But what about number two? Who goes in that spot? Peck Hickman? Bobby Watkins? W.C. Mobberly? Joe Mac Howard? Lance Gish? Ralph Mayes? Bosco Reynolds? Tommy Eades? Greg Franklin? Curtis Shelton? Not easy, is it? Query 10 people and you're likely to get 10 different responses.

Same goes for teams. Could the 1965-66 squad that went to semifinals of the state tournament beat the 1953-54 team that entered the Sweet 16 with a perfect 35-0 record? Ralph Mayes, David James and Rodney Kirtley would say yes, while Bobby Don Millard and Larry Ray would say no. Or can you overlook the 1955-56 team that very likely would have won the state title had Billy Ray Duvall not been injured? And let's not forget the 1949-50 team headed by Joe Mac Howard, Marion Tinsley and Bobby Nofsinger that also advanced to the semifinals of the state tourney. That bunch was pretty good. In truth, none of those teams can be discounted or dismissed.

Then, of course, there's the most-successful Central City team ever, the 1944-45 Bobby Watkins, W.C. Mobberly, Billy Hicks-led club that had a 37-4 record and lost to Louisville Male and the great Ralph Beard in the championship game of the Sweet 16. Was that the best team ever? Based on the number of wins and its success in the state tourney, you almost have to conclude that it was. But who knows? Who can ever say? Who's prepared to make those picks? The floor is now open, and you're free to make your own choice.

Let the debate begin.

The Story

Where, then, do we begin our story? The answer to that question is easy: we go back to the beginning, to the man who laid the foundation for Golden Tide greatness.

George Taylor.

GOLDEN GLORY

The History of Central City Basketball

Chapter 1

George Taylor

If first impressions always held true, George Taylor's time in Central City would have been extremely brief. It was no sweet movie moment, that's for sure, one where a guy like Jimmy Stewart shows up and instantly falls in love with the place. If we were watching this particular movie scene, we would be given no hint that our star would make it through the day, much less spend the rest of his life here.

As Taylor himself admitted in a 1972 *Times-Argus* interview, his initial impression of Central City left him feeling underwhelmed. One quick check of the neighborhood surrounding the train station was all it took for him to question his decision to come here in the first place.

"The area was torn up pretty bad," Taylor said. "I looked around, decided I might stay a week or two, but figured I might blow out of town any time."

Sammy Sparks, Taylor's grandson, adds a juicy (if somewhat questionable) detail relating to that particular moment. "Granddad always said the first step he took after getting off the train, he landed in a big mud puddle," Sammy said. "He said it ruined his new shoes, too. Don't know if that's true or not, but it's what he told us."

Fortunately for generations of Central City students, Taylor's initial negative impression wasn't strong enough to turn him away from a city and a school that he came to love with his heart and soul. For 47 years, he served as teacher, coach, athletic director, principal and superintendent, filling each role with distinction, honor, dignity and professionalism. If any single individual can said to be the face of Central City High School, it is George Taylor.

Young Mr. Taylor

Taylor's grandfather was a Teamster who worked closely with Gen. U.S. Grant during the Civil War. When Taylor's father was born, as a tribute to the man he admired so much, the elder Sparks named his son after the legendary general. Taylor's father, Grant, had three children, Gertrude, Bessie and George.

The Grant name would run through the next three generations of Taylor's descendants. Taylor and his wife, Virginia, named their only child Grant. His grandson, Steve Sparks, and great-grandson, Patrick Sparks, both have Grant as a middle name.

Taylor graduated from Robinson (Ill.) Township High School in 1921. Four years later, in 1925, he graduated from James Milliken College in Decatur, Ill. Taylor was a solid athlete, particularly when it came to baseball. He played that sport throughout his years at Milliken College.

As a newly minted college graduate looking for work, Taylor got word through a friend that Central City High School had an opening for a basketball coach. He came to town, interviewed with Tim Meinschein, and was offered the job, which he accepted for $150 per month. He taught history and was the men's head basketball coach. In addition to those duties, he helped coach several other sports, including baseball and track.

(Back then, Central City also had football and girls basketball teams, neither of which were very successful. By the time World War II began, those programs had been eliminated. Girls did begin playing basketball again in the 1970s when Title IX came into existence.)

Past First Impressons

Meinschein, being a wise fellow, dispatched several Golden Tide players to greet Taylor when his train arrived. Included in that group were Bishop Arnold and Charles Bennett Greenwood. Sending a welcoming committee was a shrewd move on Meinschein's part, if for no other reason than the smiling faces and firm handshakes helped offset the rundown surrounding area (and the muddy shoes?) that had Taylor wondering just how long he would hang around such a place.

Taylor came to Central City with a desire to work with, educate, coach and help young people. In the end it would be his desire to serve the youth of this community that kept him here for the remainder of his life. Regardless of his success as a basketball coach, he was always an educator first.

"Education should teach you how to think and where to get information you need," Taylor said in that 1972 interview. "It's not really necessary to have a head crammed full of little facts."

As we will soon see, Taylor's ability to coach basketball—and to motivate young athletes—was virtually unprecedented at the time. Remember, Taylor began his career before such coaching titans as Adolph Rupp, Fog Allen and John Wooden came along. He was truly a forerunner and ground-breaker in the coaching profession.

As a coach, Taylor was adamant that his players learn and perfect the game's basic fundamentals.

"Coach Taylor was the best coach in the state and was recognized as such," Bob Lawton, one of Taylor's former players, said. "He really stressed the fundamentals. We spent hours working on things like pivoting, shooting, handling the ball and defense. He really made us pay attention to every detail of the game."

According to Lawton, Taylor was also a strict disciplinarian. "There were some pretty tough guys back in those days, but he kept them in line. Even guys who had graduated knew better than to misbehave when they were around him."

Tommy Gray, who knew Taylor only as school superintendent, echoed Lawton's sentiment. "Coach Taylor could stare at you harder than any man I've ever been around. Those beady little eyes—they could cut right through you."

Along with those scary eyes, Taylor also had a voice that could quickly catch your attention, something ex-Tide player H.G. Watkins found out at the most inopportune time.

"We were playing Hughes-Kirk and I was having a big game," Watkins said. "I think I had scored all but three of our points. Anyway, a teammate stole the ball and passed it ahead to me. I was all alone, going in for an easy layup. Unfortunately, I was heading toward our bench. Just as I was about to shoot, Coach Taylor stood and screamed, 'Watkins, you had better not miss that shot!' Scared me so bad I threw the ball over the backboard."

True story or myth? We'll never know. But one thing we can be sure of—with Taylor firmly in control, Central City basketball, average by any set of standards, would soon become one of the mightiest and most-respected programs in the Commonwealth. Under Taylor's guidance, Golden Tide basketball became something special.

The 1920s

Won – 150

Lost – 49

Winning Pct. – 75.4

Player of the Decade

Bernard "Peck" Hickman

Other Notable Players

Bishop Arnold
Tom Campbell
Jerry Cates
Oral Caywood
George Connor
Arvall Eades
Harold Eades
Edgar Ray Frost
Virge Gish
Bill Hughes
Charles Hughes
William McDowell
James McEuen
John Meinschein
Frank Rice
Jim Rice
Larue Sosh
Nelson Sosh
Dorsey Wesley

Chapter 2

1921-30

Central City High School was erected in 1910 as a result of 20-year bonds floated in 1908. The first class to graduate from the new building was in 1913, consisting of five members. The high school was located on Morehead Street until a decade or so later when the new building was constructed. After that, the old building served as the elementary school.

Little is known about athletics at the time, the exception being the 1911-12 team that was made up of Bryant Lawton, Bernes Frost, Frank West, Fuqua Bennett and Paul Frost. That team's won-loss record, Central City's first victim and which Golden Tide player scored the first points in school history are details that have all vanished in the mist of time. No records or scorebooks exist for the next 11 years, not until the 1922-23 season. It is known that the 1921-22 team had a 13-3 won-loss mark, but no scorebook of that season survives. Had records been kept, or if indeed they were and they could be located, no doubt Central City's all-time win total would be higher.

The oldest scorebook in existence covers 10 games during that 1922-23 campaign, with the Golden Tide winning eight and losing two. The first officially recorded victory came against Union University 22-18, the first loss against Beaver Dam 33-22. The other loss came at the hands of Owensboro 17-8.

What's surprising is the number of points this Central City club scored. It was a team with a high-octane offense, one certainly not typical for the times. Remember, this was the era of set shots, underhand free throws, and a jump ball after every made basket. It was not unusual to see both teams fail to score in double figures.

Yet, the Golden Tide scored 61 points against Dawson Springs, 56 against Hartford and 55 against Fordsville. For the season, this team averaged 35 points per game, an almost-unheard-of figure for that era.

Equally impressive were some of the individual performances, especially those turned in by Jim Rice, who has to be regarded as Central City's first big-time scorer. Rice had 27 against Dawson Springs, 23 against Fordsville, 20 against Hartford and 12 against Union University. Rice averaged just shy of 12 points per contest in those games that were recorded.

But Rice wasn't the sole offensive weapon on that team. Arvall Eades scored 20 against Dawson Springs, while William McDowell tossed in 20 against Hartford.

Other members of that team included Clyde Lawton, Hughes Wallace, Oran Karnes and Albert Hill.

After two seasons at the helm, Tim Meinschein handed the coaching reins to R. H. Carlson, who led the 1923-24 team to a 12-4 record. This would be his only year as head coach. For the 1924-25 season, Arthur Bacon handled the coaching duties, his one and only team, finishing with a 9-8 record.

Taylor Takes Command

No scorebooks exist for either of those seasons, nor do they exist for George Taylor's first year as head coach. What is known is that Taylor's initial club ended the season with a 6-11 record, and that its team members included Bacil Swanay, Edgar Ray Frost, Harold Eades, George Connor, Bud Cates, Randolph Baker, Carl Quisenberry and John Harvey.

For Taylor's second team, which finished with a 20-5 won-loss mark, a scorebook with 18 games still exists. This would be Central City's first 20-win season, and never again would a Taylor-coached team fail to register at least 20 wins.

This was a solid club, but not a dominating one. It was certainly no match for many of the teams that would soon follow. But it did set the standard—a 20-win season—that all future Golden Tide teams would be challenged to meet.

One of this team's strengths was its balance, with no fewer than six players earning game-high scoring honors. The big scorer was Edgar

Ray Frost, who had 26 points against Utica, 19 against Calhoun and 13 against Bethel. Oral Caywood was also capable of big scoring outbursts, ringing up 14 points against Utica, 13 against Livermore and 11 against Daviess County.

Dan Baldwin led the way with 17 against Owensboro, Joe Cates had 18 against Elkton and George Connor had six against Lewisburg.

Other team members included John Harvey, Randolph Baker, Bishop Arnold, Harold Mix, Charles Bennett Greenwood, Bacil Swanay, Charles Hughes and John Louis Sandback.

There are scorebook statistics for 17 of the 30 games played by the 1927-28 team that finished with a final record of 23-7. It would be this team that made the first of Central City's 17 trips to the state tournament. This also marked the first of five consecutive appearances in the Sweet 16. This was the year Peck Hickman, a freshman guard, made his debut in a Golden Tide uniform.

In those 17 games, James McEuen was the leading scorer on 13 occasions. His best effort was a 23-point outing in a 50-20 victory over Nebo. He had 20 in a 53-19 win over Hartford and 16 in a 42-13 win over Bremen.

McEuen received solid support from Charles Hughes and Bishop Arnold, two of this club's steadiest contributors. Hughes had 16 against County High, while Arnold had 14 against Utica.

Other team members included Nelson Sosh, Larue Sosh, Sam Stringer, Frank Salsburg, Frank Rice, Randolph Baker, Harold Mix and Tom Campbell.

The Golden Tide's first visit to the state tournament was not a pleasant experience, resulting in a 53-14 pounding at the hands of Louisville St. Xavier. This would be a trend that haunted Central City hoops throughout its history, great teams advancing to the state tournament only to fall victim in first-round games.

The 1928-29 team improved to a 29-5 record while earning a second straight trip to the state tourney. Scorebook statistics exist for 29 of those 34 games. What is not available to us are the three regional tournament games and the two played in the state tournament. In the state tourney, played in Alumni Gym on UK's campus, Central City beat Henderson 30-27, then lost to Heath 22-15 in the Class A semifinal round.

Peck Hickman, now a sophomore, was named to the all-tournament team. He would earn that same honor again two years later.

Hickman was just one of many standout performers on what was a remarkably balanced team. His best scoring performance was a 16-point outing in a 45-11 win over Greenville. Others who led the team in scoring on at least one occasion were Bishop Arnold, Charles Hughes, Tom Campbell, Nelson Sosh and Frank Rice, who earned a starting nod after scoring 37 points in the first three games.

Central City breezed through the district tournament, dispatching Greenville 42-7 and Elkton 32-15. Campbell had 15 in the win over Greenville, while Arnold scored nine against Elkton.

In the regional tournament Class A section, the Tide took the big trophy by beating Hardyville Memorial 22-18 and Horse Cave 27-15, then lost 34-29 to Class B champion Woodburn. Both teams advanced to the state tournament.

Throughout its grand basketball history, 17 Central City teams have won 30 or more games in a season. To this day, that number remains the most of any Kentucky high school. It was the 1929-30 club that became the first to reach the 30-win milestone. By season's end, the Golden Tide's record was 30-4.

Only 20 of those 34 games could be found in the old archives, but what we learn from those records is simple and straightforward—this was one very powerful team, easily the strongest during the school's first full decade of competition. The average winning margin was 18.5 points per game. Among those teams crushed by Central City were Daviess County 52-10, Earlington 55-10 and 41-6, Elkton 39-7 and 48-12, Paducah 33-12 and Greenville 36-12.

Once again, this was a team with a host of players capable of leading the scoring parade. Hickman, the all-state performer now in his junior year, led the team in scoring eight times, with a season high 18 in that 55-10 romp past Earlington. He also hit double digits with 16 against Paducah and 13 against Centertown.

Other Tide players who had big scoring nights included Bill Hughes (18 against Earlington), Charlies Hughes (15 against Daviess County), Dorsey Wesley (13 against Graham), Virge Gish (10 against Greenville) and John Meinschein (nine against Earlington).

Rounding out the roster were Malcolm Sears, Wayne Millard, Glover Ellis, Joe Walling, Jerry Cates, Clarence Batsel, J.B. Hill, John Williamson, Clay Hill, Benton Holt, Cy Sweatt and Elliot "Flop" Ramsey.

The Tide reeled off four wins to capture the district crown, beating Graham 24-16, Lewisburg 19-11, Greenville 31-10 and Olmstead 33-8. They earned a third straight trip to the state tourney by topping Hardyville Memorial 23-17, Cave City 29-14 and Woodburn 21-13 to win the regional title.

But this team, powerful as it was, came up short again in the state tourney, dropping a hard-fought 24-18 decision to eventual runner-up Kavanaugh.

Despite the disappointment of that loss to Kavanaugh, nothing could dampen the excitement surrounding Golden Tide basketball. In the past four seasons, Taylor's team carved out a 102-21 won-loss record for an 82.9 winning percentage. There had been four consecutive district championships, three straight regional titles and, of course, three trips to the Sweet 16.

These were grand times for Golden Tide hoops, and they were only going to get better.

Chapter 3

Bernard "Peck" Hickman

If it's true that George Taylor is the Godfather of Central City basketball, then it's equally true that Bernard "Peck" Hickman was Taylor's first Chief Enforcer. The impact on Central City basketball by these two individuals cannot be overstated. With Taylor on the bench directing traffic and Hickman on the court leading the way, the Golden Tide's basketball reputation shot to the top faster than a rocket heading to the moon. It was on the shoulders of this dynamic duo that Central City began to distinguish itself as a state powerhouse.

The Golden Tide's success during Hickman's four-year career is simply staggering. From 1927-31, the Tide had a 116-20 won-loss record, which computes to an 85.3 winning percentage. In each of those years the Golden Tide advanced to the state tournament. Twice, in 1929 and 1931, Hickman was named to the all-tournament team. He was also an all-state player in 1930 and 1931.

Little wonder, then, that Taylor was always quick to say, "Peck Hickman is the best all-around basketball player I ever coached."

Hickman was one of those rare players who could control and dominate a game without posting high-scoring numbers.

"Peck could score if he wanted to," Bob Lawton remembers. "But it was the other things he could do that made him unique. For instance, while dribbling, he could move and pivot in such a way that the player guarding him would get all tied up in knots. Then Peck would go past the guy, spot an open teammate under the basket and get him the ball. He was a very special player."

Although Taylor would later label Bishop Arnold as "the best all-around athlete I ever coached," Hickman, in addition to excelling on the basketball court, was a four-year starter on the baseball and football teams. When it came to sports, there seemed to be no limit to the things he could do. Simply put, he was just a rare once-in-a-lifetime athlete.

Peck's Bad Boy

When did Hickman get the nickname he answered to all his life? Where did it come from? And why? With no one left who can give us those answers, we are free to make our own surmises. And in this instance, it's probably not all that difficult to come up with a reasonable guess.

In the late 1880s, George M. Peck wrote a series of highly popular newspaper stories and magazine articles in which the lead character was a young lad known for being a mischievous, incorrigible kid. He became known as "Peck's bad boy", a fitting description for countless young and rowdy males. Most likely, Hickman fell into the "Peck's bad boy" category. Hence, the life-long nickname.

Hickman may have provided us with the best evidence when he wrote an article praising George Taylor. "I know there were times when my performance and emotional stability were a source of great concern for him (Taylor), but he always managed to bring me around to his way of thinking with just a good ole heart-to-heart talk."

A Hilltopper Standout

After graduating from Central City in 1931, Hickman took his skills to Bowling Green, where he was a three-year starter for Ed Diddle's Western Kentucky Hilltoppers. In those three years, the Hilltoppers posted a 68-17 record for an 80-percent winning percentage. They captured three KIAC Tournament Championships and one SIAA tourney title. Their record in each of those three years was 16-6, 28-8 and 24-3.

Hickman, the team's captain his senior season, also collected his share of individual honors, making the Kentucky All-State team in 1933 and 1934, the All-KIAC tournament team in 1935, and the All-SIAA tournament team in 1934 and 1935.

Hickman graduated from Western in 1935 with a bachelor's degree in physical education. In 1944 he would earn his master's degree from the University of Kentucky's College of Education.

Building His Own Empire

For the next decade Hickman coached at the high school level, first at Hodgenville High, then at Louisville Valley High. His teams had a combined record of 216-49, and he twice led Valley to the Sweet 16.

In 1944, Hickman was hired as the men's basketball coach at the University of Louisville. At the time, Louisville's basketball program could politely be termed a dismal failure, having had only 11 winning seasons in 33 years. That was soon to change.

Peck Hickman was to the University of Louisville what George Taylor was to Central City, Adolph Rupp to the University of Kentucky and Ed Diddle to WKU—the father of Cardinal basketball. At Louisville, there is Before Hickman and After Hickman.

His first team went 16-4, and not once during his 23-year career did the Cardinals post a losing record. Overall, his teams were 443-183 for a 70.8 winning percentage. His 1948 club captured the NAIB championship, his 1956 team came home with the NIT title and the 1959 team earned the school its first Final Four appearance. In all, five of his teams were in the NCAA Tournament and six of his teams participated in the NIT.

That 1948 team beat John Wooden's Indiana State club in the NAIB title game. Soon after, Hickman was offered the UCLA head coaching position, which he declined. He did, however, recommend Wooden for the job. And we all know how that turned out.

For many years Hickman served as both head coach and athletics director. He graduated 82-percent of his players, and was the first basketball coach in Kentucky to break the color barrier, signing Eddie Whitehead and Wade Houston in 1962.

Despite all the success that came his way, Hickman never forgot the one man who meant so much to him—George Taylor.

"He played a very important role in my life during the impressionable years," Hickman said of his old coach. "His strength, understanding, guidance and friendship were a beacon of light for me. Most of us have someone whose memory and friendship we cherish and respect very much. For me, that person is Coach George Taylor."

Hickman, who died in 2000 at age 88, was inducted into the Helms Foundation Hall of Fame in 1967 and the National Association of Collegiate Directors of Athletics Hall of Fame in 1981.

The 1930s

Won – 278

Lost – 60

Winning Pct. – 82.2

Player of the Decade

Bernard "Peck" Hickman

Other Notable Players

Clark Bailey
Clarence Batsel
J.C. Batsel
J.T. Byars
Les Chinn
Leroy Crossman
Harold Gish
Damon Hart
Benton Holt
Charles Hughes
Bob Lawton
Buddy Lloyd
Maurice Lowe
Billy Ray Nale
Denzil Noffsinger
Roy Noffsinger
Bennie Ogden
Malcolm Sears
Harold Shrewsberry
Ermine Vincent
H.G. Watkins
Gilbert Wilkins

Chapter 4

1931-35

With its record of 34-4, the 1930-31 club ranks as one of the top four winning teams in Central City history. Only the 1944-45 team (37-4) and the 1953-54 team (35-1) won more games in a season than the 1930-31 squad. Rounding out the top four is the 1946-47 team, which also posted a 34-4 mark.

This would be the great Peck Hickman's final season for the Golden Tide, and he and his teammates made it count. Hickman was surrounded by a battalion of familiar faces, many of whom had played key roles in helping the previous team claim 30 wins and earn the Tide a third straight trip to the state tourney. Among those returning were Virge Gish, Bill Hughes, Terry Cates, Wayne Millard, Brooks Wooten, Malcolm Sears, Clarence Batsel, Joe Walling, Glover Ellis, Benton Holt, Sam Stringer, Johnny Ogden, Elwood Wallace and Nathanial Ogden.

No doubt, it was this team's experience that enabled it to survive so many close games. In all, seven games were decided by fewer than three points. Sears was a key player in several of those narrow escapes, scoring five in a 14-13 win over Paducah, six in a 13-10 win over Beaver Dam, 11 as the Tide downed Centertown 21-19 and eight in a second 26-24 win over Beaver Dam.

Batsel had eight in a 21-18 win over Graham, while Hickman's seven points were tops in a 21-20 win over Father Ryan.

The club also had its share of laughers, too, beating Daviess County 41-10, Pembroke 44-6, Greenville 35-10, Russellville 38-17, Olmstead 47-12, Graham 42-12, Horse Branch 34-12 and Lewisburg 42-16.

In those runaway wins, Sears had 15 against Daviess County, 14 against Greenville and 13 against Graham, while Wallace had 11 against Olmstead, Cates 10 against Horse Branch, Holt 12 against Lewisburg, Wooten nine against Pembroke and Hickman eight against Russellville.

Behind Hickman's game-high seven points, the Golden Tide posted an impressive 20-12 victory over perennial Louisville powerhouse St. Xavier.

The Tide opened district tournament play by dispatching Greenville 18-8. Hughes led the way with five points. Gish scored eight and Sears added six as the Tide topped Russellville 36-24 in semifinal action. In the title game against Olmstead, Gish scored 15 to lead the Tide to a 31-18 win.

Regional tourney action began with an easy 28-13 win over Glasgow. Cates led a balanced scoring attack with seven points. One night later, playing Bowling Green on the Purples' home court, the Tide overcame a three-point halftime deficit to squeeze out a 15-12 win. Hickman led the winners with six points, while Cates came up big by sinking two crucial second-half buckets.

That win sent the Tide into the championship game against an Olmstead team they had easily defeated twice during the regular season. This outcome was no different. Hughes scored nine points, Sears seven and Cates six as the Tide rolled into a fourth-straight state tournament appearance by topping Olmstead 34-23.

The Tide topped Benham 30-19 in the state tourney's opening round, then squared off against Louisville Manual in a game with a nightmare outcome that would haunt George Taylor for the rest of his life. Despite a superb five-point effort from Hickman in his final game, the Tide dropped a 16-15 decision.

"It was in the semifinals," Taylor remembered. "We were ahead the entire game, then got beat in the final seconds. That one still hurts."

For his effort, Hickman was named to the all-tournament team for the second time.

During his four years at Central City, Hickman led his teams to 116 victories, a number later matched by W.C. Mobberly. Only Corky Withrow's teams, with 119 wins, had more.

The only scorebook records that exist for the 1931-32 team cover the three regional tournament games and the one played in the state tourney. Members of this team, which had a 24-9 record, included Virge Gish, Bill Hughes, Jimmy Beeler, Clarence Batsel, Joe Walling,

Wayne Millard, Denzil Noffsinger, Clark Bailey, Merrel Franklin and Oberlan Westerfield.

Central City advanced to the regional tourney by beating Graham 38-23 and Drakesboro 48-18 in district action.

Impressive performances continued in the regional, with Gish and Beeler each scoring 13 points in a 54-19 win over Kuttawa. Beeler had 14 and Batsel 13 as the Tide crushed Drakesboro 43-24 in semifinal action. In a low-scoring title tilt, Batsel scored eight points in a 15-4 victory over Kirkmansville, a win that sent the Golden Tide to the state tourney for the fifth straight year.

The easy blowout was on the other foot once the Tide got to the state tournament. In a game that was never close, the Tide were no match for Paris, losing 44-16. Batsel and Walling each had six points in a losing cause.

Prior to the 1932-33 campaign, Taylor's teams were noted for featuring a balanced scoring attack. That would not be the case with this team, which fashioned a 24-4 record. For the first time during Taylor's tenure, a single player, Clarence Batsel, emerged as a powerful scoring force.

Although only 21 of this club's 28 games can be found in scorebooks, Batsel, an outstanding football player who later became a professional boxer, led the team in scoring 17 times. On 12 of those occasions, he hit for double figures, with a high of 16 in a 32-6 win over Bowling Green.

Along with Batsel, the roster included J.P. Stringer, Joe Keys, Benton Holt, Johnny Ogden, Arthur Murphy, J.C. Batsel and Oberlan Westerfield.

Other Batsel double-figure outings came against Earlington (12), Russellville (10), McHenry (13), Earlington (12), Owensboro (11), McHenry (13), Hopkinsville (10), Beaver Dam (11), Russellville (10) and Daviess County (14).

Stringer, Holt and Johnny Ogden each led the scoring on two occasions.

The two most impressive wins that season came against Owensboro 27-25 and Paducah 26-13.

Any hopes for a six straight trip to the Sweet 16 were quickly dashed by Drakesboro.

Playing on its home court, Central City, which entered the district tournament with a 24-3 record, suffered a stunning 17-15 loss. It marked the first time a Taylor-coached team lost a district tournament game.

Taylor's next team rebounded with an outstanding 31-3 record and another trip to the state tourney. Unfortunately, statistics for the 1933-34 season are virtually all but missing. The only ones to be found cover the three district games and the three regional games. Scoring for the state tourney game against Danville has also been lost.

Members of this team included Clarence Batsel, Harold Shrewsberry, Denzil Noffsinger, Les Chinn, J.C. Batsel, Damon Hart, Clark Bailey, J.B. Allen, Howard Mansfield and Johnny Ogden.

Clarence Batsel had a team-best nine points in a 35-10 win over Hughes-Kirk in the district tourney opener. Chinn tossed in 12 and Batsel 11 as the Tide rolled past Drakesboro 48-13 to earn a shot at another district crown. Chinn came back one night later to score 10 in a 28-15 championship-game win over Graham.

Behind 16 points from Mansfield and 15 from Batsel, the Tide coasted past Elkton 62-20 in first-round regional tourney action. Next came a pair of two-point squeakers—22-20 over Hopkinsville and 21-19 over Madisonville—that enabled the Golden Tide make another trip to the state tourney.

Once again, however, the Tide suffered a first-round Sweet 16 defeat, losing an 18-16 overtime decision to Danville.

The 1934-35 team, which finished with a 28-7 record, took Central City to the state tourney for the seventh time in the previous eight years. This was another strong aggregation that featured several players capable of posting big numbers.

The roster included Ermine Vincent, Harold Shrewsberry, Gilbert Wilkins, Merrel Robey, Denzil Noffsinger, David Lockery, Clark Bailey, J.W. Conrey, Bill Durham, Damon Hart and Leroy Crossman.

This club started strong, winning 11 of its first 13 games. The two setbacks, both nail-biters, came against Beaver Dam 17-16 and Sacramento 21-20.

Noffsinger was the big gun in the season's first two games, accounting for 11 points in a 39-2 romp past Bremen and 12 points in a 33-5 win against Drakesboro. In the Tide's next two wins—26-14 over Hughes-Kirk and 22-13 over Calhoun—Hart and Bailey led the way with 10 and eight points, respectively.

Vincent accounted for 25 points in the Tide's wins over Hartford 30-18, Caneyville 21-19 and Hughes-Kirk 19-15. Following the loss to Sacramento, Hart came through with 18 points in a 39-3 win over Calhoun, Shrewsberry had 12 in a 38-13 win over Drakesboro and Noffsinger 10 in a 26-20 win over Graham.

The Tide did avenge both early season losses, topping Beaver Dam 37-26 behind 11 points from Robey and 10 from Hart, then rode a 10-point effort from Wilkins to a 25-22 win over Sacramento.

Shrewsberry and Wilkins played particularly well during the last half of the season. Shrewsberry scored 13 in wins over Hopkinsville, Murray and Owensboro, while Wilkins had 13 against Fulton, 11 against Owensboro, 16 against Murray and 12 against Hartford and Earlington.

Hart also had a big night, hitting for 17 in a 52-12 win over Murray.

Other regular-season losses came at the hands of Henderson 38-36, St. X 35-20, Owensboro 25-22, Lynnville 30-27 and Earlington 37-34.

With Shrewsberry scoring 13 points and Wilkins contributing 11, the Tide later avenged the loss to Owensboro, winning 43-35.

Noffsinger scored 10 points as the Tide opened district tourney play by topping Drakesboro 42-15. Next, the Golden Tide set a record that still stands to this day, beating hapless Dunmor 99-5. That 94-point winning margin ranks among the biggest in Kentucky high school basketball history.

In that win, for the first time in school history, three Golden Tide players topped the 20-point mark, with Noffsinger and Shrewsberry each accounting for 26, while Wilkins added 20.

One night later, Shrewsberry scored 13 and Noffsinger 11 as the Tide beat Hughes-Kirk 40-26 for the title.

The Tide were paired off against Hughes-Kirk in the regional tourney opener, marking the fourth time the two teams met this season. The outcome of this game followed the same path as the first three, with the Tide posting a 31-23 victory. Wilkins led the Tide with nine points.

Wilkins had seven points in a 20-14 semifinal win over Hartford, then Shrewsberry came through with 11 points to lead the Tide past Owensboro 26-16 and into the state tourney.

In Lexington, squaring off against Inez, the Tide lost 20-15. Wilkins was his team's top scorer with seven.

Chapter 5

1936-40

The next two seasons remain among the most successful in Central City's long basketball history. They also rank as two of the most perplexing seasons ever. In those two years, the Tide won 60 games and lost only seven. That computes to a 90-percent winning pace. But in the end, there was nothing to show for such success, because two of those seven losses came in regional tourney action against teams the Tide were expected to defeat.

The 1935-36 team, which carved out a 32-4 record, featured another solid group headed by veterans Harold Shrewsberry, Ermine Vincent, Damon Hart, Merrel Robey and Bill Durham. Joining them were Leroy Crossman, Joe Noffsinger, Bob Lawton, Harold Gish, Charles McQuady and Boyd Crowder.

The team raced out of the gate, capturing its first 17 games before dropping a 33-21 decision to Lynnville (Ind.). During those first 17 victories, the Tide's average winning margin was 16 points per game.

Among those victims that felt the wrath of this team's high-powered offense were Bremen 54-14, Graham 38-19, Caneyville 41-19, Brownsville 35-14, Morganfield 41-21, Calhoun 41-14 and Hopkinsville 41-14.

Only teams that managed to slow the pace caused trouble. The Tide struggled to beat Sacramento twice 8-6 and 19-17, Russellville 17-9 and Hartford 13-11.

This club, like many before it, was not lacking for offensive weaponry. At various times during the season, eight different players took high-scoring honors.

Vincent was the emerging force, leading the team in scoring on 16 occasions. His best performance was a 16-point effort against Bremen. He also accounted for 14 against Graham, 13 against Fulton, 13 against Manual and 12 against Beaver Dam.

Hart also had several big nights, tagging Bremen for 13 points, Manual for 12 and Drakesboro for 10.

Shrewsberry had a season-best 14 points in a 26-19 win over Cannelton (Ind.), while Robey led with 11 points against Morganfield. Others who led in scoring were Durham (10 against Lynnville), Noffsinger (three in a 12-8 win over Beaver Dam), Crossman (nine against Owensboro) and Gish (eight against Drakesboro).

The other two regular-season losses were administered by Drakesboro 18-16 and Hartford 22-13.

The Tide coasted through the district tournament, blasting Drakesboro 36-7, Hughes-Kirk 34-5 and Bremen 45-18. Gish led with eight in the win over Drakesboro, Hart had nine against Hughes-Kirk and 13 against Bremen.

The Tide's foe in the regional tourney opener was a familiar one—Beaver Dam. The two teams had met twice during the regular season, with the Tide taking both games, 12-8 and 30-22. But in this third meeting, with everything on the line, the outcome was different. On this night, Beaver Dam claimed a 26-22 upset victory.

Vincent led the Tide with 10 points.

It was a disappointing end to what had been a magnificent season. And although no one could have predicted it at the time, next year's club would follow a similar pattern, soaring to great heights, only to fall victim to crushing disappointment when the stakes were at their highest.

Fueled by the scoring prowess of Ermine Vincent and the rapidly improving play of Harold Gish, this 1936-37 club notched 28 wins against only three setbacks. It was another George Taylor-coached team capable of putting up big scoring numbers. Twice, this team scored more than 50 points, five times it had 40 points and 14 times the 30-point mark was crossed.

Along with Vincent and Gish, this team's roster included Bob Lawton, Joe Noffsinger, Leroy Crossman, Dave Duncan, Buddy Lloyd, Boyd Crowder, Bennie Odgen and Robert Kitchens.

Vincent hit for 17 points in an opening-game 39-18 romp past Calhoun, then followed that with an 11-point outing in a 28-11 win over Fordsville. Vincent would crack double figures 17 times this season, with a high of 19 against Caneyville.

The Tide won their first 14 games before falling 23-17 to Paducah. In those victories, several Tide players played key roles, including Crossman with 10 points in a 48-13 win over Livermore, Gish with 12 in a 36-14 win over Graham and Noffsinger with 10 in a 38-9 win over Sacramento.

Rebounding from the Paducah loss, the Tide wrapped wins against Russellville 30-24, Beaver Dam 37-29, Henderson 33-16, Caneyville 52-14 and Cannelton (Ind.) 50-12 around a 13-12 loss to Hartford.

In their final three games prior to district tourney action, the Tide topped Madisonville 47-13, Henderson 36-6 and Russellville 36-12. Gish and Vincent had 11 and 10 points, respectively, against Madisonville, Vincent led with eight against Henderson and Ogden had his best game of the season, scoring 10 in the win over Russellville.

Gish hit for 17 points and Vincent added nine as the Tide took out Drakesboro 36-25 in the district opener. In the final against Hughes-Kirk, Vincent scored 11 in a tough 29-25 victory.

Regional tourney play began with Kitchens scoring seven points in a 25-14 win over Clarkson. The semifinal game against Fordsville was an easy 45-12 Golden Tide win, with Gish topping the scoring with 10 points, Noffsinger adding eight and Crowder seven.

The title game against McHenry was a see-saw thriller that saw the Tide battle back from an eight-point deficit heading into the final quarter, only to suffer a 27-26 loss. The Tide had four more field goals than McHenry, but failed to connect on all seven free throw attempts. Those misses cost the Tide a state tourney trip.

Lawton and Crowder keyed the Tide's comeback, accounting for 10 of the team's 14 second-half points. Lawton, Vincent and Crossman all finished with six points, while Crowder had four. The normally high-scoring Gish was limited to two points.

Two straight dominating seasons ended with no important hardware to show for it. This would all change in 1937-38, when a grizzled, veteran team headed by Vincent, Gish, Lawton, Odgen and Lloyd led the Golden Tide to a 31-5 record and George Taylor's eighth—and final—trip to the state tournament.

Those five veterans were joined by Roy Noffsinger, H.G. Watkins, Harold Soder, J.T. Byars and Roy McWaters.

Although Vincent continued to put up impressive numbers, this club featured a much more balanced scoring attack than the previous team. At various times, Gish, Lawton, Lloyd, Ogden, Watkins and Noffsinger all led the team in scoring. Gish was the top gun, leading the scoring parade 17 times.

Gish racked up 97 points in the Tide's first seven games, wins against Earlington 36-12, Calhoun 43-22, Sacramento 38-17, Hartford 23-20, Russellville 27-14, Lewisburg 34-24 and Beaver Dam 29-21. In those wins, Gish had 12, 17, 15, 11, 10, 17 and 15 points.

Gish wasn't the Tide's lone weapon in those games. Vincent had 10 against Sacramento and 12 against Beaver Dam, while Lawton had eight against both Hartford and Russellville.

After McHenry snapped the winning streak by claiming a 21-20 win, the Tide came back to win their next 11 games. Included among the Tide's victims were Greenville 15-9, Daviess County 32-31, Owensboro 27-18 and Tompkinsville 32-18.

Behind a 17-point effort from Gish, the Tide scored a measure of revenge by whipping McHenry 39-27.

Ogden had his best performance thus far, scoring nine against Daviess County, while the sophomore Watkins had four in that low-scoring win over Greenville.

The Tide split their next four games, beating Memorial 22-17 and Owensboro 30-22, and losing to Sharpe 29-26 and Paducah 28-26. Vincent had 13 and 11 points, respectively, against Sharpe and Memorial, Gish had nine against Owensboro and Lloyd 10 against Paducah.

Sharpe would eventually go on to capture the state championship.

In the Tide's next game, a 60-24 rout of Madisonville, Vincent had 15 points, Gish 14, Lloyd 11 and Lawton 10. This marked the first time in Central City's basketball history that four players cracked double figures in the same game.

Following a pair of easy wins over Madisonville 22-8 and Bardstown 40-20, the Tide faced off against powerful Louisville St. X, dropping a hard-fought 38-32 overtime decision. Noffsinger led the Tide with 11 points, while Vincent added 10.

This would not be the last time these two teams would see each other. They were destined to meet again three weeks later in a match-up of significant importance.

The regular season ended with Gish scoring 10 points in a 29-22 win over Horse Cave.

District tourney action began with Gish scoring 12 points and Watkins and Noffsinger eight apiece in a 38-4 win over Butler County. Vincent tossed in 11 as the Tide beat Rochester 29-12, then Gish had 13 in a 28-17 championship-game win over Drakesboro.

The Tide kicked off regional tourney play with a 36-31 win over Ekron. In that game, Gish had 10 points, Lloyd and Vincent eight each. One night later, Ogden had his best game of the season, scoring 10 in a 30-17 win over Hawesville.

That win set the stage for a showdown that never happened.

"Going into the tournament, we all figured McHenry was the team we had to beat in order to make it to the state tournament," Bob Lawton remembered. "Well, we did our part, taking care of business by winning our first two games. But McHenry must have been thinking about us, because they completely overlooked Drakesboro. And what usually happens when you overlook an opponent? You lose. And Drakesboro beat them."

With McHenry watching from the sidelines, the final against Drakesboro was no contest. Ogden scored 10 points and Lawton added nine in an easy 45-13 win over the Cardinals.

Waiting for the Tide in the state tourney was St. X, the team that posted a 38-32 overtime win earlier in the season. This time, however, the outcome wasn't close. St. X stormed to an easy 31-13 victory.

Vincent had six points and Lawton five in that loss.

During the previous three seasons Central City lost a grand total of 12 games. But the 1938-39 club wouldn't be nearly so successful, losing 13 times, the most setbacks ever suffered by a George Taylor-coached team. Although this team did post 20 wins, it turned out to be a most-difficult season, one that featured the Tide's first five-game losing skid and their first-ever loss to hated archrival Greenville.

The reason for this team's struggles can be summed up in a single word—inexperience. Ninety-eight percent of the previous season's offensive firepower had graduated, leaving a roster full of talented, but unproven, players. The results were predictable—inconsistency from game to game.

H.G. Watkins, the most-experienced returning player, was joined by Billy Ray Nale, J.T. Byars, Harold Soder, Ray Franklin, Maurice Lowe, John Withrow, Earl Latham, Marion Staples, Dave Duncan and Roy McWaters.

Watkins and Nale, both juniors, were the driving force behind whatever success this team did achieve. Both were outstanding players, and by the time they graduated, the duo ranked as arguably the best one-two punch in Central City's early basketball history.

The Tide kicked off the season by beating Drakesboro 22-12 and Earlington 34-20. Soder had 10 in each game, a number matched by Nale against Earlington.

Following a loss to Calhoun, the Tide ran off three straight wins, topping Sacramento 26-22, Hughes-Kirk 11-9 and Greenville 24-12. But this club's inexperience continued to pose problems, which resulted in losses to Russellville, Lewisburg and Louisville St. Xavier.

Despite the inconsistency, there were some solid individual efforts sprinkled in along the way. Watkins had 14, 16, 16 and 13 points in wins over Bowling Green 28-22, Clinton 34-22, Hopkinsville 36-26 and Daviess County 47-35.

Nale's best outings included 13 points in that win over Daviess County, 11 against Sacramento and 10 against Murray.

Franklin led the scoring with eight in a 17-14 win over Drakesboro, while Byars had eight in that 29-25 loss to St. X.

Watkins had 14, but it wasn't enough to keep the Tide from losing a double-overtime 27-25 thriller to Greenville. This marked the lone victory posted by the Blackhawks over a George Taylor-coached team.

The regular season ended in nightmare fashion, with the Tide losing their final five games to Owensboro 31-20, Madisonville 39-31, Murray 32-24, St. X 41-21 and Horse Cave 33-27, thus handing Taylor the longest losing streak during his tenure as head coach.

No one's confidence could have been very high as tournament time rolled around, yet this team surprised everyone by taking home another district tourney title, beating Bremen 33-22, Dunmor 28-14 and Hughes-Kirk 22-19.

Nale and Watkins had nine and eight points, respectively, in the win over Bremen, then Watkins and Franklin each tallied seven against Dunmor. Watkins was practically the whole show in the championship game, accounting for 15 of his team's 22 points.

Watkins continued his hot hand, scoring 11 points in a 33-29 win over Kyrock in the regional tourney opener. But the Tide's dream of making it to the state tourney was ended by Horse Branch, which rolled to an easy 44-30 semifinal win.

Watkins had 14 points and Nale 12 in that season-ending loss. The strong performances by those two gave Tide fans a preview of what lay on the horizon.

In the 1939-40 season, in which the Tide had a much more respectable 26-8 record, Nale scored 282 points and Watkins 276. Bernard Gary was next with 128, followed by Maurice Lowe (104), Earl Latham (93), Soder (40), Byars (34), Franklin (27), Harold Wilcox (18), David Danks (8), Roy McWaters (5) and Bobby Millard (4).

Nale and Watkins either led or shared team scoring honors in 31 of those 34 games. Nale's best effort was a 17-point performance in a 28-26 loss to Hughes-Kirk, while Watkins's top mark was 15 in a 38-29 win over Horse Branch.

The Tide opened strong, winning 13 of their first 16 games. Among the conquered were Greenville 36-15, Hopkinsville 19-17, Hodgenville 30-21, Horse Branch 38-29 and Daviess County 30-20.

After losing 36-26 to St. X, the Tide ran off four straight victories, beating Russellville 36-14, Horse Cave 25-19, Greenville 36-22 and Sedalia 32-24. Latham had his best game of the season against Greenville, accounting for 12 points in that win.

That streak ended with back-to-back losses to Morganfield 21-12 and Ashland 34-27. Then the Tide got hot again, reeling off wins against Calhoun 24-22, Owensboro 36-13, Hopkinsville 45-16, Henderson 27-22, Daviess County 39-22 and Owensboro 25-15 to close out the regular season.

Watkins hit for 12 points and Lowe 10 as the Tide whipped Graham 35-24 in the district tourney opener. In a 43-20 semifinal route of Martwick, reserves Wilcox and Danks led the scoring with 12 and eight points, respectively.

The title game opponent was Hughes-Kirk, a team the Tide split with during the regular season. On this night, however, the Tigers claimed the crown with a 35-27 win. Watkins and Latham paced the Tide with eight points each.

Unfortunately for the Tide, this would not be the last time they squared off against Hughes-Kirk. After Watkins scored seven points in a 27-26 win over Hartford in the regional tourney opener, it was another Tide-Tigers showdown. And once again, Hughes-Kirk came away with its third victory over the Tide in four tries, handily winning this encounter 45-31.

Gary led the Tide with a season-high 13 points.

Central City's overall record for the 1930s was 278-60 for an 82.2 winning percentage. There had been five trips to the state tournament and eight district tournament titles. Impressive numbers, regardless of how you assess them.

As a new decade approached, no one could have foreseen two monumental events that lay ahead—a coaching change and the most successful Golden Tide team in history.

The 1940s

Won – 263

Lost – 62

Winning Pct. – 81.0

Player of the Decade

W.C. Mobberly

Other Notable Players

Roy Atherton

Jackie Day

Bill Eades

Bud Eades

Doug Edwards

Tommy Gray

Kent Henry

Billy Hicks

Beauchamp Kirkpatrick

Gene Mercer

Jim Mohon

Hugh Vernon Smith

Jackie Sparks

Gilbert Teague

Earl Ray Tinsley

Marion Tinsley

Bobby Watkins

Chapter 6

W. C. Mobberly

Among the truly great Golden Tide players, W.C. Mobberly is without question the most underappreciated and underrated. Perhaps this oversight was inevitable, given that Mobberly's era fell between those of Peck Hickman and Corky Withrow, probably the two most-celebrated Golden Tide players ever.

But let there be no misunderstanding—Mobberly was a special player, and his many achievements certainly rank him among the elite. Only Withrow's name appears more often in the Miscellaneous Records section of this book than Mobberly's. Something else that makes Mobberly so unique is he was a groundbreaker.

Consider this: Mobberly was the first Golden Tide player to:

Score 30 points in a game (against St. Xavier on Dec. 27, 1946)
Score 500 points in a season (564 in 1946-47)
Score 1,000 career points (1,284 from 1943-47)
Participate in a post-season event (1947 East-West All-Star game)
Earn an athletic scholarship to a Division I college (Auburn)

Most important of all, during his four years the Tide won 116 games, a number matched by Hickman and surpassed by Withrow's 119 wins. He twice led the Tide to the state tournament, and was selected to the all-tournament team in 1945.

As a Golden Tide player, Mobberly battled and held his own against such standouts as Wah Wah Jones, Ralph Beard, Cliff Hagan, Frank Ramsey and Bobby Watson, all of whom went on to score more than 1,000 points apiece for the Kentucky Wildcats. In addition to that quintet, one of Mobberly's foes in that inaugural East-West game was future UK coach Joe B. Hall.

"I remember Mobberly," Hall said. "He was a good player. I know the West whipped us good in that game."

According to his old teammates, tenacity and fearlessness were at the heart of Mobberly's game.

"W.C. was aggressive in everything he did," Marion Tinsley said. "He was by far the most aggressive basketball player I played with or against. If the ball was loose on the floor, he made it his mission to go get it. He would kill his mother to get the basketball."

Tommy Gray, a guy not known as a shrinking violet, echoed Tinsley's assessment. "W.C. was one tough guy. He was a man. I can assure you that going up against him in practice every day was no picnic. He put a bunch of knots on my head."

But for all Mobberly achieved on the basketball court, what he accomplished after his playing days were over is far more impressive. He lettered four years for the Auburn Tigers while earning his bachelor's degree in Pharmacology. After that, he went to Huntington College in Montgomery, Ala., getting a second bachelor's in Biology. Next, he attended Tulane University, where he got his master's degree in Biology and his Ph.D. in Comparative Physiology.

After serving time in the Air Force, Mobberly did research and was a professor at Northeast Louisiana University.

He was diagnosed with malignant melanoma in 1960, and for the next eight years he battled against the cancer, undergoing multiple operations and skin grafts. Despite the many medical procedures, the cancer kept spreading.

During those eight years, Mobberly continued to work and to referee college basketball games when he felt up to it.

But in the end, cancer was the one opponent this ultimate warrior couldn't defeat. He died in 1968 at age 39, leaving behind his wife, Bette, daughters Deborah and Mary Jane, and three grandkids.

Still, his legacy lives on long after his death. Based on his research, which today's scientists are still using as a basis for current investigation, W.C. Mobberly was posthumously named among the Who's Who of American Scientists.

That's not a bad way to be remembered.

Chapter 7

1940-42

The new decade would get off to a rather mediocre start, with the 1940-41 team finishing with a 20-10 record. Members of this club included David Danks, Earl Capps, Bill Eades, Maurice Lowe, Bud Eades, Bill Miller, H.C. Ward, Henderson Duvall, Evan Ray, Bobby Millard, Billy Arnold, Jimmy Walker and Harold Wilcox.

This was one of the more schizophrenic teams in Central City history. The season kicked off with the Tide losing three straight games, then winning 16 of their next 17 games. That hot spell was followed by five losses in the next nine games to close out the regular season. Then if that weren't bad enough, the Tide were upended by Graham 31-21 in the district tournament opener.

That trio of season-opening losses came at the expense of Calhoun 22-17, Graham 36-11 and Sacramento 26-23. Danks and Millard each had five points in the opener, while Lowe had five against Graham and six against Sacramento.

In winning their next eight games, the Tide took care of Hopkinsville 48-21, Greenville 38-23 and 25-18, Drakesboro 32-29, Bowling Green 39-21, Elkton 49-23, Russellville 28-27 and Sacramento 57-25.

That streak was highlighted by several outstanding individual performances, including a 17-point effort by Duvall against Sacramento, 11 points by Capps and Millard against Hopkinsville and Bowling Green, respectively, and 10 points by Lowe in the win over Russellville.

After falling 35-33 to Calhoun, the Tide claimed victories over Hughes-Kirk 32-29, Clinton 27-25, Hopkinsville 25-24, Russellville 31-23, Owensboro 40-20, Elkton 36-23, Lewisburg 37-31 and Drakesboro 29-27.

Danks was the big gun during this stretch, leading the team in scoring on four occasions, with a season-best 16 against Lewisburg. Ray had his best game against Clinton, racking up 10 points.

As the season wore on, Bill Eades began to assert himself as a big scorer. The talented sophomore accounted for 12 points against Elkton, 13 against Providence and 10 against Horse Cave. He would not be the last Eades to put up impressive numbers. A generation later, sons Mark, Tommy and Penrod would account for more than 5,200 points.

Unfortunately, Eades's strong play did not translate into Golden Tide wins. Down the stretch they lost to Henderson, Graham, Bowling Green, Hughes-Kirk and Corbin.

They did manage to register wins over Providence, Owensboro, Horse Cave and Munfordville.

In the district tourney loss to Graham, Bill Eades was the top scorer with eight points.

In one of those tell-me-it-ain't-so situations, no scorebook could be located for the entire 1941-42 campaign, George Taylor's final season in the coach's chair. What makes this doubly disappointing is that this was a terrific basketball team, one that finished with a 32-3 record that included a 21-game winning streak.

This team's roster featured Bill Eades, Evan Ray, E.G. "Foo" Stevens, Bud Eades, Jimmy Walker, Bobby Millard, Earl Capps, Billy Arnold, Bill Miller and talented sophomore Beauchamp Kirkpatrick.

The only facts we know about this season are that the Tide went into district tournament action with a sparkling 28-2 record, then beat Drakesboro 24-10, Sacramento 33-28 and Graham 52-35 to notch another championship.

In regional action, the Tide easily handled Rochester 57-33, only to suffer a semifinal 40-37 loss to Graham.

At the conclusion of the season, George Taylor elected to step down as the Golden Tide coach. His reign had been remarkable, 438 wins against just 105 losses, an 81-percent winning percentage, eight trips to the Sweet 16, including one stretch of five years in a row, six teams with 30 or more wins and 14 district titles during his 17-year tenure.

The man Taylor handpicked to be his successor was no stranger to Central City or Golden Tide athletics. Delmas Gish graduated from Central City in 1925 and was a member of the basketball team. He later coached four years at McHenry High School, then returned to his alma mater to serve as assistant coach for the football and basketball teams.

Taylor's choice was a good one. Gish would go on to win more than 400 games during his years on the bench, take six teams to the state tournament, including one that finished as runner-up, and he would develop and coach the greatest player in Golden Tide history.

Chapter 8

1942-44

Delmas Gish was no novice when he took over from George Taylor in 1942. Gish had spent four years as head coach at McHenry High School, where his teams had an overall record of 62-36. Like Taylor, Gish got off to a rocky beginning—his first McHenry team could do no better than a 10-14 record—before turning things around in a quick way. Gish's next two teams went 19-5 and 21-5. In his fourth and final season, the Eagles were 12-12.

But coaching at McHenry High School was miles away from coaching at Central City, where Taylor had raised the bar of expectations to a very high level. Gish, who had been Taylor's assistant, surely understood the pressurized cauldron he was stepping into when he agreed to take over the head-coaching duties. Thanks to the enormous success during Taylor's reign, Golden Tide fans *expected* their team to win. It was now up to the diminutive Gish to make sure those fans weren't disappointed.

Gish's first team—1942-43—ended the season with a fine 21-6 record. But this turned out to be a somewhat strange campaign, one in which two key players—cousins Bill Eades and Bud Eades—were only allowed to play half the season. One day, the two Eades boys were on the team, the next day they weren't. At the time of their forced departure, the Tide's record was 12-2. (More about this odd situation later.)

Bill Eades, a three-year starter, was a superb scorer, while Bud, also a three-year veteran, was a solid all-around player. Joining them were Beauchamp Kirkpatrick, Earl Ray Tinsley, Howard Lovell, Bobby Logan, Earl Atherton, Lindle Cessna and a quartet of players—sophomores Bobby Watkins, Billy Hicks and Hugh Vernon Smith and freshman Gilbert Teague—that would later form the nucleus of Central City's most-successful team in history.

Starters in Gish's first game as Golden Tide coach were the Eades boys, Kirkpatrick, Tinsley and Watkins. In that historic game—an easy 54-19 romp past Sacramento—Bill Eades had 22 points on 10 buckets and a pair of free throws. Bud added 11 points, while Tinsley had nine, Lovell eight and Watkins four.

Tinsley had 13 and Bill Eades 12 in a 35-14 win over Drakesboro, then Bill had 11 and nine in wins over Livermore 24-21 and Hughes-Kirk 27-18. Bud Eades was the big hero in that come-from-behind win over Livermore. He scored six crucial second-half points that enabled the Tide to overcome a 17-15 halftime deficit.

Performing better in the second half became the norm for this team, which tended to start slow, then survive disaster by finishing strong.

After Bill Eades had 14 points and Watkins eight in a 39-19 win over Bremen, the Tide suffered back-to-back losses, losing to Graham 31-27 and Calhoun 37-36. In both of those games, the Tide trailed at intermission, played much better in the final two quarters, only to come up short.

Bud Eades had 10 against Graham, which was led by big Bob Gillespie with 14. Bill Eades and Tinsley scored 12 and eight points, respectively, in the Calhoun loss.

Those would be the only two setbacks the Tide suffered while the Eades boys were still on the team.

With Kirkpatrick accounting for 14 points, Tinsley and Watkins 11 each and Bill Eades 10, the Tide slammed arch-rival Greenville 61-16.

Bill Eades had 12 and 10 points in convincing wins over Hopkinsville 41-22 and Sacramento 32-16, then Bud Eades knocked in 13 points as the Tide broke away from a 19-19 halftime deadlock to slip past Russellville 34-31.

Another solid second-half effort propelled the Tide to a 33-32 revenge win over Calhoun. In that game Tinsley had nine points, Bill Eades and Kirkpatrick eight each.

More second-half magic was necessary in order to get past Hughes-Kirk 27-25. The Tide trailed 14-11 at the half, but with Bill Eades and Watkins accounting for all 16 second-half points, the Tide came away with the win. Eades paced the scoring attack with 15 points—12 in the final two quarters—while Watkins added eight, four in each half.

In what turned out to be his final game, Bill Eades scored 21 points to lead the Tide past Sharpe 44-32. Bud Eades, also in his last game, finished with nine.

It was at this point—January 1943—that the two Eades boys were no longer eligible to participate, and no one seems to know exactly why.

"Dad tried to explain it to me several times, but I never really understood it," Bill's son, Mark, said. "He said they were something called 'mid-school students', whatever that means. I can only assume that it meant they had graduated at mid-term and had no more eligibility remaining. That would almost have to be the case. Otherwise, I can't imagine Coach Gish allowing it to happen without putting up a fight."

Bill Eades would certainly have been worth fighting for. When his season ended prematurely, he had scored 173 points and was averaging 12.4 points per game.

At any rate, with the Eades boys gone, the pressure to produce points fell squarely on the shoulders of Tinsley, Kirkpatrick and Watkins. They would have to step up, or this team had little chance of succeeding. And for the most part, they did, helping lead the Tide to a 9-4 record the rest of the way.

In those 13 games, only 10 of which are found in scorebooks (the post-season games are missing), Tinsley led the scoring five times, Kirkpatrick four times and Watkins once.

The first post-Eades game resulted in an impressive 44-26 win over Owensboro. Kirkpatrick had 16 and Watkins nine in that victory. Watkins scored 15 in a 45-26 win over Henderson, then Tinsley took over, leading the scoring in the Tide's next four encounters, wins against Livermore 24-23 and Drakesboro 32-22, followed by losses to Louisville Manual 41-22 and Russellville 25-19. In those four games, Tinsley had 12, 16, 10 and 10 points.

Kirkpatrick led the charge in the next two games, scoring 10 points in a 40-24 win over Bremen and 14 in a tough 31-27 win at Owensboro.

The Tide closed out the regular season by splitting a pair of games against district rivals Graham and Greenville. Graham, again led by Gillespie with 12 points, built a 24-11 halftime lead, then coasted to a 37-25 win. Tinsley paced the Tide with nine points.

Against home-standing Greenville in the season finale, the Tide once again found themselves on the short end of a 15-12 halftime score. But with Kirkpatrick scoring seven second-half points and Tinsley chipping in with six, the Tide managed to escape with a 30-27 win. Kirkpatrick led with 13 points, Tinsley and Lovell had six each, Watkins had four and Cessna had one.

No scorebook records exist for the 23-22 district tournament win over Bevier-Cleaton or the 43-30 victory against Drakesboro in the championship game. Nor is there a record of the Tide's first-round 33-32 loss to Graham in the regional tournament. Of the Tide's six losses during the 1942-43 campaign, three were administered by Graham.

Gish's first season at the helm has to fall into the "what if?" category. What if Bill and Bud Eades had been eligible to participate during the second half of the season? How many more games might the Tide have won? How much deeper might they have advanced in tournament play? Those questions can never be answered.

With Kirkpatrick and Watkins returning along with veterans like Lovell, Atherton, Smith, Hicks, Cessna, Logan and Teague, along with a pair of new faces—W.C. Mobberly and Jimmy Mohon—the 1943-44 club's 22-10 record is something of a disappointment. And yet, despite those 10 losses, including one four-game losing streak, this team did get its act together late in the season, coming within one win of earning a trip to the state tournament.

According to Marion Tinsley, this team's struggles might have been exacerbated by the fact that the senior Kirkpatrick and the junior Watkins were constantly butting heads.

"There was definitely some friction between those two," Tinsley noted. "Both were terrific players, and both wanted to be the leader. I'm sure that what happened between them impacted the team. There was no way it couldn't have."

Rivalry or not, Kirkpatrick and Watkins performed very well that season. Kirkpatrick finished with 303 points, Watkins with 292. In 29 of the team's 32 games, those two players either led or shared scoring honors.

Behind 11 points from Kirkpatrick and 10 from Hicks, the Tide opened with a 47-17 win over Bremen. Kirkpatrick sandwiched 13 and 17 points in wins over Sacramento 37-18 and Hughes-Kirk 41-26 around a 12-point effort from Watkins in a 27-16 win over Livermore. Next came an easy 64-25 win over Drakesboro, with Kirkpatrick and Watkins scoring 14 and 11, respectively.

In that win over Drakesboro, the freshman Mobberly, who would go on to become the first Central City player to crack the 1,000-point barrier, nailed a second-half bucket for the first two points of his career.

The next two games resulted in losses, first to Gish's old school, McHenry 42-23, then to Calhoun 46-28. Hicks led the scoring with seven against McHenry, Watkins had 16 against Calhoun.

After Kirkpatrick scored 14 and Watkins 13 in a 42-29 win over Greenville, Watkins came through with 20 and Mobberly, making his first start, added 11 in a 53-30 win at Bremen. Kirkpatrick had 17 to lead the Tide past Russellville 37-25.

Those three wins were quickly followed by a pair of dismal performances, a 26-24 home-court loss to Hartford and a 21-18 loss to McHenry. Cessna had nine against Hartford, Lovell and Kirkpatrick six each in that second loss to McHenry.

Kirkpatrick scored nine points in a 33-27 victory over Livermore that kick-started a four-game winning streak. Watkins had 12, Mobberly and Lovell eight each, as the Tide topped Drakesboro 43-31 in their next outing. The streak continued with wins over Owensboro 30-19 and Henderson 38-28. Kirkpatrick had nine against Owensboro, Watkins 15 against Henderson.

Watkins kept the hot hand in the Tide's next three games, racking up 13 in a 37-30 loss to Hopkinsville, 12 in a 47-27 win over Hughes-Kirk and 12 in a hard-earned 33-30 win over Hazard in the All-Kentucky Conference Tournament.

In second-round action, the Tide dropped a 46-39 decision to Louisville St. Xavier, the start of a four-game losing streak. Kirkpatrick led the Tide with 16 points, Watkins had 12.

In the consolation game against Corbin, the Tide stormed back from a 42-30 deficit heading into the final quarter, only to lose 48-47. Kirkpatrick and Watkins each had 10 points in that loss, but it was the inspired play of Hicks and Smith that fueled the comeback. They each scored six points in that second-half charge.

The leg-weary Tide returned from the Louisville trip and immediately turned in two stinker performances, losing 34-32 to Hartford and 39-25 to Calhoun. Mobberly led with nine points against Hartford, a number matched by Kirkpatrick against Calhoun.

At this stage the Tide's record was a sub-par 14-9, with four of those losses coming at home. There was little reason to believe that some sunlight might peek through the dark clouds hovering above this team. There appeared to be little hope that this team could get out of its own way and perform at a higher level. And yet, that's exactly what happened. During the final month of the season, the Tide won eight straight, capturing another district championship in the process.

What makes this turnaround so remarkable is that with a single exception, none of the games were close. In those seven games, the winning average margin was 23 points per outing.

This run began with a 57-20 win over Sacramento. That was followed by wins over Owensboro 42-20, Russellville 53-45 and Greenville 41-22 to close out the regular season. Several superb individual performances highlighted this streak. Kirkpatrick had 19 against Sacramento, 14 against Owensboro, 13 against Russellville and 12 against Greenville. Teague also played well, scoring 13 against Russellville and 12 against Greenville, while Atherton and Mobberly each had 10 in the win over Russellville.

The district tournament proved to be little more than a turkey shoot, with the Tide crushing Bevier-Cleaton 62-28 and Bremen 52-23. Kirkpatrick led with 13 points in the opener, a game that saw nine players crack the scoring column. Lovell had 10, Mobberly nine, Smith eight, Hicks seven, Teague and Atherton five each, Watkins four and Young one.

In the title game against Bremen, Teague had 15, Kirkpatrick 14 and Watkins 10.

The regional tournament opening-round foe was a familiar one—Hughes-Kirk. The Tide twice defeated the Tigers during the regular season, and they made it three in a row by posting a 48-36 victory. Kirkpatrick led the charge with 13 points, followed by Teague with 11.

The situation was reversed in semifinal action, where the opponent was a Hartford team that had claimed two regular-season wins over the Tide. Both wins were by two points, 26-24 and 34-32. This game would also be decided by two points, only this time the Tide edged past Hartford for a 28-26 win. Kirkpatrick topped the Tide with eight points, while Watkins, Teague and Mobberly each contributed five.

With a state tournament trip at stake, the Tide faced yet another team that had won both regular-season battles. McHenry had defeated the Tide twice, once in easy fashion 42-23 and once in a thriller 21-18.

In the championship game, the Tide fell behind 24-19 at the half, pulled ahead 34-33 heading into the fourth quarter, then were outscored 19-7 in those final eight minutes, losing 52-41.

Watkins had a huge game, finishing with 20 points. Kirkpatrick closed out his career with an 11-point effort, while Mobberly added eight.

But McHenry's William Warren was the big difference in this game, ripping the Tide defense for 27 points.

Kirkpatrick and Watkins were both named to the all-regional team.

With battle-scarred veterans Watkins, Teague, Mobberly, Hicks and Smith all returning, expectations for the 1944-45 team were sky high. And those players didn't disappoint, leading the Tide to their most-successful season in history.

Chapter 9

The Great 1944-45 Team

History has always credited the 1944-45 team with a final record of 39-4. However, based on the two scorebooks, both of which are thorough and detailed, and a look at the schedule, it is clear that this club's record was 37-4. Even minus those two victories, this is the winningest team in Golden Tide history.

Here is how we know what the final—and accurate—record is: The team had a 29-game regular-season slate. A Feb. 2 home game against Drakesboro was cancelled when the Tide was invited to participate in a Louisville tournament. Of the 28 scheduled games, the Tide won 26. At Louisville, they won three and lost one, giving them a 29-3 record heading into post-season action. Two wins in the district, three in the regional and three in the state tournament—along with a loss—figures to a 37-4 record.

This also makes more sense. Forty-one games is a busy season. In fact, no Central City team other than this one played more than 40 games. The 1983-84 team comes closest with 39, while the 1930-31 and 1946-47 teams are next with 38.

(A note to those of you concerned about the loss of two victories to Central City's all-time total: Stop worrying. We'll reclaim those two wins later on down the road.)

Gish Challenges His Star Player

Prior to the start of the 1944-45 season, Delmas Gish pulled Bobby Watkins aside for a little heart-to-heart chat. Gish was well aware of two Watkins traits that tended to compete against each other—great leadership skills and a hot temper. In the past, Gish knew, Watkins was often his own worst enemy. The last thing Gish needed was for his most-experienced player to wage a season-long war against his inner demons.

Gish knew this team had the potential to be special. Watkins, Hicks, Mobberly, Smith and Teague were all returning, and they would be joined by Kent Henry, Jackie Sparks, Jimmy Mohon, Richard Morris, Harold Tudor and Billy Dukes. It was a team with size (Henry), strength (Mobberly and Teague), savvy (Hicks), defense (Smith) and a solid bunch of role players (Mohon, Sparks, Morris, Tudor and Dukes).

But for all the separate parts to blend together, the team needed a leader. And in Gish's view of things, that's the role Watkins had to fill. Hence, that pre-season heart-to-heart chat, one in which Watkins listened but didn't really hear.

In the season opener, an easy 44-21 win over Bremen, Watkins played poorly, scoring only three points. After the game, Gish entered the classroom where the players were getting dressed just in time to witness an angry Watkins slam a chair against the wall.

It was a moment in which Gish could have gone ballistic, and had every right to do so. But he didn't. Instead, he played it cool, slowly approaching his senior "leader" and then in a quiet voice, simply said, "Same old Bobby Watkins. Nothing has changed at all."

Gish's quiet rebuke must have made an impression on Watkins, because from that moment on he became the leader Gish wanted and the team needed. Watkins was done with slamming chairs; now he would lead this team to the greatest season in Central City history.

"Look, that team had some really good players," future Golden Tide great Joe Mac Howard said. "I was only in junior high that year, but I can remember watching them play. Bob Watkins was the leader. He really held that team together."

According to Tommy Gray, another key player on that team was the often-overlooked Hugh Vernon Smith. "I remember one game when Bob was not playing very well . . . I think he was having girlfriend troubles at the time. Anyway, his attention was not on the game. So what does Hugh Vernon do? He confronts Bob, his best friend, grabs him by the shoulders, shakes him and orders him to get his act together and focus on the game. After that, Bob played pretty well."

Sometimes even a good leader can use a wake-up call.

The Memorable Season Begins

Eight different players scored in that 44-21 win over Bremen, paced by Hicks with 10 points. Smith and Mobberly each had eight, Henry had seven, Teague had four, Watkins had three, Sparks and Morris two apiece.

A balanced scoring attack was one of this team's strengths. It was not unusual for nine or 10 players to contribute points. For the season, seven players would top the 100-point mark.

Watkins had 12 points and Henry, a 6'3" sophomore, had eight in a difficult 31-24 road win at Drakesboro, then Teague and Watkins each had 11 as the Tide pounded Graham 48-15.

Teague continued his hot hand, single-handedly outscoring Beaver Dam in 47-10 romp. Teague finished with a dozen points. Watkins had nine and Mobberly eight in that win.

Mobberly and Watkins hit for 12 points each and Hicks added 10 as the Tide crushed Livermore 53-24. Three nights later, Watkins scored 12 points, Teague 11, Smith nine and Mobberly eight in a 57-17 win over Hughes-Kirk.

After a 52-22 win over Hartford in a game that saw 10 players hit the scoring column, headed by Watkins with 11, the Tide suffered their first loss of the season, falling 34-26 at Calvert City. The game was knotted 12-12 at intermission, but the Wildcats, who could manage only an 11-12 record that season, pulled away in the final two quarters to post the upset.

Watkins led the Tide with 11 points.

The Tide came back from that setback to beat Dawson Springs 34-31 before easily blasting Calhoun 57-34. Mobberly and Smith had eight points apiece against Dawson Springs, while Teague and Watkins had 19 and 18, respectively against Calhoun.

Next up was one of the most memorable games in Golden Tide history.

Welcome to Central City, Mr. Jones

At the time, the most popular and most recognizable prep player in Kentucky was Wallace "Wah Wah" Jones, the 6'4" man-child who led Harlan to the state championship in 1944. In fact, the Green Dragons went to the state tournament in each of Jones's four years at the school. As a freshman he scored 16 points in a 44-32 loss to Lexington Lafayette in the title game. As a junior in 1944 he had 23 points in a 40-28 title win over Dayton.

All Kentucky high school basketball fans knew about Wah Wah Jones and, naturally, they all wanted to see him play in person. With that in mind, Harlan coach Joe Gilly scheduled a Western Kentucky road trip for his defending state champs. Included among the games set for this excursion was a Dec. 22, 1944, stop at Central City.

This was a huge game for the Golden Tide, and in a story Watkins often recounted with great pride, this was the moment when it became crystal clear that this was a fearless basketball team.

"When we were in the dressing room prior to the game, Coach Gish asked who wanted to guard Wah Wah," Watkins said. "Every player in that room raised his hand."

While it's not known who actually drew the assignment, judging by the results we can assume that it most likely was the result of a total team effort. Jones was limited to three points by Golden Tide defenders. All Jones could manage was a single field goal and one free toss, all coming in the opening half. Jones was shut down completely during the final two quarters.

Watkins scored 12, Henry eight, Smith three, Teague and Mobberly two each in a low-scoring 27-19 Tide victory.

This was a monumental win for the Golden Tide. It would also not be the last time they faced off against Jones and his Harlan teammates. The two teams would get together again in March.

Continuing to Roll Along

With the exception of a single blip—a 26-23 loss at Leitchfield—the Tide seemed to get stronger with each outing. After topping Harlan, the Tide won 11 of their next 12 scheduled games, beginning with a 42-24 revenge win over Calvert City. In that game, Henry and Watkins were the top scorers with nine points each.

Teague had 16 points in a 57-16 win over Russellville, then Mohon, Teague and Watkins had five each in that Leitchfield loss.

Every Tide player scored, with four cracking double digits in a 75-28 won over Graham. Mobberly and Mohon each had 12, while Hicks and Smith both had 10.

The next three Tide games resulted in easy wins—Greenville 36-20, Bremen 71-24 and Owensboro 44-31. In each of those three victories, a pair of Golden Tide players hit for double figures. Teague and Watkins had 12 apiece against Greenville, Hicks had 16 and Teague 14 against Bremen, and Watkins had 14 and Mobberly 10 against Owensboro.

Mohon picked a good night to have his best game of the season, scoring 13 points in a tough 42-40 win over visiting Louisville Manual. Teague had nine, Mobberly eight and Hicks seven in that win, which kept the Tide's perfect home-court record alive. For the year the Tide would go 14-0 at home.

After that narrow escape against Manual, the Tide rolled to four easy wins, topping Henderson 53-21, Livermore 51-15, Hopkinsville 39-22 and Russellville 52-21. Teague led the scoring in those first two games, getting 12 against Henderson and 10 against Livermore. Mobberly had 10 in the win over Hopkinsville, which got eight points from future UK football coach Jerry Claiborne, then Mohon and Mobberly each had 11 and Watkins 10 against Russellville.

Hello Louisville, Hello Ralph Beard

As noted earlier, Central City cancelled a home game against Drakesboro after receiving an invitation to participate in the prestigious All-Kentucky Conference Tournament played in Louisville Male's gym. This event proved so popular that it later became the Louisville Invitational Tournament, the LIT.

Male, which made it to the 1944 state tournament, was regarded by most observers as the team to beat in 1945. This experienced club featured a trio of standout performers, headed, of course, by the great guard Ralph Beard. Joining Beard were Gene Rhodes and Ed Mudd, both superb players.

The Tide opened against Middlesboro, grabbing a 22-14 halftime advantage, then holding on for a 42-37 win. Mobberly was terrific, racking up 16 points. Teague chipped in eight.

A similar scenario followed in quarterfinal action against Danville, with the Tide cruising to a 22-11 halftime lead, only to watch that lead quickly diminish. The Tide, thanks to nine points each from seniors Smith and Watkins, managed to hang on for a 33-29 victory. A late Hicks bucket sealed the win.

In a second bitterly contested battle against Louisville Manual, the Tide, after trailing 14-12 at intermission, rode hot hands from Hicks and Watkins to a 33-30 semifinal win. The score was tied 11 times, the last one coming at 28-28. A Watkins bucket broke the tie, then Hicks came up with a steal and layup to ice the victory.

Watkins finished with 12 points, while Hicks had 10. Those two players each had eight second-half points to lead the comeback win.

Later that evening, in the championship game, Male, led by Beard's 21-point performance, showed why the experts picked the Bulldogs to win it all. With Rhodes scoring 10 points and Beard nine, the Bulldogs raced to a 28-16 halftime lead and then never looked back, claiming a 52-35 win.

Beard received solid support from Rhodes with 12 points and Mudd with 10.

Watkins was the lone Golden Tide standout, accounting for 18 points. Teague had eight, Mobberly five and Hicks four.

As it was with Harlan, this would not be the Golden Tide's last encounter with Beard and his Male buddies. The two teams would collide again a month later.

Finishing Strong Down the Homestretch

Although the Tide won three games in Louisville, the fact is they had not played particularly good basketball. That trend continued in their first post-Louisville game, a narrow 36-34 win over Calhoun. Once again the Tide watched as a solid 24-19 halftime lead melted away during the final two quarters. Calhoun closed to within two points before time ran out, thus allowing the Tide to keep a perfect home-court record.

Teague and Mobberly led the Tide with 12 and 11 points, respectively.

After barely avoiding disaster against Calhoun, the Tide rediscovered their mid-season form by winning their final four games in convincing fashion. Smith had nine in a 36-22 win over Hartford, before Mohon had 12, Watkins 10 and Hicks eight as the Tide pounded Greenville 48-22.

The Tide closed out the regular campaign by beating Owensboro 50-30 and Hughes-Kirk 55-43. Watkins had 18 against Owensboro, Teague had 20 against Hughes-Kirk, including 14 in the second half, while Hicks, who always seemed to play well against tougher opponents, had 11 in the win over Owensboro and 10 against Hughes-Kirk.

Eyeing a Return Trip to Louisville

The trio of Teague, Hicks and Watkins stayed hot, combining for 34 points in a 50-26 win over Drakesboro in the district tournament opener. The game was close for a half, with the Tide only holding a slim 18-16 advantage at the break. Hicks accounted for all 10 of his points in those opening two quarters.

A smothering defense in the second half proved to be the difference. During those final 16 minutes, the Tide limited Drakesboro to a single field goal and eight free throws.

Teague paced the winners with 14 points, 13 coming after intermission. Watkins matched Hicks with 10 points.

In a 51-29 title game blowout over Bremen, eight Golden Tide players dented the scoring column, led by Teague with 11. Smith and Watkins had nine each, Mobberly and Hicks eight each, with Sparks, Morris and Henry adding a bucket apiece.

The regional tournament opener in Leitchfield pitted the Tide against Caneyville, a team they had not faced during the regular season. The game proved to be much closer than expected, but the Tide, behind 10 points from Watkins and six each from Teague and Mobberly, managed to slip away with a 28-21 win.

Home-standing Leitchfield, a club that handed the Tide one of their three losses, was expected to be the big challenge. However, that predicted match-up never took place, thanks to Graham's stunning 36-31 upset win over Leitchfield.

In semifinal action, the Tide faced Hartford, a team they had handled on two occasions without much trouble. In this outing, the Tide held a narrow 19-15 lead at the intermission. In the second half, propelled by the strong play of Teague and Mohon, the Tide advanced to the championship game with a 44-34 win.

Teague led the scoring with 12 points, including nine after the break. Watkins had 11, Mobberly nine and Mohon eight, six coming in the decisive second half.

Traditionally, championship tussles are down-to-the-wire thrillers in which the outcome isn't decided until the final seconds. That was not the case on the night of March 10, 1945. This title game was a laugher from start to finish.

The Tide, sparked by Hicks with 16 points, routed Brownsville 66-26. This one was over not long after the opening tip-off. By halftime, the Tide owned a commanding 29-8 lead. The Tide's defense was dominant, holding Brownsville to a pair of first-half field goals.

Watkins and Henry hit for double figures with 13 and 12 points, respectively. Other Tide players who scored included Teague with eight, Smith with seven, Mohon and Mobberly with four each and Tudor with two.

This victory sent the Tide back to the Sweet 16 for the first time since 1938. It also provided Delmas Gish with the first of his six trips to the state tournament.

Chapter 10

The 1945 State Tournament

According to the Louisville *Courier-Journal*, the 1945 state tournament shattered all previous Sweet 16 attendance records. During the four-day event, more than 35,000 fans packed into the Jefferson County Armory to watch the action. Both the semifinal and final rounds were played in front of sold-out capacity crowds of 7,000.

Such excitement is understandable when you consider that the 1945 tourney featured the state's top two teams (Male and Central City), the defending champs (Harlan) and two of the most-celebrated and recognizable individual players in Kentucky hoops history (Wah Wah Jones and Ralph Beard).

But that's only the tip of the iceberg. From top to bottom, the 1945 state tournament was loaded with exceptional teams. Check out these opening-round match-ups and team records heading into the Big Show.

Elkhorn City (36-8) vs. Valley (24-3); Harlan (33-6) vs. Covington (24-4); Central City (34-3) vs. Rineyville (28-5); Madison (22-2) vs. Paducah Tilghman (21-6); Providence (37-2) vs. Vicco (29-8); Danville (22-6) vs. Dawson Springs (17-8); Bowling Green (23-2) vs. Clark County (22-5); Male (22-5) vs. Maysville (19-5).

In all, that computes to a record of 365-78 for an 82.4 winning percentage.

The Big Show Begins

With two exceptions, form held true in the tournament's first round—Elkhorn City bumped off favorite Valley 39-31 and top-ranked Male only managed to ease past upset-minded Maysville 44-41.

Other first-round scores were: Harlan 43, Covington 33; Madison 53, Paducah Tilghman 51; Providence 45, Vicco 34; Danville 54, Dawson Springs 30; Bowling Green 46, Clark County 40.

The Tide opened with a relatively easy 54-36 win over Rineyville. After racing to a 28-18 halftime lead, the Tide coasted into the quarterfinal round.

Watkins topped a balanced scoring attack with 14 points. Mobberly and Teague each had 12, Smith seven, Mohon six, Hicks two and Dukes one.

The next two games tested the Tide to the limits, and each one easily could have ended in defeat were it not for late-game heroics by Hicks and Mohon. In both of those games, the Tide trailed deep into the fourth quarter, only to find a way to escape with a win.

A dreadful first-half effort that included a single second-quarter point nearly doomed the Tide in their 32-28 win over Madison. At intermission, the Tide were on the short end of a 13-10 score.

Madison continued to hold a 24-21 advantage heading into the final eight minutes. With their backs squarely against the wall, this Golden Tide team did what it had done all season—it simply refused to lose.

Hicks sparked the comeback, scoring all six of his points late in the second half. Hicks had late-game help from Mobberly and Watkins, who combined for 10 second-half points.

With his team trailing 27-25, Hicks nailed one from long range to even the score. After a free throw by Dick Webb put Madison back in front 28-27, Hicks scored again, this time on a crip shot, to give the Tide a one-point advantage. A Watkins free throw and another bucket by Hicks sent the Tide into the semifinal round.

Watkins and Teague each scored eight for the winners, while Mobberly had seven, Hicks had six and Mohon had three.

Hello Again, Mr. Jones

What that exercise in survival against Madison did was earn the Tide a second meeting against Wah Wah Jones and his Harlan teammates. In their second-round game, the Green Dragons, led by Jones with 19 points, manhandled Elkhorn City 49-36.

Those 19 points by Jones were a far cry from what he scored in Harlan's first meeting with the Tide. In that December match-up, which the Tide won 27-19, Jones was held to three points.

Legend has it that sometime later a sportswriter asked Jones about that game. According to the legend, Jones said, "the only place Central City could beat us is in that cracker box gym of theirs."

Is that legend fact or fiction? Who can ever know for sure? But true or not, it is a great story.

Jones did get his second shot at the Tide, and for much of the game it appeared as if his prognostication would come true. The Tide led 11-10 after one quarter, and the score was tied 19-19 at the half. In those opening two quarters, Watkins accounted for 12 of his team's points, while Jones had eight, six coming from the charity stripe.

Plagued by foul problems—Watkins and Teague fouled out—the Tide fell behind 27-23 heading into the final quarter. Now in desperation mode, the Tide upped their defensive intensity, limiting the Green Dragons to just three fourth-quarter points.

Inside the final minutes, with Watkins and Teague watching helplessly from the sidelines, Hicks accounted for four crucial points, Henry had a basket and a free throw, and Mohon dropped in three big free tosses to lift the Tide to a 34-30 win.

Watkins led the way with those 12 first-half points, while Hicks finished with nine. Mobberly, Teague, Mohon and Henry all had three points apiece and Smith had one.

Jones topped all scorers with 17.

The Tireless Ralph Beard

While the Tide was forced to expend considerable energy in the win over Harlan, Male was able to take it easy in its semifinal game, a 50-20 romp past Danville. The outcome of that game was decided so early that Male coach Paul Jenkins was able to rest his starters for much of the second half.

Tired legs may have played a role in the outcome of the championship game, a fact alluded to by *Courier-Journal* assistant sports editor Ken Taylor. "The Golden Tide would never admit defeat...but they just didn't have enough to play two hard games in one day. Their victory over Harlan left them leg-weary."

"Yes, we were plenty tired and Male was well-rested," Watkins would later say, adding, "but I'm not sure we could have beaten them even if we were rested. Male beat us twice that year. They were just a better team, that's all you can say. And that rascal Beard *never* got tired. When everyone else was bent over grabbing their shorts and gasping for air, Ralph would be running around like the game had just begun."

Beard would score 19 points, Dale Powell 13 and Gene Rhodes 12 as Male captured the state crown with a 54-42 victory.

The game was close early, with the Bulldogs on top 8-5 after one quarter. But the second quarter proved to be the difference. In those eight minutes, Male unleased a deadly fast break, outscoring the Tide 21-13 to take a 29-18 lead at intermission.

Male's lead eventually stretched to 20 points before a late Golden Tide flurry cut the difference to that final 12-point margin.

Teague led the Tide with 13 points. Hicks and Watkins each had eight, Mohon seven, Mobberly four, Smith and Dukes one apiece.

After Mobberly opened the scoring by sinking a free throw, Male reeled off six unanswered points, two each from Ed Mudd, Beard and Powell, to grab a 6-1 lead. Teague and Watkins countered with back-to-back buckets to make it 6-5, before Mudd scored again just before the first quarter ended.

In that decisive second quarter, Beard registered seven points, while Rhodes and Powell added four each as the Bulldogs took command. The two teams played on fairly even terms in the third stanza—Male had a 15-13 advantage—but with the gas tank now completely empty, the Tide were in no position to mount a comeback.

The Tide would have to settle for the runner-up trophy.

Watkins, Teague and Mobberly were named to the all-tournament team. Also named were Beard and Jones, who scored 80 points in his four games, giving him an all-time state tournament total of 223 points, a record that stood until Clay County's Richie Farmer broke it more than 40 years later.

For the season, seven Golden Tide players scored more than 100 points, led by Watkins with 400. Others included Teague (358), Mobberly (277), Hicks (235), Smith (190), Mohon (147) and Henry (108).

A Truly Special Saturday

On a single Saturday in 1945, Central City went up against two of the greatest players to ever play the game of basketball—Wah Wah Jones and Ralph Beard. Those two players would go on to lead the University of Kentucky to incredible success. During the four years Jones and Beard played, the Wildcats won two NCAA championships, one NIT title, had an overall record of 130-10 and went 55-0 against Southeastern Conference foes. Then, of course, they helped the U.S. win a gold medal in the 1948 Olympic Games played in London.

But during this remarkable 1944-45 season, the best that talented duo could manage against the Tide was to break even. Two wins, two losses. Splitting four games against Jones and Beard ranks as one of the major accomplishments in Golden Tide history. Never again would a Central City team face two players of their caliber on the same day.

Chapter 11

1945-46

Despite losing Bobby Watkins, Billy Hicks and Hugh Vernon Smith to graduation, expectations for the 1945-46 season were fairly high. And why shouldn't they be? After all, several key veterans were returning, headed by all-state performers W.C. Mobberly and Gilbert Teague. Also back were Kent Henry, Jimmy Mohon and Jackie Sparks, three players with plenty of experience. Joining them were Richard Morris, Royce McDowell, Gene McDonald, Sonny Son, Billy Dukes, Ronnie Milam, Harold Tudor and Tunney Jones.

This club would finish with a fine 23-6 record that included impressive wins over Owensboro, Madisonville (twice), Hazard, Henderson, Hopkinsville and Leitchfield.

But two factors kept this group from achieving greatness—lack of depth and a missing all-state player.

The usual starting five, Mobberly, Henry, Mohon, Sparks and Morris, logged the vast majority of playing time. There was occasional help from the bench, but for the most part those five starters were iron men.

Factor number two was even more profound, and it had a huge impact on this team's results. Teague, a senior and a three-year starter, left school to enter the military. The absence of a player projected to be one of the top two scorers left a huge hole for this team to fill. Teague would return to action in 1946-47 to finish his career.

In Teague's absence, much of the scoring burden fell on Mobberly's shoulders. Mobberly, now in his junior season, would step up and do his share. But one is left to wonder how good this team might have been had Teague remained in school.

The Tide opened the campaign by beating Bremen 35-29. Henry paced the Tide with 12 points. Mobberly added eight.

Mobberly hit for 14 in a tough 36-32 win over Graham, then came back to score 15 in a 36-25 win over Drakesboro. The Cardinals' Paul Riley led all scorers with 18.

Henry tossed in 12 points, Mohon and Mobberly added 11 each as the Tide remained undefeated by topping Dawson Springs 46-38. Next came a 36-25 win over Livermore, with Mobberly's 13 points leading the way.

A miserable three-point second quarter was enough to land the Tide on the short end of a 42-41 score against Bremen. The Tide led 21-12 after the first eight minutes, only to find that advantage whittled down to 24-22 by intermission. The lead held at 34-33 going into the last quarter, but the Eagles, paced by Rip Gish's 13 points, pulled out the narrow victory.

Henry had 11 for the Tide, while Mobberly added 10.

Behind 18 points each from Henry and Mobberly, the Tide bounced back with a 58-36 win over Calhoun. Mobberly had 15 and Mohon 10 as the Tide stopped Greenville 42-32, then with Mobberly scoring 13 and Sparks 10, the Tide slipped past Hartford 37-33.

Traveling out of state, the Tide fell victim to Metropolis (Ill.) 46-36. This game was never close, with the host team jumping to a 26-13 half-time lead and never looking back.

Morris paced the Tide with 11 points.

Now sporting an 8-2 record, the Tide would edge past Paducah St. Mary's 33-30 to kick off an impressive nine-game winning streak. Mobberly had 11 points and Henry 10 in that road victory. Of those nine wins, five were in enemy territory.

In an easy 54-33 home win against Leitchfield, Mohon led a balanced attack with 18 points. Mobberly had 10, Henry nine and Morris eight in that win.

After leading 20-19 at halftime, the Tide broke away in the final two quarters to slam Madisonville 46-28 in the first of back-to-back road wins. Mobberly had 13 points, Morris 10, Mohon nine and Henry eight against the Maroons.

With nine different players scoring, the Tide traveled to Hughes-Kirk and won a 44-18 laugher. Milam paced the attack with a career-best 11 points.

Morris got the hot hand in the Tide's next two outings, accounting for 31 points in wins over Hartford 41-28 and Owensboro 52-42.

Morris had 15 against the Mustangs, and 16 against the Red Devils. In the win over Owensboro, Morris received help from Mobberly with 14 points and Mohon with 10.

All-state standout J.M. Gipe led Owensboro with 15 points.

Henry scored 13 and Sparks added nine in a 41-27 win at Henderson, then Mobberly erupted for 21 as the Tide pounded Livermore 48-17. The win over Henderson proved to be a costly one. Henry, the Tide's tallest starter, suffered an injury that sidelined him for the remainder of the regular season.

With Henry now unavailable, the Tide traveled to Louisville to face Hazard in the first round of the All-Kentucky Conference Tournament. Mohon stepped up big, scoring 20 points to lead the Tide to a 46-36 victory.

One day later, St. Xavier, fueled by George Silliman's 14 points, claimed a 39-36 win. Mobberly led the Tide with 10 points, while Sparks, Morris and Milam each contributed seven.

Returning closer to home, the Tide, behind 18 points from Morris, ripped home-standing Drakesboro 52-28. Sparks also hit double digits with 10 points.

Morris stayed hot, hitting for 16 points in a 50-33 win over Hopkinsville. Mohon had 10 points and Mobberly nine in that win.

Hopkinsville was led by future UK football coach Jerry Claiborne's 11 points.

Still minus Henry, the Tide dropped a 37-30 decision at Calhoun before coming back to beat Madisonville 45-22 and Hughes-Kirk 68-23. Mobberly had 21 points against the Maroons, then Mohon scored 15, Mobberly and newcomer Tunney Jones each had 11 against the Tigers.

The Tide split their final two games of the regular season, losing 47-32 to Owensboro and then beating Greenville 31-28.

Against Owensboro, Morris topped the scoring with 10 points. Mobberly added nine, Jones six and Mohon four.

In the win over Greenville, Morris finished with nine points, Sparks and Mobberly seven apiece.

District play opened with a second straight battle against arch-rival Greenville, this one taken by the Tide 37-30. Mobberly had 11 points to lead the winners, while Mohon had nine and Morris eight. Henry, returning to action for the first time in a month, chipped in with seven.

One night later, in a nip-and-tuck thriller, Drakesboro, led by Paul Riley's 13 points, overcame a 21-17 halftime deficit to edge past the Tide 32-31.

The Tide's scoring was topped by Mohon with 11 and Mobberly with nine.

This season is another that fits nicely into that "what-if?" category. What if Teague had played? What if Henry hadn't missed so many games due to injury? Once again we are left holding a bag of questions and no way to offer any answers.

What we do know is that next year's team, hoisted squarely on Mobberly's shoulders, recorded one of the winningest seasons in school history.

Chapter 12

1946-47

It was during this season that W.C. Mobberly established some record-breaking numbers, becoming the first Golden Tide player to score 30 points in a game, 500 points in a season and surpass the 1,000-point career mark.

And of even more importance, while Mobberly was setting those personal milestones, he was also leading the Tide to a 34-4 record and another trip to the state tournament. Those 34 wins would tie the 1930-31 team for the third most in school history, topped only by the 1944-45 team's 37 wins and the 1953-54 team's 35 wins.

In every way this was a solid team, one with a nice blend of veterans and newcomers, and a deep bench—it was not uncommon for substitutes to put up big scoring numbers. There was excellent size inside—Kent Henry, Marvin Dossett and Tommy Gray were all big, strong players. Plus, there was a familiar face—Gilbert Teague, who had returned from the service.

Rounding out the roster were Tunney Jones, Jackie Day, Royce McDowell, Sonny Son, Doug Edwards, Wallace Noffsinger and Gene McDonald.

Behind 17 points from Mobberly, 10 from Henry and eight from McDowell, the Tide opened the campaign by whipping Graham 59-40. Joining that trio in the starting lineup were Jones and McDonald.

Teague made his return to the starting quintet, replacing Jones, and although he went scoreless, the Tide managed to ease past Sacramento 31-29. McDonald led the winners with 10 points, while Mobberly and Dossett each had six.

Teague scored 10 points, Dossett nine, Mobberly seven and Gray six in a 41-30 win over Drakesboro. Henry came through with 14 points and Mobberly added 11 as the Tide improved to 4-0 by ripping Livermore 46-22.

The next two Tide wins were anything but easy. During this testy stretch, they faced a tough challenge from Paducah St. Mary's before finally prevailing 44-37, thanks to 23 points from Mobberly, and then slipped past Hughes-Kirk 30-28, led by Jones, who came off the bench to score 11 points.

Mobberly racked up 40 points in the Tide's next two outings, scoring 15 in a 40-27 win over Calhoun and 25 in a 51-38 win over Dawson Springs. Teague also hit for double figures, scoring 12 against Dawson Springs.

Home-standing Greenville slowed the pace, yet the Tide were able to get away with a 25-21 win. Mobberly's 11 points led all scorers.

Nine Golden Tide players hit the scoring column in an easy 52-21 win over Hartford. Dossett and Mobberly each had 10, Jones had eight, Teague and Henry six apiece, McDowell four, Edwards and Gray three each and Noffsinger two.

Next, the Tide traveled to Louisville for a battle against a strong St. Xavier club, and it was in this game, a 60-51 Tide win, that Mobberly hit the 30-point mark. To achieve his total, Mobberly had 12 field goals and hit six of seven free tosses.

Mobberly received help from Teague and Jones, who scored 13 and 12 points, respectively.

The Tide's first loss came a few days later when Leitchfield, led by Marion Rau's 22 points, posted a 44-43 win. Rau scored 19 of his points in a first-half outburst that had the Bulldogs on top 27-19 at intermission. Mobberly had 15 and Jones 10 for the Tide.

Time For a Lineup Change

It was following the Leitchfield setback that Delmas Gish felt the time had come to make a permanent change in the starting lineup, and in particular, the backcourt. That meant a promotion for sophomore Jackie Day.

"Before practice one day Mr. Gish called me into his office," Day said. "Mr. Taylor was also there. I was on the "B" team at the time, but I guess Mr. Gish wasn't pleased with the way his guards were playing. He asked me if I had any interest in moving up to the varsity. I nodded and quickly said, 'you bet I do.' After that, I started every game for the rest of my career."

Day scored four points in his debut effort, a 34-28 win over Sacramento that kicked off a 10-game winning streak. Dossett had 10, Mobberly and Jones eight each in that win.

Mobberly went on a scoring rampage in the Tide's next nine wins, accounting for 153 points. His best efforts were 20 points in wins over Livermore 55-27 and Dawson Springs 43-36, 19 against Manual (60-33), 18 against Henderson (40-37) and 17 against Bremen (59-31).

Several of Mobberly's teammates also contributed in a big way during this impressive run. Jones had 13 against Manual and 10 in a 49-46 win over Owensboro, while Henry and McDowell each had 11 in that win over Bremen.

The last two of those 10 straight wins came in the first two rounds of the All-Kentucky Conference Tournament. In the opener, the Tide had a second meeting against Manual. With Teague scoring 14 points, Mobberly 13 and Jones 10, the Tide advanced with a 50-31 win.

Led by battle-hardened veterans Teague and Mobberly with 16 points each, the Tide broke away from a 32-32 tie heading into the final quarter to post a 49-43 victory over Murray. Jones had eight points and Day six in that win.

Corbin, led by Curt Selvy's 12 points, snapped the Tide's winning streak by claiming a 44-41 win. The Tide led 8-7 after one quarter, but fell behind 25-21 at the half and were never able to catch up.

Mobberly topped all scorers with 17 points in what would be the Tide's last loss during the regular season. They would capture their final eight games, all in impressive fashion.

This late surge began with Mobberly scoring 13 points, Dossett and Jones eight apiece in a 53-43 win over Drakesboro. Mobberly scored 12, Henry 11, Dossett eight and Gray seven in a 59-19 blowout of Hopkinsville that saw all 10 Tide players get in on the scoring.

Mobberly had 18 points, Jones 13 and McDonald eight in a surprisingly easy 63-29 win over Greenville. This marked the second straight game in which all Tide players scored.

Next came back-to-back wins against two of the state's top teams—Madisonville, led by Frank Ramsey and Ches Riddle, and Owensboro, led by J.M. Gipe, Bobo Foster and Bobby Watson.

In what turned out to be a low-scoring affair, the Tide used a strong second-half performance to beat Ramsey and his home-standing Maroons 38-24. The Tide were on the short end of a 16-14 halftime score, but with Mobberly accounting for 10 of his game-best 16 points after the break, the Tide roared back to get the win. Ramsey and Riddle led the Maroons with seven points each.

The Tide's 59-53 win over Owensboro was the virtual opposite of the Madisonville game. After building a 35-25 halftime lead, the Tide had to hang on during the final 16 minutes to escape with the win. Gipe, who would join Mobberly as a first-team all-state selection, led the Red Devils with a game-high 21 points.

Four Tide starters cracked double figures, led by Mobberly with 18. Teague, Henry and Jones each had a dozen, while Day added five.

The Tide closed out the regular season by beating Hughes-Kirk 63-29, Bowling Green 52-41 and Calhoun 78-40. A different Tide player led the scoring in those three wins. Teague had 18 against Hughes-Kirk, Mobberly 21 against Bowling Green and Henry 20 against Calhoun.

A Shocking Loss, A Strong Finish

Heading into district tournament action at Drakesboro, the Tide were heavily favored to claim another crown. After all, they owned a 29-2 record highlighted by a perfect 8-0 mark against district foes. And after posting easy wins over Dunmor 63-14 and Hughes-Kirk 53-40, it appeared as though the script was being followed to perfection.

Dossett had 16 and McDonald 13 in the Dunmor romp, while Mobberly had 18, Jones 11 and Henry 10 in the win over Hughes-Kirk.

But it turns out that someone forgot to send the script to Greenville, a team the Tide had crushed 63-29 less than a month earlier. On this night, with the title trophy on the line, the Blackhawks used a smothering defense to hold the high-scoring Mobberly to three points en route to a 46-40 upset victory.

Bobby Summers and Irvin Gary led the Blackhawks with 13 points each. Dossett and Jones topped the Tide with seven points apiece.

Feeling the sting of that loss to Greenville and playing on their home turf, the Tide began regional tournament action by beating Beaver Dam 51-31. Mobberly rebounded from his worst effort of the season by ripping the Beavers for 24 points. Jones finished with seven, Day and Henry six each in that win.

Waiting for the Tide in the semifinal round was Greenville, a 52-25 winner over Caneyville in opening-round action. Once again, the

Blackhawks slowed the pace, and once again, their defense did a number on Mobberly, limiting him to four points.

But it wasn't enough. Big second-half performances from Henry and Teague helped propel the Tide to a hard-earned 33-25 win. The two bitter rivals were knotted 11-11 at the break, but with Henry scoring eight of his 11 points and Teague six of his 11 after intermission, the Tide managed to pull away for the win.

The title game against McHenry was a nail-biter from the opening tip to the final buzzer, with the Tide hanging on for a 43-40 win. Mobberly scored 18, including 13 in the final half, to pace the Tide. Henry also came through with a big game, scoring 14 points, eight after intermission.

In the state tournament opening round, the Tide were matched up against a deep, talented Clark County club headed by all-state performer Billy Puckett. Joining Puckett were a trio of superb players—Jim Winburn, Howard Rogers and Lindle Castle.

Clark County jumped to a quick 13-8 first-quarter lead and never looked back. Still trailing 23-19 at the half, the Tide did close to within a single bucket (34-32) heading into the final frame, but they could never grab the upper hand.

The final: Clark County 53-43.

Puckett lived up to his billing, leading all scorers with 18. Winburn had 12 and Rogers 11 for the winners.

Teague led the Tide with 14 points, while Mobberly added 13. Jones had five, Henry four, Dossett three, Day and McDonald two each.

The loss left the Tide with a final record of 34-4.

Mobberly closed out his career with 1,284 points, the most scored by a Golden Tide player up until that time. He accounted for 564 points during his final campaign for an average of 14.8 points per game.

For his efforts, Mobberly was named to the Louisville *Courier-Journal's* first-team all-state squad.

Chapter 13

1947-48

Losing veterans W.C. Mobberly, Gilbert Teague, Kent Henry and Marvin Dossett left some big holes Delmas Gish had to fill if he entertained any hopes that the 1947-48 team could be successful. Yes, there were several experienced returning players, including the backcourt duo of Tunney Jones and Jackie Day, along with Tommy Gray, who would be counted on to provide rebounding and inside defense.

Rounding out the roster were Roy Atherton, Doug Edwards, Gene Mercer, Marion Tinsley, John Bastin, Hubert Francis, Ray Watkins and a pair of extraordinarily gifted freshmen, Joe Mac Howard and Bobby Nofsinger.

With the exception of the 6'2" Tinsley, this was not a team with much size. It was, however, a team with plenty of strength. Gray, Mercer and Atherton were strong guys who were not shy about mixing it up with bigger opponents.

The Tide kicked off the season by blasting Bremen 52-18. Edwards led a balanced scoring attack with 14 points, while Jones added nine. Other starters that night included Atherton, Gray and Day.

A balanced scoring attack was one of the chief reasons why this team would go on to post an excellent 25-6 record. In all, seven different Tide players would lead the team in scoring.

Atherton had 11 points and Gray 10 in a 41-26 win over Sacramento, then Gray knocked in 12 points and Jones had 11 in a 63-26 pasting of Dawson Springs. In that game, all 10 Tide players scored: Edwards had seven, Atherton and Watkins six each, Day, Tinsley and Bastin five each, Francis four, Nofsinger two.

Traveling to Hartford, the Tide were upended 59-58 in a two-overtime thriller. The score was 55-55 at the end of regulation and 57-57 after the first OT period, before the Mustangs scored the final two points to secure the victory.

Gray led the Tide with 15 points. Tinsley came off the bench to score 13, Atherton had 11 and Day 10 in that losing effort.

After suffering that loss, the Tide bounced back with a 57-35 win over Drakesboro, which turned out to be the first in an 11-game winning streak. Edwards had 14 points against the Cardinals, Day added 11.

Next, the Tide made a Western Kentucky trip, beating Benton 58-42 and Paducah St. Mary's 63-22. In those two wins, Edwards racked up 40 points, 19 against Benton and 21 against St. Mary's. In the Benton game, Jones had 13 points, Day 11 and Gray 10. Against St. Mary's, Jones and Gray also hit double figures with 15 and 12 points, respectively.

Calhoun proved to be a difficult challenge, but with Gray scoring 23, Jones 16 and the red-hot Edwards 14, the Tide pulled out a 62-55 win.

Edwards scored nine and Jones eight in a 34-27 win over Greenville, then Gray had 10, Jones nine and Day eight in a 40-34 victory over Louisville St. Xavier.

The Tide continued to roll, topping Newburg (Ind.) 60-33, Drakesboro 33-22, Louisville Manual 59-38, Leitchfield 55-26 and Hughes-Kirk 67-45, pushing their winning streak to 11.

Jones scored big during this stretch with 13 against Newburg, 14 against Manual and 12 against Hughes-Kirk. Gray's best outing was 18 in the win over Leitchfield, while Edwards and Day had 16 and 12, respectively, in that Hughes-Kirk laugher.

A powerful Owensboro gang came to Central City and posted a convincing 58-44 win over the Tide. Thanks to 10 first-half points from Bobby Watson, the Red Devils blew out to a 27-14 lead at intermission and were never threatened during the second half. Watson finished with 14 points, Cliff Hagan and Dwane Morrison each had 11 and Billy Miller added 10.

Edwards paced the Tide with 15 points. Gray chipped in with 13.

The Tide then hit the road to Henderson, where they were handed another convincing defeat—51-34. Dave Epling had 18 to lead the Purple Flash, with future WKU All-American quarterback and Hall of Fame coach Jimmy Feix adding 10.

Gray had nine, Edwards eight in that loss.

Jones Out, Tinsley In

Following the Henderson loss and heading to the Louisville Invitational Tournament, the Tide's roster was now short one player. Tunney Jones left the team for personal reasons, opening a spot in the starting lineup that was filled by Tinsley. Actually, replacing the 5'8" Jones with the 6'2" Tinsley gave the Tide a much more imposing inside presence. It also allowed Gish to move Edwards back to his more-natural guard position.

That revamped lineup worked well in the LIT opener, a 48-39 win over Manual. Gray had 14, Edwards 12 and Tinsley, making the most of his debut start, finished with 11.

However, this win proved to be a costly one. During a scramble for the ball, Edwards sustained an injury that sidelined him for the next four games.

Waiting for the Tide in second-round action was mighty Owensboro, and although this game was much more hotly contested than the first encounter, the result was the same: The Red Devils notched a 43-39 win.

Once again, Watson did the heaviest damage, scoring 13 points. Morrison had 10, while the magnificent Hagan was held to seven.

Tinsley had a monster game, leading all scorers with 18. Day had nine and Gray eight in a losing cause.

Tinsley and Gray were both named to the all-tournament squad.

After losing for the second time to Owensboro, and playing four games with Edwards watching from the sidelines, the Tide went on another winning streak, this one covering seven games. The streak began with a 58-39 win over Hopkinsville and concluded with a 47-44 win over the Frank Ramsey-powered Madisonville Maroons.

Four players hit for double figures in the win over Hopkinsville, headed by Tinsley with 18. Others included Gray (14), Atherton (13) and Day (10). Gray came through with 20, Tinsley 15 and Day 13 in a 66-50 win at Bowling Green. Then in a 46-23 romp past Greenville, Francis, starting in place of the recuperating Edwards, had his best game with a team-high 14 points.

With Gray scoring 13, Atherton 12 and Edwards 11 in his first game back, the Tide gained a measure of revenge by beating Hartford 53-42.

The streak extended to six straight with wins over Calhoun 53-39 and Hughes-Kirk 46-39. Edwards scored 16, Tinsley 13 and Day 10 in the Calhoun win, then Day had 14 and Edwards 12 against Hughes-Kirk.

Sparked by Gray's 14 first-half points, the Tide built a 30-20 advantage at the break, then had to hold on inside the final minutes to secure that 47-44 win over Madisonville. Gray gave a giant effort, leading all scorers with 20 points.

Ramsey had 15 and Ches Riddle 10 for the Maroons.

The Tide closed out the regular season with a third meeting against Owensboro, which meant yet another confrontation with all-state performers Cliff Hagan and Bobby Watson. In this one, played in Owensboro, the Tide held a slim 19-15 lead at the half. Then Hagan took command, scoring 14 of his game-high 19 points after intermission, enabling the Red Devils to come away with a 37-35 victory.

Edwards and Tinsley had 12 and 10 points, respectively, for the Tide. The normally high-scoring Watson was limited to just five points.

District tournament play got underway with Gray and Edwards each scoring 13 points and Atherton 11 in a 47-38 win over Drakesboro. One night later, Gray had 14 points and the freshman Howard added 10 as the Tide overcame a 20-16 halftime deficit to beat Greenville 45-36. Gray led the comeback charge, scoring 11 of his points in the second half.

In the title game against Hughes-Kirk, the Tide found themselves in even more early trouble, trailing 20-12 at halftime. The Tigers' Billy Carver exploded out of the gate, scoring 14 points in the opening half. Carver would finish with a game-best 25 points.

While no Tide player could match Carver's heroic individual performance, a balanced second-half attack proved to be the difference. Led by Gray, the Tide came back to claim the trophy with a 40-38 overtime win. Gray finished with 11 points, nine coming in the second half. Edwards scored all six of his points in those final two quarters, while Howard came through with all four of his points after the break.

The Tide had to feel upbeat heading into the regional tournament. They had won 10 of their final 11 games, and their opening-round foe was Leitchfield, a team they clubbed 55-26 earlier in the season.

But in the second meeting, the one that counted, the Tide team that had been playing so well was nowhere to be found. Leitchfield, with a dreadful 4-23 record, pulled off the big 39-38 win.

The Tide were undone by poor shooting at the free throw stripe. For the game, they hit just 14 of 24 attempts. In the second half, they connected on five of 11 free tosses.

Gray led the Tide with 10 points, while Edwards and Day each had eight.

The loss left the Tide with a final 25-6 record.

Chapter 14

1948-49

Although this club put together a respectable 20-8 record, given the number of experienced players coming back, the season has to be rated as something of a disappointment. This team never really went on a red-hot run, nor was it a team that succeeded in post-season play.

Whatever kept this team from succeeding remains a mystery, but the failure can't be blamed on lack of talent. Starters in the opening game were Marion Tinsley, Jackie Day, Gene Mercer, Roy Atherton and Joe Mac Howard, all players with plenty of experience. Plus, there was a deep bench that included Bobby Nofsinger, Eddie B. Moore, John Bastin, Hubert Francis and Charlie Day.

On paper, at least, this should have been a strong team.

It did open strong, capturing its first six games, beginning with a 52-39 win over Sacramento that saw Tinsley lead the way with 14 points. Jackie Day had 12 and Howard 11 in that win.

Moore scored 10 in a 57-22 win over Bremen, then Tinsley accounted for 18 points, Howard 12, Bastin 11, Mercer and Moore 10 apiece in an easy 78-25 laugher against Dawson Springs.

The next three wins came against district foes, Drakesboro 37-34, Greenville 54-39 and Hughes-Kirk 61-42. Day had seven in the win over Drakesboro, Tinsley 17 against the Blackhawks, Nofsinger 17, Howard 13 and Moore 10 against Hughes-Kirk.

The Tide split their next four games. Calhoun upended the Tide 43-40 despite 11 points from Day and 10 from Tinsley, then Howard and Tinsley pitched in 15 apiece, Day 11 and Nofsinger 10 in a hard-fought 59-49 win over Louisville Manual.

After dropping a 44-29 decision to Louisville St. Xavier, the Tide came back to beat Newburg (Ind.) 65-36. In that win, Mercer had 14, Nofsinger 13, Howard 12 and Moore 10.

Accepting an offer to participate in the Paducah Invitational Tournament, the Tide headed west, scoring a 60-52 victory over St. Mary's in first-round action. Nofsinger led the winners with 13 points, while Tinsley and Mercer each had 12 and Day added 10.

In the second round, Murray broke away from a 23-23 halftime deadlock to notch a 46-40 win. Accuracy at the free throw stripe was the difference in this game. The Tide had more field goals (16-13), but Murray hit 20 of 28 freebies while the Tide made good on eight of 20, including a dismal three of 13 effort in the second half.

Bastin had his best game, coming off the bench to score 14 points in a 67-26 win over Benton. Tinsley had 11, Nofsinger and Howard 10 each.

Next, the Tide claimed a pair of victories over Western Kentucky foes, edging Paducah St. Mary's 50-48 and Mayfield 53-41. Mercer topped the scoring against St. Mary's, finishing with 13 points. Tinsley and Howard chipped in with 12 and 10 points, respectively. Nofsinger had 18 points, Howard 12 and Mercer 10 in the win over Mayfield.

Eventual state champion Owensboro, led by Cliff Hagan's 17 points, pulverized the Tide 54-32. The Red Devils ran out to a 26-12 halftime lead and never looked back. Hagan received strong support from Bill Cook with 14 points.

Moore and Howard each had seven for the Tide.

Tinsley and Howard took control in leading the Tide to wins over Henderson 44-33 and Calhoun 43-37. Tinsley had 16 against Henderson and 15 in the win over Calhoun, while Howard scored 10 points in each outing.

Atherton had a big game against Bowling Green, scoring 11 points as the Tide rolled to a 49-37 victory. Then the Tide, after trailing 25-20 at the half, roared back in the final two quarters to beat Greenville 39-35. Tinsley and Howard each had 12 points for the winners.

The Tide's winning streak ended with a 41-38 loss at Hopkinsville. Howard paced the Tide with 14 points. Hopkinsville's Billy Sparks torched the Tide for 24 points.

Howard came up big again in the Tide's next two games, wins over Drakesboro 40-35 and Hughes-Kirk 52-49. The sophomore guard scored 14 against the Cardinals, 15 against the Tigers.

Hagan, Ramsey and a Weak Finish

For the second time this season, Cliff Hagan led Owensboro to a convincing 50-41 win over the Tide. Hagan proved to be unstoppable, racking up 26 points. Day and Howard each had eight for the Tide.

Hagan's future UK teammate, Frank Ramsey, was equally destructive in leading Madisonville to an easy 53-44 win over the slumping Tide. Ramsey tossed in 23 points for the Maroons, while Ches Riddle added 13.

Day was the only Tide player to hit double figures, ending the night with 11.

Behind 14 points from Howard and 11 from Nofsinger, the Tide closed out the regular season with a 44-34 road win over Louisville Male. Atherton finished with eight points, all coming in a first-half blitz that saw the Tide build a 29-18 lead at the break.

In the district tournament opener, the Tide gave a solid effort in defeating Bremen 51-30. Day had 13 for the winners, Atherton 10 and Tinsley nine.

Jimmy Eades had a game-best 15 points for the Golden Eagles.

In semifinal action, Drakesboro, a club the Tide had beaten twice during the regular campaign, came out on the winning end of a 46-44 two overtime heart-stopper. The game was tied 22-22 at intermission, 42-42 at the end of regulation and 44-44 after the first OT period.

The victorious Cardinals were led by the strong duo of Nookie Hope and Jimmy Mitchell, with 16 and 13 points, respectively. Howard had 18 for the Tide.

With this final loss, the Tide could only watch from the sidelines as district rival Hughes-Kirk, another team they had defeated twice during the regular season, advanced to the state tournament.

This loss also sent all eyes looking toward next season, one that had the potential to be super successful. With Tinsley, Howard, Nofsinger, Mercer, Atherton and Moore all set to return, there was no reason for the team be anything but special.

And it would be.

Chapter 15

1949-50

Several past Central City teams featured duos that packed a solid one-two scoring punch. H.G. Watkins and Billy Ray Nale, Bill Eades and Bud Eades, Beauchamp Kirkpatrick and Bobby Watkins come most quickly to mind.

But the 1949-50 team was blessed with an added element—three players who could put points on the board in flurries. During this season, senior Marion Tinsley and juniors Joe Mac Howard and Bobby Nofsinger combined for 1,253 points, making them the most-productive trio Golden Tide fans had seen thus far. With them leading the way, this team finished with a 29-5 record and a trip to the state tournament, where it notched a pair of victories.

Only the 1944-45 team, and later, the 1965-66 team, performed as well in the Sweet 16.

Tinsley, Howard and Nofsinger may have been the big-time scorers, but they weren't the only familiar faces on this squad. Joining them were battle-tested veterans Gene Mercer, Eddie B. Moore and Roy Atherton, three players who never shied away from a tough encounter.

Other members of the team were Charles Day, John William Gray, Charles Stewart, G.W. Anderson and Bobby Calvert.

Tinsley shot out of the gate with a 24-point effort in a 50-27 win over Graham. Next, in one of those blowouts that saw all players score, the Tide ripped Bremen 70-30. Mercer, Howard and Tinsley each tallied 12 points for the winners.

Future Bremen coach Bobby Joe Rickard scored 16 points to lead invading Sacramento to a 45-37 win on the Tide's home floor. Sacramento led 26-17 at the half and was never seriously threatened. Tinsley had nine in a losing effort.

After that stunning loss, the Tide came back to post 12 straight victories, beginning with a come-from-behind 51-49 win over Hughes-Kirk. In this game, the Tide trailed 36-35 heading into the final frame before Howard and Nofsinger came to the rescue, accounting for 11 fourth-quarter points that enabled the Tide to sneak away with the win. Howard finished with 16 points, Nofsinger 11 and Tinsley 10 for the Tide.

Tooter Norris led the defending regional champs with 14 points.

Moore scored 13 and Atherton added 10 in a 48-29 win over Calhoun, then Howard had 17, Tinsley 12 and Nofsinger 11 in a 62-35 pasting of Drakesboro. Nookie Hope matched Howard for game-high honors with 17.

Playing Manual in Louisville, the big three racked up 40 points to lead the Tide to an impressive 55-39 win. Nofsinger had 15, Tinsley 14 and Howard 11. Atherton also played well, contributing seven points.

Adhering to standard procedure, Greenville slowed the pace on the more fast-break oriented Golden Tide. The ploy worked for a half—the Tide led 14-13—but in the end, the Blackhawks came out on the short side of a 39-31 score.

Nofsinger and Howard paced the winners with 13 and 10 points, respectively. Greenville's Tommy Gross also hit for 13 points.

In a second early match-up against dangerous Hughes-Kirk, Howard threw in 15 points, Tinsley 13, Nofsinger and Moore 11 apiece in a decisive 66-45 win. The Tigers' Tooter Norris led all scorers with 20 points.

Rolling On, Beating Cliff

Nofsinger erupted for 28 points as the Tide topped Paducah St. Mary's in a high-scoring 83-69 affair. Those 28 points by Nofsinger represented the most scored by a Tide player since W.C. Mobberly had 30 against St. Xavier in 1946. Howard finished with 19 points, Tinsley 16 and Atherton 11.

After Atherton scored 14 points and Mercer, Howard and Nofsinger each added 10 in a 49-42 win over St. Francis, the Tide once again faced the daunting task of trying to stop Cliff Hagan and the defending state champion Owensboro Red Devils. Hagan was scheduled to graduate at mid-semester, so this would be the Tide's final look at one of the state's all-time greatest players.

After one quarter, it looked as though the Tide would be no match for Hagan and company. The Red Devils owned a 16-10 lead heading into the second period. It was in these eight minutes that the Tide turned things around, outscoring the visitors 20-10 to take a 30-26 advantage into the dressing room at the half. Tinsley, Nofsinger and Howard each had five points in that quarter.

The Tide outscored Owensboro 16-12 in the third quarter, then pulled away in the final frame to post a 58-45 win. Hagan, as expected, did not disappoint the onlookers, scoring a game-high 26 points. But Hagan had little help from his teammates, while the Tide once again rode a balanced scoring attack to victory. Tinsley had 17, Howard 13, Moore 11 and Nofsinger nine for the winners.

Nofsinger came up big in the Tide's next two wins, 56-46 over St. Xavier and 59-29 over Greenville. He had 19 against St. X and 14 against the Blackhawks. Howard had 18 in that win over St. X.

On tap next was a trip to the Louisville Invitational Tournament, where the Tide would open with a second meeting against Manual. This game was anything but easy. Trailing 24-19 at the half, the Tide managed to pull even at 36-36 heading into the last quarter. In those crucial eight minutes, thanks to seven points from Moore, the Tide came away with a 49-48 win. Moore paced the winners with 11 points, while Nofsinger added 10. Manual was led by all-state performer Don Whitehouse with 13.

In quarterfinal action, Male, led by its all-state standout Jimmy Sedbrook's 18-point performance, sent the Tide home with a 49-46 win. Tinsley had 17 for the Tide, while Nofsinger finished with 14.

Once again the Tide responded to a setback by putting together another winning streak, this one covering seven games. The streak began in Bowling Green with a 60-42 win over the Purples. Nofsinger and Tinsley each scored 17 points in that win. Howard also hit double figures with 11.

The Tide's solid play continued with impressive wins over Hopkinsville 54-24, Paducah 67-57 and Drakesboro 60-34. Howard had 14 points in the win over Hoptown, and Tinsley had 22 against Paducah. Against Drakesboro, Howard had 13, Nofsinger 12 and Atherton 11.

Owensboro and Madisonville were the Tide's next two opponents, and for the first time in four years, they would not have to worry about such standouts as Cliff Hagan, Frank Ramsey or Bobby Watson. Thankfully, that trio was now firmly planted in Lexington, where they would soon lead the Wildcats to an NCAA title.

The Red Devils, without Hagan, were simply no match for the Tide, who rolled to an easy 67-49 win. In this game, the Tide led 42-18 at the half. Atherton had his best game with 23 points. Howard and Nofsinger added 14 and 12, respectively.

Madisonville, without Ramsey, proved to be a little more stubborn, but the Tide, with four players hitting for double digits, claimed a 60-49 win. Nofsinger led with 18 points, followed by Tinsley with 12, Mercer and Howard with 11 apiece.

Behind 16 points from Nofsinger and 15 from Tinsley, the Tide's winning streak hit seven with a 57-41 victory over Calhoun. Moore chipped in with nine points in that win.

For the second time this season, it would be Male that halted the Tide's winning ways, coming to Central City and escaping with 55-54 win. This was a classic thriller, with the two clubs deadlocked at 40-40 heading into the last quarter. But the Bulldogs, riding a 19-point effort from Hank Brinkerhoff, left town with the win.

In the Tide's regular-season finale, Nofsinger had 15 points, while Tinsley and Howard each contributed 13.

Blowing Opponents Away

Delmas Gish always said a basketball season is in reality three seasons—the regular season, the district and regional tournaments are the second season, and the state tournament is the third season. Gish, like every coach who ever sat on a bench, lived with the hope that his team would be performing at its highest level when it mattered the most—at tournament time.

History is written by winning armies, just as sports legacies are written by winning teams. Success in the post-season is the number-one requirement for a winning legacy.

This 1949-50 team certainly fulfilled Gish's hopes. For the next six games—three in the district tourney, three in the regional—this club turned in a series of devastating performances, winning all six games by an average margin of 30 points per outing. Not only does this qualify as total dominance, it is, in post-season tournament play at least, a rarely seen display of power.

In the district opener, Howard erupted for 25 points to guide the Tide to a 75-45 win over Hughes-Kirk. Mercer finished with 13 and Atherton 11 in that win.

Next, it was Nofsinger's night to do the most damage. He scored 19 points in a 71-34 romp past Graham. Mercer again played well, coming through with a second-straight 13-point performance. Moore and Howard each had 10 points.

Greenville managed to make it interesting for a while, but the Tide simply had too much firepower, eventually pulling away for a 51-40 championship game win. Nofsinger matched his semifinal total with another 19 points. His 12 first-half points helped stake the Tide to a 27-16 lead at the break.

Tommy Gross led Greenville with 16 points.

If winning the district title was easy, capturing the regional crown was *ridiculously* easy. In three games, the closest an opponent could get was 17 points. The Tide's wins were by 50, 17 and 35 points.

All 10 Tide players scored in the opener, an 83-33 win over Sunfish, a game that saw the winners take a 33-7 lead after one quarter. Howard had 18 points, Nofsinger 14, Tinsley and Anderson 12 each. Others who scored were Moore with seven, Mercer and Stewart with six each, Day with four, Atherton with three and Calvert with one.

In the semifinals, the Tide raced to a 22-9 first-quarter lead and then rolled to a 58-41 victory over Clarkson. Nofsinger had 22 and Tinsley 10 in that win.

That set up a championship battle against a home-standing Leitchfield squad that reached the finals by dispatching Rockport and Hartford.

According to Marion Tinsley, this was a Leitchfield team that went into the game with a high level of confidence.

"Those people were absolutely convinced that they were going to beat us," Tinsley said. "They acted like it was going to be a walk in the park. Well, it didn't turn out that way, did it?"

No, it didn't. With five players hitting for double figures, topped by Tinsley with 22, the Tide shattered Leitchfield's dream of making it to the state tournament by storming to an 85-50 win. Nofsinger had 18 that night, Howard 13, Mercer 12, Moore 10, Atherton eight and Calvert two.

That easy win sent the Golden Tide to the state tournament for the third time in the past five years.

A Solid State Tourney Showing

The one thing missing from Central City's magnificent basketball resume is a state championship. That quest proved to be both frustrating and illusive. The 1944-45 team came close, finishing in the runner-up sport. This 1949-50 team and the future 1965-66 team would also make deep runs into the Sweet 16, only to come up short.

Part of the reason for this hole in the resume is simple: Central City rarely got a favorable first-round opponent. In 13 of 17 Sweet 16 appearances, the Tide lost to teams that won the title, finished as runner-up or advanced to the semifinal round.

The Tide's opening-round foe in the 1950 state tournament was Tompkinsville, a tough challenge by any standards. The Bears entered the event with a tournament-best 32-1 record. Other standout teams included Corbin (30-2), Central City (27-3), Lexington Lafayette (24-3), Paducah Tilghman (26-3) and Clark County (29-6).

The opener was a tale of two halves. Tompkinsville led 30-28 at intermission before the Tide, riding big halves from Howard and Tinsley, came back to get a 60-51 win. The third quarter was pivotal; in those eight minutes, the Tide outscored Tompkinsville 19-8 to seize control.

Howard led the attack with 22 points. Tinsley ended the night with 18 and Moore added 10.

Campbellsville, a 69-49 winner over Bush in the opening round, was the Tide's quarterfinal opponent. This was the Eagles' 30th win against only nine setbacks.

For the second straight game, the Tide played chicken with disaster, once again trailing at the half. This time, however, they were also trailing 33-32 going into the final stanza. A timely offensive outburst by Nofsinger, combined with a stifling defense, provided just enough momentum for the Tide to bump off Campbellsville 45-41.

Nofsinger accounted for nine of his game-high 15 points in the final frame, while the Golden Tide defense held the Eagles to eight fourth-quarter points.

Howard also played well, scoring 12 points. Mercer and Tinsley each had nine.

Clark County, headed by the gifted duo of Linville Puckett and Lewis Snowden, was the Tide's Saturday-morning semifinal opponent. Puckett was a crafty 6'1" sophomore guard who would make the all-tournament team three times, while the 6'5" Snowden gave the Cardinals great inside size.

The Tide trailed at every stop—16-11, 26-23 and 40-35—before mounting a serious comeback charge late in the fourth quarter. But each time the Tide drew close, Puckett had an answer, scoring eight of his 15 points in the final frame. Behind Puckett's heroics, the Cardinals managed to hang on for a 59-55 win.

Tinsley had 16 for the Tide, with Howard chipping in 14.

Jim Wells also had 15 points for Clark County, while Elmer "Bubba" Pelfrey and Joe Rogers each had 10.

Later that night, in the consolation game, Corbin, after trailing 57-53 heading into the last quarter, eeked out a 71-69 win on a last-second shot by Roy Kidd. It was a disappointing loss for a Tide club that felt it had let victory slip from its grasp.

"We could easily have won either of those two games," Tinsley said. "But we definitely should have handled Corbin. We had them beat, and then we blew it."

If someone had said prior to the game that Frank Selvy would be limited to a dozen points, all betting money would have been on the Tide coming away with the win. Selvy would go on to earn All-America honors at Furman—once scoring 100 points in a game—and later play professionally in the NBA. In short, the guy could play. In fact, he was so good that a future UK star, Jerry Bird, was his backup.

But in this game, it was Bobby Terrell with 21 points and Bob Barton with 17 who did the most damage. Kidd, who later became the hall-of-fame football coach at Eastern Kentucky University, finished with 11.

The Tide also had a trio of players in double figures, including Nofsinger with 19, Mercer 16 and Howard 12.

Howard would be named to the all-tournament team.

The fourth-place finish left the Tide with a 29-5 record. For the season, Nofsinger was the leading scorer with 450 points, Howard had 413 and Tinsley 391.

With Nofsinger and Howard returning, Tide fans were optimistic that the 1950-51 team could have an even better season. But a bad break snuffed out those hopes.

Chapter 16

1940s Sideline Shots

Billy Hicks—Walking Tall

Billy Hicks was a quiet hero on that 1944-45 Golden Tide team that advanced to the championship game in the state tournament. He was one of those players who always seemed to play his best when defeat was knocking at the door. In short, Hicks stepped up when it counted the most.

But it was only by the grace of God—and a bicycle—that Hicks could step up at all. Or walk, for that matter. Had fate dealt him a crueler hand, Hicks might have been walking with the aid of crutches. Or even worse, confined to an iron lung.

Billy Hicks, you see, was stricken with infantile paralysis when he was 11 years old.

Polio.

Get that diagnosis and your future as a basketball player is an almost-impossible dream.

The Hicks family was living in the small coal mining community of Echols in Ohio County when Billy was first diagnosed. His father, Leslie, took him to a doctor in Beaver Dam. The doctor said the best thing would be to buy Billy a bicycle and let him ride as much as possible. That exercise, the doctor predicted, would help strengthen Billy's legs.

A few days later, Billy was the only kid in Echols with a bike.

The doctor's prescription worked; Billy's legs got stronger and stronger. In 1940, after Louisville Electric and Gas closed, Leslie Hicks moved his family to Central City, which turned out to be a good break for Coach Delmas Gish and Golden Tide fans.

Five years later, the only kid in Echols with a bicycle was helping lead the Tide to their most-successful season in school history.

Jackie Day—Paid Defender

For several seasons in the late 40s, going up against Owensboro meant having to defend against Bobby Watson and Cliff Hagan. This was not easy; those two guys were pretty good. No, those two guys were great.

Hagan is one of a handful of athletes to win championships at the high school (Owensboro), college (UK) and pro levels (St. Louis). And Watson, well, Adolph Rupp was forever trying to keep him out of the starting lineup, claiming lack of size was a hindrance. Watson always proved the Baron wrong, starting all three years and scoring more than 1,000 points for the Wildcats.

Prior to one game against Owensboro, Tide players made a deal with Jackie Day, who was the guy counted on to slow Watson down. The deal involved a somewhat professional approach to the situation.

Pay for play.

"The guys took up a collection the afternoon of the game," Day said. "Couldn't have been much money, because nobody had much money back then. But they told me I would get the money if I held Bobby Watson scoreless. Well, I was all over Watson that night. Held him scoreless until the last few seconds of the first half. I had the ball, three Owensboro players swarmed me, stole it from me and got it to Watson, who went in for a layup. That was his only basket that night. He did hit a free throw in the second half, giving him three points for the game."

And the money?

"Yeah, they gave it to me," Day said. "I guess they were satisfied that I'd done a good job."

Battling Frank and Cliff

While Jackie Day was tasked with stopping backcourt ace Bobby Watson, Tommy Gray drew the difficult assignment of trying to shut down big inside players Frank Ramsey and Cliff Hagan, two players who had a three- or four-inch size advantage.

Also, they remain two of the most-successful players in basketball history. As noted, Hagan won titles at all three levels, while Ramsey won an NCAA title at UK and collected enough championship rings with the Boston Celtics to open a jewelry store.

To put it mildly, Gray had his hands full, especially when dealing with Hagan.

"I could handle Frank OK," Gray said. "He was a great player, but he wasn't overpowering. Cliff, on the other hand, was. He had that big body—those wide shoulders—and it was almost impossible for me to get in front of him and deny him the ball. Cliff was a handful."

Gray recalled one game when he was doing a good job against Hagan, until…

"I held him in check during the first half," Gray said. "But in the second half, Owensboro Coach (Lawrence) McGinniss ordered Cliff to play out on the floor, away from the basket. Since I was our best rebounder, Coach Gish told me to stay down low. Well, that turned out to be a mistake, because Cliff killed us in the second half. He burned it up from the corners."

Don't feel bad, Tommy. Cliff Hagan burned plenty of teams before his playing days were finished.

The Rowdy Bunch

From about 1947 thru 1951, it's safe to say the Central City roster had a bunch of guys who could best be described as forerunners to the World Wrestling Federation. This group included Tommy Gray, Jackie Day, Gene Mercer, Roy Atherton, Marion Tinsley, Bobby Nofsinger and Joe Mac Howard.

To call this gang combative is putting it mildly.

"I don't know what it was about that group of boys, but they sure did like to fight a lot," Mary Day said, shaking her head. "They must have had incredible energy. And they didn't have to be angry with each other for something to start up. Two of them would be standing there, laughing and joking, and the next thing you know they were on the ground wrestling."

And according to Joe Mac, it started early. "Tommy Gray and Robert Armstrong used to chase me down and whip my butt," Joe Mac said. "I was a little guy then, so I couldn't put up much of a fight. I just had to take it."

Sometimes the horseplay had unexpected—and negative—consequences, as it did when Gray and Day got into it.

"We were walking home from practice," Day remembered. "We were down behind the old Coca-Cola plant. Tommy picked me up and slammed me into some bushes. Made me about halfway mad. Anyway, he took off running and I chased him down and tackled him from behind. When Tommy fell, he broke his wrist."

Ouch!

"Of course, Tommy didn't bother to see a doctor," Day continued. "He just taped it up. We had a game a day or two later, and every time Tommy went for the ball, that wrist was just flapping. You have to be tough guy to play basketball with a broken wrist. And Tommy Gray was plenty tough."

Joe Mac offered a reason why those guys tended to be a little on the wild side.

"We all grew up in the pool room," Joe Mac said. "Things were just different back in those days... there wasn't all that much to do in Central City. We'd either play pool or break into the school and play basketball. That was about it."

Break in?

"Well, change that to 'we'd sneak in,'" he corrected. "That does sound a little better, doesn't it?"

So the question begs: How did Delmas Gish, who stood maybe 5'3" on a good day, handle such a wild bunch of hooligans?

"Oh, I don't think he had much trouble with those older guys," Joe Mac said. "He was mostly worried about Bobby and me."

Day recalls one instance when Gish intervened in a painful way.

"Joe Mac and I got into it one day at practice," Day said. "I was a little stronger than he was, and I had him pinned down. Mr. Gish saw us fighting, ran onto the floor, grabbed me by the back of my neck and began pulling me off Joe Mac. Well, Mr. Gish had these really long, sharp fingernails. He raked my neck pretty good, too. Blood was running down my back."

Let Joe Mac have the final word: "We were just a different breed back then."

The Greatest Player Sidelined

Although Central City is noted for producing terrific basketball players, it should also be pointed out that the town has turned out its share of superb baseball players as well. Corky Withrow spent time with the St. Louis Cardinals, while Bobby Don Millard, who hurled a no-hitter in the minor leagues, had an excellent shot at making it to the Big Show until an arm injury ended his career. Marvin Dossett also inked a pro contract.

Along with those three, there have been others who excelled on the baseball diamond.

But ask any of the old-timers who was the best of the best and the answer is unanimous—Tommy Gray. He was to Central City baseball what Corky Withrow was to Central City basketball—the all-time greatest.

As a teenager, Gray was good enough to play for the Central City Reds, a semi-pro team that had older players like H.G. Watkins, Marvin Dossett and John Withrow on the roster. Even against those veterans, Gray more than held his own. As a high school player, he helped lead the Tide to their first-ever appearance in the state tournament.

Gray was what baseball people now call a "five-tool" player: He could run, throw, hit, hit with power and play defense. In particular, Gray, an outfielder, had a cannon for an arm.

"Tommy Gray could stand against the centerfield fence and throw a strike to the catcher at home plate," Bobby Nofsinger once said.

After graduating, Gray signed a pro contract with the Detroit Tigers. In only his second year of pro ball, playing for Richmond, Ind., he produced the kind of numbers that marked him as a can't-miss prospect for the big leagues.

That season he led the club in batting, runs scored and outfield assists, while becoming the first player in team history to drive in more than 100 runs.

Gray's roommate on the road that season was future Hall of Fame pitcher and U.S. Senator Jim Bunning.

Then, just days before leaving for spring training, tragedy struck. Gray, like most professional baseball players in those days, had to work during the off-season to make ends meet. Gray worked for the Illinois Central Railroad.

At around 10:30 p.m. on an April night, while coupling two railroad cars, his right arm got caught between the two cars. The arm was crushed to such an extent that it could not be repaired. He was taken to the hospital, where surgeons amputated just above the wrist.

Suddenly, the career of Central City's greatest baseball player was finished.

But Tommy Gray wasn't. He teamed with his buddy Robert Armstrong, bought a few hens and started a new business—the A&G Egg Farm. The business, which began as a basically local supplier of fresh eggs, soon became a huge success, both reputation-wise and financially.

In the end, Tommy Gray did all right for himself.

Still... one is left to ask the question: Does Tommy think he would have made it all the way to Detroit?

"All the scouts said I would," Tommy said.

So does everyone else who ever watched him play.

The 1950s

Won – 251

Lost – 86

Winning Pct. – 74.5

Player of the Decade

Corky Withrow

Other Notable Players

Lewis Chaney
Don Coleman
Billy Ray Duvall
Pat Franklin
Lance Gish
Earl Goode
H.L. "Hub" Hope
Joe Mac Howard
Carl Ray Jamison
Johnny Lile
Billy Mason
Terrill Mayes
Frankie Mercer
Bobby Don Millard
Bobby Nofsinger
Larry Ray
Billy Lee Robinson
Jimmy Simmons
Sonny Stone
Winfred Thompson
Marion Tinsley
Roy Lee Toll
Bobby Joe Withrow
Roy (D.D.) Withrow
Dick Wolfe

Chapter 17

The Great One

Corky Withrow.

Even now, many decades after playing his last game for Central City High School, his name retains the same power and evokes the same awe it did when he was performing heroic feats on the basketball court. No Muhlenberg County player before or since comes close to matching his accomplishments. Simply put, Withrow was the greatest of the greats, the standard against which all other Muhlenberg County players are measured.

When hoops historians chronicle the list of the greatest players ever to play in the Commonwealth, Withrow's name will surely rank among the elite.

It should come as no surprise, then, that he was voted into the Kentucky High School Athletic Association's Hall of Fame, the Sweet 16 Hall of Fame and the Kentucky High School Basketball Hall of Fame.

Memorable Performances

During his great career, Withrow gave some of the most memorable performances ever recorded in Kentucky high school basketball history. The 38 points he scored in the Louisville Invitational win against top-ranked Newport Public; the 34 points he scored against Carr Creek in the 1956 state tourney; the 51 points he had against a Hughes-Kirk team coached by his brother, Roy "D.D." Withrow; and, of course, the legendary night when he and "King" Kelly Coleman each scored 40 points in Central City's win over Wayland.

However, if you ask Withrow to choose the game that stands out first and foremost in his mind, his answer will likely come as a surprise.

"It was a junior varsity game against Drakesboro," Withrow remembers. "I didn't play until the fourth quarter. I went in and scored 17 points."

He was in the seventh grade.

"That gave me the confidence that I could play the game," Withrow said, adding, "and that maybe I could be pretty good at it."

Pretty good is putting it mildly, to say the least. For four years, from 1952 thru 1956, he played the game at the highest level possible, carving out numbers and ringing up individual achievements that are simply staggering. He scored 3,136 career points, which still ranks 19th on the all-time Kentucky scoring list. He scored more than 1,000 points and averaged more than 30 points per game in each of his final two seasons. He scored 40 or more points nine times, going above the 50-point mark on three occasions.

But those are just numbers. Consider these other achievements:

- Led Central City to a 119-20 record and three straight state tourney appearances.
- Was chosen to *Dell Magazine's* first five All-America team in 1956. Another member of that quintet was the great Oscar Robertson. Also, Withrow and Kelly Coleman were chosen as All-Americans by *Scholastic Magazine*, making Kentucky the only state with two players on the first team.
- Named Player of the Year in 1956 by the *Paducah Sun*, and co-Player of the Year (with Coleman) by the Lexington *Herald-Leader*. Also named to the *Courier-Journal's* first team all-state squad. This marked the second straight year he had been named to the all-state team in each of those publications.
- Was a two-time all-state tournament selection, and a two-time All-Louisville Invitational Tournament pick.
- Three times named to the all-district team and three times to the all-regional team.

Georgetown and Stan 'the Man'

In late 1955, while playing in the Louisville Invitational Tournament, Withrow became the first player in that talented 1956 class to ink a scholarship with the University of Kentucky. UK coach Adolph Rupp, who had been pursuing Withrow for two years, finally landed his primary target. Later, Rupp would also sign Greenville's Roger

Newman, Berea's Don Mills and a 6'7" lefty from Louisiana named Jackie Moreland. It was by any definition a great class.

But in mid-summer, Withrow opted instead to fulfill his life-long dream of playing professional baseball, signing with the Milwaukee Braves. By putting his signature on the baseball contract, Withrow immediately became ineligible to play at UK. In those days, professional athletes were not allowed to participate at the Division I level. Still, Withrow wasn't ready to completely abandon basketball. He considered playing at Murray State and Kentucky Wesleyan before finally ending up at Georgetown College, where he played for two seasons.

Kelly Coleman, who played three years at Kentucky Wesleyan, commented that "had Corky come to Kentucky Wesleyan, we would have had the best team in Kentucky, bar none."

During those two years at Georgetown, Withrow scored 1,378 points. In the 1958-59 season opener against Louisville in Freedom Hall, he scored 26 points to lead the Tigers to an 84-78 upset victory. (Later that season, Louisville defeated UK 76-61 in the NCAA tourney.)

That same year, Withrow played a key role in Georgetown's win over Tennessee A&I, which was led by Dick Barnett. It proved to be the lone loss for an A&I club that went on to capture the NAIA national championship.

Withrow spent 10 years playing pro baseball, and not without his share of success. He hit more than 325 home runs during his career, and was twice named Minor League Player of the Month.

In 1963, he made it to The Show, getting called up by the St. Louis Cardinals late in the season. There, he was able to play alongside his boyhood idol, Stan "the Man" Musial.

"He was the first guy to greet me in the clubhouse," Withrow says of his hero. "Stan couldn't have been nicer or more helpful."

Retirement and Beyond

These days, Withrow spends most of his time with wife, Barbara, their two children, Keith and Kelly, and the grandkids. Although long retired, Withrow helps out with Keith's successful plumbing business in Owensboro.

"Keith works me to death," Withrow says, chuckling. "No, that's not true. He doesn't trust me enough to let me do very much. Mainly, he lets me drive the truck."

Looking back on his career, Withrow seems less surprised by what he accomplished than he is by the fact that so many people remember him at all.

"That was a long, long time ago," he said. "There were a lot of great Muhlenberg County players before I came along, and there have been plenty more since I left the scene. To have people remember me as one of the best is a great honor.

"I am proud to have played for the Golden Tide," he adds. "I'm proud to have played for a coach like Delmas Gish. I had great teammates, and I'm proud of all that we accomplished. Those were great times for all of us."

Chapter 18

1950-51

The 1950s are considered by many to be not only the golden age of Central City basketball, but also the golden age for Muhlenberg County and the entire Commonwealth. Those 10 years featured some of the most powerful teams ever and many of the state's all-time greatest players. From Linville Puckett to Howie Crittenden to Vernon Hatton to Johnny Cox to Don Mills to Billy Ray Lickert to Charlie Osborne to Harry Todd to Bobby Rascoe to Tom Thacker to Randy Embry, the Kentucky basketball landscape was littered with supremely gifted players.

And, of course, there was "King" Kelly Coleman, the most prolific scorer in the history of Kentucky high school hoops.

Closer to home, Muhlenberg County also had its share of superb players, guys like Nookie Hope, Tommy Gross, Joe Roop, Jim Williams, Dave Shutt, Denny Wester, Carl Carver, Glenn Mohon, T.R. Newman, Larry Sparks, Don Raymer, Joe Robert Divine, Robie Harper, Jimmy Harper, R.C. McElwain, Johnny Roark, Jerry Shanks, Doug Strader, Leroy Willis, John Frazier, Larry Cary, Curtis Shelton, Wayne Divine and Buddy Casebier, just to name a small handful. To name them all would fill up dozens of pages.

And then there's the two greatest of them all—Corky Withrow and Roger Newman. A pair of players, the equal of any who played in this decade (or any decade), separated by a mere seven miles... how fortunate for those of us who watched them play, who had the chance to marvel at their exploits.

The basketball gods definitely did us all a big favor by putting those two giants so close together.

As for the Golden Tide, the decade began with much excitement and anticipation. And why not? The Tide were fresh from a successful state tournament appearance, and that club's two standout performers—Joe Mac Howard and Bobby Nofsinger—were returning for their senior season. Having that pair in the starting lineup virtually assured a successful campaign.

Joining those two were Don Coleman, Bobby Joe Withrow, G.W. Anderson, Benny Dukes, Charles Stewart, Dick Wolfe, Charlie Day, Frankie Huddleston, Roy Lee Toll and Tommy Jamison.

But this team, which finished with a 20-9 record, rarely had the chance to show just how good it might have been. Once Nofsinger went down with a broken leg that sidelined him for much of the season, this team was never at full strength.

Howard did his share picking up the slack, ending the season with 531 points and an 18.3 scoring average. Withrow also stepped up, averaging just over 10 points per contest. Other players also made contributions, but without Nofsinger's scoring and rebounding, this Golden Tide team was only a shell of what it might have been.

The Tide began the season with a low-scoring 48-36 win over Bremen. Howard had 14 and Nofsinger 13 to lead the way. Other starters that night included Anderson, Jamison and Withrow.

Howard scored 26, Nofsinger 17 and Withrow 14 in a 67-49 romp past Graham, then Howard came back with 22 and Nofsinger 14 in a 57-40 win at Drakesboro.

Trailing 37-34 after three quarters, the Tide, sparked by Dukes, outscored Frankfort 29-10 in the final eight minutes to post a 63-47 victory. Howard led the way with 19 points. Withrow had 15 and Dukes added 10, nine coming in the decisive fourth quarter.

Howard scored 14 and Nofsinger 11 in a 47-30 win over Calhoun, then in the game that saw Nofsinger go down with his injury, the Tide topped Greenville 52-35. Howard had 16 points, Withrow 13, Dukes nine and Anderson seven in that costly win.

Lexington Lafayette, the defending state champs, paid a visit to Central City and walked away with an easy 76-54 victory. All-state performers Charley Hadden and Jim Hutchens had 25 and 15 points, respectively, for the winners, while Howard's 25-point effort matched Hadden for top honors.

What this game showed was that without Nofsinger in the lineup, any game against a top-flight opponent was going to be a struggle.

Surprisingly, against a strong Hughes-Kirk squad, the Tide turned in a sterling performance, easily beating the Tigers 55-35. Howard had 14, Jamison 11 and Anderson 10 in that win.

Facing off against St. Xavier in Louisville Male's gym, the Tide suffered a 58-45 loss. Withrow paced the Tide with 12 points, while the normally high-scoring Howard was limited to nine.

The Tide remained on the road, traveling to Winchester to meet powerful Clark County in the Optimist Club Tournament. Unlike the previous year when the two clubs met in the Sweet 16, this game was never close. The host Cardinals, led by Lewis Snowden with 27 points and Linville Puckett and Elmer Pelfrey with 20 apiece, rolled to an easy 93-61 win.

Withrow had 25 points and Howard 19 for the Tide.

Clark County would go on to capture the state title.

Following that loss, the Tide split their next four games, beating Somerset 62-51 and St. Francis 49-34, and losing to Bourbon County 50-47 and Owensboro 47-40. Howard had 21 points and Stewart 17 against Somerset, then Howard had 15 for the Tide, which blew a fourth-quarter lead in the loss to Bourbon County.

Withrow scored 13, Dukes and Stewart 11 each against St. Francis, while Howard had 16 against the Red Devils.

Behind 27 points from Howard, the Tide began a modest four-game winning streak by beating Hazard 74-59. Withrow finished with 13 points, Anderson eight and Coleman seven in this impressive win.

The Tide's defense held all-state performer Dickie Keffer to eight points.

In the Tide's next game, a 63-31 win over Greenville, Howard scored 24 points and Anderson added 17 for the winners. Lynn Wilkins, an eighth-grader, led the Blackhawks with 10 points.

An easy 66-45 win against Bowling Green was followed by a narrow 50-49 victory at Hopkinsville. Against Bowling Green, Howard led a balanced attack with 12 points. Coleman and Stewart each had 11, Day and Withrow eight apiece, Dukes seven, Anderson five, Wolfe and Jamison a bucket each.

Against Hopkinsville, Howard scored 13 points before being ejected from the game in the third quarter for "disorderly conduct against the referee." With Howard watching from the bench, the Tide, which led

30-22 at the intermission, managed to hang on for the win. Anderson came up big for the Tide, scoring 11 points.

Led by first-team all-state performer Lynn Cole's 20 points, Paducah Tilghman came to town and pounded the Tide 92-65. Howard had 22 and Coleman 12 for the Tide in what was the first of three setbacks in their next four games.

The Tide's next game, a 70-68 loss at Hughes-Kirk, was memorable on two fronts: first, it marked the first loss to a district foe since 1949, and, second, it was the first time Hughes-Kirk defeated a Delmas Gish-coached Central City team.

Wayne "Slim" Ewing led the Tigers with 20 points, while Dave Shutt, Dude Shutt and David Hinton each scored 12 points. Howard was the game's top scorer with 29 points.

Thanks to 10 fourth-quarter points from Howard, the Tide came from behind to edge Owensboro 58-57. The Tide trailed 46-43 heading into the final stanza. Howard finished with 25 points.

Jimmy Mitchell blistered the Tide's defense for 31 points, leading Madisonville to a 62-49 victory. Mitchell, an all-state selection, had 12 field goals and seven free throws.

Howard scored 16 for the Tide. Nofsinger, in his first game back since sustaining his leg injury, chipped in with eight points.

The Tide closed out the regular season by beating Drakesboro 52-41 and Calhoun 61-43. Howard had 16 points and Nofsinger 10 against the Cardinals, then Howard came back with 22 in the win over Calhoun.

In the district tournament opener, the Tide faced off against Muhlenberg Central, a team they had not met during the regular season. This game proved to be no contest, with the Tide winning easily 78-27. Ten different Tide players scored, headed by Nofsinger with 12. Howard had 11, Withrow and Dukes 10 each, Stewart nine, Anderson, Coleman and Jamison seven each, Day three and Wolfe two.

The semifinal game against Greenville was not so easy, but a solid first-half effort was enough to earn the Tide a 44-40 victory. The Tide led 25-20 at the break, maintained a five-point advantage going into the final quarter, then managed to hang on for the win.

Howard had 12 points and Nofsinger 10 for the Tide. Kenny Richardson led the Blackhawks with 13 points.

Giving one of their finest performances of the season, the Tide, riding a big 26-point effort from Howard, captured the district crown by beating Hughes-Kirk 68-48. The game was close at intermission—the Tide led 26-25—but a big second half that saw the Tide outscore Hughes-Kirk 42-23 was more than enough to secure another district trophy.

Howard received plenty of help from Withrow, who finished with 14 points, and Dukes with 11. Nofsinger had nine points, all coming after intermission.

Dave Shutt led Hughes-Kirk with 13 points, while Ewing finished with 12.

Nofsinger, Howard and Withrow were named to the all-district team.

Howard kept the hot hand, scoring 24 points in a 72-56 win over Kyrock in the regional tournament opener. This one was never close; the Tide held a commanding 33-16 lead at the half.

Nofsinger ended the night with 14 points, while Stewart also hit double digits with 11.

On deck was a familiar foe—Hughes-Kirk. The two clubs had met three times, with the Tide claiming two wins. But on this night, Dave Shutt was not about to let the Tide hang a third loss on the Tigers.

Shutt burned the Tide for 28 points in a 59-56 Hughes-Kirk win. The Tide led by seven at the half and two as the final quarter got underway, but the Tigers won the fourth-quarter battle 13-8 to secure the win. In those final eight minutes, Miller accounted for seven points and Shutt four.

The Tide had two more field goals than Hughes-Kirk, but the Tigers hit 21 free tosses to the Tide's 14, which proved to be the difference.

Howard had 15 points for the Tide, while Nofsinger and Stewart each had 11.

This is another of those "what-if" seasons that show up every so often. What if Nofsinger had not missed 15 games due to injury? That's more than half the games played that season. Of those 15 games, the Tide lost seven. How many might have gone the other way had Nofsinger been healthy? We'll never know.

What is known is that the Golden Tide would move into a brand new home, and they would do so with an inexperienced, untested team. And the results would be less than impressive.

Chapter 19

1951-52

For the previous two years George Taylor and Delmas Gish had been lobbying hard for the construction of a new gymnasium, arguing that the current gym, once one of the state's most spacious, was now too small, thus putting Golden Tide teams at a disadvantage when playing opponents in larger venues. Construction of the new gym began in 1950 and was completed in time for the start of the 1951-52 season. For the first time in more than four decades the Golden Tide had a new home, one that could accommodate 2,500 fans.

What the Golden Tide didn't have, however, was a roster featuring many experienced players. With the exception of Bobby Joe Withrow and Don Coleman, there were virtually no players on hand who had logged much playing time. This was one of the most untested, inexperienced Golden Tide teams to come along in many years.

And predictably, that lack of experienced reared its ugly head pretty much from start to finish. This club would finish with a 19-13 record, thus making it the first Golden Tide team in 25 years that failed to win 20 games in a season. And those 13 losses equaled the 1938-39 team for the most setbacks in a single season.

What killed this club was its inability to win close games. Of the 13 losses, nine were by six points or less.

OK, a couple of trivia questions: Who scored the very first field goal in the new gym? Answer: Roy "D.D." Withrow in the junior varsity game. Who scored the first field goal in the varsity tilt? Answer: Bobby Joe Withrow.

Prior to the season opener against Bremen, in between the JV and varsity games, there was a dedication ceremony in which several distinguished individuals spoke. The headline speaker was long-time

Kentucky Athletics Commissioner Ted Sanford. Other dignitaries included Joe Billy Mansfield, Sanford's special assistant, SEC official Bob Forsythe, Muhlenberg County Superintendent Robert Shaver, Central City Mayor Albert Harding, school board chairman Crandall Bastin and CCHS Superintendent George Taylor.

The game itself lacked the luster of the pre-game ceremonies, with the Golden Tide claiming a less-than-titillating 40-35 win. Withrow led the Tide with 13 points, while Roy Lee Toll had 10 and Frankie Huddleston had eight.

Joining that trio in the starting quintet were Coleman and Dick Wolfe. Other team members were Benny Creel, Charles Gray, Forrest Shown, Junior Howerton and Bobby Don Millard.

It didn't take long for fans to discover that the new gym was not going to be a safe haven for this team. In only the second game played in the new facility, the Tide fell to Dunmor 47-46, courtesy of a big 22-point effort by the Wildcats' Glen Mohon. Withrow, with 11 points, was the only Tide player in double figures.

This game did provide a brief glimpse into the future. Millard, a sophomore, scored three points, and Corky Withrow, an eighth-grader, made his first varsity appearance, failing to score while committing one personal foul.

Bobby Joe Withrow tallied 13 points and Toll added 10 as the Tide beat Graham 44-37. The Tide were behind 35-31 after three quarters, then held the Nighthawks to a pair of fourth-quarter free throws to pick up the win.

After beating Graham, the Tide dropped four of their next five games, the lone win coming against Calhoun 60-40. In that game, Coleman and Withrow each had 15 points.

The losses were to Drakesboro 50-47, Hughes-Kirk 45-39, Bourbon County 46-45 and St. Xavier 50-41. Against Drakesboro, the Tide led 41-35 going into the final stanza, only to watch the Cardinals, paced by Joe Roop with 14 points, come back to notch the win.

Coleman had 13 and Creel 12 for the Tide.

Hughes-Kirk got 16 points each from Alvis Parsons and Bill Miller in its win over the Tide, who were paced by Withrow with 11 and Huddleston with 10.

Withrow played well in the next two setbacks, scoring 18 against Bourbon County and 20 against St. X.

In a 55-53 double-overtime win over Greenville that began a three-game winning streak, Withrow led the attack with 21 points. Coleman also played well, ending the long affair with 14 points.

Toll tossed in 20 points, Withrow 12 and Shown 10 as the Tide got revenge against Bremen with a 58-37 win. Toll scored 16 of his points after intermission.

In the inaugural Central City Invitational Tournament, the Tide took the title by beating Cromwell 59-52 and Graham 48-40. Coleman had 23 points and Withrow added 18 in the win over Cromwell. Against Graham, Withrow had 17 points and Shown 11.

Despite 23 points from all-state performer (and future University of Louisville All-American) Charlie Tyra, the Tide posted an impressive 52-47 win over Louisville Atherton. The Tide got standout efforts from Millard with 17 points and Shown, now a starter, with 10.

On a road trip to Eastern Kentucky, the Tide split a pair of games, losing 58-47 to London before beating Hazard 59-58. Against London, Withrow and Coleman each had a dozen points. In the win over Hazard, Withrow had 18 and Shown 11.

Roscoe Shackleford and Dickie Keffer led Hazard with 18 and 16 points, respectively.

In their next three outings, the Tide wrapped wins over Owensboro Catholic 46-36 and Bowling Green 54-44 around a 52-47 loss to Owensboro. Withrow scored 14 points in the win over Catholic, then had 16 against Owensboro, which was led by Billy Bibb's 33-point performance. Coleman had 16, Withrow 13 and Toll 10 against Bowling Green.

The win at Bowling Green was one of the best efforts turned in by the Tide, yet it failed to generate any positive momentum. Instead, what followed was a three-game losing streak, beginning with a 69-55 setback at Paducah Tilghman. Withrow scored 22 points and Shown had 14 in that loss.

David Mercer knocked down 25 points to lead Drakesboro past the Tide 66-45.Withrow had 15 and Coleman 10 in a losing cause.

The old story of fading in the later stages of the game came back to haunt the Tide in a 53-49 home loss to Daviess County. The Tide led 21-17 at the half, and the score was knotted 37-37 going into the final frame, which saw the Panthers, led by Paul Johnson, pull away for the win. Johnson had 16 points, 12 coming after intermission.

Shown had 15 and Withrow 14 for the Tide.

The Tide responded to those three losses by going on a season-best four-game winning streak, kicked off by a surprisingly easy 65-33 win over a good Hughes-Kirk club. In this game, for the first time all season, five Tide players hit for double figures. Toll led with 13, Shown had 12, Withrow 11, Coleman and Wolfe 10 each.

Bill Miller had 14 for the Tigers.

Giving another superb effort, and reversing a trend by winning the fourth quarter, the Tide upended a good Madisonville team 47-39. Behind 34-32 after three quarters, the Tide, getting clutch late-game performances from Shown and Withrow, outscored the Maroons 15-5 in the final eight minutes to earn the victory. Coleman led the winners with 14 points, Shown had 13, seven in the final frame, and Withrow added 11, four of his total coming in the last quarter.

All-state standout Jimmy Mitchell paced the Maroons with a game-best 17 points.

In their next two games, both wins, the Tide continued to display a tough grittiness in late-game situations, coming out on top after heading into the final quarter with the score knotted. Those wins came against Calhoun 57-55 and Greenville 47-39.

Coleman and Shown each scored 19 points against Calhoun, then Coleman and Withrow each had 13 against Greenville.

The Tide closed out the regular season by dropping a pair of hard-fought encounters against Louisville Male 53-48 and Owensboro 62-61. Coleman was superb in those two games, accounting for 14 points against Male and 17 against Owensboro. Toll and Withrow each had 15 points in that loss to the Red Devils, who were once again led by Billy Bibb with 27 points. It was a Bibb free throw with six seconds remaining that was the difference.

With a mediocre 6-4 record against district foes, and a season-long history of inconsistent play, no oddsmaker was about to give Central City much of a chance at succeeding in post-season play. And yet this team managed to fool everyone, reeling off three straight wins to capture the district title.

Playing at home, the Tide opened tourney play by pounding Dunmor 71-47. Coleman led a balanced attack with 16 points. Shown had 14, Withrow 13 and Toll 12 for the Tide.

Glen Mohon had 16 for the Wildcats.

In semifinal action against Graham, with a record crowd estimated at 2,600 looking on, the Tide trailed until the final two minutes, before pulling out a 52-49 victory. Tide defense, which limited Graham to seven fourth-quarter points, was the big difference.

Coleman topped the winners with 16 points. Withrow and Toll had 12 apiece.

Bob Arnett led Graham with 14 points.

The championship match-up against Drakesboro presented an exact opposite scenario. In this game the Tide held a commanding 43-30 lead heading into the final quarter, then had to hang on down the stretch to preserve a 50-47 win.

With just under five minutes remaining, a bucket by Toll extended the Tide's advantage to 50-35. Those would be the last points scored by the Tide. As the Tide's offense was slipping into the deep freeze, the Cardinals, sparked by Joe Roop and David Mercer, began to chisel into the lead, their charge coming up just short as time expired.

Despite what had been an up-and-down season, the Tide somehow found a way to take home another district trophy.

Withrow and Coleman were both named to the all-district team.

In regional tournament action, also played in Central City's new gym, the Tide open against a Cromwell team they had beaten by seven points in the CCIT. This encounter wasn't close. Behind 19 points from Withrow and 12 each from Coleman, Toll and Millard, the Tide rolled to a convincing 61-46 victory.

Cromwell's Reathal Goff led all scorers with 23.

The Tide's semifinal battle against Breckinridge County offered a scenario that would play out in eerily similar fashion one year down the road—a heart-breaking loss that easily could have gone the other way.

Breckinridge County ended the Tide's season by posting a 42-40 win. The Tide trailed 36-30 after three quarters, then made a late charge. But with five players having fouled out, the Tide lacked the muscle to complete the comeback.

Coleman had 14 to lead the Tide. Withrow had 12 and Toll 10.

This club's 19-13 record was the worst since George Taylor's first team finished with a 6-11 mark in 1925-26. And with so many of this year's players set to graduate, the outlook for 1952-53 couldn't have been particularly bright. After all, next year's team would have only one returning player (Wolfe) who had logged any meaningful minutes, and he would be surrounded by a very young and inexperienced supporting cast.

But next year's team would be different in more ways than you can count, primarily because those young and inexperienced players turned out to be very good basketball players.

Bobby Don Millard, Larry Ray and Roy "D.D." Withrow were rock solid players, smart, tough, tenacious. They knew how to win.

And joining them would be freshman Corky Withrow, who, by the time his career ended, established himself as the greatest player in Golden Tide history.

Chapter 20

1952-53

It's difficult to recall any Golden Tide season beginning under a bigger cloud of uncertainty than this one. To be sure, given the youth and inexperience on this roster, there was much more reason for doubt and skepticism than there was for excitement or enthusiasm. This season, the Golden Tide were truly venturing into the unknown.

Dick Wolfe, at 6'4", would anchor the pivot. Bobby Don Millard and Corky Withrow were set to handle the forward spots, while Roy "D.D." Withrow and Larry Ray took care of the backcourt duties. Those five would play the bulk of minutes during a season that turned out to be something of a surprise.

This team finished with a 24-9 record, claimed another district title and came within a questionable call of making it to the state tournament. Not a bad resume for a club that began with modest expectations at best.

Joining the five starters on the team were Junior Howerton, Charles Gray, Stanley Ruby, Eddie Houston, Bobby Mercer and Billy Lee Robinson.

Although no one was aware of it at the time, this season also began what later became known as the Corky Withrow Era, during which the Golden Tide won 119 games and lost just 20.

However, based on the Tide's season opener against Bremen, any hopes for a golden era were about as unlikely as snow in Florida. In this game, a 53-52 home-court loss, neither the Tide, the Withrow Era nor Withrow himself offered any hints that success might be waiting somewhere down the road.

Bremen beat the Tide despite the absence of starting guards Gene Anderson and Joe Robert Divine, who were injured in an automobile accident and couldn't play.

The Tide led at the end of the first three quarters, only to watch as the Golden Eagles battled back to take a 51-50 lead with less than two minutes remaining. Moments later, Corky Withrow scored his only bucket of the night (and the first two of his 3,136 points) to give the Tide a 52-51 lead. Then Wayne Neal nailed a pair of free tosses to give Bremen the win.

Wolfe led the Tide with 14 points, while Roy Withrow and Millard had 13 and 12, respectively.

(To simplify matters, the Withrow brothers will be referred to as D.D. and Corky.)

Jay Bird Jones paced Bremen with 14 points. Neal had 12, six coming in the final quarter.

The Withrow brothers combined for 38 points—D.D. had 20, Corky 18—and Millard added 10 in a 79-34 win at Muhlenberg Central, the start of a four-game winning streak. In this easy win, nine different players scored. Others included Wolfe with nine, Gray seven, Houston five, Mercer and Howerton four each, and Ray with two.

Millard scored 14 points, Corky and D.D. 10 each in a 54-43 win over Graham, then Wolfe had 18 points, Corky 13, Millard 11 and D.D 10 as the Tide crushed Calhoun 76-37. The fourth consecutive win came at Drakesboro 79-45, with D.D. burning the nets for 23 points. Millard had 17 and Wolfe 16 in that victory. Mercer also played well, coming off the bench to score eight points.

The streak was snapped when Dunmor came to town and upended the Tide 52-48. Bobby Driskill did the most damage, scoring 16 points, 14 coming after intermission.

Wolfe had 16 and Millard 14 in a losing effort.

The Tide struggled in their next game before finally managing to put away Hughes-Kirk 48-42. Millard and D.D. each had 13 for the winners, while Wolfe added 10.

Carl Carver paced the Tigers with 10 points.

Traveling to Bremen, the Tide avenged their opening-game loss by ripping the Golden Eagles 68-45. The Tide's backcourt tandem of Ray and D.D. was splendid, each player racking up 17 points. Millard finished with 11, Wolfe with 10.

Led by D.D. with 13 points and Wolfe with 10, the Tide topped Greenville 46-31. Ray chipped in with eight points, six coming in the final stanza.

Murrell Cobb had 10 points for the Blackhawks.

Wolfe erupted for 22 points to lead the Tide to a 68-40 win over Drakesboro in the Central City Invitational Tournament opener. Wolfe received strong support from the Withrow brothers, D.D. with 16 and Corky with 14.

The Tide captured the title while also extracting a measure of revenge by edging past Dunmor 64-58. Leading 52-40 after three quarters, the Tide had to fight off a Glen Mohon-driven comeback in order to secure the championship trophy. Mohon had 19 points, 11 coming in the final frame. Driskill also had 19 for the Wildcats.

The Tide's balanced scoring attack was enough to offset the Mohon-Driskell scoring parade. Wolfe had 16, Ray 12, D.D. 11 and Millard 10 for the winners.

Sparked by eight second-half points from Howerton, the Tide took care of Louisville Atherton 60-53. Wolfe scored 20 points for the Tide, a number matched by Atherton's 6'8" all-state performer Charlie Tyra. Millard also hit double digits with a dozen points.

With Millard scoring 15 points, Wolfe 14 and D.D. 10, the Tide beat an improving Muhlenberg Central squad 65-50. Muhlenberg Central made it somewhat interesting, thanks to a 23-point effort from Gene Evitts.

Unable to win at home, the Tide lost to visiting London 59-54. This was the Tide's third loss, all coming on their own court. Ray paced the Tide with 17 points.

Behind 18 points from Corky, 14 from D.D., and 10 each from Millard and Wolfe, the Tide dismantled home-standing Greenville 69-55. The Tide led 40-28 at the half, saw the advantage close to within 50-46 after three quarters, then outscored the Blackhawks 19-9 in the final quarter to notch the win. All fourth-quarter Greenville points came on free throws.

Larry Sparks and Tommy Mercer topped Greenville scoring with 15 points each.

For those of you wondering about the Corky Withrow-Roger Newman rivalry, you'll have to wait a little longer. In these first two Central City-Greenville games, Newman did not play.

Thanks to another balanced scoring attack, the Tide easily handled Owensboro Catholic 68-48. Millard led with 16 points, followed by Corky with 15, Ray with 11 and D.D. with 10. Gray came off the bench to score nine points, all in the second half.

Facing Owensboro in the Sportscenter, the Tide, fueled by Millard's 20 points, beat the Red Devils 69-58. This game was never close, with the Tide sitting on a 53-34 advantage at the end of the third quarter.

The Tide did their best to drop another home game, trailing Bowling Green until late in the fourth quarter before finally managing to subdue the visitors 55-52. D.D. and Millard led the comeback effort, combining for 12 fourth-quarter points. D.D. ended the night with 13 points, Millard and Wolfe with 12 apiece.

After 18 games, this team that began the season under such a cloud of uncertainty now sported a surprising 15-3 record. In every way, this group had surpassed all expectations. With that in mind, what occurred over the next three weeks was both shocking and inexplicable.

The team that was sailing along lost five of its next six games. What happened? What caused this downward spiral? Perhaps this team had simply been playing above its head all season, or maybe it was just a mid-season funk that many teams go through. But whatever it was, things got so bad that after the last of those five losses, Delmas Gish told his players he was calling it quits.

The long trip into darkness began with a 68-64 loss at Hughes-Kirk. Bill Miller had 29 points and Carl Carver 23 for the Tigers, who, despite having five fewer field goals than the visitors, made good on 28 free throws to 14 by the Tide. That proved to be the difference.

Ray paced the Tide with 19 points. Corky had 14, Millard and Wolfe 11 each.

All-state performer Kenny Sidwell dumped in 22 points to lead Caverna to an 80-73 win. Sidwell, who later coached at Greenville, had eight buckets and six free throws. Wolfe and Millard led the Tide with 18 points, while D.D. added 15.

The Tide tried to make it three losses in a row, but somehow managed to snatch victory from the jaws of defeat, edging Daviess County 51-50 in the Sportscenter. Up 41-36 after three quarters, the Tide had to hang on down the stretch to sneak out with the win. Millard had 14 points, Wolfe 13 and D.D. 11 for the Tide.

In another home-court disaster, the Tide blew a six-point lead against Paducah Tilghman, eventually losing 53-51. Dwain McIntosh, another all-state performer, paced the Tornado with 15 points.

For the Tide, D.D. had 14, Corky 13 and Millard 12.

Madisonville, behind 33 points from Jimmy Mitchell, pulled away in the final stanza to post a 66-50 victory. Mitchell, a first-team all-state selection, was simply unstoppable. His 10 fourth-quarter points killed any chance the Tide could pull off the win.

At this stage, just when it looked like things couldn't get much worse, they did. Worse in a monstrous way. If the Tide had previously been a sinking ship, it was now the Titanic.

Traveling to Louisville, pitted against the best player they would see all season, the Tide suffered a humiliating 94-49 loss to Male. This one was over about a minute after tip-off. By the end of the first eight minutes, Male led 26-9. After that, it only got worse.

Kenny Kuhn, only a sophomore, was a man among boys, leading all scorers with 37 points. He had 13 field goals and 11 free throws. David Kuhn had 15 for the Bulldogs.

Wolfe was the only Golden Tide player to hit double figures, finishing with 13 points.

It was after this humbling experience that Delmas Gish told his players he was calling it quits. His players, however, were not about to let that happen. They banded together, went to see their coach and promised him that if he would stay, they would turn things around.

And they did. Of the Tide's next 44 games, they lost only once.

The turnaround began with a tough 53-44 win over Drakesboro. It took a big fourth quarter for the Tide to put this one away. D.D. paced the winners with 14 points. Millard and Corky each had nine, while Gray came off the bench to chip in seven.

The Cardinals were led by H.L. Hope with 15 points. Hope, who only played during the second half of the season, would become a very familiar name to Golden Tide fans in less than a year.

The Tide closed out the regular season by beating Owensboro 61-52 and Calhoun 65-60. Against the Red Devils, Corky scored 17 points, Ray 15 and D.D. 13. In the win over Calhoun, Wolfe was the top gun with a season-best 25 points. Millard had 16 points in that game.

Post-season action began with the Tide facing Drakesboro for the fourth time. Having won the first three encounters, the Tide were expected to win this one as well, which they did, coming out on top 57-49 after trailing 42-39 heading into the final frame.

Corky led the winners with 16 points. Wolfe had 14, Millard 11 and D.D. 10.

Drakesboro's Denny Wester topped all scorers with 28 points.

In semifinal action against Greenville, the Tide won 52-48 despite losing all five starters to foul problems. In all, the Blackhawks only had eight field goals, but thanks to 32 free throws (in 51 attempts), they made things interesting.

Millard had 17 points and D.D. 11 for the Tide, who benefited greatly from six Billy Lee Robinson fourth-quarter points.

Larry Sparks led the Blackhawks with 16 points.

In their first head-to-head match-up, Roger Newman had nine points, Corky had four.

Wolfe scored 22 points and D.D. added 14 in a 65-58 championship game win over Dunmor. Corky had eight, Millard and Gray seven each, Ray six and Robinson one in that win.

Dunmor's one-two punch of Mohon and Driskill had 19 and 15 points, respectively.

The regional tournament opener against Butler County turned out to have a touch of déjà vu. In fact, it was almost a carbon copy of the Tide's district game against Greenville. The Tide escaped with a 58-56 win despite losing four players via the foul route, while watching Butler County, playing on its home court, make good on 34 of 39 free tosses. For the game, the Tide had 22 field goals to Butler County's 11.

Wolfe led the winners with 17 points. Ray contributed 11.

Butler County's J.C. Phelps was the game's top scorer with 24, 14 coming at the charity stripe.

Next up was a fourth match-up against dangerous Dunmor and its high-scoring duo of Mohon and Driskill. A big first half, which saw the Tide build a 36-24 advantage, proved to be more than Dunmor could overcome.

The Tide advanced to the championship game with a 71-63 win. Corky had 16 points, Ray 15, Wolfe 12 and Robinson 10 off the bench for the winners.

Driskill had 20 and Mohon 16 to lead Dunmor.

The championship game, a 67-66 loss to Breckinridge County, is one that will forever live in infamy for Golden Tide fans. It was a game that saw the Tide lead early, fall behind, reclaim the upper hand late, and then just when it appeared that a win was on the horizon, a questionable call—a foul on Millard—was made by one of the officials, Roy Settles.

A pair of free throws later and Breckinridge County was on its way to the state tournament.

"That was a terrible call," Corky said. "They called the foul on Bobby Don and he was *behind* the guy he supposedly fouled. That's the only time in my life that I ever heard Mr. Gish curse."

Ray had a superb game for the Tide, ending the night with 16 points. Millard had 15 and Wolfe 14.

Carlos Irwin led all scorers with 24 points.

For their efforts, Ray and Wolfe were named to the all-regional team.

This season, which the Tide carved out a surprising 24-9 record, had been far more successful than anyone could have imagined. With Wolfe being the lone senior, it meant next year's club would feature a roster filled with returning veterans. Expectations were sure to be sky high. But even with all that returning talent, no one could have expected what eventually transpired.

A perfect season.

Chapter 21

1953-54

Prior to the start of the 1953-54 season, most basketball observers predicted the Golden Tide to be one of the state's premier teams. In the first Litkenhous (Lit) Ratings, the Tide were ranked 15th. With four returning starters, such confidence in the Tide's chances for success was not unwarranted.

Back for their final season were seniors Larry Ray, Bobby Don Millard and D.D. Withrow. Also returning was sophomore Corky Withrow. The loss of Dick Wolfe to graduation was off-set by what can only be termed a lucky—and timely—set of circumstances.

Of course, Central City opponents tossed out lucky and timely, replacing those terms with pure recruiting.

H.L. "Hub" Hope, a 6'2" forward, decided to transfer from Drakesboro, where he played half the year in 1952-53, and join the Golden Tide for his final season. Hope, younger brother of Cardinal great Nookie Hope, had relatives living in Central City, and that's who he chose to live with in order to be eligible to play for the Tide.

To say Drakesboro fans were not pleased with what they viewed as a traitorous act is putting it mildly. In their eyes, Central City had recruited Hope, pure and simple.

Is that what happened?

"Well, there may have been some recruiting going on, but I'm not aware of it," Corky Withrow said. "I'm positive Mr. Gish didn't recruit H.L. In fact, I think he was as surprised as everyone else was when he found out H.L. was transferring. Probably, H.L. looked at the situation and realized he had a better chance of being on a winning team if he came and played with us. And since he had relatives in Central City, he was able to do it."

Whatever the circumstances that brought Hope to Central City, his arrival on the scene provided the missing piece to what was already a strong puzzle. He would handle one of the forward slots, with the rapidly maturing Corky Withrow, now close to 6'4", shifting into the pivot position.

Millard, Ray, Hope and the Withrow brothers would be the starters on a team that wrote itself into the record books by becoming the first and only Golden Tide club to go through an entire regular season without suffering a single defeat. Finishing 35-0, this would be one of only a handful of teams to enter the state tournament with an unblemished record.

Other team members included Billy Lee Robinson, Eddie Houston, Johnny Swann, Jerry Calvert, Buddy Lear, Stanley Ruby and Buddy Fuller.

The road to perfection began with a less-than-sterling 55-45 home win over Graham. It was not a close call, but neither did it offer any hint that this team would be something special.

Millard led the winners with 13 points. The Withrow brothers each contributed 11, Ray nine and Hope six in his Golden Tide debut.

After that unimpressive win, the Tide began to flash some serious firepower, beginning with a 79-48 romp past Bremen. Corky scored 24 and Millard 15 in that win.

Millard came through with 19 points and Corky added 18 in a 75-49 win over Dunmor, then Ray picked up scoring honors by tossing in 18 points to lead the Tide past Muhlenberg Central 72-43. Against MC, Millard chipped in 16 points and the Withrow brothers had 11 apiece.

Don Perkins led Muhlenberg Central with 15.

Corky scored 23 points, D.D. had 15 and Ray 11 as the Tide demolished Drakesboro 77-45. In their next outing, a 92-54 win at Hughes-Kirk, five Tide players cracked double figures, led by Corky with 20 and D.D. with 19. Swann came off the bench to score 14 points, while Robinson finished with 12 and Ray 11.

Hughes-Kirk's Carl Carver claimed game-high honors with 29 points.

At Calhoun, Hope had his breakout performance, hitting for 18 points in a 57-46 Tide win. Ray had 13 and Millard 11 in that victory.

Sparked by 16 points from Robinson, the Tide easily took care of visiting Louisville Atherton 69-49. Robinson, a cat-quick little guard, had four buckets and eight free throws after coming off the bench. He received strong support from Millard and Corky, both of whom had 13 points.

In the first of four hard-fought tussles against arguably the greatest Greenville team of all-time, the Tide somehow managed to escape with a 74-73 overtime victory. Although this was Greenville's home game, it was played in Muhlenberg Central's gym in order to accommodate the enormous crowd.

With the Blackhawks leading 68-66 and just eight seconds remaining in regulation, D.D. hit his only bucket of the night to tie the score and send the game into the extra frame. A Ruby free throw, his only point of the game, turned out to be the difference.

A total of 55 fouls were whistled in this battle, with the Tide losing four players and Greenville two. The Blackhawks connected on 31 of 43 free throws, while the Tide hit just 16 of 33.

Ray and Corky each had 20 points for the Tide, with Hope adding 11. Larry Sparks had 20 and Roger Newman 18 for the Blackhawks.

D.D. scored 19 points, Hope 13, Corky 12 and Millard 10 as the Tide beat Graham 60-38 in the first round of the Central City Invitational. What that win did was get the Tide a second confrontation with Greenville in the title game. Unlike that first match-up, this one ended with the Tide winning easily 71-48, thanks to 20 points from Corky, 16 from Hope and 15 for D.D.

Roger Newman paced the Blackhawks with 10 points.

Behind 27 points from Corky, the Tide made it 12 in a row with a 64-51 road win over Drakesboro. D.D. and Ray finished with 14 and 12 points, respectively.

Denny Wester topped the Cardinals with 19 points.

The Tide's next seven games, beginning with a 71-54 win over Butler County, were a showcase for excellent and overpowering basketball. In those seven victories, the Tide's average winning margin was 21.6 points per game.

Corky had 25, Millard 15 and Ray 11 against Butler County, then Corky came back to score 17, Ray 15, Millard and Hope 12 each, and D.D. 10 in a 76-56 win over Owensboro Catholic.

Sedalia, a dangerous club, came to town, but with Millard tossing in 22 points, Ray 16 and Corky 11, the Tide notched an impressive 74-58 win. In that game, the Tide limited Sedalia to 13 field goals.

Member of the 1911-12 team include (l-r): Charlie Banks, manager, Bryant Lawton, Bernes Frost, Frank West, Fuqua Bennett, Paul Frost, J.R. Kirk. This was Central City's first team.

The 1912-13 team, front row (l-r): Fuqua Bennett, Neal Barnes, Henley Napier. Back row (l-r): W.B. Frost, Paul Frost, Bryant Lawton, J.R. Kirk.

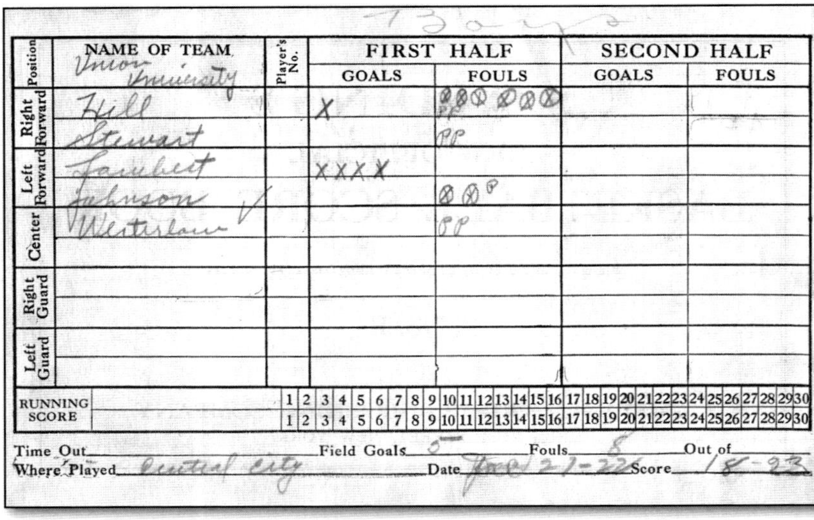

Position	NAME OF TEAM Union University	Player's No.	FIRST HALF GOALS	FIRST HALF FOULS	SECOND HALF GOALS	SECOND HALF FOULS
Right Forward	Hill		X			
	Stewart					
Left Forward	Lambert		XXXX			
	Johnson					
Center	Westerlaw					
Right Guard						
Left Guard						

RUNNING SCORE 1 2 3 4 5 6 7 8 9 10 11 12 13 14 15 16 17 18 19 20 21 22 23 24 25 26 27 28 29 30

Time Out Field Goals 5 Fouls 8 Out of
Where Played Central City Date Jan 27-23 Score 18-23

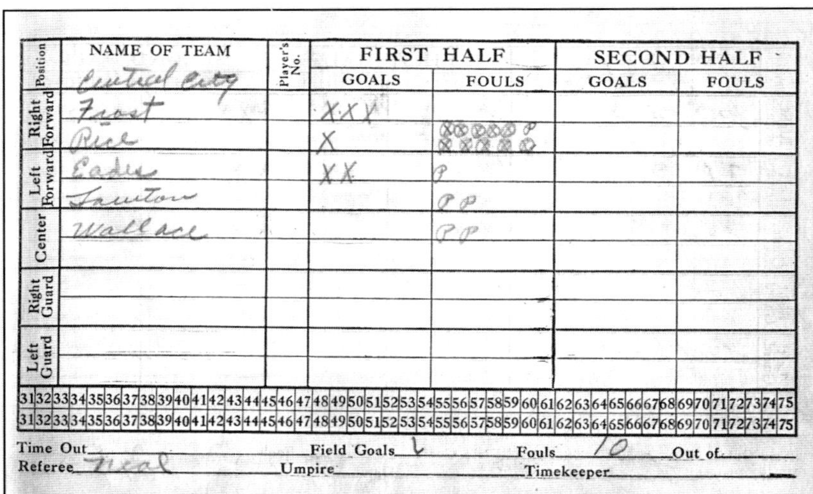

Position	NAME OF TEAM Central City	Player's No.	FIRST HALF GOALS	FIRST HALF FOULS	SECOND HALF GOALS	SECOND HALF FOULS
Right Forward	Frost		XXX			
	Rice		X			
Left Forward	Eades		XX			
	Tainton					
Center	Wallace					
Right Guard						
Left Guard						

31 32 33 34 35 36 37 38 39 40 41 42 43 44 45 46 47 48 49 50 51 52 53 54 55 56 57 58 59 60 61 62 63 64 65 66 67 68 69 70 71 72 73 74 75

Time Out Field Goals 6 Fouls 10 Out of
Referee Neal Umpire Timekeeper

Oldest Scorebook…1923

The 1925-26 team, sitting (l-r): Bacil Swanay, Edgar Ray Frost, Harold Eades, George Connor, Bud Cates. Standing (l-r): Randolph Baker, Carl Quisenberry, John Harvey, George Taylor. This was Coach Taylor's first team.

The 1928-29 team, front row (l-r): Norval Davis, Glover Ellis, Sam Stringer, William Hughes, Tom Campbell, Peck Hickman, Larue Sosh, Frank Rice, Charles Hughes. Bishop Arnold. Back row (l-r): Joe Walling, J.B. Hill, James Cates, Elliot Ramsey, Nelson Sosh, Wayne Millard, Malcolm Sears, John Meinschein, Virgil Gish. Back: George Taylor.

The 1933-34 team, front row (l-r): Clark Bailey, Johnny Ogden, Harold Shrewsberry. Middle row (l-r), Clarence Batsel, Red Almond, Les Chinn, J.C. Batsel. Back row (l-r): George Taylor, Damon Hart, Denzil Noffsinger, Unknown, E.P. Malloy (manager).

The 1934-35 team, front row (l-r), Ermine Vincent, Merrel Robey, Harold Shrewsberry, G. Wilkins, Denzil Noffsinger. Middle row (l-r), David Lockery, J.W. Conrey, Bill Durham, Damon Hart. Back row (l-r), George Taylor, Leroy Crossman, E.P. Malloy (manager).

The 1937-38 team, sitting (l-r), Buddy Lloyd, Harold Gish, Ermine Vincent, Bob Lawton. Standing (l-r), Roy Noffsinger, J.T. Byars, H.G. Watkins, Roy McWaters, Bennie Ogden. In back, George Taylor and E.P Malloy (manager).

The 1941-42 team, front row (l-r), Jimmy "Jug" Walker, Evan Ray, Earl Ray Capps, E.G. "Foo" Stevens, Bill Eades, Bud Eades. Back row (l-r), George Taylor, Beauchamp Kirkpatrick, Billy Arnold, William Miller, Bobby Millard, Red Kelly (manager).

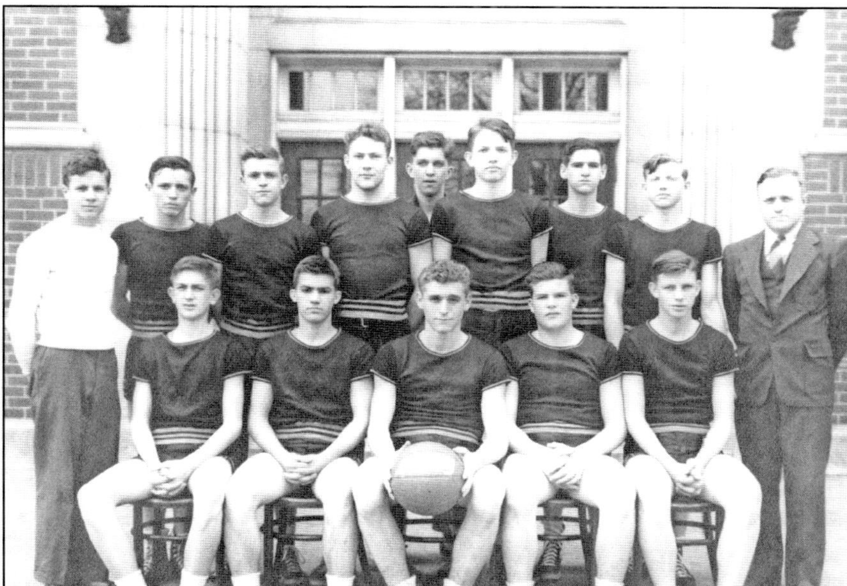

The 1942-43 team, front row (l-r), Hugh Vernon Smith, Billy Hicks, Earl Ray Tinsley, Gilbert Teague, Earl Atherton. Back row (l-r), Jimmy Van Sickle (manager), Lindle Cessna, Beauchamp Kirkpatrick, Billy Eades, Bud Eades, Howard Lovell, Bobby Watkins, Bobby Logan, Delmas Gish.

The 1943-44 team, front row (l-r), Howard Lovell, W.C. Mobberly, Bobby Watkins, Beauchamp Kirkpatrick, Gilbert Teague. Back row (l-r), Connis Young, Billy Hicks, Hugh Vemon Smith, Earl Atherton, Jimmy Mohon, Delmas Gish.

CENTRAL CITY HIGH SCHOOL

Runner-Up

Front Row: Tudor, H. V. Smith, Sparks, Teague. Second Row: Dukes, Mohon, Henry, Watkins, Mobberly. (C. Hicks and Coach Gish were absent).

DELMOS GISH, Coach SEASON'S RECORD: Won 29, Lost 3 COLORS: Black and Gold

District Tournament Games Won

Central City	50—Drakesboro	26
Central City	51—Bremen	29

Regional Tournament Games Won

Central City	28—Caneyville	21
Central City	44—Hartford	34
Central City	66—Brownsville	26

Name	No.	Age	Hgt.	Semester
Tudor	21	16	5-8	6
H. V. Smith	20	10	5-10½	8
Sparks	24	16	5-11	6
Teague	29	17	5-11½	6
Dukes	23	16	6-1	6
Mohon	26	16	6-1	6
Henry	22	15	6-3	4
Watkins	27	18	6-1	8
Mobberly	28	16	6-0	4
Hicks	25	17	5-8	8

State Tournament

Central City 54—Rineyville 37
Central City 32—Madison 28
Central City 34—Harlan 30
Central City 42—Male 54

The 1944-45 team, front row (l-r): Billy Hicks, Gilbert Teague, Bobby Watkins, W.C. Mobberly, Hugh Vernon Smith. Back row (l-r): Jimmy Van Sickle (manager), Richard Morris, Jimmy Mohon, Kent Henry, Jackie Sparks, Harold Tudor, Delmas Gish.

FAIRDALE

High And Consolidated School

Charles W. Blake, Principal

CORAL RIDGE, KY.

205 Esplanade Drive
Kenwood Village
Louisville 8, Ky.
March 21, 1945

Mr. George Taylor
Supt., Central City Schools
Central City, Ky.
Dear George:

This letter is written to congratulate you on one of the finest groups of boys I have ever had the pleasure of officiating for.

During all of the games of the Regional and the two games I worked for Central City in the State Tournament I had the deepest respect for your boys because of the manner in which they conducted themselves. They were, indeed, the best of sportsmen.

Your coach and my friend, Delmas Gish, deserves two commendations -- one for his team of champions and the other for teaching sportsmanship, thus developing men as well as ball players.

I value my association with you, Delmas, and Mr. Kiper most highly and feel most grateful for the fine cooperation you fellows have always given me.

With kindest personal regards I am

Sincerely your friend

Charlie

Charles J. Vettiner

CJV:VC

CLASS OF SERVICE

This is a full-rate Telegram or Cablegram unless its deferred character is indicated by a suitable symbol above or preceding the address.

WESTERN UNION

A. N. WILLIAMS
PRESIDENT

SYMBOLS

DL=Day Letter
NL=Night Letter
LC=Deferred Cable
NLT=Cable Night Letter
Ship Radiogram

The filing time shown in the date line on telegrams and day letters is STANDARD TIME at point of origin. Time of receipt is STANDARD TIME at point of destination

OB186 8=CENTRALCITY KY 17 454P

CENTRAL CITY BASKET BALL TEAM=

CARE COACH GISH=KY HOTEL=LVILLE= 1945 MAR 17 5 35

EVERY MEMBER OF LIONS CLUB ROARS FOR YOU=

CENTRAL CITY LIONS CLUB.

OB214 14= CENTRALCITY KY 16 436P 1945 MAR 16 PM 5 36

CENTRALCITY BASKETBALL TEAM=

CARE COACH DELMAS GISH KY HOTEL LVILLE=

NICE GOING GANG SEE YOU IN THE MORNING DONT FORGET WE BEAT HARLAN TOMORROW=

BOB LEACH.

OB220 9= CENTRALCITY KY 16 445P 1945 MAR 16 PM 5 45

CENTRALCITY BASKETBALL TEAM=

CARE GISH KY HOTEL LVILLE=

HEARD GAME BROADCAST. PROUD OF YOU BEAT HARLAN TOMORROW=

MR AND MRS E E MASSIE.

The filing time shown in the date line on telegrams and day letters is STANDARD TIME at point of origin. Time of receipt is STANDARD TIME at point of destination

OB185 13=CENTRALCITY KY 17 420P 1945 MAR 17 PM 5 38

GOLDEN TIDE BASKET BALL TEAM=

CARE GISH=KY HOTEL LVILLE=

THE ENTIRE MEMBERSHIP CENTRAL CITY COMMERICAL CLUB IS BACKING YOU HEART AND SOUL=

L M ROSS SECRETARY.

The filing time shown in the date line on telegrams and day letters is STANDARD TIME at point of origin. Time of receipt is STANDARD TIME at point of destination

OB213 11= CENTRALCITY KY 16 435P 1945 MAR 16 PM 5 35

CENTRALCITY BASKETBALL TEAM=

CARE COACH DELMAS GISH KY HOTEL LVILLE=

WE LOVE YOU ALL. KNEW YOU COULD DO IT. SEE YOU TOMORROW=

THELMA GRANT BOBBY OTTISE.

Central City Tops Harlan 34-30 and Rips Danville 50-20 to Gain State

By KEN TAYLOR, Assistant Sports Editor.

Kentucky was assured of a new and different high school basketball champion this year when Central City and Male advanced through semi-finals of the annual State Tournament Saturday afternoon before a full house at Jefferson County Armory.

Central City eliminated Harlan, the defending champion and the only past title holder to survive district and regional competition, by 34-30 and Male won the most lopsided game of the first 14 contests of the meet by 50-20 from Danville.

Central City's conquest was one of the greatest of all Kentucky High School Athletic Association Tournament games. And the Green Dragons were put out of the campaign by a defense through which they just could not often break.

Harlan and Danville were to play for the third and fourth places in the state Saturday night, before Male and Central City tangled for the crown given over by Harlan.

* * *

Male 50,
Danville 20

Male simply didn't let Danville have a look-in as it won its semi-final game 50-20 and hand the Admirals the worst licking of the tournament.

Danville thus had the distinction of winning and losing the greatest margin games. In the first round the Admirals defeated Dawson Springs by 25 points, 55-30.

The handwriting was on the wall right from the start as Don Martin, Ed Mudd and Gene Rhodes threw in field goals in four minutes. And just to make it absolutely certain that Danville should have no false ideas, Martin dumped in a short one, Dale Powell made two free throws and Mudd looped in a long one from the side to make it 12-0.

Finally Danville scored on Joe Brummett's tip in, but Rhodes hit a long one from center and Male was ahead 14-2 at the quarter.

At the end of the half, Male led 26-9 and was ahead 44-12 going into the fourth. Paul Jenkins let his subs play all the fourth period and they were outscored only 10-8 by the Admirals, several of whom also were subs.

Seven Male players starred in the scoring, with Mudd making 12 and Rhodes 11. Jim Hughes strove manfully, but hopelessly, for Danville and wound up with nine points.

FIRST PERIOD.

Player—Shot.	Male.	Danville.
Hughes, missed free throw	--	--
Martin, short side shot	2	0
Mudd, short	4	0
Brummett, missed one free throw	--	--
Mudd, missed one free throw	--	--
Rhodes, crip	6	0
Brummett, missed one free throw	--	--
Martin, short	8	0
Powell, two free throws	10	0
Mudd, long	12	0
Brummett, tip in	12	2
Rhodes, long center	14	2
SECOND PERIOD.		
Hughes, two free throws	14	4
Mudd, missed free throw	--	--
Rhodes, two-hand overhead	16	4
Hughes, under basket	16	6
Brummett, one free throw	16	7
Beard, medium center	18	7
Acton, long center	18	9
Martin, missed one free throw	--	--
Mudd, long side	20	9
Rhodes, one free throw	21	9
Rhodes, one-hand side	23	9
Acton, missed 2 free throws	--	--
Powell, one of 2 free throws	24	9
Hughes, missed free throw	--	--
Robinson, long center	26	9
Rhodes, missed free throw	--	--
THIRD PERIOD.		
Powell, free throw	27	9
Rhodes, long side	29	9
Acton, long side	29	11
Powell, tip in	31	11
Powell, free throw	32	11
Robinson, long	34	11
Mudd, one-hand side	36	11
Mudd, throw back	38	11
Hughes, one of 2 free throws	38	12
Beard, free throw	39	12
Robinson, free throw	40	12
Mudd, long side	42	12
Martin, one-hander front	44	12
FOURTH PERIOD.		
Hughes, crip	44	14
Hughes, free throw	44	15
Shannon, free throw	44	16
Robinson, free throw	45	16
Robinson, one-hander front	47	16
Hughes, free throw	47	17
Brummett, free throw	47	18
Cain, under basket	49	18
Gibson, missed free throw	--	--
Brummett, short	49	20
Robinson, missed free throw	--	--
Robinson, missed free throw	--	--
Farley, missed free throw	--	--
Shannon, missed free throw	--	--
Robinson, free throw	50	20

Male (50)	Pos.	(20) Danville
Mudd (12)	F	(6) Brummett
Rhodes (11)	F	(4) Acton
Powell (7)	C	(9) Hughes
Beard (3)	G	Massey
Martin (6)	G	Daugherty

Substitutes: Male—Robinson 9, Cain 2, Kinniard, Phelps, Gibson. Danville—Volmer, Shannon 1, Anderson, Farley.

Centr…
Harla…

A yo… so well… turned… tral Ci… Harlan… game.

With… the Go… had the… free th… City w… Again… was th… Kentuc…

The… tuted f… Friday… quite… sank th… score a…

TH…

That… end fo…

For… Hicks,… game… the sen… droppe… the sid… it 31-2…

Clar…

Conti…

Central City Tips Harlan By 34-30

Continued from First Page

For m… of the third period, it looked as though Harlan would be the winner, for the Green Dragons pulled into a four point lead at 25-21 and held it to the end of the period at 27-23.

Five minutes before the end of the game, Jones made a free throw and boosted the score to 29-24. Then Central City began the surge that put the Tide over. Hicks made a free throw and Smith added another to bring the score to 26-29, Central City trailing.

That is when Mohon took over to tie the score and set the stage for Hicks and Henry to put on the clincher.

In the full game, Central City made 10 field goals and 14 of 20 free throws. Harlan scored seven field goals and 16 of 23 free throws.

Reading about all those free throws one might judge that the game was rought. It wasn't. It was the best defensive game of the tournament and fouls naturally followed the tight defense.

free throws, but Central City still was ahead by a point with 2 minutes and eight seconds to go. Kent Henry slipped in for a crip shot and a few seconds later made one of two free throws. That made the score 34-30 and Central City took the ball outside rather than to risk immediate loss of possession of the ball.

Twice more i nthe last minute, Central City took the ball outside on fouls and played only to protect that four-point lead.

The battle was point-for-point from start to finish. Central City got a 6-1 lead in the first five minutes, but twice Harlan tied the score and Central City was ahead by only 11-10 at the quarter.

TIED 19-19.

Harlan made up that point in the second period, and the score was tied at 19-19 at the half. During the first two periods, Harlan made nine of nine free throws and only five field goals. Central City, on the other hand, made only three of five free throws and eight from the field.

The game was a battle between Wallace Jones, all-state center of last year and of 1942, and Billy Watkins, the guiding light of the team on the floor. In the first half, Watkins made five field goals and two of two free throws. Jones made one field goal and six of six free throws.

Jones, however, came out in the final count ahead, making 17 points on three field baskets and 11 of 13 free throws. Watkins did not score in the second half.

HARLAN LEADS

Hicks, long side	31	29
Bailey, one of two free throws	31	30
Rice, fouled out	--	--
Coldiron for Rice	--	--
Smith missed free throw		
Henry, crip and one free	34	30
Thompson, fouled out	--	--
Jemley for Thompson	--	--
Central City took ball out on foul	--	--
Central City took ball out on foul	--	--
Jemley missed free throw		
Final	34	30

Harlan (30)	Pos.	(34) Cen. City.
Rice (2)	F	(8) Hicks
Thompson (4)	F	(4) Teague
Jones (17)	C	(3) Mobberly
Yessin (4)	G	(1) Smith
Bailey (3)	G	(12) Watkins

Substitutes—Harlan: Coldiron, Jemley. Central City: Mohon (3), Henry (3).

* * *

Friday Night Games.

Danville 40
Providence 38

Danville's 40-38 victory over Providence was almost a matter of swap-point-for-point and the crowd was on edge from the start.

Providence scored first on a crip shot by T. C. Stone and when Willis Simpson sank an extra long shot there might have been those who believed the Admirals were sunk, too. But they reckoned not on the aggressiveness of the Admirals.

Milton Massey put Danville in the lead 7-6 a minute before the end of the first period and from then on it was hammer-and-tongs between two big teams that could play hard and fast basketball. Wayne L. Brown tied the score at 7, but John Acton made a free throw just as the period ended with Danville ahead 8-7.

Providence regained the lead on Brown's slap back and ran the score to 13-8 on Stone's one-hander and Brown's one-hand push-up. And the Bulldogs kept the lead until the half, which ended at 25-23.

Danville gained the lead on three free throws, one by Massey and two by Jim Hughes and that might have been the deciding of the issue. Just before the third period ended, Simpson's long one from the front put Providence ahead 31-30.

Joe Brummett tied it on a free throw and Daugherty and Simpson squared off free throws. Hughes scored on a spinner to make the count 34-32 and Danville had the lead for keeps.

With a minute to go, Danville led 38-36. Twice Danville took the ball outside on fouls, but just before the end Massey got clear for a crip shot to make it 40-36. Brown dropped in a short one just a second before the end.

* * *

Louisville Male 31
Bowling Green 23

After Ralph Beard and Ed Mudd got to clicking in the second period there was little doubt about the outcome of Male's 31-23 victory over Bowling Green.

Bowling Green led right up to the final seconds of the first period, but Beard and Mudd soon put a quietus on Bowling Green's hopes.

For three minutes of the second period, the teams sort of sparred for an opening. Then Beard slipped through for a crip shot and in less than a minute he hit a one-hander to put Male in front 13-9.

Three minutes before the end of the half, Beard made a free throw and then Mudd took over. With a minute more before intermission, Mudd scored from the baseline and in just a moment or two more he hit a long side shot to double the score at 18-9 as the half ended.

Male kept the score doubled at 22-11, 26-13 and 28-14 during the third period, but allowed Bowling Green to close some of the gap in the fourth quarter.

The 1945-46 team, front row (l-r): Jackie Sparks, Jimmy Mohon, Kent Henry, W.C. Mobberly , Richard Morris. Back row (l-r): K.T. Downs (manager), Royce McDowell, Gene McDonald, Sonny Son, Billy Dukes, Ronnie Milam, Harold Tudor, Delmas Gish.

W.C. Mobberly

The 1946-47 team, front row (l-r): Tunney Jones, Gilbert Teague, Kent Henry, W.C. Mobberly, Jackie Day. Back row (l-r): K.T. Downs (manager), Royce McDowell, Sonny Son, Doug Edwards, Marvin Dossett, Tommy Gray, Wallace Noffsinger, Gene McDonald, Delmas Gish.

The 1947-48 team, front row (l-r): Marion Tinsley, Tommy Gray, Roy Atherton, Jackie Day, Doug Edwards. Back row (l-r): Delmas Gish, Gene Mercer, John Bastin, Bobby Nofsinger, Joe Mac Howard, Ray Watkins, Hubert Francis, James Givens (manager).

The 1947-48 club enjoyed a steak dinner prior to participating in tournament action. From the left, Doug Edwards, Jackie Day, Eddie B. Moore, Bobby Nofsinger, James Givens, manager, Hubert Francis, Joe Mac Howard, Ray Watkins, John Bastin, Roy Atherton, Marion Tinsley, Tommy Gray, Delmas Gish.

Tommy Gray (center, back row), was only a teenager when he played for the Central City Reds in 1948. Gray, who played professionally for two years in the Detroit Tigers organization before an accident ended his career, is regarded as the finest baseball player in Central City history. To Gray's right is ex-Golden Tide standout H.G. Watkins. Other former Tide players are Marvin Dossett (first player on the bottom row) and John Withrow (middle of bottom row).

The 1948-49 team, front row (l-r): Roy Atherton, Jackie Day, Marion Tinsley, Gene Mercer. Middle row (l-r): Delmas Gish, Eddie B. Moore, Bobby Nofsinger, James Givens (manager). Back row (l-r): Joe Mac Howard, John Bastin, Hubert Francis, Charlie Day.

The 1949-50 team, front row (l-r), Roy Atherton, Gene Mercer, Marion Tinsley, Eddie B. Moore, Bobby Nofsinger, Joe Mac Howard. Back row (l-r), Delmas Gish, Bobby Calvert, Charlie Day, Charles Stewart, G.W. Anderson, John Gray, Carlos Vincent (manager).

The 1952-53 team, kneeling (l-r), Billy Lee Robinson, Larry Ray, Eddie Houston, Roy "D.D." Withrow, Junior Howerton. Standing (l-r), E.P. Doom (manager), Bobby Mercer, Bobby Don Millard, Stanley Ruby, Dick Wolfe, Corky Withrow, Charles Owen Gray, Delmas Gish.

The 1953-54 team, front row (l-r), Freddie O'Donohoe (manager), Bobby Don Millard, H.L. Hope, Corky Withrow, Larry Ray, Roy "D.D." Withrow, Delmas Gish. Back row (l-r), Eddie Houston, John Swann, Jerry Calvert, Buddy Lear, Stanley Ruby, Billy Lee Robinson, Buddy Fuller.

The 1955-56 team, front row (l-r), Carl Ray Jamison, Billy Duvall, Corky Withrow, Winfred Thompson, Billy Mason. Back row (l-r), Delmas Gish, Eddie Brand, Donnie Moore, Jimmy Swann, Earl Goode, Johnny Lile, Bob White (manager).

1955

ALL-TOURNAMENT TEAM—These 10 players were selected by sports writers, sportscasters and officials as the All-Tournament team for the 38th annual State meet which ended last night after a four-day grind at Memorial Coliseum. Front row (left to right) Terry Randall, Adair County; Ed Huffman, Newport Public; Byron Pinson, Henderson Barret; Arnold Feltner, Hazard. Back row, Don Mills, Berea; Ralph Shearer, Adair County; Corky Withrow, Central City; Joe Viviano, St. Xavier; Johnny Cox, Hazard, and Ralph Gilliam, Pikeville. (Herald-Leader Photo).

Record-Smashing Johnny Cox Leads Balloting For All-Tournament Team

By Jerry Finch

Unstoppable Johnny Cox, holder of a new state basketball tournament scoring record that's likely to stand for many years, is the No. 1 member of the All-State Tournament team.

The Bulldogs' bulldozer led the balloting by the 16 participating coaches, tournament officials and members of press and radio which selected the 10 boys for the honor squad at the conclusion of the 38th annual tournament last night.

Six seniors, three juniors and a sophomore made up the All-State list, which included two repeaters from last year in Ed Huffman of Newport and Ralph Shearer of Adair County.

The roll of All-State stars in order of selection, with heights in parentheses:

Johnny Cox (6-4) of Hazard.

Joe Viviano (6-2) of St. Xavier.

Corky Withrow (6-4) of Central City.

Ralph Shearer (6-3) of Adair County.

Byron Pinson (6-2) of Henderson.

Don Mills (5-7) of Berea.

Terry Randall (5-10) of Adair County.

Ed Huffman (6-4) of Newport.

Ralph Gilliam (5-11) of Pikeville.

Arnold Feltner (6-0) of Hazard.

Cox, Viviano, Randall, Huffman, Gilliam and Feltner are seniors. Withrow, Shearer and Mills are juniors and Pinson is a sophomore.

Thus the finalists, champion Hazard and runner-up Adair County, were the only teams to place two players on the All-Tournament squad. Two of the

Where They're From

Although Adair County was making its second successive appearance in the State Tournament and Hazard had been here 15 times before winning the crown in 1932, many telephone calls were received by The Herald-Leader last night from persons asking the location of the two schools—particularly Adair County.

Adair County, whose largest town is Columbia, population 2,167, is located just below the mid-section of the state in the southernmost tip of Region 6. Columbia, the county seat, is about 40 miles south of Springfield and about 70 miles east of Bowling Green.

Hazard, population 6,985, is in Perry County near the state's mountainous southeastern border, in Region 14.

record on game totals of 25, 33, 37 and 32 points, and put together 42 fielders and 94 free throws for the sum.

Puckett in playing with the Clark County team which took third place in 1952, had games of 47, 26, 23 and 6 points, the last figure registered in the consolation when he saw action for only 16 minutes.

For the tournament, Cox tried 94 shots from the field and hit on 44.6 per cent. He made 43 of 61 free throws for a blazing percentage of 70.4. Too, he committed but 10 fouls in the tourney and never more than three a game.

After all of the awards had

cheerleading crew for the best performance and crowd-control of the tourney.

Runner-up was the Henderson Barret group and third was Mayfield's team.

The Berea cheerleader champs are Frances Andrews, Pat Porter, Patsy Marcum, Jean Wilson and Imogene Combs.

Six of the 16 groups were disqualified, said Mrs. Elmer Gilb, who headed the presentation committee, because school principals failed to reply by letter with confirmation that their cheerleaders would be chaperoned throughout the tourney.

Infirmary report—All cagers injured or ailing during the tourney are now doing very well, thank you, say the coaches.

Among the battered were St. Xavier's Joe Shaw, who received a head gash that required two stitches when he met an elbow in a quarter-final with Newport; Hazard's Davis Copeland, who lost two teeth in a first-round clash with Glasgow; Berea's Francis Boggs, who suffered a shoulder dislocation in the first round against Mayfield and Mayfield's Orby Arnold, who had the misfortune to suffer a sinus attack that bothered his breathing at just the wrong time.

Arnzen ailing, too—Not feeling well at all is Newport's Coach Stan Arnzen, but his difficulty doesn't derive from any germ or crash. He couldn't understand how his two tall aces, 6-4 Huffman and 6-3 Paul Bergman, could foul out in two straight tourney games.

Newport lost both boys in a quarter-final against St. X, but had enough lead to hold on. But when

Sharpshooting Joh[illegible] To Pace Goebel R[illegible] Henderson Trims [illegible]

By [illegible]

"Yo' all come, but not [illegible]

That was Hazard's dep[illegible] night as the Bulldogs from [illegible] of Kentucky put the bite [illegible] the championship game of [illegible] Basketball Tournament.

With a howling overflow [illegible] Ritter's sharp-toothed Bulldogs [illegible] quarter and picked up an insu[illegible] best Indian effort after that w[illegible] points on two occasions at the [illegible]

Paced by Johnny (The Spr[illegible]) Cox, whose 32 points in the [illegible] game gave him a new individ[illegible] record for four tourney appe[illegible]ances, Hazard thus captured [illegible] coveted crown for the sec[illegible] time. The Bulldogs first won [illegible] title in 1932 with Pat Payne [illegible] the helm, defeating Louisv[illegible] Male, 15-13, in the final gam[illegible]

By the way of contrast, Ha[illegible] and Adair County [illegible] points, shading by three the [illegible]vious record for both teams [illegible] the championship game. The [illegible] mark was set when Lafay[illegible] bested Paducah Tilghman, 8[illegible] in 1953.

Adair County, the canny [illegible]gion 6 champ tutored by J[illegible] Burr, cracked the record for [illegible] points by a losing finalist w[illegible] Newport Public held after lo[illegible] to Inez, 63-55, last year.

Almost overshadowed by [illegible] Hazard victory and the var[illegible] records was the fact that R[illegible] Shearer, talented Adair Co[illegible] forward, flipped through 29 po[illegible] before going to the bench [illegible] fouls near the close of the g[illegible] Hitting 15 of 18 throws at [illegible] charity line—12 of them wit[illegible] a miss—Shearer fouled out [illegible] time when Cox had lobbed [illegible] 28 of his total points.

The Indians cashed 30 ou[illegible] 35 gratis throws in all to st[illegible] the battle while the Bulldogs [illegible] outhitting them by a margi[illegible] 26-18 from the field. In the [illegible] half, when Hazard emerged [illegible] a 38-32 bulge, the Tribe h[illegible] perfect mark with 10 free th[illegible] in the same number of tries.

Hazard gained the finals [illegible] a 72-62 verdict over highly [illegible]garded Newport while [illegible] County earned its berth in [illegible] title tilt by whipping Hend[illegible] Barret 66-54, in games yeste[illegible] afternoon.

The Henderson team [illegible] to oust Newport, 68-62, for [illegible] place in a preliminary to [illegible] championship game.

Sharing the glory with [illegible] were a host of other Bull[illegible] foremost of whom was [illegible] Ward. He ripped the [illegible] which Cox lashed out from [illegible] north goal for 14 points. [illegible] Gary Gabbard contributed 1[illegible] Stidham nine, Arnold Feltne[illegible] and Sammy Burlow two. The [illegible] other Hazard player to see [illegible] was David Copeland, who g[illegible] good account of himself d[illegible] the fact that he failed to sc[illegible]

Ritter also brought Haza[illegible] the big Dribble Derby in [illegible] after completing his own [illegible] as an Eastern Kentucky Stat[illegible]lege and professional New[illegible] player. The present quinte[illegible] the 16th to represent Haza[illegible] the meet.

Adair County, which [illegible] fourth place in its initial ap[illegible]ance a year ago, came throu[illegible] a district runner-up and ca[illegible] the fancy of the fans w[illegible] heady play.

In addition to Shearer, t[illegible]dians displayed chubby [illegible] Randall with 18 timely [illegible] and his efforts almost suc[illegible] in bringing the Tribe back

Pinson, Shepherd Head Herald's All-Sta

By Billy Surface
Herald Sports Writer

The little man is rapidly being shoved out of the basketball picture—or at least that's what the results of The Herald's first annual All-State selections reveal.

Every member of the honor squad stands above the six-foot mark and the shortest cager picked on the first team is Flaget's Mickey Kelly, a 6-1 guard.

In fact, the 10-man team, which includes eight seniors, averages nearly 6-4, a pretty lofty bunch.

The Herald, in naming its first All-State selections, did away with the usual popularity system in which every coach in the state was entitled to vote, but instead compiled the choices of 32 veteran coaches and officials—two from each region. Thus the committee members, who voted only for the boys they'd seen in action, were in a position to compare the top athletes and make an unbiased decision.

Wayland's Kelly Coleman and Central City's Corky Withrow left little doubt as to their ability by being named on every ballot.

Coleman, whose fantastic scoring feats are somewhat legendary, and Withrow, good enough to merit the University of Kentucky's first cage scholarship this winter, also were named to the All-State Tournament team recently.

Third choice was Berea's ace pivotman, Don Mills, who was named on 30 of the 32 ballots. Touted by many as the best big man in the Commonwealth, the 6-7 flagpole led his team to the No. 1 ranking in the final regular-season poll.

Byron Pinson, classy Henderson performer, was the pick of 26 voters and his recent State tourney play verified his right to be accorded the high position, just ahead of Carr Creek's Bobby Shepherd, who finished fifth with 24 votes.

Sixth position went to Richard Newman of Greenville, a Fourth Region quintet. The Fourth incidently, was the only region to land two players on the first team.

Charlie Osborne, 6-5 junior from Flat Gap was the choice of 19 voters, while Kelly was eighth and College High's David Denton, ninth. Tenth place went to Earlington's Harry Todd, the only sophomore selected.

Carr Creek's affable pilot, Morton Combs, is the recipient of the "Coach of The Year" accolade, although his selection wasn't a runaway by any means. Combs received backing from nine of the 31 voters, while the runner-up spot ended up in a tie between Heath's Bill Carter and Cooper John Campbell of Wayland. Carter piloted his team to 30 straight victories, while Campbell's team finished third in the State tourney.

T. L. Plain of Henderson and Elmer (Baldy) Gilb of Henry Clay each received two votes, while the following had one backer each: Jim Riffey, Manual; Henderson Wilson, Sonora; Charles Finnell, Nicholas County, and Jim Connor, Newport Catholic.

Montgomery County's Kenny Meyer was the top second-team choice, winning in a narrow race over Lafayette's Billy Lickert, Ken Cornelius of Mount Vernon and Martin Holland of Heath.

Here are thumbnail descriptions of the "Top Ten":

Coleman: Shattered virtually every scoring record in posting the highest average ever compiled in Kentucky prep circles. The Wayland wonder had a four-year average of 33 points a game and a 48-point average for his senior season. Broke State tourney four-game total with 185, and made 68 in third-place game. A fine rebounder for his size (6-2) Coleman can practically name his college, although his coach says he's narrowed his choice to Kentucky and West Virginia.

Withrow: Led his team to State tourney berths for three straight years and in so doing, achieved all-tourney honors each time. Broke the 1,000-point barrier two straight seasons and accumulated 3,036 points during his four-year career. Season high was 53 points recorded against Bremen. Already accepted a grant-in-aid at UK.

Mills: Posted a 24-point average this season with Berea and his rebounding and defense was equally brilliant. Tied the Louisville Invitational Tournament scoring mark with 38 points while leading his team to the title. His steady improvement each season is a point that has impressed college coaches. Like Coleman, he can almost name his own meal ticket.

Pinson: Probably the most evasive center in the State for his 6-2 frame, a factor that has lured college scouts to Henderson like a magnet. An All-State Tournament choice two straight years, Pinson has received scholarship offers from Kentucky, Vanderbilt, Illinois, Murray and Western, according to his coach.

Shepherd: A husky mountain lad whose rebounding is his most valuable asset, Shepherd virtually swept the boards clean in pacing Carr Creek to the State title. Owns a 24-point average and has Dayton, Furman, Morehead, and West Virginia bidding for his services but will probably attend Kentucky.

Newman: Any time a boy receives a scholarship from Adolph Rupp as early as Newman did, he's bound to be outstanding. Touted by many as even a better cager than Withrow and outscored him during the last two meetings, despite having been sidelined with a chipped ankle bone.

Osborne: Only a junior but he rivalled Coleman for the mountain scoring mark by posting a 35-point average and swished in 64 in a regional skirmish. His coach, Francis Stapleton, claims that Morehead, Furman, West Virginia, South Carolina and several other colleges are already after him.

Kelly: Shortest member of the honor squad at 6-1, but nevertheless is rated as a fine guard. Led all Louisville prepsters with a 22-point average. Will attend either Louisville or Xavier.

Denton: Even though he played on the Western campus (College High) this 6-2 sharpshooter is expected to follow his high school coach, Ed Diddle Jr., to Middle Tennessee. Relies on a one-hand shot as his most valuable weapon.

Todd: This 6-7 pivotman should undoubtedly develop into one of Kentucky's finest centers. Is only a sophomore now but already has college coaches drooling for his services. Has an effective hook shot and is equally dangerous with his jump shot.

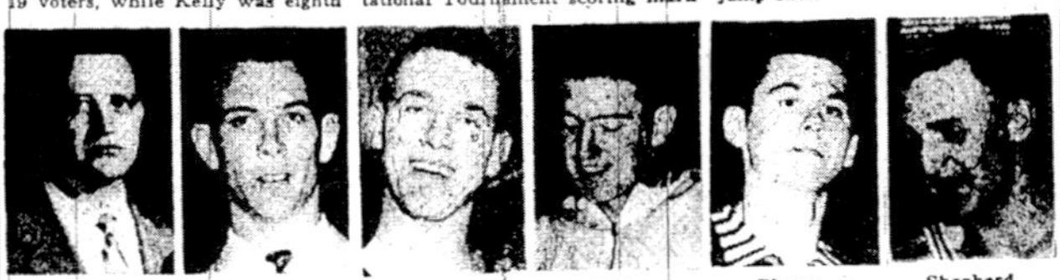

Combs — Withrow — Coleman — Mills — Pinson — Shepherd

Herald's All-S

FIRST TEA

Player	Pos.	Class
Corky Withrow	G	Sr.
Kelly Coleman	G	Sr.
Don Mills	C	Sr.
Byron Pinson	C-F	Sr.
Bob Shepherd	C	Sr.
Richard Newman	C	Sr.
Charles Osborne	C	Jr.
Mickey Kelly	G	Sr.
David Denton	G	Sr.
Harry Todd	C	Soph.

SECOND TEA

Player	Pos.	Class
Kenny Meyer	G	Sr.
Billy Lickert	C	Jr.
Ken Cornelius	G	Sr.
Martin Holland	C	Sr.
F. A. Couch	G	Sr.
Fred Hynson	C	Sr.
John Turner	C	Sr.
Calvin Bird	F	Jr.
Ned Jennings	C	Jr.
Lowell Hughes	F	Sr.

THIRD TEAM

Dave Eakins (Henderson)
Jim Mitchell (Valley)
Billy Gilley (Carlisle)
Gene Herndow (Almo)
Darrell Bicknell (Berea)
George Carroll (Ashland)
Herbie Kays (Shelbyville)
Ralph Davis (Vanceburg)
Louis Crigler (Boone County)
Rex Story (Mayfield)

PRESSB

By BILL

Morton Combs Was Named Even Though One of His Fa

It was surprising that "politi ballots were received for The State high school team.

One of the ballot sender-inn Year" space blank.

Instead of inserting a coach's na footnote, which read

"I'd like to vote for Combs, but

But both Combs and Chandler sailles was elected governor of Kentuc of State champion Carr Creek India "Coach of the Year."

As Billy Surface relates in the le it was a close race — of which Co customed during the State Tourname

For quite some time The Herald All-State team and members of the s venture into the field is a successful

West All-Stars Nudge East

Shively To Speak At Waylan

MAN, THAT'S SHOOTING — Hal Lear, Temple guard, scored 48 points Friday night as the Philadelphia club whipped Southern Methodist, 90-81 — setting a new NCAA Tournament record, and also an individual high scoring single game mark. Here he holds Temple's third-place cup and a plaque. (AP Wirephoto)

Lear, Russell Now Pc

By Jerry Liska

EVANSTON, Ill., March 24 (AP)—The San Francisco Dons, enjoying the glory of spearing their second straight NCAA cage crown, had only one wish left today — that their brilliant Bill Russell does as well for the United States in the Olympics.

That of course, also goes for stellar K. C. Jones, who had to watch from the sidelines as his Dons teammates capped their NCAA championship surge with Friday night's 83-71 title conquest of Iowa.

Jones missed San Francisco's tourney triumphs over UCLA, Utah and Iowa because he was ineligible under NCAA rules.

But Russell is the man who appears the best collegiate bet to make the Olympic squad in the college-military-AAU "shakedown" tourney at Kansas City, April 2-3-4.

The 6-10 Russell, who roamed the press box of McGaw Memorial Hall with coach Phil Woolpert and other Dons after their championship triumph Friday night, took a pretty sage view of the Olympic Games at Melbourne late this year.

"Too much has been said about the rivalry between the United States and Russia," commented the Dons' big defensive "umbrella" man.

"That isn't the idea of the Olympic Games. Competition for competition's sake is the important thing.

"I want to compete for America in the Olympics. That's what I'm pointing for now."

Russell is a 6-7 high jumper and hopes he can also make the U. S. Olympic track squad.

Bucky O'Connor of Iowa's very fine runners-up will substitute for Woolpert as coach of the 14-man collegiate squad in the Kansas City Olympic Trials.

Bucky should ... Russell, who ... against Iowa ... anguish by his ... ing and batting ... Hawkeye shots.

Woolpert elect... Kansas City coa... cause, if the coll... the Trial tourne... unable to get ... handle the coach... Melbourne.

The eventual 1... will be composed ... and seven membe... ning team at K...

Withrow, Mills, Coleman Top All-State Team Named By Paducah Sun-Democrat

PADUCAH, Ky., March 24 (AP)—Two repeaters and Kentucky's all-time scoring champion dominated the Paducah Sun-Democrat's 1956 all-state high school basketball team announced today.

Corky Withrow of Central City won the Player-of-the-Year award for polling a record 301 votes of a possible 378. Close behind were Don Mills of Berea with 294 and Kelly Coleman of Wayland with 292.

Withrow and Mills are the only repeaters from the 1955 squad.

The fabulous Coleman, who wound up his high school career this year, shattered practically every Kentucky scoring record, both in season play and in the state tournament.

Also on the first 10 and their votes were Martin Holland of Heath (147), Roger Newman of Greenville (141), John Turner of Newport Public (132), Byron Pinson of Henderson (108), Mickey Kelly of Louisville Flaget (106), E. A. Couch of state champion Carr Creek (97) and David Denton of College High, Bowling Green (96).

All members of the team are seniors.

"Coach-of-the-Year" honors went to Bill Carter of Heath, whose team won 30 consecutive games before being upset in the semi-finals of the First Region tournament. Last year, with the same club, Heath had a 13-13 record.

Carter was a popular choice, receiving 110 votes. T. L. Plain of Henderson was second with 51 and John Campbell of Wayland third with 32.

Only coaches were eligible to vote on players nominated by the newspaper's all-state board. The team was based on regular season play and ballots were cast before the tournaments got under way.

The second team.

Billy Lickert, Lexington Lafayette; Calvin Bird, Corbin; Harry Todd, Earlington; **Ken Cornelius, Mt. Vernon; Lowell Hughes, Prestonburg; Ken Meyer, Montgomery County;** Dave Eakins, Henderson; **Herby Kays, Shelbyville;** Freddie Luigs, Paducah Tilghman, and **Darrell Bicknell, Berea.**

The third team:

Rex Story, Mayfield; Ronnie Bridewell, Newport Public; **Dickie Baugh, Somerset; Bobby Shepherd, Carr Creek;** Wally Johnson, Butler County; **Fred Hynson, Lexington Henry Clay;** Jerry Vest, Sedalia; **Charles Osborne, Flat Gap,** and **Ned Jennings, Nicholas County.**

State Weight-Lifting Meet Set Here Today

The Kentucky State AAU Weight-Lifting meet will be held at 2:30 o'clock this afternoon at the University of Kentucky Euclid Avenue classroom, across from Alumni Gymnasium.

Malicks Gym of Louisville is the defending team champion. The host UK team is favored to dethrone the champs.

Two Lexington boys, representing UK, are expected to break the state records in their classes. They are Ronald Lacy, in the 198-pound class, and Allen Nickell in the 181-pound class.

Nineteen entries will compete in the seven classes.

Seixas, Flam Advance

MIAMI, Fla., March 24 (AP) — First-ranked Vic Seixas of Philadelphia and Herb Flam of Berkeley, Calif., No. 6, emerged today as finalists in the Good Neighbor Tennis tournament.

MYSTERY: GUES... pictures. At the le... Al Glaza (16) and ... as the Flyers lose...

DELL MAGAZINE

All-Americans: 500 top high

NOMINATED BY COACHES AND SPORTS EDITORS . . . . players in bold type are preseason choices as

Dave Denton (College of Bowling Green) 6-2; Roger Newman (Greenville) 6-2.

LOUISIANA

Jack Moreland (Minden) 6-7; Harriman Morgan (New Orleans De La Salle) 6-4; Jon Peebles (New Orleans Fortier) 6-4; Dave Corson (Fortier) 6-5; Billy Castilaw (Baton Rouge Istrouma) 6-5; Bobby James (Ruston) 6-5; Eddie Burt (Shreveport Byrd) 6-1; Fred Holt (Jena) 6-9; Carey Guglielmo (Baton Rouge Catholic) 6-1; Joe Scaffi (New Orleans) 6-0; George Kelt (New Orleans Holy Cross) 6-2.

MAINE

Danny Drinon (Bangor) 6-0; Carl Daigle (Bangor) 6-3; Ricgard Bishop (Morse of Bath) 6-1; Paul Davenport (Houlton) 6-2; Ed Marchetti (Morse) 6-1; Roland Gagne (Lewiston) 6-1; Don Sturgeon (Old Town) 6-0; Brian Murray (Bangor John Bapst) 5-11; Wayne Rogers (Ellsworth) 5-10; Carlo Cimino (Portland Cheverus) 6-1; Bob Fallon

MICHIGAN

Herb Wood (River Rouge) 5-8; Dan Potter (Hazel Park) 6-4; Bob Skrzycki (Detroit Catholic) 6-4; Chester Hicks (Inkster) 5-8; Bob Zimmerman (Jackson) 5-10; Ed Burton (Muskegon Heights) 6-4; Ed Reynolds (Benton Harbor) 6-1.

MINNESOTA

Ron Johnson (New Prague) 6-7; Tom Idstrom (Fairmont) 5-9; Ken Excel (Minneapolis Roosevelt) 5-11; Roger Plantikon (St. Louis Park) 6-2; Skip Fointaine (Proctor) 6-0; Paul Mortella (Hibbing) 6-3; Tom Moe (Edina) 6-2; John Wage (Aurora) 6-1; Dave Dragotis (Hopkins) 6-1.

MISSISSIPPI

Bobby Kitchens (Natchez) 5-10; Denton Ducker (Roxie) 6-1; Shelby Watts (Brookhaven) 5-9; Bobby Avant (Greenwood) 6-2; Jack Mitchell (Corinth) 5-10; Tommy Alexander (Laurel) 5-10; Charles Parson (West Lincoln) Jimmy

Smith (Omaha Tech) 5-7; Lynn Nelson (Ord) 6-4; Dan Arnold (Minden) 5-11; Bob Moore (Clarkson) 6-3; Dennis Mullins (Omaha Central) 6-3; Larry Feaster (Grand Island) 6-3; Dick Haggerty (Omaha Holy Name) 6-3.

NEW HAMPSHIRE

Bob Dickson (Manchester Central) 5-8; Dick Loiselle (Manchester Bradley) 6-0; Bill Smith (Berlin) 6-6; Bob Maloney (Dover) 6-0; Mike Pendergast (Portsmouth) 6-0; R. Hanson (Concord) 6-2; R. Breen (Nashua) 5-11; L. Harper (Laconia) 5-10.

NEW JERSEY

George Ramming (Union Hill) 6-5; Art Matson (North Arlington) 6-4; John Crotty (Jersey City St. Peter's) 6-0; Myron Magarro (Lodi) 6-4; Harp Junta (Pompton Lakes) 6-7; John Purcell (Bayonne) 6-2; Cliff Ehrlich (Teaneck) 6-4; Joe Russo (Paterson Bosco) 5-7; John Saxenmeyer (Belmar St. Rose) 6-4; Frank Michener (Passaic Valley) 6-0; Bill Collier (Newark West Side) 5-10.

NEVADA

Chub Quilici (Smith Valley) 5-8; Jin Rice (Panaca Lincoln County) 5-8; Do Ashworth (Las Vegas) 6-2; Georg Allison (Carson City) 6-1; Bob Brad (Panaca Fernley) 6-1; Don Helm (La Vegas) 6-4.

NORTH CAROLINA

Grey Poole (Raleigh) 6-5; Dann Casteen (Wilmington New Hanover 6-0; Charles Wilson (Asheville Le Edwards) 5-10; Poe Rochelle (Kingsto Grainger) 6-0; Hal Edwards (Greenville 6-3; Hal Gilbert (Rocky Mountain) 5-6 Ray Bender (Burlington Williams) 6-1 Rick McDonough (Charlotte Central 6-4; Carroll Younkin (North Davidson 6-5; Bradley Anderson (Greensbor Senior) 6-0; Reggie Heavener (Gas tonia) 6-1; Winston Wiggins (Youngs ville) 6-5.

NORTH DAKOTA

Ronald Schiff (Sherwood) 6-1; Maurice Railing (Lansford) 5-10; Otto Riel

THE HIGH SCHOOL ALL-AMERICA SQUAD

1955-56 FIRST TEAM:

A. C. Black (Crozier Tech of Dallas, Tex.) 6-9; Corky Withrow (Central City, Ky.) 6-4; Horace Walker (Chester, Pa.) 6-3; Oscar Robertson (Crispus Attucks of Indianapolis, Ind.) 6-5; George Ramming (Union Hill of Union City, N. J.) 6-5.

1955-56 SECOND TEAM:

Jack Moreland (Minden, La.) 6-7; Albert Ellison (Linden, Tenn.) 6-4; Dennis Price (Norman, Okla.) 6-1; Fred LaCour (St. Ignatius of San Francisco, Cal.) 6-4; Earl Nau (Mt. Pleasant, Iowa) 6-2.

(Rumford Stephens) 6-1; Bill Bragdon (Westbrook) 6-0.

MARYLAND

Barry Shetrone (Baltimore Southern) 6-1; Dick Brown (Silver Spring Montgomery-Blair) 6-2; Carl Pakulski (Baltimore Patterson) 6-1; Charles Keller (Frederick) 6-2; Howard Beeman (Frostburg Beall) 6-6; George Miller (Baltimore Calvert) 5-10; Al Budnichuck (Towson Catholic) 6-1; Phil Kulinski (Baltimore Poly) 6-2; Dick Marshall (Easton) 6-3; Barrie Lindenbaum (Franklin) 6-2; Johnny Hoerr (Kenwood) 5-11.

MASSACHUSETTS

Charles Chevalier (Charlestown) 5-10; Al Attar (Fall River Durfee) 6-1; Don McGillicudy (Reading) 6-0; Joe Bellino (Winchester) 5-8; Peter Clarey (Malden) 6-1; Joe Lane (Worcester St. John's) 6-2; Rudy Williams (Cambridge Rindge Tech) 6-3; Dick Whalen (Somerville St. Clement's) 6-2; Jack Tierney (Cambridge Latin) 6-2; Bernie Sidman (Lynn Classical) 6-5.

Whetstone (Natchez) 6-3; Paul Jones (Goodman) 6-4; Louis Griffin (Meridian) 6-6.

MISSOURI

Jim Hoffman (Kansas City Northeast) 6-4; Jack Pirrie (Maplewood) 6-5; Geore Burkel (St. Louis Cleveland) 6-7; Jim Daily (Joplin) 5-10; Dick Chartrand (St. Louis U.H.S.) 6-0; Don Costello (St. Louis Beaumont) 6-4; Ivan Richmann (Fisk) 6-6; Gene Jordan (Malden) 6-3; Jack Wolff (Webster) 6-1.

MONTANA

Dennis Reber (Missoula) 6-3; Dan Balko (Great Falls) 5-9; Dan Burns (Missoula Loyola) 6-0; Bob Hurley (Anaconda Public) 6-3; Jack Watson (Helena Public) 6-1; Floyd Henderson (Bozeman) 6-0; Mike Freebourn (Butte) 6-1; Dave Johanson (Sidney) 5-8.

NEBRASKA

Dick Harvey (Omaha Creighton Prep) 6-6; Keith Ozanne (Cozad) 6-5; Jim

NEW MEXICO

Kim Nash (Hobbs) 6-1; Sulo Mattson (Carlsbad) 6-2; Barry Stone (Portales) 6-5; Dave Miller (Rosewell) 6-2; Doug Anderson (Los Alamos) 6-0; Ed Lopez (Santa Fe St. Michael's) 6-3; Billy Cates (Lovington) 6-5; Floyd Donham (Hobbs) 6-0; Clyde Chaney (Antesia) 6-6.

NEW YORK

STATE: **Hugh Gallagher** (Mineola) 5-10; Al Siegel (Long Beach) 6-0; George Bird (Freeport) 6-0; Bob Kerzner (Valley Stream) 6-1; Monty Stickles (Poughkeepsie) 6-4; Richard Kenney (Binghamton Central) 5-11; Pete Corbett (Syracuse CBA) 6-10; Ray Mossey (Schenectady Mott Terrace) 6-4; Al Handley (Syracuse Assumption) 5-10.

CITY: **Bernard Cabey** (De Witt Clinton) 6-4; Ira Sussman (Taft) 6-0; Alfred Paine (Commerce) 6-0; Tommy Smith (St. Francis) 6-2; Tommy McNamara (St. Agnes) 6-3; Dick Rodin (Jamaica) 6-3; Robert Jones (Lane) 6-4; Gerald Kaufman (New Utrecht) 5-11.

(Ashley) 6-3; Al Roisum (Grand Fork Central) 6-1; Ray Smith (Enderlin 6-4; Jack Bergene (Fargo Central) 6-0 Sy Vermillion (Ft. Yates) 6-1; Dale Leathers (Lansford) 6-3.

OHIO

Roland Bolds (Lockland Wayne) 6-0; Lee Patrone (Bellaire) 6-0; Ron Dykes (Middletown) 6-2; Gary Kessler (Wilshire) 6-9; Ray Apple (Cincinnati Hughes) 6-2; Earl Frederick (Lockland Wayne) 6-3; Spud Hornsby (Hamilton) 6-4; Bill Ralich (Steubenville) 6-7; Ron Godfrey (Martins Ferry) 6-5; Henry Josefczyk (Yorkville) 6-5; Joe Roberts (Columbus East) 6-6; Jim Parfitt (East Liverpool) 6-3; Mallie McCarthy (Milford) 6-3; Verlyn Witte (Reading) 6-6; Willie White (Springfield) 6-0; John Middendorf (Cincinnati McNicholas) 6-2.

OKLAHOMA

Dennis Price (Norman) 6-2; Bill Gary (Putnam City) 6-3; Dick Urban (Blackwell) 6-6; Dick Soergel (Oklahoma City Capitol Hill) 6-4; Floyd

National School Paper Names Corky On All-American Basketball Team

Corky Withrow of Central City and Kelly Coleman of Wayland have been named on Scholastic magazine's All-American High School Basketball Team. This is the third All-American team Withrow has been named on. Last year he was named on Dell's All-American team and previously this year he had been named on Newspaper Enterprise Association All-American team. Also he made the All-State tourney team, the Paducah Sun-Democrat, the Louisville Courier-Journal and the Lexington Herald all-state teams.

Scholastic is a national educational magazine.

The Windup of A Big Basketball Weeken

WHERE'S KELLY? . . . Here is the Kentucky State High School All-Tournament team. We almost, that is. Conspicuous by his absence (and by his attractive sister who subbed for him) is Wayland's Kel Coleman whose four-game total of 185 points shattered several tourney records. Linda Carol Coleman (circle explained that Kelly was "too shy" to face the crowd and receive his trophy. The team: (kneeling, left to righ Rex Story, Mayfield; Dave Eakins, Henderson; E. A. Couch and Bobby Shepherd, Carr Creek, and Pascal Benso Henderson. Standing (from left) are Harry Todd, Earlington; Byron Pinson, Henderson; Linda Carol Colema Wayland; Corky Withrow, Central City, and Billy Lickert, Lafayette.

This Freddie Maggard jumper gave Carr Creek a 70-68 OT win over the Tide in the 1956 state toumey.

The 1956-57 team, front row (l-r), Johnny Lile, Lance Gish, Frankie Mercer, Winfred Thompson, Jimmy Swann, Earl Goode, Lewis Chaney. Back row (l-r), Delmas Gish, Byron Bailey, Lewis Carr, Eddie Brand, Carroll Harrison, Tommy Barnett, Bob White (manager).

The 1957-58 team, front row (l-r): Tommy Barnett, Frankie Mercer, Lewis Chaney, Earl Goode, Lance Gish, Carroll Harrison. Back row (l-r): Delmas Gish, Byron Bailey, Lewis Carr, Terrill Mayes, Ben Mac Wolfe, Eddie Vincent, Jack Simpson, Wendell Decker (manager).

Ben Mac Wolfe blocks a shot as Jerry Mayes closes in.

Hitting the road, the Tide, behind 21 points from Corky, 17 from Millard and 16 from Ray, took care of Bowling Green 75-60. Returning home, the Tide blasted Owensboro 67-39, with Corky accounting for 22 points and Hope 20.

At this stage of the season, reasons for this club's success were becoming apparent. First, this was a tremendous defensive team. Second, it was a team with dead-eye marksmen. Third, Corky was becoming a genuine offensive force. He was not yet the scoring machine he would later become, but he was certainly giving a preview of what lay ahead.

In the Tide's next two wins, 81-58 over Hughes-Kirk and 90-58 over Daviess County, Corky racked up 43 points, giving him 86 in the past four games. He had 22 against the Tigers, 21 against Daviess County.

But he wasn't the only Tide player putting up big numbers. Hope had 16 points, D.D. 12 and Millard 10 in the win over Hughes-Kirk, while Millard and Ray each had 16 and D.D. added 13 as the Tide put away Daviess County.

Visiting Caverna, again led by all-state performer Kenny Sidwell, became the first team in more than a month to give the Tide a run for their money. The Tide led by only three at the half (36-33), upped their advantage to nine after three quarters (53-44), then held on down the stretch to get away with a 74-67 victory.

Tide forwards Millard and Hope did the most damage, combining for 42 points. Millard had 23 and Hope 19. Corky offered support with 15 points.

Sidwell finished with 20, 18 in the second half, but Caverna's Jim Godwin took game-best honors with 28.

Owensboro, a team the Tide easily defeated by 28 points in the Sportscenter, came to town and turned out to be a stubborn foe. The Tide won this outing 71-63 to improve their record to 21-0. Millard led the way with 21 points. Corky had 15 and Robinson 13 in yet another solid effort off the bench.

Heading west, the Tide began a two-game road trip by crushing Murray 98-64. Millard keyed the onslaught with 28 points, while Hope had 23 and Corky 19. Those 98 points turned out to be the most scored by the Tide this season.

With the exception of the first game against Greenville, the Tide's encounter with a deliberate Paducah Tilghman club came closest to ending any hopes for perfection. This game was a toss-up all the way, mainly because the Tornado played at a deliberate pace. Leading by a single point (48-47) going into the last quarter, the Tide, thanks to Corky and Hope, kept their perfect record intact with a 60-57 win. Corky and Hope accounted for all 12 fourth-quarter points for the Tide.

Corky ended the night with 19 points. Hope had 16 and Ray 12 in a surprisingly close call.

Four players hit double digits as the Tide once again flashed overwhelming force by smashing Madisonville 77-54 at home. Corky paced the Tide with 25 points, while others in double figures included Hope (16), D.D. (12) and Robinson (11).

That dominance continued in an 87-47 win at Bremen. This game, in which nine different players scored, was also Delmas Gish's 300th win as Golden Tide coach.

In the win over Bremen, Corky had 29 points, Millard and D.D. 10 each. Other Tide scoring included Swann with nine, Hope and Robinson eight each, Fuller six, Ray five and Calvert two.

Joe Robert Divine tied Corky for game-high honors with 29.

Those Blackhawks Again?

Round three against Greenville ended up being exactly what everyone expected—a down-to-the-wire thriller. Trailing late, the Tide parlayed four Hope free throws and two more from Corky inside the final 2:37 to come away with a 56-52 win. Hope was clutch, scoring nine of his 14 points in the fourth quarter, including going seven-for-seven at the charity stripe.

Ray paced the Tide with 17 points, Corky added 10.

T.R. Newman had 18 for the Blackhawks, with Sparks and Roger Newman scoring 13 and 10, respectively.

While the Tide was in Louisville preparing to take on St. Xavier, it was announced that Delmas Gish had been named Coach of the Year. This was just the first of many coaching honors that would come his way. A few days later, Gish was presented with a new automobile in recognition of his tremendous coaching job this season.

St. X was a solid team, but with Corky knocking in 28 points, Millard 16, Hope 11 and D.D. 10, the Tide won handily 76-60. A big key to this win was the Tide's defense, which held all-state candidate Joe Viviano to 11 points. Jack Ramsey led the Tigers with 26 points.

Only two opponents—Muhlenberg Central and Calhoun—stood between the Tide and a flawless regular-season campaign, and neither of those clubs came close to derailing the train. The Tide cruised past MC 90-46, then blasted Calhoun 85-57.

Corky had his best night of the season against MC, torching the Musketeers for 35 points. This marked the first 30-point performance of his career. It would not be his last.

Millard and D.D. each had 13 against MC.

In the season finale against Calhoun, Millard had 24 points, Corky 23, D.D. 11 and Robinson 10.

The Final Stretch

As fate would have it, Central City and Greenville drew each other in the district tournament's opening round. These two teams were so formidable that many observers were convinced that the winner of this game would go on to capture both the district and regional crowns. And they had every right to have that belief. After all, Central City was undefeated and Greenville had only five losses, three coming at the hands of the Tide.

But this game was far different than the first three. This one was for all the marbles. This was sudden death. Win and keep advancing, lose and pack away the uniforms until next season. This one had everything riding on it.

Greenville led 13-12 after the first quarter, then the Tide put together a solid second eight minutes to take a 32-29 lead into the dressing room at intermission. Thanks to eight third-quarter points from Millard, the Tide upped their lead to 53-47 heading into the home stretch.

The Tide extended their advantage to 56-47 at the six-minute mark and appeared to be on their way to a convincing win. But this Blackhawks team was simply too good to lie down and die without putting up a fight. They battled back, and with two minutes remaining, they had narrowed the difference to a single bucket—63-61.

Now the pressure was back on the Tide's shoulders, and on this night, Millard, who played the game of his life, was not going to let this win slip away. The always-steady and reliable Millard scored a game-high 23 points, five coming in the final quarter, to help the Tide sneak out with a 69-64 victory. This was win number 30.

Corky tallied 18, while Ray, who also came up with four key fourth-quarter points, finished with 11.

Big T.R. Newman had a huge game for the Blackhawks with 19 points. Younger brother Roger chipped in with 13.

In semifinal action, the Tide did as expected, slugging Muhlenberg Central 72-49. Corky led the way with 20 points. D.D. had 19 and Ray 14 for the Tide.

Muhlenberg Central's two Dons—Raymer and Perkins—led the Musketeers with 19 and 18 points, respectively.

The championship tilt against a pesky Graham squad was never as close as the final 76-62 score indicates. The Tide, behind 14 points from Corky and 13 from Ray, raced to a big 39-22 lead by intermission. The lead was 56-36 after three quarters. As time wound down, Graham was able to slice the difference to that final 14-point margin.

Ray had a monster game, ending with 25 points. Corky also came up big with 24.

Buddy Newton had 20 points to lead the Nighthawks.

Millard and Corky were both named to the all-district team.

Now within three wins of reaching the state tournament, the Tide took on Hartford in the regional opener. A quick start, again sparked by Corky and Ray, enabled the Tide to take an 18-6 lead after one quarter. In those opening minutes, Corky accounted for seven points and Ray had six.

After that, the outcome was never in doubt, with the Tide advancing 69-56 thanks to a balanced attack led by Corky with 19, Hope 18, Millard 13 and Ray 11.

For the second straight night, the Tide used a huge first quarter to essentially put Meade County away and move on to the championship game. The Tide led 25-8 after the opening quarter, then went on to win with ease 70-38.

Hope was the Tide's top gun with 18 points. Millard and Corky each had 15, with Ray adding nine.

Another rush from the starting gate was the difference in the Tide's 79-63 title win over Butler County. The Tide raced to a 10-2 lead, sat on a 25-16 advantage after the first stanza, then claimed win number 35 without ever really having to look in the rearview mirror.

Corky, who finished with 28 points, keyed that early charge with 20 first-half points. Hope and Millard had 17 and 16, respectively, while D.D. tossed in 11.

Bobby Green scored 19 for the Bears.

Corky, Millard and Hope were voted to the all-regional squad.

With that 35-0 record, Central City became just the 17th team to enter the state tournament with a perfect slate. Incidently, this has happened only four times since the Tide did it.

The Tide's opening-game opponent was a tough one—Inez, the 15th region champs. In the pre-season Lit Ratings, the Indians were ranked 12th, and with a 29-2 record they had lived up to their billing.

The Indians were led by lefty Billy Ray Cassady, a first-team all-state performer who later signed to play at UK, and by diminutive guard Herbie Triplett. Both players would acquit themselves well in this match-up with the Tide.

As for the Tide, well, this game was nothing less than the worst nightmare imaginable. The ability to consistently hit the bucket, this club's trademark all season, was nowhere to be found. To say the Tide were slightly icy is putting it mildly. On this night, they were colder than cold, connecting on 25 of 96 field goal attempts for 26 percent.

Such frigid shooting doomed them to a 72-57 loss.

The Tide had a brief moment of glory, jumping to a quick 6-0 lead. But following an Inez timeout, and three quick fouls on Millard, things went bad in a hurry. By the end of the first quarter, Inez was ahead 21-14 and firmly in control. The Indians extended their lead to 40-25 at the half, and although the Tide trimmed the difference to eight points on three occasions in the fourth quarter, their cold shooting prevented them from making a serious charge.

All the Tide could do was foul and hope the Indians failed to connect at the charity stripe. That didn't happen. The Indians made good on 26 of 30 free throw attempts.

Despite their cold night from the floor, the Tide had two more field goals (25-23) than Inez. But Inez committed just eight personal fouls, sending the Tide to the stripe 10 times, where they hit seven.

Cassady led all scorers with 27 points, 11 coming on free throws. Triplett added support with 17.

Inez would, of course, go on the capture the state title.

Millard, in his final game, had 19 points to lead the Tide. Hope, another senior, finished with 14, while Corky, who came into the tournament with a hot hand, was limited to 10. D.D. and Ray, the Tide's superb backcourt duo, had seven and four points, respectively, in what was also their last game. Robinson, a junior, had three points.

Despite that sudden and disappointing finish, this had been a season for the ages. This team's 97.2 winning percentage still rates as the best in school history. And those 35 victories rank second behind the 1944-45 team's 37 wins.

Losing such stalwarts as Millard, Ray, Hope and D.D. Withrow would normally be more than enough to keep a coach up at night wondering just what's around the corner. That would be akin to a poker player losing four of a kind. Any coach, even the consensus Coach of the Year, wouldn't be immune to some serious concerns.

But Delmas Gish's hand was far from empty. He was in possession of a pretty good hole card, an ace up his sleeve. Coming back was a player who was soon to shatter all Central City—and Muhlenberg County—scoring records.

Chapter 22

1954-55

For the second time in three years, Delmas Gish welcomed back only one returning starter from the previous season. But unlike the earlier situation, this time the player was one who would soon break all previous scoring records.

Throughout the decades, no Central City or Muhlenberg County player scored 1,000 points in a season. None had come close to averaging 30 points per game. Yet over the next two seasons, Corky Withrow would score 2,138 points and average 30.5 points per outing. As a junior, his numbers were 1,086/30.2 and as a senior they were 1,052/30.9. Even more important, the Tide won 60 of those 70 games, going to the state tournament each year.

Withrow was surrounded by a cast of talented players, including: Billy Lee Robinson, Billy Mason, Carl Ray Jamison, Winfred Thompson, Billy Duvall, Jimmy Swann, Stanley Ruby, Eddie Houston, Donnie Moore, Jerry Calvert and Lawrence Simpson.

For the opener against Muhlenberg Central, Gish opted to go with a starting lineup of Ruby and Houston as the forwards, Withrow in the middle, and Robinson and Mason in the backcourt. This was not a quintet that would last the season. Eventually, Thompson and Jamison replaced Ruby and Houston.

Withrow and Mason were the big guns in the Tide's first two games, both easy wins. Withrow had 36 and Mason 15 as the Tide opened with a 76-26 win over Muhlenberg Central, then Withrow came back with 36 and Mason 16 in a 74-58 victory over Graham.

At Drakesboro, the Tide were down 43-42 heading into the final stanza, but with Robinson scoring nine fourth-quarter points, Withrow eight, Mason six and Duvall one, the visitors came back to post a 66-57 victory. Withrow led a more balanced attack with 22 points. Robinson had 16, Mason 13 and Duvall six for the winners.

Gale Buchanan paced the Cardinals with 20 points.

In the Tide's next two games, wins over Dunmor 86-52 and 86-41 over Bremen, Withrow became only the second Muhlenberg County player to surpass the 40-point mark in a game. He had 40 against Dunmor, 42 against Bremen.

Hughes-Kirk's Carl Carver was the first to achieve that feat, hitting for 44 points in a 1954 game against Utica.

Jamison had 14 in the win over Dunmor, while Mason registered 12 in each game.

Withrow scored 34 points, Mason 12 and Robinson 10 as the Tide made it six wins in a row by blasting Hughes-Kirk 89-51. Duvall and Jamison came off the bench to contribute nine points apiece in that easy romp.

Hughes-Kirk was led by Robie Harper's 19 points, with 16 by Jimmy Harper. The Harper brothers would go on to set a few scoring records before their playing days were finished.

Always dangerous Louisville St. Xavier paid a visit to Central City, but with Withrow throwing in 39 points, Robinson 13 and Ruby a season-best 12, the Tide claimed a 76-63 victory. In this game, Withrow made good on 19 of 22 free throw attempts.

Facing a Greenville team playing without the injured Roger Newman, the Tide scored an easy 70-52 win. Withrow had 34 and Mason 18 for the winners.

Senior Larry Sparks did his best to make up for Newman's absence, ending the night with 27 points. Kenny Arbuckle and Percie Gossett each had 10.

Behind 25 points from Withrow, 18 from Mason, 12 from Robinson and 10 from Houston, the Tide easily defeated Hartford 78-58 in the Central City Invitational opener. This was, of course, the first of two meeting against the Mustangs, and the second encounter would turn out to be among the most memorable in Golden Tide history.

One night later, Withrow scored 34 points, Mason 20 and Robinson 10 as the Tide captured the title by topping Graham 76-48.

The Withrow-Mason-Robinson trio continued to score well, racking up a combined 66 points as the Tide cracked the century mark with a 102-69 win over Calhoun. In this game nine different Tide players scored.

Withrow led with 40, Mason had 14, Robinson 12, Jamison nine, Thompson and Ruby eight each, Swann six, Duvall three and Houston two.

Withrow tossed in 28 points and Mason added 14 as the Tide beat Hughes-Kirk 63-38 to improve their season mark to 12-0.

Robie Harper paced the Tigers with 22 points.

A Mid-Season Slump

Any dream of a second straight undefeated regular season was laid to rest by home-standing Butler County. In a thriller that went down to the wire, the Tide, now ranked third in the state, were upended 65-64. The loss ended the Tide's regular-season winning streak at 47.

Withrow had 35 points for the Tide, while Ruby chipped in with 11.

Butler County was led by Radean Hammers with 17.

Withrow had 30 points, Robinson and Mason 12 each as the Tide bounced back to defeat stubborn Owensboro Catholic 69-59 at home. The Tide only led 34-30 at the break, then with Robinson scoring 10 of his dozen points in the final quarter, they were able to pull away for the win.

With Thompson scoring 14 points in his initial start, the Tide beat Wingo 84-73 in the first of a two-game road swing. Thompson, a sophomore, played particularly well after intermission, scoring 10 points in those final two quarters.

Withrow had 27 to lead all scorers. Robinson scored 17 and Mason 12 for the Tide.

Hampered by foul problems that had Withrow, Robinson and Mason spending time on the bench, the Tide lost a 75-59 decision to Sedalia, which was led by Bob Wilson's game-high 23 points.

Withrow had 20 points before fouling out, Mason had 17 and Thompson, in another solid performance, finished with 13.

In a tune-up prior to the Louisville Invitational Tournament, the Tide, triggered by Withrow's 37 points, ripped Owensboro 80-57. Mason was the only other Tide player in double digits with 10.

Having dropped to 10th in the Lit Ratings, the Tide were paired against No.2-ranked Newport Public in the LIT. What transpired in this game—a 69-62 loss—was easily the most-perplexing performance turned in by the Tide this season.

The Tide led 28-18 after one stop, pushed their lead to 32-18 on a Thompson bucket, were in front 44-37 at intermission, then managed to score only 18 points in the second half. Even despite a dismal seven-point third quarter, the Tide were still in front 51-49 after three quarters. But Newport, fueled by all-state performer Ed Huffman's 16 points, gained the upper hand early in the fourth quarter and never looked back.

Withrow led the Tide with 31 points, 16 coming in the opening stanza. Mason finished with 14.

At this stage, Delmas Gish decided it was time for another lineup change, replacing Ruby with Jamison. Thompson, Jamison, Withrow, Robinson and Mason would be the starters for the remainder of the season.

That lineup got off to a good start, beating a solid Drakesboro club 68-55. Withrow led the way with 26 points, while Thompson added 15. Jamison, in his first start, had eight points, a number matched by Mason.

Bobby Bradley had 21 points for the Cardinals.

Traveling to Owensboro to face Daviess County, Withrow broke all existing Central City and Muhlenberg County single-game scoring records with a 51-point effort in a 103-83 victory. Withrow had 22 field goals—two better than the previous record of 20 he shared with Muhlenberg Central's Don Raymer—and seven free throws to account for his total.

Mason had 16 points, Thompson 15 and Robinson 12 in that win.

Withrow came back to score 33 in a 70-31 win over Muhlenberg Central and 35 in a 79-72 win over Heath. Against Heath, Jamison knocked in 20 points and Mason 12.

Deciding that running with the Tide was not a strategically sound plan, Paducah Tilghman slowed the pace, a ploy that paid big dividends, a surprising 56-51 win. The Tide held a 46-44 advantage after three quarters, but when Withrow went to the bench with five fouls, the tables quickly turned the visitors' way. In that final stanza, the Tide could only manage five points while the Tornado were scoring 12.

Withrow had a game-high 24 points before fouling out. Mason added 10.

Withrow scored 24 points, Mason 21 and Robinson 18 to lead the Tide past Madisonville 74-50. In a 70-49 win over Bremen, Withrow racked up 34 points, Jamison 16 and Robinson 10.

Strange Happenings in Greenville

In what must surely rank among their most bizarre performances ever, the Golden Tide dropped a 51-49 double-overtime sudden-death decision to archrival Greenville. The Blackhawks won it when Roger Newman connected on a pair of free throws in the second OT. Newman was brilliant, finishing the game with 25 points, 17 coming at the free throw stripe. For the game, the Blackhawks only managed eight field goals. They won it by making good on 35 free tosses.

What made this game so bizarre is that the Tide did not score a single point in the fourth quarter or in either OT period. The Tide led 49-42 heading into the final frame, then the faucet was shut off. It was zilch from that point on.

Withrow had 16 for the Tide. Mason added 12.

Adair County, led by all-state standout Ralph Shearer's 31 points, came to town and almost pulled off the upset, eventually coming out on the losing end of a 73-69 score. The Tide led 61-49 after the third quarter, but Withrow, who tallied 28 points, fouled out and did not score in the final eight minutes. Still, the Tide hung on despite not registering a field goal in the fourth period.

Robinson had 16 points and Mason 10 for the Tide.

Adair County would go on to advance to the finals of the state tournament, losing to Hazard in the title game.

Withrow scored 29 points and Mason 10 as the Tide smothered outmanned Calhoun 79-30. Then in the regular season's final game, the Tide, behind 21 points from Withrow, beat Owensboro 62-54 in the Sportscenter.

Robinson had 14 and Mason 12 in that win.

A Tough Tournament Road

The Tide's path through the district tournament was not an easy one. Unlike the previous year, when the Tide and Greenville met in the opening round, this time the two rivals were in opposite brackets. Even with that bit of good fortune, the Tide had to face a good Drakesboro team led by Gale Buchanan and Bobby Bradley.

The game was tough, but with Withrow scoring 23 points, Mason 20, Robinson 14 and Jamison 11, the Tide pulled through for a 77-69 victory.

Buchanan and Bradley led the Cardinals with 18 and 14 points, respectively.

If the Drakesboro game had Tide fans nervously chewing their fingernails, then the semifinal battle against Graham had them keeping their eyes closed and whispering silent prayers. The Tide were clinging to a 48-46 lead after three quarters, then used a stifling defense to limit Graham to a pair of fourth-quarter field goals en route to a 66-57 victory.

Withrow had 25 points, Robinson 14 and Mason 10 for the winners, who would now square off against Greenville in the championship game.

In the rubber match, the Tide jumped to a 24-16 first-quarter lead, only to watch as the Blackhawks trimmed the difference to 38-35 at the half. The Blackhawks outscored the Tide 16-10 in the third quarter to take a 51-48 advantage into the final eight minutes. In that last quarter, with the game on the line, Withrow had seven points and Thompson six, as the Tide claimed their sixth consecutive district title with a 66-62 win.

Withrow and Newman each scored 27 points. Sparks had 20 for Greenville, while Thompson had 14 and Robinson 11 for the Tide.

Withrow, Mason and Robinson were voted onto the all-district team.

Central City's regional tournament draw couldn't have been tougher. The Tide would open against Butler County, a club that won a January match-up 65-64. Looming ahead, should they get past the Bears, was Greenville, another team that owned a win over the Tide. Get past those two difficult foes, Tide fans felt, and the final game should be a piece of cake. But cakes have a way of sometimes turning out poorly, and this one almost did.

The Tide opened by giving one of their best performances of the season, beating Butler County 87-72. Withrow paced the winners with 26 points, while Mason had 16, Jamison 15, Thompson and Duvall nine each, Robinson eight and Simpson four.

Wally Johnson led Butler County with 20 points.

Squaring off against Greenville in one of those all-or-nothing contests, the Tide rode a strong second-half effort to a 69-54 victory. Greenville, on the strength of 26 first-half points by Roger Newman and Larry Sparks, owned a 29-28 lead at intermission. In that half, Newman had 14 points and Sparks 12.

But the second half was ruled completely by the Tide, who outscored Greenville 43-25 in those final 16 minutes. If Newman and

Sparks dominated the opening half, it was Withrow who owned the second half, scoring 18 of his game-high 28 points after the break.

Robinson and Jamison each had 12 points for the Tide.

Newman ended the night with 23, while Sparks had 15.

A Houdini-Like Escape

Having dismissed powerful clubs like Butler County and Greenville left only Hartford standing between the Tide and a second straight state tournament appearance. Based on the existing evidence, few observers felt this game would be close. After all, the Tide defeated Hartford 78-58 during the regular season. Also, Hartford had barely escaped in the tourney opener, edging past Leitchfield 55-54 in overtime.

For much of this game, it appeared as though the observers knew what they were talking about. The Tide roared to a 14-8 lead after one quarter and were ahead 31-19 at the half. But then things began to unravel, thanks primarily to foul problems. The Tide's two top guns, Withrow and Mason, would both foul out.

Still, the Tide led 39-33 going into the final eight minutes. Midway through the quarter, Hartford went on top 46-45. A Mason bucket put the Tide back in front before an exchange of free throws over the next few minutes had Hartford holding a 50-49 lead. Thompson connected on two free tosses to give the Tide a 51-50 advantage. Seconds later, Donnie Barrass hit a pair of freebies to give the lead back to Hartford 52-51.

What happened next falls into that I-can't-believe-what-I-just-witnessed category.

Hartford, leading by a single point, came up with a crucial steal and began holding the ball. With 11 ticks remaining, Hartford's Glenn Mills was fouled, sending him to the free throw line for a pair of free tosses. If Mills hit one, the best the Tide could hope for was a late bucket that would send the game into overtime. If Mills hit them both, well, this was long before the three-point shot, so the Tide would go home and Hartford go to Lexington.

Incredibly, Mills missed both shots. When the second one rimmed out, Thompson snared the rebound and quickly passed it ahead to Jamison. With time winding down, Jamison sent a pass to Duvall, along with the order to "shoot it now!"

Duvall caught the ball, glanced at the clock—"there were three seconds left"—and let it fly from 30 feet away.

Swish!

A no-doubter, Duvall says of his only basket in the game.

"I knew the second I shot the ball that it was going to be good," Duvall said. "I could tell the moment it was in the air."

In a most miraculous way, thanks to the most-memorable shot in school history, the Tide prevailed 53-52 to earn a berth in the Sweet 16.

Another Disappointing Loss

For the second straight year, the Golden Tide drew another tough Eastern Kentucky mountain team as a first-round Sweet 16 opponent. Last year it was Inez; this year it was Pikeville, the 15th region champs.

According to the final regular-season Lit Ratings, Berea was the team to beat, followed in order by Newport Public, Henderson, Adair County, Mayfield, Central City, Louisville St. Xavier, Pikeville, Somerset, Clay County, Hazard, Shelbyville, Bracken County, Olive Hill, Dawson Springs and Glasgow.

Proving that ratings don't mean much, Hazard, the 11th-ranked team, went on to capture the title.

There were several teams in the tourney that the Tide were familiar with. They owned wins over St. X and Adair County, and had suffered a loss to Newport Public.

This was a tournament loaded with terrific individual players, including Withrow, Hazard's Johnny Cox, Berea's Don Mills, Newport's Ed Huffman, St. X's Joe Viviano, Adair County's Ralph Shearer and Terry Randall and Pikeville's Ralph Gilliam.

Against Pikeville, the Tide, keyed by 10 Withrow points, ran out to a 22-20 lead after one quarter. That advantage quickly melted when the Panthers went to a defense the Tide had not seen all season—a 1-2-1-1 full-court press. This defensive set-up, which later became known as a "diamond" press, had been created by Pikeville coach John Bill Trivett.

With the score knotted at 27-27, the pressing Panthers forced several Tide turnovers, which they quickly converted to points, building a 38-27 lead. The Tide finally found their footing, but Pikeville, with Gilliam accounting for 12 second-quarter points took a 46-41 lead at halftime.

Despite facing mounting foul problems, the Tide, behind seven Mason points and five from Withrow, fought back to take a precarious 61-59 lead going into the final frame, courtesy of a 25-foot Jamison jumper at the horn.

Pikeville opened the last quarter by rattling off four unanswered points to take a 63-61 lead. After Withrow tied it with a bucket, Pikeville scored four straight points to go on top 67-63. But back-to-back buckets by Mason and Thompson tied it for the last time at 67-67. From that point on it was all Pikeville.

The final: Pikeville 78, Central City 74.

Withrow had 28 points for the Tide before fouling out in the game's final minutes. Mason, who also fouled out, finished with 15, while Thompson added 11.

Pikeville's Gilliam led all scorers with 33 points, hitting 11 field goals and connecting on 11 of 19 free throws. For the game, Pikeville won the field-goal battle 30-28, one of the few times all season the Tide were outgunned from the floor.

Withrow was named to the all-tournament team. He was also a first-team selection by the Louisville *Courier-Journal*, *Paducah Sun* and the Lexington *Herald-Leader*.

History has always credited this team with a 28-6 record, which is not accurate. The correct record is 30-6. This is where we get back those two wins taken away from the 1944-45 team.

If there had been questions prior to the start of this season, there would be none as Tide fans looked ahead. Three starters and miracle-maker Duvall were set to join Withrow, who would continue to write his name into the record books.

Chapter 23

1950s Sideline Shots (Part One)

The Happy Gunner

Joe Mac Howard will be the first to admit (freely, it must be added) that he never met a shot he didn't like. Or was hesitant to take. It has always been understood that when Joe Mac crossed the center stripe, he was instantly in range.

"Yeah, I did like to jack that ball up there a lot," Joe Mac says, chuckling at the memory. "I could never be accused of being bashful about shooting."

Legend has it that the shot chart was first used at Central City during Joe Mac's senior year. The shot chart, usually kept by one of the team managers, has a diagram of the basketball court on it. When a player takes a shot, the statistician finds the place on the chart that corresponds with the spot on the court where the player took the shot. If the shot is good, the chart keeper circles the player's number; if it misses, the number is not circled.

At the conclusion of the first game in which the shot chart was utilized, as the teams headed for the locker room, the young chart keeper waded through the Golden Tide players until he found Joe Mac. Proudly holding up the chart, a big smile on his face, the young man said, "Look, Joe Mac. You took twenty-four shots and you made three."

At which time, as the legend goes, Joe Mac grabbed the shot chart, ripped out the page, tore it in half, then handed the chart back to the young man, saying, "Don't tell that to anybody."

"I don't know if that story is true or not," Joe Mac says. "I kind of doubt it. It sounds like something someone made up along the way. But like I said, I wasn't afraid to take a shot."

And how did Delmas Gish feel about having a player with such a quick trigger?

"Coach Gish never got on me," Joe Mac says, "except for one time. It was during summer practice and we were scrimmaging. I took so many shots that Mr. Gish stopped the game, made everyone on my team get off the floor, and then he ordered me to play against all five defenders by myself. But other than that one time he never got on my case for shooting too much."

That's probably because Joe Mac had a knack for putting the ball in the bucket.

Coach Gish the Motivator

As a coach, Delmas Gish was known as a terrific motivator. And as with all good motivators, Gish would say whatever it took to get his players fired up and ready for battle. This was especially true when the Golden Tide squared off against those infidels from Greenville.

Back in the late '40s and early '50s, Greenville's best player was Tommy Gross, whose father just happened to be a minister. For Gish, this was a scenario begging to be used as a motivational tool.

"He would get us in the dressing room prior to the game and he would be really fired up," Bobby Nofsinger said. "He hated Greenville, and could not stand losing to them. And he would always end his speech by saying, 'Fellows, you simply cannot lose to a team whose best player is a preacher's son. You cannot let that happen. That would be embarrassing.' When he finished speaking, we were charged up and ready to fight tigers."

Gish Almost Calls it Quits

The 1952-53 season is most notable because it was the start of the Corky Withrow Era at Central City. Withrow, a freshman, was a starter that season, along with senior Dick Wolfe and juniors Bobby Don Millard, Larry Ray and Roy "D.D." Withrow.

Wolfe was the only starter returning from the previous season, and of the four newcomers, only Millard had logged much playing time as a sophomore. In short, this was a very young and inexperienced club.

Despite its youth, this team, for much of the season, acquitted itself extremely well. There were a few bumps in the road along the way, like an embarrassing home-court loss to Bremen in the season opener, but after the first 18 games, this team's record was a very good 15-3.

Then all of a sudden, those bumps in the road turned into massive pot holes. Of their next six games, the Tide lost five. Suddenly, in the span of two weeks, that once sterling record now stood at 16-8.

The last of those five setbacks was a humiliating embarrassment: Male 94, Central City 49. When the slaughter was over, Delmas Gish came into the locker room and hit his players with a surprising bit of news.

"He told us that if he couldn't prepare a team better than this, if he couldn't do a better job of motivating us, it was time for him to quit," Bobby Don said. "He was really down, and I'm sure he meant what he said."

But according to Bobby Don, the players weren't about to let that happen.

"We all got together and went to see Mr. Gish," Bobby Don said. "We told him that if he would stick with it, we wouldn't lose another game the rest of the season."

And were it not for a questionable call against Breckinridge County in the regional tourney final, the players' promise to their coach might have come true.

"Of our next 44 games, we only lost one," Corky said. "And we shouldn't have lost that game. We were ahead by one point when Roy Settles called a foul on Bobby Don. And Bobby Don was *behind* the guy he supposedly fouled. That's the only time I ever heard Mr. Gish curse. He also promised that Settles would never again call a game in Central City, and I don't think he ever did."

Proving once again that coaches have long memories.

Remembering the Inez Disaster

Central City entered the 1954 state tournament with a perfect 35-0 record. In that tourney's opening round, the Tide faced Inez, the eventual champs. Inez won 72-57 primarily because the Tide, normally a good-shooting team, couldn't throw the ball in the ocean, much less make a bucket. For the game, the Tide shot 26 percent from the field.

Back then, some in the media wondered if perhaps the Tide had been vastly overrated, if maybe that 35-0 mark resulted from having played a mediocre schedule. However, given the fact Inez went on to claim the crown should be more than enough to silence the skeptics.

And how do the Golden Tide players feel about it? Well, Larry Ray says anybody who doubts that Tide team's ability doesn't have a clue.

"Look, Inez beat us that night," Larry said. "They were the better team in that game. But we didn't play very well, and we had a miserable shooting night. It happens. If we played Inez 10 times, I'm confident we could win five of those games. They weren't that much better than we were."

Corky Withrow says much of the blame for the Tide's poor effort should be placed on his shoulders.

"If I had a halfway decent game we might've had a chance of winning that night," Corky said. "I was averaging close to 20 points a game and I scored 10. But I was simply overwhelmed that night. Playing in the state tournament, being in Memorial Coliseum... I was just out of it."

Despite what the critics might have said, Larry concluded by saying, "If you go 35-0, you're pretty darn good."

Tough Battles Times Four

A few years ago, during a celebration honoring Corky Withrow's induction into the KHSAA Hall of Fame, two old warriors—Larry Ray and T.R. Newman—were reminiscing about past times. In particular, they were discussing the 1953-54 season, during which Central City and Greenville did battle four times.

That was a terrific season for both schools. Without question, those were two of the strongest teams ever produced by either Central City or Greenville. The Tide defeated Greenville in the district opener, then went on to the state tournament. Many observers felt that had the Blackhawks won that game, they would have made it to the Sweet 16.

It's hard to argue against that point of view. Greenville was a solid club.

"You know, we only lost six games that season," T.R. said, adding, "and four of those losses were to Central City."

To which Larry simply replied, "Yeah, I know. I was there."

Facing Jim Host

Ashland native Jim Host will most certainly go down as one of the most astute and successful businessmen in Kentucky history. As CEO of Host Communications, he helped developing marketing for collegiate athletic programs. He was the founding chairman of the Alltech FEI World Equestrian Games, and he was instrumental in helping get the KFC Yum Center built.

In 1971, he ran for lieutenant governor.

Among his many honors, Host was inducted into the National Collegiate Basketball Hall of Fame in 2012.

Host was also an outstanding pitcher, both at Ashland High School and later at the University of Kentucky. In fact, he was good enough to sign a professional contract.

In the 1955 Kentucky baseball state tournament, Central City faced off against Ashland in the opening round. As expected, Host, the ace of the Tomcats' staff, took the mound against the Golden Tide.

While Host may have been enormously successful in virtually every area of his life, he failed miserably when it came to facing Corky Withrow.

"I went three-for-three that day," Corky recalls. "I had a single, then a double my first two times up. The last time I hit one off the wall for a triple."

And the outcome?

"We won 3-2," Corky said. "Winfred Thompson was the winning pitcher."

And like all successful hitters, Corky isn't shy about rubbing salt into a pitcher's wound.

"I saw Jim Host not too long ago," Corky said, "and I reminded him about that game. That I had rattled the walls my last time at bat. He didn't deny it. But he's a pitcher; I'm sure he thinks I just got lucky."

Upping the Tempo

Both Corky Withrow and Billy Mason are quick to agree that the 1954-55 season gave rise to a new style of play for the Golden Tide. According to them, things went from fast to supersonic.

"That team relied almost totally on the fast break," Corky said. "Get the ball and run with it. Central City teams always preferred to play up-tempo, but in 1954-55 we took it to a new level. Even the undefeated 1953-54 team didn't really run all that much. That team won because it had such great shooters, not because it outran anybody."

Billy concurs. "All we knew was to run and gun. Billy Duvall and I were talking just a few days ago, and I asked him if could ever remember Coach Gish giving us a set play once we got into the half court. He couldn't remember one, and neither could I. You've got to throw up a lot of shots to score as many points as we did. That 1955-56 team likely would have averaged close to 100 points a game if our opponents hadn't started holding the ball on us late in the season."

Like Corky, Billy is also convinced that the Golden Tide would have won the 1956 state championship had Duvall not been injured.

"Well, we'll never know for sure, but I really think we could have won it all," Billy said. "I certainly think we would have gotten past Carr Creek. They beat us by two points; Duvall would have been worth anywhere from eight to 12 points. That would have been the difference."

According to Billy, Duvall wasn't the only gimpy Golden Tide player on the floor during the Carr Creek game.

"Winfred (Thompson) was heavily taped," Billy remembers, "and I had a stress fracture in my left leg. Thing is, I didn't know that until the next year when I went off to college. While I was there, the leg was injured and had to be X-rayed. The doctor came out and asked me when it had been broken. I told him it had to have happened during my senior year in high school. So I played against Carr Creek with an injury that I wasn't aware of."

And how does Billy remember those days?

"There were things we could have done better," he said. "But we played hard and we ran with the ball. Also, there was no jealousy on those teams. We all knew who buttered our bread, and that was Corky. Get him the ball and there was a good chance he would score. But I never once heard Mr. Gish tell us to get the ball to Corky. Not once. We did because it gave us the best chance of winning.

"Those were great times," he added. "I think those guys I played with, we all had big hearts. Bigger than these kids today. They are great athletes, but now it's all about me, me, me. We always thought team first. That's how Mr. Gish wanted it, and that's how we played."

Chapter 24

1955-56

Several years ago, Delmas Gish made a statement to Billy Ray Duvall that came as a surprise to Billy. "Coach Gish told me he thought the 1955-56 team was the best in Central City history. There have been some great Golden Tide teams, so that's a big compliment for us."

No doubt, players on three previous Central City teams, and one that was waiting down the road would disagree with Gish's assessment. After all, the 1944-45 team advanced to the state tournament's championship game, the 1949-50 team made it to the semifinals, the 1953-54 team had a perfect 35-0 regular-season record, and the 1965-66 team also advanced to the semifinals.

A strong case can be made that any one of those teams was the school's all-time best.

But there is no denying that the 1955-56 club belongs in the debate. This was a veteran team that saw the return of starters Billy Mason, Winfred Thompson and Carl Ray Jamison, along with regional tournament hero Billy Ray Duvall. Backing them up were Donnie Moore, Jimmy "Duck" Swann, Eddie Brand, Earl Goode, Johnny Lile and Carroll Harrison.

And at the center of it all was Corky Withrow, who scored 1,086 points and averaged 30.2 points per game as a junior, earning All-America and all-state recognition for his efforts. As a senior, his numbers virtually matched those of his junior campaign, and would have been even more impressive had teams not begun holding the ball late in the season. Despite those slow-down tactics, Withrow scored 1,052 points and averaged 30.9 points per game, leading the Tide to a 30-4 record.

Many long-time observers rank the 1955-56 season as one of the greatest, most-exciting in Kentucky high school hoops history. No wonder. That season, there were an abundance of strong teams and a legion of terrific players, headed by four gifted seniors—Withrow, Wayland's "King" Kelly Coleman, Greenville's Roger Newman and Berea's Don Mills. Among the many talented underclassmen were Lafayette's Billy Ray Lickert, Earlington's Harry Todd, Newport's John Turner and Flat Gap's Charlie Osborne, just to name a few.

In every way this was a special year.

For the Golden Tide it turned out to be yet another successful season that ended in bitter disappointment. There were some big victories, record-shattering performances by Withrow, the slaying of a King, a No. 1 state ranking and a three-week suspension midway through the season. No one can accuse the 1955-56 campaign of being ordinary.

The season began with a 66-47 win over Bremen. In that opener, Withrow had 29 points, Jamison 15 and Duvall 11. Withrow came back to score 38 in an 89-55 win over Calhoun and 35 in an 81-54 win over Dunmor.

Jamison and Thompson each had 13 and Mason 11 against Calhoun, then Mason dropped in 22 and Thompson a dozen in the win over Dunmor.

In what had to be an uncomfortable situation, Withrow tied his all-time scoring record with 51 points in a 107-63 win over Hughes-Kirk. What made this a strange situation was the fact that Hughes-Kirk was coached by Roy "D.D." Withrow, Corky's older brother who, just two short years earlier, was his teammate on that undefeated club. Only in his second year of college, D.D. was at the helm of a good Hughes-Kirk team headed by the Harper brothers, Robie and Jimmy.

But on this night, no one could stop Withrow, who had 22 field goals and seven free throws. Mason finished with 14 points, Thompson and Jamison had 13 each, and Moore added 10.

Robie Harper had 29 points for the Tigers.

Withrow had 35 points and Thompson 10 as the Tide pounded Drakesboro 74-49. In an 87-46 win over Muhlenberg Central, Withrow had 30 points, Thompson 19 and Mason 10.

An 88-69 win over Graham wasn't so easy. The Tide trailed 35-34 at the half before breaking the game open in the third quarter. Withrow fouled out with 24 points, but he received strong support from Jamison with 21, Mason with 15, Thompson with 14 and Duvall with 10.

Graham's Bobby Oldham led all scorers with 28 points.

At Greenville, the Tide again rode a strong second-half effort to a 69-51 victory. The Tide led by a single point (33-32) at the break, then broke away during the second half to secure the win. In the first head-to-head match-up of their final season, Roger Newman outscored Withrow 30-22. The difference in the game was Withrow's supporting cast, which was far more productive than Newman's. Mason had 16 points, Duvall 10, Jamison nine and Thompson eight for the winners.

A King Comes to Town

No Central City Invitational before or since was more exciting or more memorable than the one played on Dec. 23-24, 1955. Joining the Tide in the CCIT field were Graham, Elkton and Wayland, which, of course, meant "King" Kelly Coleman, the state's all-time leading scorer, was in town. Before this tournament concluded on Christmas Eve, a game would be played that remains to this day the most talked about in Muhlenberg County sports history.

Wayland vs. Central City. Corky vs. a King.

For that showdown to happen, the Tide and Wayland had to take care of business in the opening round, which they did. Coleman, who came in averaging 46 points per game, scored 40 to lead the Wasps to a 65-53 win over Graham. In the nightcap, Withrow had 26 points, Mason and Thompson 16 apiece, Jamison 13 and Duvall 10 as the Tide topped Elkton 85-63.

In that famous head-to-head confrontation, Withrow and Coleman each scored 40 points, Withrow on 15 field goals and 10 free throws, Coleman on 14 field goals and 12 freebies. Over the years, this game, which the Tide won handily 83-75, has taken on a life of its own. So have the performances of Withrow and Coleman.

"Of all the games I played, this is the one people ask me about the most," Withrow says. "And if everyone who tells me they were at the game really were there, then about 20,000 people were able to get inside a gym that held about 2,500."

As with the Greenville game, the difference was Withrow's supporting cast. Jamison racked up 14 points, while Duvall and Mason each contributed 12.

With that trophy securely in hand, the Tide, now ranked 4th in the state, went in search of more hardware, this time traveling to Louisville for a second straight appearance in the Louisville Invitational Tournament, where their opening-round foe would be St. Xavier. Behind 20 points from Jamison and 17 each from Thompson and Withrow, the Tide advanced with a 65-49 win.

This game marked the only time all season that Withrow wasn't the team's leading scorer.

Next up for the Tide was Newport Public, the state's top-ranked team. But in a game that was essentially over two minutes after tip-off, the Tide, behind 38 points from Withrow, crushed Newport 90-60. The Tide led 23-6 after one quarter and 44-15 at the half. Withrow's 38 points tied the LIT record set the previous year by Kenny Kuhn. That record would be matched later that night by Berea's Don Mills.

Newport was led by John Turner's 21 points.

Berea, led by the 6'7" Mills, halted the Tide's winning streak at 12 by posting a 72-64 semifinal win. Mills led all scorers with 27 points. Dave Singleton and Darrell Bicknell ended the game with 19 and 13 points, respectively.

Withrow led the Tide with 22. Jamison had 14, Mason 12 and Duvall 10.

Withrow and Thompson were named to the all-tournament team.

That loss to Berea sent the Tide into something of a funk that saw them lose two of their next four games, including one that would have huge repercussions. The first of those four games was an easy 85-66 win over Roy "D.D." Withrow's Hughes-Kirk team. In this outing against his brother, Corky had 30 points. Jamison scored 16, Thompson 14 and Duvall 11 for the Tide.

Jimmy Harper had 23 points and Robie Harper 22 for the Tigers.

Basketbrawl Leads to a Suspension

It was in the next game, a fight-marred 54-47 home loss to Butler County that the Tide put their entire season in jeopardy. In the closing minutes, following a missed free throw, Withrow and Radean Hammers got into a fight. Within seconds players from both benches were on the floor, along with spectators from the two schools. It was an ugly, scary moment in which a fan pulled a knife and threatened one of the officials. Later, after order was restored and the visitors were leaving, Central City fans reportedly threw rocks at the departing bus.

As for scoring honors, combatants Withrow had 23 points and Hammers 21 to lead their respective teams.

A report of the nasty incident was sent by the two officials to the KHSAA for review. It would take two weeks before a decision was handed down.

The Tide split their next two games, beating Owensboro Catholic 64-56 before losing 87-83 to Sedalia. Withrow had 22, Duvall 18 and Thompson 11 in the win over Owensboro Catholic, then Withrow came back to score 36, Thompson 19 and Duvall 14 against Sedalia, which was paced by Jimmy Vest with 29 points and John Key with 26.

With all five starters cracking double figures, the Tide set a school record with a 116-77 win over Wingo. Withrow led with 32, followed by Mason's 21, Jamison's 19, Duvall's 14 and Thompson's 12.

Playing in the Sportscenter, the Tide, behind 39 points from Withrow, blasted Owensboro 85-58, unaware that this would be their final game for the next three weeks. In this win, Duvall had 16 points, Mason and Thompson 10 apiece.

Following this game, KHSAA Commissioner Ted Sanford announced his decision, dropping the hammer on Central City. His verdict: a three-week suspension and one year on probation. In his report, Sanford singled out Withrow for "committing an apparent flagrant act of unsportsmanlike conduct against a Butler County player, Radean Hammers, for which he was ejected from the game by officials Norman and Eugene O'Nan."

Butler County was also placed on one-year probation.

Despite being sent to detention, the Tide were able to reschedule several of the missed games. The suspension ended with a bang, Withrow breaking his own record by pouring in 53 points in a 104-63 win over Bremen. Withrow had 21 field goals and 11 free throws.

Mason had 14 and Thompson 11 in that win.

Incredibly, the Tide, having watched from the sidelines, came out of their exile ranked No. 1 in the state.

Withrow remained hot in the Tide's next three games, wins over Madisonville 81-47, Greenville 63-27 and Calhoun 68-28. In those three wins, Withrow had 42 against Madisonville, 29 against Greenville (to Roger Newman's 10) and 35 against Calhoun.

Thompson also scored well in those three games, accounting for 39 points.

After Withrow had 38 points, Mason 18, Jamison 14 and Thompson 13 in a 93-79 win over Daviess County, Drakesboro became the first of several teams to decide that running against the Tide was not a strategically sound plan. Slowing things to a crawl, the Cardinals were still no match for the Tide, losing 47-27. Withrow scored 18 and Thompson 14 for the winners.

Bobby Beasley paced the Cardinals with 10.

The Tide ended what had been a turbulent season by beating Owensboro 77-65 and Muhlenberg Central 84-55. Withrow tossed in 38 points, Duvall 12 and Jamison 11 against the Red Devils, then Withrow had 34 and Mason 14 in the win over MC.

Jerry Shanks led Muhlenberg Central with 16 points.

Corky vs. Roger One Last Time

By now opposing coaches decided that the best way to stop the Tide was to put the ball in the deep freeze. And that's exactly what happened in four of the Tide's next six games. Only Dunmor chose to run with the Tide, to disastrous results.

In a game that took just 68 minutes to play, the Tide opened defense of their district title by topping Hughes-Kirk 48-22. The Tigers tried to hold the ball but turnovers kept getting them in trouble. Trailing 25-8 heading into the final quarter, Hughes-Kirk had no choice but to up the tempo, which is precisely what the Tide wanted. In that final frame, with Withrow accounting for 11 of his game-high 22 points, the Tide pulled away for the easy win.

Once again, Central City and Greenville found themselves in the same bracket, meaning one of the two clubs would head to the regional tournament, the other would head home. This would also be the final showdown between Withrow and Roger Newman, still the two greatest players in Muhlenberg County history.

Newman easily won the individual battle, outscoring Withrow 22-10. But in a game that was tied on numerous occasions, the Tide, thanks to a late steal and bucket by Mason, managed to slip away with a 32-31 victory.

Greenville was in front 29-26 before Thompson connected on a jumper to make it 29-28. The Blackhawks had the lead and possession of the ball when Mason came up with his crucial steal, which he converted by laying in a crip shot. With 39 ticks remaining, Newman launched a shot that missed, then fouled Withrow while going for the rebound. Withrow hit both free tosses to make it 32-29. A bucket by Jerry Thomasson at the buzzer accounted for the final score.

The win was a costly one for the Tide, who lost Duvall for the remainder of the season. The Tide's senior sharpshooter suffered a broken ankle in the fourth quarter when his foot came down on Newman's. Without Duvall, this Tide team simply wasn't as good, and his absence would be profoundly felt in less than two weeks.

If nothing else, Dunmor deserves credit for fearlessly running-and-gunning with the Tide in the district championship game. Unfortunately, it was primarily the Tide doing the running and gunning, claiming the title with a 94-49 romp.

Withrow had 42 for the Tide, while Swann, filling in for Duvall, and Mason each contributed 14. Jamison also hit double figures with 10.

R.C. McElwain led Dunmor with 16.

Withrow, Thompson and Jamison were voted onto the all-tournament team.

Deep Freeze, Revenge and Ultimate Heartbreak

In sports, fate and circumstances have a way of making things interesting. For the Tide, the road to the state tournament had to go through Morgantown, site of the regional tournament. This meant that in all likelihood the Tide would have to beat a Butler County club they had lost to on their home court in that fight-marred game.

For the regional opener, the Tide caught a break, drawing district foe Dunmor, a team that was clearly outgunned and outmanned. This game was an almost-carbon copy of the district championship game. Withrow scored 38 points, Jamison 15, Thompson and Swann 10 each in a 96-51 win.

If previous teams elected to put the ball in the deep freeze, Clarkson chose to bury it in an iceberg. After a first quarter that ended with the Tide on top 9-7, neither team scored again until Clarkson's Allen Herron tied it with two minutes remaining. The Tide held for the final shot, which Withrow took and made with six seconds left to give his team an 11-9 victory.

Withrow had eight points and Thompson three to account for the Tide's point total. Herron scored all nine of his team's points.

In a jam-packed, tension-filled gym, the Tide sought revenge against a Butler County team that was not only very formidable, but was also playing at home. Getting past the Bears was no easy task, and for much of the game, it appeared as though it wasn't going to happen.

With both clubs playing at a deliberate, cautious pace, the score was tied 27-27 at the half. The Bears, behind five points from Wally Johnson, forged a 41-37 advantage with just eight minutes remaining. Those eight minutes would be all Central City.

Butler County did not score in the final quarter.

Buckets by Mason and Withrow tied the score at 41-41. After a Butler County miss, the Tide held the ball until the seven-second mark. Then Withrow hit a short jumper to make it 43-41.

The Bears launched a desperation shot at the buzzer that wasn't close. Outscored 6-0 in the final quarter, the Bears could only look on as the Tide cut down the nets, took home the trophy and earned a third-straight appearance in the state tournament.

Withrow led all scorers with 22 points. Thompson finished with 11 and Mason eight for the Tide.

Radean Hammers had 14 and Johnson 11 for Butler County.

Withrow and Mason were named to the all-tournament team.

For the third straight year, the Tide drew a tough mountain team for an opening opponent in the Sweet 16. This time it was Carr Creek, the 14th region champs.

This was an historic state tournament, one in which "King" Kelly Coleman scored 185 points in four games, including 68 against Bell County. This was the tournament Freddie Maggard etched his name into Sweet 16 lore by becoming a two time last-second assassin. This was also the tournament most experts predicted that the Central City-Carr Creek survivor would be the team that took home all the marbles.

And the experts were correct.

In an overtime thriller, Carr Creek, thanks to a buzzer-beating Maggard jumper, knocked off the Tide 70-68. It was then, and it remains so to this day, perhaps the most painful loss in Central City history.

Playing without Duvall, and with Withrow slowed by early foul troubles, the Tide fell behind 31-19. With the game slipping away, Delmas Gish elected to put Withrow back in the game. Fueled by six Thompson points and four from Withrow, the Tide narrowed the gap to 33-28 by intermission.

The third quarter belonged to Withrow, who scored 20 of his team's 27 points as the Tide forged ahead 55-52 heading into the final frame. In his third-quarter explosion, Withrow made good on 10 of 11 field goal attempts.

The Tide led throughout most of the fourth quarter, and were sitting on a 68-66 lead with 13 seconds remaining after Jamison made good on the first of two free tosses. But when the second attempt missed, the Indians' E.A. Couch rebounded and was fouled by Jamison. Couch calmly sank both freebies to send the game into overtime.

The Tide controlled the tip but committed a turnover before getting off a shot. The Indians held the ball until Maggard sent up his dagger with nine seconds left. That was the deciding bucket.

Two days later, Maggard did the same thing to Kelly Coleman, hitting a last-second jumper to beat Wayland 68-67. Without Maggard's heroics, no way does Carr Creek win it all.

Withrow, in his final game, led all scorers with 34 points. Thompson, a junior, finished with 18.

Bobby Shepherd had 26 points for the Indians, while Maggard ended the game with 15, 10 coming in the fourth quarter and the OT.

The big question that haunts: What would have been the outcome of this game had Duvall been able to play? In a game so close, his 10-point scoring average looms pretty big.

Withrow was named to the all-tournament team. He was also named first-team all-state by the Louisville *Courier-Journal*, Lexington *Herald-Leader* and the *Paducah Sun*. In addition to those honors, he was a first-team All-America selection.

The Corky Withrow Era was now officially over. Gone was the player responsible for 3,136 points, 119 victories and three trips to the state tournament. And his absence resulted in back-to-back seasons that were far from impressive.

Chapter 25

1956-57

Corky Withrow's absence was felt immediately and with great force. The next two Central City teams had a combined won-loss record of 38-29, and with rare exceptions, seldom performed at a high level. There were some talented players, but the positive results simply weren't there. Something kept these two Golden Tide teams from achieving consistent success.

"Those two teams weren't very good," Frankie Mercer said. "We had some good players, but something was missing, something that kept us from winning more than we did. What was missing was chemistry. Those teams didn't have good chemistry."

At the end of this unsuccessful two-year period, Delmas Gish would call it quits, handing the reins to ex-Tide player Jackie Day.

The 1956-57 team, which ended with a 20-15 record, had one returning starter, and he was a good one. Winfred Thompson, now a senior, was the clear leader of this team. Also returning were Johnny Lile, Jimmy Swann, Earl Goode and Carroll Harrison. The new faces included Frankie Mercer, Tommy Barnett, Lewis Carr, Byron Bailey, and a pair of very talented sophomores—Lance Gish and Lewis Chaney.

For the opener at Bremen, the starting quintet featured Thompson, Swann, Lile and rookies Gish and Chaney. The Tide struggled to a 62-56 win thanks to 12 second-half points from Barnett. Chaney led the winners with 14 points, while Swann had 11 and Thompson 10.

Thompson broke loose for 27 points, Gish added 16 and Lile 12 in a 75-67 win over Livermore, then Thompson tossed in 17, Gish 14, Lile 13 and Chaney 11 as Tide beat Calhoun 65-56.

Dunmor had closed its doors after 1956 and merged with Hughes-Kirk. This meant ex-Dunmor star R.C. McElwain was now a Tiger, and with him scoring 27 points and Jimmy Harper adding 17, Hughes-Kirk beat the Tide 67-62.

Chaney had 23 points for the Tide, with Lile and Thompson adding 14 and 11, respectively.

Behind 33 points from Thompson and 12 from Gish, the Tide got back on the winning track by beating Drakesboro 61-50. Those winning ways didn't last long, though, thanks to a 26-point effort from Johnny Roark that lifted Graham past the Tide 62-61.

Thompson had 19 and Lile 18 in a losing effort.

With Mercer, another talented sophomore, replacing Swann in the starting lineup, the Tide began a five-game winning streak by beating Muhlenberg Central 70-55. Thompson led a balanced scoring attack with 16 points. Gish and Lile each had 14 and Chaney added 13. Mercer, in his debut start, finished with six points.

Larry Cary led all scorers with 19 points.

In an historic game that saw the first African-American athlete compete against a Muhlenberg County team, the Tide, riding a 31-point performance from Lile, beat visiting Somerset 76-70. Lile received plenty of help from Gish and Chaney, who had 14 and 13 points, respectively.

Howard Cunningham, the player who broke the color barrier, had 14 for Somerset.

Facing a Greenville team now coached by ex-Tide player Hugh Vernon Smith, it was Thompson who put up the big numbers—30 points—as the Tide claimed a 66-63 victory. Gish also hit double figures with 12.

Kenny Arbuckle led the Blackhawks with 18 points.

Traveling to Louisvlle to participate in the Fern Creek Invitational, the Tide opened with a solid 75-65 win over the host school. Chaney had 27 points in this win, followed by Thompson with 20 and Lile with 11.

Behind 25 points from Lile and 23 from Chaney, the Tide advanced with a superb 81-62 win over Louisville Southern. Gish had 11, Thompson 10 and Swann, now back as a starter, added eight.

The Tide's run to the title ended with a 74-58 loss to Earlington. Pat Kirkwood paced the winners with 23 points, while 6'8" first-team all-state performer Harry Todd had 19.

Lile, in another strong effort, led all scorers with 24.

That setback sent the Tide into a downward spiral that saw them drop seven of their next 10 games, including both outings in the Central City Invitational, making this the first time they had failed to win their own tourney.

In the CCIT, the Tide lost to Hartford 54-46 and Hughes-Kirk 66-65. Thompson had 17 against Hartford and 16 against Hughes-Kirk, a total matched by Gish. Chaney and Mercer each contributed 10 in that loss to the Tigers.

Jimmy Harper had 21 for Hughes-Kirk.

The Tide won their next two games, beating Owensboro Catholic 83-70 behind 22 points from Gish, 20 from Thompson, 14 from Chaney and 10 from Mercer. Next, the Tide pounded a good Beaver Dam squad 82-64 to up their record to 11-5. Thompson and Chaney were the big guns, finishing with 26 and 20 points, respectively. Gish chipped in with 16, while Lile added 15.

Jimmy Brown and Jerry Singleton paced Beaver Dam with 23 points each.

After giving a strong performance against Beaver Dam, the Tide slipped off the edge, dropping five of their next six games. The lone victory was a 70-68 win over Bowling Green. In that game Lile led with 21 points.

The losses were administered by Sedalia 83-72, Hartford 63-53, Owensboro 73-68, Graham 61-57 in overtime and Daviess County 99-78.

There were some decent individual efforts along the way, particularly from Chaney, who had 26 against Sedalia, 18 against Hartford, 17 against Owensboro and 32 against Daviess County. Goode also had a couple of nice outings, scoring 15 in the Owensboro loss and 10 against Graham, while Brand, subbing for Thompson, scored 15 in the loss to Daviess County.

The problem was several opponents were putting up better numbers. E.C. Guthrie and John Key scored 27 and 26, respectively, for Sedalia; Gerald Daniel had 20 for Hartford; Johnny Roark 24 for Graham; Ronnie Wells 21, Bobby Rascoe 20 and Don Crosley 18 for Daviess County.

Making matters worse, the Tide were now without Thompson, who went down with an injury, causing him to miss three games.

Following the Daviess County debacle, the Tide managed to right the ship by notching wins over Drakesboro 84-54 and Paducah Tilghman 59-55. In the win over Drakesboro, Chaney led a balanced attack with 19 points. Others in double figures included Lile (16), Goode (13), Swann (11) and Gish (10). Against Paducah, Lile had 19, Gish 17, Chaney and Goode 11 each.

Once again, the Tide, after taking one step forward took two steps back, losing to Heath 58-54 and Madisonville 69-66. Chaney continued to sizzle, accounting for 21 points in the loss to Heath. Thompson, in his first game off the disabled list, added 14. Against Madisonville, Thompson scored 24 points and Chaney had 18.

At this stage, with a 14-12 record and no guarantee of a winning season, the Tide actually began to play much better basketball, ending the regular season with four victories in their final five games, beginning with a 78-64 win over Muhlenberg Central. In that game, Lile had 23 points, Thompson 21, Chaney 13 and Gish 11.

The Spartans were led by Frank Fitzhugh's 16 points.

A 33-point effort by Chaney wasn't enough to keep Greenville from handing the Tide an 83-70 setback. Chaney had 11 field goals and 11 free throws to account for his season-best outing. Thompson and Gish each had 14 points in that loss.

Kenny Arbuckle paced the winners with 23 points, while Donald Addison added 19.

The Tide managed a measure of revenge in their next three games, beating Hughes-Kirk 78-73, Earlington 75-67 despite 40 points from Harry Todd, and Owensboro 81-66 in the Sportscenter.

Todd's 40 points matched "King" Kelly Coleman for the most scored against a Central City team. Their record would be broken a year later by Hughes-Kirk's Jimmy Harper.

Lile led the way against Hughes-Kirk with 25 points. Gish ended the game with 19 and Chaney had 10.

The Tigers' R.C. McElwain topped all scorers with 28 points.

Against Earlington, Thompson scored 29 points, Chaney 17 and Lile 13. In the win over Owensboro, Thompson had 28, Lile 19, Gish 14 and Chaney 10.

More revenge was necessary if the Tide hoped to advance in post-season play. Their district tournament opening-round foe was Graham, a team that owned a pair of wins over the Tide. In this third meeting, the Tide used a strong fourth-quarter effort to post an 80-69 win. Leading 54-51 heading into those final eight minutes, the Tide got 12 points from Lile and eight from Chaney to break the game open.

Lile finished with 24 points and Chaney had 18, a total matched by Gish.

Chaney scored 25 points and Lile had 20 as the Tide beat Muhlenberg Central 82-64 to earn a spot in the title game and a ticket to the regional tournament. This was another solid all-around effort by the Tide, with Gish scoring 14, Thompson 10, Swann seven and Goode six.

Jerry Shanks led MC with 16 points.

In the championship game, Greenville's Donald Addison scored 29 points and John Smith added 22 to lead the Blackhawks to an 81-67 victory. This was Greenville's second win in three games against the Tide, marking the first time the Blackhawks captured the season series.

Thompson paced the Tide with 18 points. Chaney had 16 and Gish 12.

Hartford, a team with a pair of wins over the Tide, was the regional tournament opponent. This time, however, there would be no payback. The Mustangs built a big lead, then held on down the stretch to escape with a 66-64 win.

Thompson, playing his final game, led all scorers with 25 points. Chaney was the only other Tide player in double figures with 14.

The Tide finished the season with 20 wins and 15 losses. Those 15 losses were the most ever suffered by a Golden Tide team up to this point.

Scoring for this team was very interesting. Thompson's numbers were 542 points for a 16.9 average. Others were Chaney 538/15.8, Lile 470/13.4 and Gish 416/11.9.

Here's another interesting tidbit: This was the first Golden Tide team to have more than one player score 30 points in a game. Thompson and Chaney did it twice, Lile once.

Although Thompson, Lile, Swann and Brand would be departing via graduation, a solid group was set to return, including Chaney, Gish, Mercer, Goode and Barnett. The nucleus for a strong team was definitely present. A big turnaround was seen as a real possibility.

But that turnaround never happened. An even more dismal season lay ahead, one that would be the swan song for Delmas Gish.

Chapter 26

1957-58

Delmas Gish's final season as Central City's head coach was not a good one. Despite the presence of several talented and experienced players, this club could do no better than an 18-14 record. Eighteen wins were the fewest by a Golden Tide team since 1925-26.

Perhaps this team's poor showing was rooted in that "lack of chemistry" pointed out by Frankie Mercer. Whatever the cause, this team was just not very good.

Juniors Mercer, Lance Gish, Lewis Chaney and Tommy Barnett were all back, along with senior Earl Goode. Those five would be the starters for much of the season. Joining them were Carroll Harrison, Jack Simpson, Lewis Carr, Terrill Mayes, Ben Mac Wolfe, Byron Bailey and Eddie Vincent.

Even the majority of wins for this team were a struggle, beginning with a 68-60 victory over Bremen. Gish led the Tide with 23 points, followed by Chaney's 21.

Gish hit for 23 points, Chaney 19 and Goode 13 as the Tide beat Hughes-Kirk 66-58 despite 24 points from the Tigers' Jimmy Harper. In their next outing, Gish scored 20 and Chaney 14, but the Tide dropped a 55-53 home-court decision to Dawson Springs.

Mike Ridley led Dawson Springs with 17 points.

The Tide improved to 4-1 with wins over a pair of district foes, getting past Graham 82-66 and Drakesboro 62-39. Goode had 20 points, Gish 18, Chaney 14 and Barnett 10 in the win over Graham, then Gish scored 20, Chaney 17 and Barnett 11 against the Cardinals.

In the Graham game, Doug Strader burned the Tide for 33 points.

Early in the Tide's next game, Gish went down with an injury that sidelined him for two games. Not surprisingly, without their leading scorer the Tide lost all three games. All three setbacks were on the road, starting with a 56-39 loss at Somerset. Chaney, with 11 points, was the only Tide player in double figures.

On the second leg of this road trip, Clay County slapped the Tide 76-63. Barnett scored 20 points and Goode had 18 for the Tide.

At Greenville, the Blackhawks made it three in a row over the Tide with a 69-58 win. Donald Addison and Jerry Smith led the winners with 18 points apiece. Goode and Barnett each had 14 and Chaney 12 for the Tide.

With Gish back in the lineup, and with all five starters hitting for double figures, the Tide easily disposed of Calhoun 80-47 in the first round of the Central City Invitational. Chaney paced the winners with 24 points, while Mercer had 13, Goode 12, Barnett 11 and Gish 10.

In the title game, the Tide overcame a 39-point performance from Bobby Bland to edge past Leitchfield 78-70 in overtime. The game was knotted 69-69 at the end of regulation, but the Tide won the OT 9-1 to get the victory.

Once again all five starters hit for double digits, led by Chaney with 24. Others included Barnett with 17, Mercer 13, Goode and Gish 11 each.

Chaney continued to sizzle, hitting for 20 points in a 65-47 win over Owensboro Catholic in the Sportscenter. Gish chipped in with 14 points, Mercer 12 and Barnett 11.

Playing at Beaver Dam, the Tide gave a strong performance before falling 67-63 to the eventual 4th region champs. The Tide trailed by eight heading into the final quarter, closed the difference to a bucket, only to come up short.

Chaney and Gish paced the Tide with 25 and 22 points, respectively. Beaver Dam was led by Jimmy Brown and Donnie Hoskins with 16 points each.

In another overtime thriller, Jerry Shanks knocked in a bucket and Dwain Jones hit a pair of free throws to lift Muhlenberg Central to a 65-63 victory. With the game tied 61-61, Shanks and Jones wrapped their four points around a lone Gish field goal to account for the difference.

Larry Cary led all scorers with 23 points, while Shanks added 15. For the Tide, Chaney had 22, Gish 15 and Mercer 13.

Gish exploded for 34 points to lead the Tide past Hartford 83-61. Gish hit nine field goals and 16 free tosses against the Mustangs. Goode had 17 and Chaney 11 for the Tide.

Cecil Goff led Hartford with 19 points.

Turning in another superb effort, the Tide blasted home-standing Bowling Green 76-43. Gish had 21 points, Chaney 18, Barnett 15 and Goode 12 for the winners.

For much of the next game it appeared as if the Tide would continue their winning ways. They led Owensboro 53-48 after three quarters, then were outscored 21-12 during the final eight minutes to suffer a 69-65 loss. Harold Pugh led the Red Devils with 21 points.

Goode scored a game-high 23 in a losing effort.

At home, with four starters hitting for double figures, the Tide posted a 59-50 revenge over Clay County. Goode paced the Tide with 15 points, while Barnett had 12, Chaney and Mercer 11 apiece.

All-state standout and future WKU star Bobby Rascoe banged in 27 points to lead a strong Daviess County team to a come-from-behind 81-76 win in Central City. The Tide led 44-41 at intermission, but with Rascoe scoring 19 of his points in the second half, the visitors proved to be too strong. This Panthers team would eventually advance to the championship game of the state tournament, losing to St. Xavier in the title tilt.

Rascoe received plenty of support from Ronnie Wells and 6'8" Don Crosley, both of whom had 14 points.

Gish had 22 for the Tide, followed by Chaney with 20 and Mercer with 13.

Giving a less-than-standout performance, the Tide did just enough to get past Calhoun 52-47. Chaney topped the scoring with 19 points. Gish had 16 and Mercer 12 for the winners.

Nine different Tide players scored in an easy 74-25 romp past Drakesboro. Gish had 17 points, Goode 16, Mercer 14, Chaney 11, Barnett six, Harrison four, Bailey three, Wolfe two and Mayes one.

Unable to defend their own court, the Tide dropped back-to-back home games, losing to Paducah Tilghman 80-65 and Madisonville 66-65. Chaney scored 20, Barnett 19 and Gish 13 in that loss to Paducah.

Paul Holland had 23 for the winners.

Against the Maroons, the Tide led at the end of the first three quarters, only to fold in the final stanza. Gish paced the Tide with 22 points, Mercer and Chaney each had 13 and Goode 12.

With a 12-10 record and the regular campaign heading for the finish line, this team needed to turn things around and play with more consistency if it entertained any hopes for post-season success. And that's exactly what happened. The Tide won four of their next five games, including an 81-62 win over Greenville.

The Tide began their run by beating Muhlenberg Central 88-79 in Powderly. They won it despite a 30-point performance from MC's Larry Cary, who didn't even start the game.

To get this win, the Tide got a huge boost from Harrison, who came off the bench to score 10 points. In this game, six Tide players cracked double figures, led by Gish with 25. Others included Barnett (14), Chaney (13), Mercer (12) and Goode (10).

Behind 22 points from Gish and 21 each from Goode and Barnett, the Tide snapped their three-game losing streak to Greenville by posting that 81-62 win. The Blackhawks, who were without the services of Addison, were led by Charlie Summers with 22 points.

Chaney snapped out of a mini-slump to score 20 points in a 78-68 victory over Hughes-Kirk. Chaney received support from Goode with 15 points, Gish 13 and Barnett 10.

Jimmy Harper led the Tigers with 25 points.

Earlington hit town, and thanks to a 41-point performance from Harry Todd, left with an 84-65 win. The game was up for grabs after three quarters, with the visitors clinging to a 58-56 lead. But in the final stanza, Earlington outscored the Tide 26-9 to pull away for the win.

Todd's 41 points were the most scored against a Central City team, breaking the old mark of 40 he shared with "King" Kelly Coleman.

Chaney led the Tide with 20 points, while Goode finished with 16 and Barnett 12.

With Goode hitting for 29 points, Barnett 22, Gish 20 and Chaney 18, the Tide stormed to a convincing 104-76 victory at Graham.

Doug Strader led Graham with 23 points, while Ralph Evitts, a future Golden Tide assistant coach, added 10.

In the season finale, Owensboro's Harold Pugh scored 34 points to lead the Red Devils to a 75-72 win. The Tide had three more field goals (30-27) than the visitors, but lost it at the charity stripe, where Owensboro won that contest 21-12.

Gish scored 20 for the Tide. Chaney finished with 18, Mercer 16 and Barnett 10.

The district tournament opener against Hughes-Kirk turned out to be a win for the Tide and a record-shattering showcase for Tiger guard Jimmy Harper. The Tide claimed a 78-58 win despite 53 points from Harper, who had 17 field goals and hit 19 free throws. It was a singular performance, one player scoring all but five of his team's total points.

Harper's 53 points remain the most scored by a Golden Tide opponent.

Goode was splendid for the winners, knocking down 27 points. Gish and Barnett added 20 and 14, respectively.

Facing Drakesboro Community for the first time, the Tide advanced to the district title game with an 83-62 win. This marked the first appearance in district action by the Buffaloes, who were led by John Frazier's 29 points.

With Gish injured and unable to play, the Tide had little chance of beating a strong Muhlenberg Central team in the championship game. And they didn't, losing 81-68. Frank Fitzhugh paced the Spartans attack with 24 points. Larry Cary and Jerry Shanks each contributed 16.

Barnett had 20 to lead the Tide. Mercer scored 16, Goode 11 and Wolfe, coming off the bench, added 10.

Paired off against Beaver Dam in the regional tournament opener, the Tide, in what had to be the most-exciting game—and most-heartbreaking loss—of the season, dropped a 75-74 overtime decision.

The Beavers were in front 39-30 at the half but the Tide fought back to take a 51-50 lead after three quarters. Regulation play ended with the two teams knotted at 66-66. In OT, Beaver Dam won it by hitting seven free throws and one field goal, while the Tide made good on three buckets and a pair of free tosses.

Gish and Barnett shared scoring honors for the Tide with 18 points each. Chaney added 12 and Goode, in his final game, had a dozen.

Beaver Dam's powerful duo of Jimmy Brown and Dickie Curtis led all scorers with 31 and 28 points, respectively. Twenty-three of Brown's points came at the free throw stripe.

The loss left the Tide with a final 18-14 record.

Following the game, Delmas Gish announced that he was stepping down as Golden Tide coach, handing the job to Jackie Day, a former Golden Tide player and assistant coach. Gish certainly didn't walk away from a busted flush. No, Gish departed while still holding a stacked deck.

And Day, in his debut season, would turn it into a winning hand.

Chapter 27

1958-59

Jackie Day had been a three-year starter on Tide basketball and baseball teams, helping lead both sports to the state tournament. In fact, Day is the only Golden Tide player to hit a home run in state tourney action.

Day earned his degree at WKU and then returned to Central City to serve as assistant basketball coach and head baseball coach for the 1954-55 season. During that year, he guided the Golden Tide to the semifinals of the state baseball tournament. Following three years in the Air Force, he answered the call to step in and replace Delmas Gish as head basketball coach. It's a position he would hold for the next 14 years, during which his teams won 333 games and made two appearances in the Sweet 16, with his 1965-66 club advancing to the semifinals.

Day was welcomed on board by a senior-heavy, experienced group of players, headed by a trio of three-year starters—Lance Gish, Lewis Chaney and Frankie Mercer. Tommy Barnett, another veteran, was also back, along with Terrill Mayes, Ben Mac Wolfe, Jack Simpson and newcomers Jerry Mayes, Sonny Stone, Carl White, Eddie Vincent, Gene Dillingham, Dick Kirtley, Jimmy Lynch and Lloyd "B.B." Williams.

This was a team with all the necessary requirements for success—experience, size, strength, depth and offensive firepower. There was a lingering question, however. Would this group somehow pass the chemistry test that Mercer says haunted the previous two teams?

Seniors Gish, Chaney, Mercer and Barnett, along with junior Wolfe, were the starters in the Tide's opening-game 79-64 win at Bremen. Gish led a balanced scoring attack with 17 points, followed by Mercer with 16, Chaney 15, Barnett 13, Wolfe and Terrill Mayes six each, Vincent with four and Simpson with two.

Bremen was paced by Wayne Burch's 14 points. R.T. Jarvis and Carroll Nelson each contributed 12.

In a tense struggle against visiting Dawson Springs, the Tide, with Gish and Mercer scoring 25 and 20 points, respectively, edged to a hard-fought 89-85 victory. Barnett chipped in with 18 points, Chaney 14 and Terrill Mayes 11.

Dawson Springs' Billy Seibert led all scorers with 28.

Gish erupted for 32 points as the Tide ripped Leitchfield 80-43 in the first of six straight runaway victories. Chaney had 13 points, Barnett 11 and Wolfe 10 in that win over Leitchfield.

The Tide followed that outing with wins over South Hopkins 89-64, Calhoun 94-57, Drakesboro Community 85-53, Graham 75-56 and Drakesboro 85-44. At this stage, the Tide, sitting on an 8-0 record, had moved up to No. 4 in the Lit Ratings.

Against South Hopkins, Gish had 24 points and Chaney added 21. Barnett and Mercer also cracked double digits with 19 and 11, respectively. Chaney took scoring honors with 24 points against Calhoun, with Gish adding 22, Mercer 16 and Wolfe 13.

In the Tide's first regular-season meeting against Drakesboro Community, Gish scored 18, Barnett 15, Mercer and Chaney 13 each.

Leroy "Kilroy" Willis paced the Buffaloes with 23 points.

Mercer hit for 22 points to lead the way in the win over Graham. Gish finished with 19 and Chaney 14 in that victory. In the romp past Drakesboro, Gish led with 28 points, while Chaney and Wolfe contributed 13 each.

In an odd twist that proves winning doesn't always matter, the Tide, still undefeated, dropped to No. 15 in the Lit Ratings.

The First Tournament, the First Loss

Few Central City teams before or since were more tournament-tested than this one. In all, counting post-season action, this Tide club participated in six tournaments, beginning with a visit to the Beaver Dam Invitational, where they would fall from the ranks of the unbeaten.

Despite a career-best 41 points from Gish, the Tide were upset by Hartford 80-78 in the tourney opener. Gish scorched the nets, hitting for 15 field goals and all 11 of his free throw attempts. Chaney, with 13 points, was the only other Tide player to hit double figures.

But Gish's total was overwhelmed by the combined 70 points scored by Hartford's Cecil Goff, Jim Stanley and Dave Cordrey. Goff and Stanley each had 25 and Cordrey 20 for the winners.

With Chaney and Gish each registering 23 points and Mercer 12, the Tide bounced back to beat Breckinridge County 75-64 in the consolation game. This would be the first of two meetings against the Bearcats, with much more riding on the second one.

Minus the injured Chaney, the Tide got 32 points from Gish and 19 each from Mercer and Terrill Mayes in an easy 96-50 win over Greenville. Wolfe hit for 11 points and Simpson eight in this win.

Greenville was led by Roger Hedrick with 16 points.

For the second time, the Tide suffered a stunning opening-round tournament loss, this one a 68-66 decision to Hughes-Kirk in the Central City Invitational. With the count knotted 53-53 after three quarters, George Mohon scored seven of his 17 points in the final stanza to lift the Tigers to the win. Shelby Pogue led the winners with 23 points.

Gish had 26 and Chaney 13 for the Tide.

Facing a good Hopkinsville team in the consolation game, the Tide claimed another third-place trophy with a convincing 82-63 victory. Gish topped the scoring with 24 points, while Barnett had 22, Mercer 19 and Chaney 10.

Gish racked up 31 points and Mercer added 18 as the Tide clubbed Owensboro Catholic 92-57 to improve their record to 12-2. This game also served as a tune-up for the season's first encounter with a very strong and talented Muhlenberg Central squad.

Choosing to slow the pace rather than run and gun, the Spartans built a slim lead and then managed to hang on during crunch time to claim a 54-52 win. The Spartan trio of Larry Cary, Dwain Jones and Jerry Shanks did virtually all the damage, accounting for 52 of their team's 54 points. Cary and Jones each had 18, with Shanks tossing in 16.

Mercer paced the Tide with 18 points.

Teams were now being evaluated for a bid to the prestigious Louisville Invitational Tournament, and Central City was in the mix. But with three losses in their past seven games, the Tide, if they didn't want to see their opportunity slip away, needed to win and win impressively.

That's exactly what they did, beginning with an 84-68 win over a strong Beaver Dam club. Chaney snapped out of the doldrums to pour in 30 points for the winners. Gish finished with 21 and Barnett 13.

Jimmy Brown led Beaver Dam with 23 points, while Dickie Curtis added 21.

The win over Beaver Dam must have convinced the LIT selection committee, because the next day the Tide received an invitation.

With the LIT question now answered, Gish scored 25 points, Wolfe 19 and Chaney 14 as the Tide earned a bit of revenge by beating Hartford 66-61 in Beaver Dam.

Hartford's Cecil Goff tied Gish for game-high honors with 25.

It took an all-around sold effort for the Tide to get past Owensboro 75-69 in the Sportscenter. Four Tide players hit double figures, led by Gish's 21. Others included Chaney (18), Barnett (17) and Mercer (14).

Future Kentucky Mr. Basketball Randy Embry led the Red Devils with 20 points.

Staying in Owensboro, the Tide, fueled by 23 points from Gish and 20 from Mercer, beat Daviess County 65-56. In their final game prior to the LIT, Gish had 25 points, Mercer 14, Barnett 12 and Chaney 11 in an easy 74-52 win over Graham.

The LIT and Those Spartans Again

The Tide's opening-round opponent in the LIT was Ahrens, and the game was never in doubt. Thanks to 13 first-quarter points from Gish, the Tide raced to a 25-12 lead after one stop and never looked back, winning easily 93-50.

Gish ended the game with 27 points. Chaney had 16, Mercer and Barnett 12 apiece.

In quarterfinal action, powerful Louisville Male, led by the trio of Everett Stallworth, Henry Jones and Melvin Green, rolled to a convincing 94-66 win over the Tide. Stallworth and Jones each had 28 points, Green had 24.

This would be the Tide's last loss until the Sweet 16.

Gish, who earned a spot on the All-LIT squad, led the Tide with 32 points. Mercer contributed a dozen.

Making matters worse, Wolfe suffered a broken hand in the loss to Male, an injury that sidelined him for the next eight games.

With a second showdown against Muhlenberg Central looming on the horizon, the Tide first had to take care of Madisonville, which they did, winning 75-64 on the road. Gish had 29 points for the Tide. Chaney tossed in 22, Barnett 13 and Mercer 11 against the Maroons.

The Tide hosted Muhlenberg Central seeking revenge for an earlier loss and their 20th win of the season. As expected, the game was a war with neither team able to establish clear-cut authority. After a 32-32 deadlock at intermission, the Tide eased in front early in the third frame, then hung on in the waning minutes to post a 79-73 win.

Mercer was a man in this game, scoring 24 points before fouling out. In all, four Tide starters went to the bench with five fouls. Gish aided Mercer with 20 points, while Chaney had 18 and Barnett 13.

Jerry Shanks and Larry Cary paced the Spartans with 23 and 22 points, respectively.

These two teams would meet a third time in an infamous game that will forever be remembered for a strange and questionable coach's decision.

Behind 19 points each from Mercer and Gish and 18 apiece from Chaney and Terrill Mayes, the Tide won an 88-70 decision at Greenville. A huge third quarter that saw the Tide outscore Greenville 32-16 was enough to break the game open.

Johnny Vogler led the Blackhawks with 18 points.

Even without Chaney, the Tide had no trouble with Drakesboro, winning 72-47. Gish had 27 points and Mercer 18 in that win. A second encounter with Dawson Springs proved to be as challenging as the earlier one. But with Chaney back in uniform and racking up 26 points, the Tide won 70-65. Barnett and Gish each ended the night with 12 points, while Mayes added 11.

Chaney sizzled for 25 points to help the Tide maul Calhoun 101-48. In all, 11 Tide players scored, including Gish with 21, Mercer 15, Barnett and Mayes eight each, Stone with five, Simpson, Jerry Mayes, Lloyd "B.B." Willams and Bobby Tatum all with four apiece.

Twenty points each from Chaney and Gish were enough to power the Tide past South Hopkins 76-65. Barnett scored 14 points, Mercer 12 and Mayes eight in the win.

In the final regular-season game, the Tide were pushed to the limit before finally getting away with a 67-63 overtime win over Owensboro.

Chaney had another big night, ending with a game-best 22 points. Barnett scored 16 and Gish 14 in a winning effort.

The Post-Season Journey Begins

The Tide's district tourney opening-round foe was a dangerous one, a Hughes-Kirk team that owned a win in the only meeting during the season between the two squads. And that win came on the Tide's home court during the CCIT. This second meeting would take place on neutral territory—MC's gym.

But in this crucial meeting, seniors Gish, Chaney and Mercer were not about to lose a second time to the Tigers. Gish scored 25 points, Chaney 21 and Mercer 13 as the Tide advanced with a 74-61 win.

Shelby Pogue paced the Tigers with 24 points.

The semifinal game against Graham was a different story. In this one the Tide had to struggle in order to get past a team they had twice destroyed during the regular season. Thanks to 24 points from Gish, with Barnett and Mercer contributing 16 and 12, respectively, the Tide stayed alive by nipping upset-minded Graham 63-58.

Wayne Earle led the Nighthawks with 15 points.

That victory set up not only a title-game battle against Muhlenberg Central but also the rubber match between the two teams, who split the two regular-season games. This was a highly anticipated game that everyone agreed would likely be a down-to-the-wire battle for supremacy.

But it never happened. The battle ended before it began, thanks to the line-up card turned in by Spartan coach L.B. Gaston. In one of the most mystifying, uncalled for and asinine decisions ever made by any coach, Gaston chose to keep his three best players on the bench for the entire game.

Why Gaston elected to make such a move is anyone's guess. Presumably, given that the Spartans were going to the regional tournament regardless of the outcome of the championship game, his only reasoning could have been to prevent an injury to a key player.

But with talented players Larry Cary, Jerry Shanks and Dwain Jones watching helplessly from the sidelines, the Spartans had no chance. The outcome of this game was decided before the tip-off.

The Tide won it 77-54. Gish led the Tide with 24 points, while Chaney had 14 and Wolfe, now off the injured list, added 11.

Gish and Mercer were voted onto the all-district team.

Not surprisingly, Gaston's strange move did not go over well with Spartan fans, many of whom whistled and booed during the game, then demanded a refund when the contest was over. It's safe to say Gaston could not have been elected dog catcher after that game. Only a trip to the state tourney could have saved his reputation, and that didn't happen.

A familiar face was missing when the regional tournament rolled around. For whatever reason, Barnett was suddenly MIA. Why he was absent remains something of a mystery, although the official party line said he was ill with the flu.

At any rate, with Barnett out, this meant that for the second time this season, a Mayes was asked to step in and fill some big shoes. This time it was sophomore Jerry Mayes who would handle Barnett's guard spot in the tourney opener against Breckinridge County.

After a slow start in which they found themselves on the short end of a 16-9 first-quarter score, the Tide exploded for 29 second-quarter points to take a 38-26 lead at the half. In that decisive quarter, Gish tallied eight points, Chaney seven, Mercer and Wolfe six each.

Now firmly in control, the Tide cruised to an 86-71 victory behind a 32-point effort by Gish. Chaney and Mercer each finished with 18 points, and Jerry Mayes, in his first start, scored eight points while successfully running the offense.

The semifinal game against Flaherty was expected to be little more than a walk-through practice session for the Tide. But when the game got underway it quickly became clear that the Flaherty players hadn't received that message.

Playing fearlessly against the higher ranked Tide, the upstart Blue Devils took a 31-28 lead into the locker room at the half. It was a game that had the feel of upset written all over it. If the Tide hoped to avoid disaster, they needed to take control in the third quarter, which they did, carving out a slight 50-47 advantage with the final eight minutes still to go.

The Blue Devils never gave in, but with Chaney accounting for eight fourth-quarter points and Gish seven, the Tide managed to survive with a hard-earned 66-60 win.

Gish led all scorers with 25 points, with Chaney tossing in 19 and Wolfe 12.

All that stood between the regional title and a trip to the Sweet 16 was home-standing Beaver Dam, a club the Tide handled 84-68 during a regular-season meeting. Once again, it was seniors Gish and Chaney who provided the firepower that carried the Tide to a 71-58 victory.

The two veterans combined for 56 points—Gish with 30, Chaney 26—to send the Tide to the state tournament for the fifth time in the 1950s and the 15th time in school history.

This was not an easy win; the Tide only led 48-42 heading into the final quarter. With the outcome still very much in doubt, Chaney and Gish went to work, combining for 21 of the Tide's 23 fourth-quarter points. In those eight minutes Chaney had 11 points and Gish 10.

Jimmy Brown led Beaver Dam with 17 points.

Gish and Chaney were named to the all-regional squad.

The Tide's first-round state tourney opponent was highly ranked Louisville Manual, the team picked to claim the title. It was also a team the Tide would have to face with the Barnett mystery hanging over their heads. Mystery or not, even with Barnett back in uniform, it was Jerry Mayes who remained in the starting lineup.

The first quarter belonged the Tide, who built a 19-13 lead on the strength of 12 Gish points. The second quarter was a flip-flop, with Manual outscoring the Tide 19-13 to make it 32-32 at the break.

But the second half was all Manual, which steadily pulled away for a 77-65 win.

Gish, who later was named to the all-tournament team, scored 25 points in his final game, while Chaney and Mercer, two more who were bowing out, added 13 and 11 points, respectively. Wolfe ended the game with 12 points and Jerry Mayes had four.

Gerald Glur and Tommy Milton led Manual with 18 points each.

The loss left the Tide with a final record of 32-5.

Gish had a monster senior season, scoring 893 points for a 24.1 average. As a senior, Gish never failed to hit double figures. For his career, Gish scored 1,817 points.

Chaney also had a big senior year, scoring 569 points for an average of 16.3. During his career, Chaney amassed 1,610 points.

Day had certainly been successful in his debut season at the helm. But with Gish, Chaney, Mercer, Barnett and Terrill Mayes saying goodbye, the prospects for 1959-60 looked iffy at best. Wolfe and Jerry Mayes would be the only returning players with much game-time experience.

But in what can only be described as a fortuitous stroke of luck, two players with size and talent decided to join the team for their senior year, while another player who would be a junior, opted to transfer to Central City.

With them on board, the 1959-60 team would be the tallest in Golden Tide history.

Chapter 28

1959-60

Along with 5'9" Jerry Mayes, the Tide did have two players returning with good size—Ben Mac Wolfe and Sonny Stone, both of whom stood about 6'4". But those were the only players with any height. Beyond those two the roster consisted of a group of small, scrappy guys who were virtually identical size-wise. Carl White, Lloyd "B.B." Williams, Dick Kirtley, Bobby Tatum, Jackie Welborn and Johnny Lewis all fit into the 5'9" to 5'11" range. Jimmy Lynch, at 6'1", had some size but no experience.

As the season approached, it appeared as if this was going to be a quick, guard-oriented team. But the Tide caught a break when a pair of seniors—6'4" Jimmy Simmons and 6'2" Pat Franklin—decided to put on the black and gold uniform. And if that weren't enough, Oscar Perry, a 6'2" junior and a deadly shooter, chose to transfer to Central City from Drakesboro.

Suddenly, the Tide had perhaps the tallest team in school history.

This would not be a great Golden Tide team, but with a final record of 23-10 it was certainly a club worthy of some merit.

Despite the influx of players with size, it was Mayes, the team's smallest starter, who bailed out the Tide in their season opener. With just seconds remaining, Mayes came through with a steal and layup to give the Tide a 50-49 win over Bremen. Mayes led the winners with 16 points, while Wolfe added 15.

Rounding out the starting quintet were Simmons, Stone and Kirtley.

Future Golden Tide coach Wayne Divine led all scorers with 21 points.

The Tide's three newcomers had very little impact in this game. Perry had six points, Franklin three and Simmons two.

Stone scored 21 points and Wolfe added 17 as the Tide made it two in a row by beating Drakesboro Community 65-55. For this game, Perry replaced Kirtley in the starting lineup.

Leroy "Kilroy" Willis had 25 points for the Buffaloes, while Curtis Shelton, whose son Curtis would later become a standout Tide player, scored 16.

The Tide upped their record to 4-0 with wins over South Hopkins 75-59 and Graham 58-44. Wolfe led the scoring in both outings, getting 23 against South Hopkins and 15 against Graham. In the first of those two games, Mayes scored 13, Simmons 12 and Perry 11. Simmons also hit for double figures with 11 against Graham.

Visiting Christian County handed the Tide their first setback by overcoming a 39-30 halftime deficit en route to a 75-63 victory. The Tide remained on top 52-49 after three quarters, but the Colonels blew it open in those final eight minutes.

Jackie Ladd led the winners with 21 points.

All five Tide starters hit double digits, led by Wolfe with 16. Stone had 15, Franklin and Mayes 11 each and Simmons 10.

The Tide jumped to a 22-14 first-quarter lead and never looked in posting a 63-56 win over Muhlenberg Central. Simmons paced the Tide with 19 points, with Wolfe and Mayes adding 18 and 14, respectively.

J.R. Goff was the game's leading scorer with 25 points.

Wolfe scored 16 points, Simmons 13 and Stone 12 to help send the Tide to a convincing 76-42 victory at Hopkinsville.

Sacramento, fresh from its visit to the 1959 state tournament, built a 35-28 first-half advantage, then held on to edge the Tide 70-68. Sacramento had five fewer field goals than the Tide, but won it by connecting on 28 free tosses.

Charlie Walls led the winners with 19 points. Lonie Frailey and Jackie Knight had 18 and 15, respectively.

Stone, Simmons and Mayes all had 16 points for the Tide.

Opening in the Central City Invitational, the Tide, sparked by 21 points from Wolfe, moved on to the title game by whipping Hartford 64-57. In the finals, Louisville Male, a team featuring three all-state players, captured the trophy with a 63-46 win.

Ronnie Phelps had 14 for Central, while big Everett Stallworth was limited to nine.

Wolfe had 13 and White 10 for the Tide.

Simmons knocked in 30 points to help the Tide get back on the winning track with an easy 85-46 laugher against Owensboro Catholic. Simmons, "Simo" to his teammates, had 12 field goals and six free throws to account for his total. Wolfe scored 15, with Stone and Mayes each chipping in 11.

At Muhlenberg Central, with Simmons tossing in 16 points and Stone 15, the Tide clipped the Spartans 59-53 in another tight, low-scoring affair. Wolfe also helped out with a 12-point effort.

Jerry Wright paced the Spartans with 19 points.

Staying on the road, the Tide fell to Beaver Dam 74-70 after owning the advantage heading into the final stanza. In that quarter, the Beavers, paced by Butch Hill, outscored the Tide 25-19 to get the victory. Hill led all scorers with 20 points, nine coming in those decisive eight minutes.

Mayes had 19 points, Simmons 18 and Stone 12 for the Tide.

Ohio County foes made it two straight when Hartford came to town and downed the Tide 66-54 behind a 23-point performance from Chip Combs. After leading 16-15 at the end of the first quarter, the Tide fell behind and were never able to catch up.

Wolfe was the lone standout for the Tide, ending with 21 points.

White, now Mayes' backcourt running mate, dropped in 17 points to help lift the Tide to a 61-50 win at Greenville. Stone had 14, while Simmons, who suffered a broken leg in this game, had 10.

Roger Hedrick scored 14 for Greenville.

With Simmons sidelined indefinitely, someone had to step up and fill his shoes, which Franklin did by coming off the bench to score 19 points in a 67-56 win over Drakesboro. Franklin scored 13 of his points in a second-half run that saw the Tide ease away for the victory.

Wolfe had 18, Mayes 12 and Williams nine in a superb effort off the bench.

Revenge is always sweet, and the Tide got a measure of it by outscoring Sacramento 21-6 in the final frame to earn an ugly 56-48 win. Wolfe and Mayes each had 11 points to lead the Tide.

Charlie Walls had 22 and Jackie Knight 20 for Sacramento.

Another fourth-quarter comeback and some solid play in overtime was enough to give the Tide a 57-54 win over visiting Daviess County. Trailing 47-39 after three quarters, the Tide limited Daviess County to five fourth-quarter points while managing to knot the count at 52-52. In OT, Wolfe hit a bucket and Mayes added three pressure-packed free throws while the defense held the Panthers to a pair of freebies.

Wolfe finished with 22 points. Mayes had 11 and Perry 10 for the Tide.

Franklin and Wolfe each scored 17 points, Mayes had 14 and White 11 as the Tide got the best of Graham 67-60 in the first of back-to-back wins.

Buddy Casebier led Graham with 19 points.

The Tide followed up by giving one their best performances of the season in winning at Trigg County 80-65. A smoldering first half that saw the Tide build a 49-33 advantage was the difference.

In this win, Wolfe had 26 points, Stone 20, White and Mayes 14 apiece.

The road trip ended in a split when Paducah Tilghman nipped the Tide 51-49. This would be the first of three losses in the Tide's next four outings.

Mayes and Stone paced the Tide with 14 and 10 points, respectively.

With four players hitting in double figures, topped by all-state performer Doug Walsh's 21 points, Madisonville crushed the Tide 74-48 in Central City. Walsh received plenty of help from Barry Teague with 15 points and Dave Maddox with 14.

Wolfe's 13 led the Tide.

In another thriller, the Tide survived to clip Bremen 61-57 in a big road win. Stone and Mayes were the chief architects of this victory, scoring 19 and 18 points, respectively.

Budgie Wilkins had 15 points for the Golden Eagles, while Bobby Creager added 14.

Greenville parlayed a big 17-8 first-quarter advantage into a 61-58 win on the Tide's home court. Roger Hedrick led a balanced Greenville attack with 14 points. Johnny Vogler and Roger Nofsinger each had 13 and Louie Stuart had 11.

Wolfe scored 14 for the Tide, Stone 11, Franklin and Mayes 10 apiece.

With Simmons now back and available for action, the Tide began a two-game winning streak by gliding past Drakesboro 55-50 in yet another ugly win. Stone paced the Tide with 14 points. Wolfe contributed 13, Franklin 10 and Simmons two in his first game back.

Drakesboro's Charlie Taylor led all scorers with 21 points.

Giving consecutive strong performances, the Tide blasted Dawson Springs 85-62 and South Hopkins 74-50. Wolfe had a big 23-point effort against Dawson Springs, getting help from Stone with 16, Franklin 15 and Simmons 10.

Against South Hopkins, it was Stone's turn to put up big numbers, finishing with 19 points. Wolfe had 14 points and Franklin 12 in that win.

Eddie Ford led South Hopkins with 18 points. Three decades later, the Tide would have to deal with Eddie's son, Travis, a standout at Madisonville-North Hopkins who went on to play at the University of Kentucky.

Closing out the regular season in the Sportscenter, the Tide ended on a down note, losing 58-48 to the Red Devils. Randy Embry had 17 points for the winners, who would later advance to the semifinals of the state tournament.

Stone and Wolfe each had 14 to lead the Tide.

In the district tournament opener against Muhlenberg Central, Franklin came through with 17 points, including 10 in the final quarter, to lift the Tide to a 67-57 victory. Wolfe chipped in with 15 points, Mayes 14 and Stone 10.

The Spartans were led by J.R. Goff with 12 points.

Facing a Greenville team they had split with during the regular campaign, the Tide claimed the rubber match with a surprisingly easy 61-45 win. Simmons led the way with 14 points. Stone and Wolfe each had 13 and Franklin added 10 for the Tide.

Johnny Vogler topped the Blackhawks with a dozen points.

Looming ahead in the championship game was Hughes-Kirk, a club the Tide had not met during the regular season and one many experts felt was the region's premier team, an assessment the Tigers came within a last-second shot of proving to be correct.

Playing one of their most-inspired games, the Tide battled powerful Hughes-Kirk down to the wire, eventually dropping a 75-73 overtime decision. This was a game of missed opportunities for both teams—for Hughes-Kirk to win more comfortably, for the Tide to pull off the upset. In the fourth quarter and the OT period, the two teams misfired on 10 free throws, five by each club.

The Tiger trio of Shelby Pogue, Donnie McDonald and Lamar Holland put the most hurt on the Tide combining for 64 points. Pogue had 27, McDonald 21 and Holland 16.

Wolfe scored 17 for the Tide, Simmons 16, Mayes 12 and Perry 11.

In the regional tournament opener, veterans Stone and Wolfe provided enough firepower to lift the Tide past Meade County 66-60. Stone led with 20 points and Wolfe added 19.

Bill Ditto had 19 points to lead Meade County.

The Tide's firepower continued as they built a 35-29 halftime lead over Hughes-Kirk in semifinal action. But the Tide's guns fizzled in the second half, with all the firepower now coming from the Tigers, who would storm to a comfortable 72-57 win.

Once again, the Tigers' big three did the damage, with Lamar Holland scoring 23 points, Pogue and McDonald 17 each.

The Tide also got superb performances from a trio of seniors. Wolfe closed out his career with a 21-point effort, while Simmons had 16 and Stone 10 in their final game.

Hughes-Kirk was denied a trip to the Sweet 16 when Gerald Hoskins nailed a last-second jumper to give Beaver Dam a 45-44 win in the title game.

The Tide, who ended the campaign with a final 23-10 record, would be saying farewell to their four tallest players, meaning that Jackie Day was not only staring at a rebuilding year, he was staring at a team with virtually no size or inside presence.

The start of a new decade was going to be interesting.

Chapter 29

1950s Sideline Shots (Part Two)

Black and Gold Wars

If Corky Withrow has a challenger as Muhlenberg County's greatest player, it would be Greenville's Roger Newman. According to Withrow, Newman rivaled the very best.

"I played against some of the greatest basketball players ever," Withrow said. "Oscar Robertson, Kelly Coleman, Jerry West, Dick Barnett, Jackie Moreland and Don Mills, just to name a few. And I can promise you, Roger was as good as any of those guys."

Not only did the basketball gods pit such supremely gifted players as Withrow and Newman against each other, they also placed them on a stage separated by a mere seven miles. For four years, in what is arguably the high point in Muhlenberg County basketball, these two bitter rivals (and good friends) engaged in a series of epic struggles, battling for team supremacy and personal bragging rights. Each game was nothing less than a war.

Withrow and Central City won all but one of those struggles against Newman's Blackhawks, yet it's the lone setback that still burns in Withrow's soul.

"At Greenville, sudden death," Withrow recalls, as if it happened yesterday. "Roger hit two free throws to beat us 51-49."

Withrow does have a single regret, one that would have been viewed as blasphemy by both Golden Tide and Blackhawks fans—that he and Newman weren't teammates.

"It's a shame we didn't go to the same school our senior year," Withrow said. "Either Central City or Greenville. If we'd been on the same team, no one would have touched us."

Corky vs. Roger

In the years between 1952 and 1956, Central City and Greenville faced off against each other 14 times. Withrow played in all 14 games, while Newman played in 11. In those 11 head-to-head battles, here is the scoring breakdown:

Year	Withrow	Newman
1952-53	4	9
1953-54	20	18
	20	10
	10	10
	18	13
1954-55	16	25
	27	27
	28	23
1955-56	22	30
	29	10
	10	22
Totals	**204**	**197**

All-Star Summer

During the summer of 1956, the two Muhlenberg County greats were teammates in a series of high-profile All-Star games. They were on the Kentucky All-Star team that competed against Oscar Robertson and his Indiana cohorts. They were on the West squad that was involved in a three-game series against an East team led by "King" Kelly Coleman. (Withrow scored 72 points in the series to earn MVP honors, while Newman tallied 24 points in a game three win by the West.) They were also members of the Kentucky All-Star team that faced off against West Virginia's best players, led by the great Jerry West. (Withrow was voted Kentucky's Star of Stars for his performance in that game.) In a game against Ohio's All-Stars, Withrow had 28 points and Newman had 28 rebounds. Later, at Murray, they participated in the North-South All-Star classic.

Most fans saw this as only the beginning of the Withrow-Newman on-court partnership. Both players had inked scholarships to play for Adolph Rupp and his Kentucky Wildcats. Withrow was the first player in the 1956 class to sign on at UK; Newman added his name a few months later.

Wildcat fans were thrilled by the prospect of having Withrow, Newman, Jackie Moreland and Don Mills coming in to wear the blue and white. However, things didn't turn out quite the way UK fans hoped they would. Late in the summer of '56, Withrow signed to play professional baseball with the Milwaukee Braves. To those who were surprised by Withrow's decision, they shouldn't have been.

"I always considered myself a baseball player who just happened to play basketball," Withrow says. "Baseball was always my first love."

The Duvall Miracle

The necessary ingredients required to create something truly memorable include setting, circumstance and timing, with a big dash of desperation and panic liberally sprinkled on top. With those criteria in mind, there can be no challenge to the conclusion that Billy Ray Duvall's last-second bucket against Hartford is the most-memorable field goal in Golden Tide basketball history.

Over the years, there have been many crucial buckets. But Duvall's stands alone at the top.

Let's break it down, beginning with:

Setting: Muhlenberg Central gym, regional tournament championship game, fourth quarter, final seconds.

Circumstance: Hartford 52, Central City 51, Golden Tide All-American Corky Withrow on the bench with five fouls, the Mustangs' Glenn Mills at the charity stripe waiting to shoot a pair of free throws.

Desperation? You betcha.

If Mills converts one of the free throws, the best the Tide can hope for is a basket that will send the game into overtime. If Mills hits them both, well, this was decades before the three-point shot was introduced, so the game is out of reach.

Hartford goes to the state tournament.

Panic? You betcha... times 10.

The odds of Central City winning this game are minimal at best, impossible at worst. This is one of those situations where dreams melt away faster than ice cream on a summer day. This is the place where hopes go to die.

Mills lets the first free throw go. It misses.

Hope lives. Maybe, just maybe, even if Mills connects on the second one, the Tide can somehow get this thing into overtime.

Mills puts up the second freebie. Another miss.

The Tide now has a chance. All that's needed is a miracle.

Tide forward Winfred Thompson grabs the rebound, gets the ball to Carl Ray Jamison, who passes it ahead to Billy Ray Duvall along with the loud command to "shoot it now!"

Duvall catches the ball, gives a quick glance up at the clock—"there were three seconds left"—and then from approximately 30 feet away, he lets it fly.

And had no doubt about the outcome.

"I knew the second I shot the ball that it was going to be good," Billy said. "I could tell the moment it was in the air."

So could Delmas Gish, who many years later said, "I had picked up the ball bag and was ready to head for the dressing room. I was certain we had lost the game. But when I saw Billy's shot on the way, I set the bag back down. It was good from the moment the ball left his hand."

For Withrow, it was a falling over moment.

"I was on the bench, leaning over," Withrow said. "I kept leaning and leaning while the ball was in the air. When it went through the basket, I fell flat on my stomach."

Of course, with that shot giving the Tide a miraculous victory and a trip to the state tournament, what had only seconds earlier been panic was instantly transformed into pandemonium and bedlam. At that moment, Duvall, known to his teammates as "Dilly-ball," learned that being a big-time hero can be a dangerous occupation.

"As soon as the shot went in, Buddy Fuller leaped off the bench and began running straight at me," Billy recalls. "When I saw him coming, I said, 'oh, no' because I knew what was going to happen next. Buddy jumped on me and took me down; Buddy was a big, strong guy. Then everybody began to pile on. I was at the bottom and I couldn't breathe. Dan Carroll and (*Times-Argus* sports editor) Bobby Anderson were pulling people off me. That was a great moment. And a wild one."

How did Duvall fare after the mob had been peeled away?

"I had a slight concussion and a bloody nose," he said. "But all in all it was definitely worth it. People still ask me about that shot. I suppose that's what I'll always be remembered for."

According to our hero, the miracle shot shouldn't have been needed.

"We had a 12-point lead on Hartford at the half," Billy said. "It looked like we were going to win it easy. Then Corky fouled out and we kinda folded. With him out, Hartford began to come back on us. Eventually, they took the lead. I guess you can say we were lucky to win that game."

Proves again that you don't have to travel to Lourdes to witness a miracle.

One final footnote: Corky says he occasionally runs into Glenn Mills, the Mustangs player who missed those two free tosses. Each time Corky see Mills, he always hits him with the same line.

"I tell Mills he's the only outsider in the Central City Hall of Fame," Corky says, laughing.

Shutting Down Corky

During the 1954-55 season, Corky Withrow scored 51 points in an easy win over Daviess County. The following year, prior to playing Central City, Daviess County's Benny Horrell approached his coach, Buck Sydnor, with a specific request.

"I told Coach Sydnor that if he let me guard Withrow, I could promise him that he wouldn't score 51 points against us," Benny said.

And did Benny live up to his promise?

"Yes, I did. I held Corky to 38."

More From the King and the Killer

A few years ago, during a visit to Wayland, Corky Withrow was asked about the game in which he and "King" Kelly Coleman each scored 40 points. Central City won that game 83-75.

"Of all the games I played, this is the one people ask me about the most," Withrow says. "And if everyone who tells me they were at the game really were there, then about 20,000 people were able to get inside a gym that held 2,500."

At some point the conversation turned to "King" Kelly's autobiography, in which he claimed the officiating was decidedly in Central City's favor. Corky was having none of that, saying, "the way I remember it, we didn't really have all that much trouble with Wayland. And I certainly don't think the refereeing played any role in the outcome."

But what do the facts say? Well, here are the facts.

The Tide led all the way, once by as many as 18 points. Corky scored his 40 points by connecting on 15 field goals and 10 of 12 free throws. Coleman had 14 field goals and hit 12 of 19 free tosses.

For the game, Wayland, the team that trailed all the way, attempted 34 free throws to just 24 by the Tide.

Despite being faced with those numbers, "King" Kelly stuck to his story. During a marvelous interview session featuring Corky, Kelly, Freddie Maggard and the late Howard Crittenden, Coleman good naturedly pointed out that "during my entire career I was never once called for travelling. In that Central City game they called it on me five times."

Of course, this interview put Corky and Kelly in the same room with Freddie Maggard, whose last-second buckets beat Central City and Wayland in the 1956 state tournament.

During the interview, Freddie had the best line, once again slamming Corky. The topic of the interview turned to the three-point shot, which didn't exist back when those guys played. All four said they liked it. Freddie, in particular, said it would have really benefited his game.

"Many of the shots I made would have been three-pointers," Freddie said. "The shot that beat Wayland was a three-pointer, and so was the one that beat Central City."

To which Corky roared, "No, it wasn't. I have a photo at my house that shows you taking that shot. It was definitely not a three-pointer."

"Well, that's OK, Corky," Freddie answered, "because I only needed one."

Five decades later and Freddie is still hitting winners against Corky.

Earl Goode...a Success Story

As a basketball player at Central City and later at Georgetown College, Earl Goode was known as a grinder, one of those down-in-the-trenches guys who thrive doing those hard things like rebounding and playing defense. Earl was never a spectacular player, but he was always steady and dependable. Coaches could count on him to perform whatever tasks were needed in order to win.

"Every team needs a player like Earl Goode," Dr. Bob Davis, Georgetown's Hall of Fame coach, said. "A player who is not afraid to mix it up, to do the kinds of things that often go unnoticed. Earl was that kind of player for us."

Earl says Delmas Gish relied heavily on him to pull down a good share of the rebounds, which he normally did. In one game, however, even Earl was shocked by his rebound total.

"(Wendell) Decker, the team manager, was keeping the rebound chart," Earl says, "and after the game, he comes up and tells me I had forty-one rebounds. Now, I did have a bunch of rebounds that night, but I certainly didn't have forty-one. I think Decker padded my numbers to make me look good."

As for defense, well, Earl generally was assigned to stop the opponent's biggest and best inside player. Like Earlington's 6'8" Harry Todd.

"We played Earlington in the Fern Creek Invitational Tournament," Earl said, "and Mr. Gish came up with a defense designed to stop Todd, which we did. We held him to 19 points, way below his average. Trouble was, his teammates went wild and they beat us. Later that same year we played them again. This time Mr. Gish told me to guard Todd and to do my best against him, but the focus this time was on shutting down those other players. Todd scored 40 that night but we won by eight points."

Professionally, Earl has to rank among the most-successful ex-Golden Tide players ever. Here are just a few of his accomplishments: President of GTE Information Services Corp. and GTE Directories Corporation; Chief of Staff to Indiana governor Mitch Daniels; Commissioner of the Department of Administration for Indiana; President of GTE Telephone Company of the Southwest; Chairman of Indiana Sports Corporation; Chairman of Georgetown College Board of Trustees; Chairman of Indiana Sports Commission; served on the Boards of The Chase Bank of Texas, NBD Bank of Indiana, Meridian Insurance Company and Williams Manufacturing.

And that's just a partial listing.

"I have managed to stay busy," Earl said. "But I always think about those days playing for the Golden Tide. Those were great times. I was watching a college game on TV and the guy broadcasting the game mentioned Central City High School and how we had more wins than any school in the United States except for one. Hearing that really filled me with a great sense of pride."

Jack Simpson...Computer Inventor

Jack Simpson's road away from Central City has been paved with one success after another. In fact, few ex-Golden Tide players have been more successful.

Jack graduated Summa Cum Laude from UK with an EE degree in 1963, finishing first in his class. While working on his master's degree, which he received in 1966, he taught computer science classes at UK as a favor to his employer, IBM. By 1981, Jack was Lab Director at IBM in Austin, Texas.

Some of his other major accomplishments include:

- Inventor or co-inventor of six patents for IBM. Twice he received Outstanding Invention Awards.
- President of Lexis-Nexis in Dayton, Ohio, where, within in a 10-year period, he grew the business from $31 million to $500 million while overseeing 4,000 employees.
- Chairman of the Board of Micromedex, Inc., Senior Vice President of Satellite Communications for Scientific Atlanta and President of Ross Technology.
- Testified twice before Congressional committees to oppose National Security Agency over-reach in the 1980s.
- Served on the Steering Committee in National Institute of Science and Technology to improve Computer Security in government agencies.

Jack is married, has three sons and two grandchildren. He's an amateur musician, video editor and, for good measure, still shoots free throws on occasion.

Final Thoughts on Delmas Gish

When Delmas Gish decided to hand over the coaching job to Jackie Day after 16 seasons at the helm, his Golden Tide teams had a 407-120 won-loss record, a 77.2 winning percentage. He guided six teams to the state tournament, coached five all-state players and one All-American. In short, he was amazingly successful.

Golden Tide players are universal in their respect and admiration for the diminutive Gish, who did indeed chew dozens of wadded up paper balls during games. You would have to look deep and far to find a player with an unkind word for their old coach.

"I am proud to have played for a coach like Mr. Gish," Corky Withrow said. "He always taught us that the team came first, and that's how we played."

Frankie Mercer, having played on Gish's last team and Day's first team, offers a unique perspective on the difference between the two coaches.

"Mr. Gish was always very serious," Frankie said. "He rarely ever smiled, and he almost never laughed. He usually had the look on his face of someone wearing pants about three sizes too small. Mr. Day was different. He was younger, more in tune with the players. He could relate to us a little better than Mr. Gish could. And he could laugh about things. But Mr. Gish was an excellent coach."

Joe Mac Howard says appreciation for Gish's coaching abilities came after his playing days were finished.

"I didn't realize how good a coach Mr. Gish was until I graduated and went into the service," Joe Mac said. "I played a lot of basketball while I was in the military. Played against guys who were all-state and All-American who didn't know the first thing about the fundamentals of the game. I knew how to do things those guys couldn't begin to do. They had never been taught the basic fundamentals, which Mr. Gish drilled into us on a daily basis. He was a terrific coach."

The 1960s

Won – 234

Lost – 101

Winning Pct. – 69.9

Player of the Decade

Ralph Mayes

Other Notable Players

Sonny Alexander
Joe Bowen
Jimmy Davis
Eddie Devine
Mark Eades
Chuckie Gary
Larry Joe Higgs
David James
Ricky Johnson
Rodney Kirtley
Ben Lake
Kenny Lindsey
Jimmy Lynch
Freddie Mayes
Jerry Mayes
Gary Noffsinger
Oscar Perry
Steve (Bosco) Reynolds
Taylor Sparks
Joe Stone
Lee Stone
Lucian "Boat" Taylor
Gary Thompson
Ricky Turley
Mike Venerable
Jimmy Walker
Jackie Welborn
Carl White
Lloyd "B.B." Williams

Chapter 30

1960-61

The 1960s saw two seismic changes that profoundly impacted Muhlenberg County basketball—integration and a re-alignment of regions. Those changes would forever alter the basketball landscape, both positively and negatively.

Team-wise, integration began in 1959, when Drakesboro Community started playing Muhlenberg County teams and competing for the district title. Individual-wise, integration came about during the 1963-64 season at Central City and Greenville. Robert Lee Hunter was the first black player to wear the Golden Tide uniform, and although his on-court contribution was small, he was the forerunner for future standouts like Mike Venerable, Sonny Alexander, Steve "Bosco" Reynolds and Carlos "T.T." Hampton, just to name a few. Greenville's first group included talented players John Drake, Wayne Jernigan and the Elliott brothers, John and Larry.

The re-alignment of regions, which took place during the 1965-66 season, didn't do Central City or other Muhlenberg County teams any favors. The KHSAA decided to split the seventh region—the Louisville schools—into two regions, the sixth and seventh. In so doing, the majority of forth region teams were shifted into the third region—the Owensboro region. This shift coincided with an influx of Division I talent at Owensboro High School, where, for the next two decades, the Red Devils dominated. Over the next 20 years, Owensboro went to the state tournament 14 times. And in three of those years when Owensboro failed to make it to the Sweet 16, their cross-city neighbor Apollo was there. Along with having great talent, Owensboro schools benefited from playing the majority of regional tournaments in the Sportscenter.

It is safe to conclude that had there been no region re-alignment, several Golden Tide teams likely would have made it to the state tournament. The same can be said of Drakesboro, Bremen and Greenville, all of whom had powerful teams in the 1970s.

For Central City, the 1960s was a roller-coaster ride—a slow start, a sudden plummet to the bottom, a slow crawl upward, then a long stay at the top. The first four years featured two above-average teams, one horrendous team and one rebuilding team. From 1960-64, the Tide's record was 66-66. It was by far the worst four-year period in Golden Tide history.

But the final six seasons were much different, with the Tide putting together a 168-35 record. This included three 30-win seasons, and a team that many still regard as the best in Central City history—the great 1965-66 team that advanced to the semifinals of the state tournament.

The first Golden Tide team in the new decade was loaded with small, feisty guards but short on height and inside presence. At 6'3", Oscar Perry, a senior, and Gary Thompson, a 6'2" junior, were the only players with size. Back-ups Jimmy Lynch, Ben Lake and Ricky Johnson were all in the 6'1" to 6'2" range, but none of them had much experience.

The guards included veterans Jerry Mayes, Carl White, Dick Kirtley, Lloyd "B.B." Williams, Jackie Welborn Bobby Tatum and newcomer Glenn Adkins. Ball-handling and defense would not be a problem for this club. Rebounding and inside defense would be.

The Tide opened the campaign by getting past a 30-point performance from future coach Wayne Divine to beat home-standing Bremen 69-62. Kirtley came off the bench to pace the Tide with 15 points, while Perry and Mayes each had 12 and Williams 11.

Starters in the opener were Perry, Williams, Thompson, Mayes and White.

Mayes and Thompson each scored 13 points, Kirtley 12 and Williams 10 as the Tide won for the second time by topping Drakesboro Community 65-51.

Roland "Nick" Dunn had 17 for the Buffaloes.

Against South Hopkins, Mayes turned in a career-best 31-point performance to lead the Tide to an 80-68 win. Mayes hit for nine buckets and 13 free throws en route to his total. Thompson chipped in with 15 and Perry 13 in that victory.

Playing at Christian County, the Tide were no match for the tall and talented Colonels, losing 93-67. Roger Putty led the winners with 21 points, while Jackie Ladd had 20 and Robert "Snake" Grace 17.

Mayes had 14, White 13 and Perry 11 for the Tide.

After Perry and Mayes scored 18 points and Thompson 17 in a 74-60 win over Drakesboro, the Tide suffered back-to-back losses, falling to Beaver Dam 67-66 and Hopkinsville 65-59. Close games were the norm for this Tide team, in which 12 games were decided by six points or fewer.

Mayes led the scoring in both losses, getting 21 against Beaver Dam and 15 against Hopkinsville. Thompson accounted for 19 and 12, respectively, in the two games. Perry added 13 against the Beavers, Williams 11 against Hoptown.

The Tide bounced back from those two losses to go on a seven-game winning streak, beginning with an easy 73-43 romp past Sacramento. Perry tossed in 22 points in this win, followed by Thompson with 13 and Mayes 11.

Graham was the Tide's next victim, falling 74-62. Mayes again led the attack with 21 points. Kirtley had 13, White and Lynch 10 each.

Thanks to 33 points from Perry, the Tide opened the Central City Invitational by pounding Hartford 90-53. One night later, the Tide took the title by edging Greenville 53-50. In this game, the Tide, trailing 45-38 after three quarters, limited Greenville to five fourth-stanza points to post the win. Perry had 18 points and Mayes 17 for the Tide. Louie Stuart led the Blackhawks with 18.

With their sights set on capturing a second trophy, the Tide clipped Owensboro 48-46 in the Owensboro Invitational. Once again defense was the key to success; the Tide held Owensboro to 16 second-half points. Thompson had 17, Mayes 14 and Perry 11 for the Tide. Future Mr. Basketball Randy Embry led Owensboro with 22.

In the championship game, the Tide overcame a 17-4 first-quarter deficit to battle back and nip Hawesville 65-64. Perry had a big night, scoring 26 points. He received support from Mayes with 14, Thompson 12 and Williams 11.

Perry stayed hot, hitting for 23 points in a 68-37 win over Muhlenberg Central.

The Tide's second match-up against Beaver Dam wasn't a nail-biter like the first one. This time the Beavers scored 36 fourth-quarter points to register a convincing 97-74 win. First-team all-state performer Butch Hill led Beaver Dam with 30 points.

Mayes had 25 for the Tide.

Down 53-48 heading into the final eight minutes, the Tide, thanks to 12 fourth-quarter points from Perry, came back to nip Hartford 65-64. Perry finished the night with 28 points. White chipped in with 11.

Jerry Bush scored 19 points and Gary McDonald added 13 as Greenville beat the Tide 57-53 in Central City. Perry had 12 points and Williams 10 for the Tide.

With Welborn replacing the injured White in the starting line-up, the Tide kicked off a five-game winning streak with a 66-51 win over Bremen. Perry scored 24 points, Mayes 16 and Welborn nine in his debut as a starter.

Thompson racked up 17 points, Perry 16 and Kirtley 10 in a 69-52 win over Sacramento, then Mayes came through with 16 points to help the Tide get past Daviess County 49-45. Next, it was Welborn's turn to lead the offense by ringing up 17 of his game-high 18 points in the second half to help the Tide fight past stubborn Graham 57-50. Perry had 13 and Thompson 12 in the win.

After holding visiting Trigg County to 13 first-half points, the Tide rolled to an easy 62-39 win. Thompson had 18 points and Mayes 16 for the winners.

It was at this stage that the Tide's season came unglued. They would lose their next four games, beginning with a 62-60 double-overtime setback at Madisonville. The Tide led 34-26 at intermission but couldn't hold on for the win. Barry Teague, who would go on to play for Davidson College, led the Maroons with 17 points. Thompson had 19, Perry 17 and Mayes 10 for the Tide.

The Tide's two-game road trip turned out to be a double spanking, getting crushed by Vine Grove 85-55 and Larue County 70-53. Perry was the Tide's top scorer in both games, hitting for 13 against Vine Grove and 14 against Larue County.

Roger Nofsinger scored 17 points and Gary McDonald added 16 as Greenville made it two straight against the Tide with a 59-58 win. McDonald did the late damage, ringing up nine points in the fourth quarter.

Lynch, now a starter, led the Tide with 16 points. Perry added 15.

Lynch and Perry were instrumental in the Tide's next three

games—wins against Drakesboro 68-48, Owensboro Catholic 66-58 and Muhlenberg Central 44-43. Lynch had 19 and Perry 16 against Drakesboro, then each player had 17 against Owensboro Catholic. In that game, Williams and Thompson both contributed 13.

Perry, with 11 points, was the only Tide player to hit for double digits against MC. J.R. Goff led the Spartans with 16 points.

In the regular-season finale, Randy Embry showed why he was named Mr. Basketball by scoring 33 points in a 72-56 Owensboro victory. For the game, Embry hit for 16 field goals and a lone free throw.

Lynch led the Tide with 21 points.

Drawing a first-round bye, the Tide met Muhlenberg Central in semifinal action with a trip to the regional at stake. Giving one of their best performances of the season, the Tide, riding a 28-point effort from Perry, rolled to an impressive 77-49 victory. Thompson had 14 and Lynch 13 in this win.

J.R. Goff again led the Spartans with 20 points, while Ronnie "Hortney" Maddox added 16.

In the title game, Hughes-Kirk, getting 26 points from Lamar Holland, 14 from Harold Hardison and 13 from David Holland, claimed the district crown by beating the Tide 70-56. The Tigers trailed 47-45 after three quarters, then outscored the Tide 25-9 in the final frame to win going away.

Mayes and Perry each had 17 points for the Tide, with Thompson adding a dozen.

The Tide had a long game that resulted in a short stay in the regional tournament. In the tourney opener, Todd Porter nailed a last-second bucket to give Butler County a 71-69 double-overtime victory over the Tide. Billy Warren had 24 points and Porter 17 for Butler County.

Lynch finished with 22 and Perry with 20 for the Tide, who ended with a 21-12 record despite missing starting guard White for more than half the season.

The Tide would say farewell to eight seniors, meaning the 1961-62 squad was destined to be young and inexperienced.

Chapter 31

1961-62

With the lone exception of Gary Thompson, this season's starting five, along with the remaining cast of characters, was comprised of new and unfamiliar faces. Ben Lake, Ricky Johnson and Glenn Adkins had been on the previous team but had virtually no game experience. Other new faces included Chuckie Gary, Eddie Devine, Gary "Ching Ching" Noffsinger, Jimmy Davis, Joe Bowen, David Moore, Larry Joe Higgs, Rodney Kirtley, Lee Stone, William "B.O." Keown, David James and Jimmy Walker, who returned after sitting out his junior year and who would go on to become a world-class musician.

Given so much inexperience, this club actually performed fairly well, finishing with a 20-14 record. This included another district tournament championship and three wins over a good Muhlenberg Central team by a total of four points.

But there was also plenty of inconsistent play, resulting in losing streaks of four and three games, respectively. This team was good at times but seldom did it achieve excellence.

Adkins came off the bench to score 14 points in the Tide's 57-44 opening-game win over Bremen. Lake contributed 13 points, Thompson and Gary 10 each and Walker eight. Thompson, Lake, Walker, Gary and Johnson were the starters for this game.

Thompson racked up 28 points, Lake added 15 and Johnson 10 as the Tide topped Drakesboro Community 70-50. A big 24-9 second quarter outburst, fueled by 12 Thompson points, broke the game open.

Billy Ray Parker led the Buffaloes with 19.

In the first of those three squeakers against Muhlenberg Central, the Tide led 54-47 after three quarters, then managed to hang on for a 66-64 victory. Thompson again came to the rescue, scoring 17 points, eight in the final stanza. Johnson had 14 and Gary 10 for the winners.

Joe Pentecost and Denny Slinker paced the Spartans with 23 and 14 points, respectively.

A second straight squeaker resulted in a 62-61 loss to South Hopkins. After leading 36-33 at intermission, the Tide were done in by a poor nine-point third-quarter output. Johnson had 16, Lake and Thompson 14 each in a losing effort.

Christian County paid a visit to Central City, smacking the Tide 94-81. Lake had 19 points, Thompson 16, Johnson 15 and Walker 14 for the Tide. Tommy Porter, a future UK player, led the Colonels with 18.

All five Tide starters hit for double figures in a 77-63 victory over Drakesboro. Thompson led with 18, followed by Walker's 17, Johnson's 16, Lake's 14 and Gary's 10.

Losing for the second time at home, the Tide fell to Beaver Dam 57-52. Walker paced the Tide with 13 points, while Thompson and Adkins added 11 and 10, respectively.

Playing better on the road than at home, the Tide claimed wins at Hopkinsville 65-51 and Sacramento 58-52. Thompson was the top gun against Hoptown, finishing with 16 points. Walker chipped in with 15, Johnson 12 and Lake 10. Against Sacramento, Lake and Adkins each had 17, with Thompson adding 16.

The Tide's two-game winning streak ended with a 73-50 loss at Graham. Lake had 13 points and Adkins 10 for the Tide.

In the annual Central City Invitational, Greenville got 24 points from Eddie Rose and 18 from Gary McDonald to post a 66-58 win. Lake had 19 and Johnson 15 for the losing Tide.

Thompson, held to a single point in the Greenville loss, erupted for 30 to lead the Tide past Drakesboro 68-59 in the consolation game. Lake also hit for double digits with 14.

Facing Owensboro Catholic in the Owensboro Invitational, the Tide, getting 22 points from Lake and 21 from Thompson, advanced to the championship game with a 71-63 win. Walker ended the night with 11 points.

One night later, host Owensboro captured the title by beating the Tide 64-59. This would be the first loss in a four-game losing streak for the slumping Tide, who saw their record fall to 8-9.

John Harralson had 21 points and Frank Ballard added 13 for the Red Devils. The Tide were led by Thompson with 19 and Gary with 14.

The next three losses were administered by Beaver Dam 86-73, Hartford 72-59 and Greenville 54-49. Thompson scored 22, Walker 19 and Adkins 11 against Beaver Dam, then Lake came back to lead the scoring in the next two losses, getting 14 against Hartford and 18 against Greenville.

Eddie Rose had 20 for Greenville. Gary McDonald and Melvin Van Hooser finished with 16 and 13, respectively.

The Tide turned things around by bumping off Bremen 61-44 to kick off a four-game winning streak. Gary led the Tide with 17 points. Lake had 13, Thompson 12 and Johnson 11 in a solid all-around Tide performance.

Thompson tallied 20 points and Gary 16 in a 61-60 win at Sacramento that saw the Tide overcome a 53-48 third-quarter deficit, then Lake pumped in 23 points, Johnson 12 and Thompson 11 as the Tide slipped past Daviess County 65-58. Behind 21 points from Lake and 16 apiece from Thompson and Gary, the Tide made it four straight by scoring an 81-47 revenge win over Graham.

A disastrous two-game road trip resulted in back-to-back losses at Trigg County 64-61 and Calloway County 60-38. Thompson led the scoring in both games, coming through with 18 against Trigg County and 13 against Calloway County. Adkins had 17 in the first outing, Lake had 10 in each game.

David Wells scored 26 points as Madisonville spoiled the Tide's return home by notching a 60-51 win. Lake paced the Tide with 15 points.

With their record now 12-12, the Tide showed some serious moxie down the stretch, winning five of their final six regular-season games, beginning with two-point victories over Butler County 53-51 and Greenville 61-59.

Thompson had 15, Johnson 14 and Lake 12 in the win over Butler County, which was led by Billy Warren with 16 points. Johnson put up the big numbers against Greenville, scoring 17 points. Lake ended the game with 14, while Thompson and Adkins each had 10.

Gary McDonald had 22 and Melvin Van Hooser 17 for the Blackhawks.

All five starters hit double figures, led by Gary with 18, in an 80-60 rout of Drakesboro. Johnson and Thompson each had 17, Lake 15 and Adkins 10 in that win.

Jerry Mayhugh had 15 to lead the Cardinals.

With Thompson tossing in 22 points and Johnson adding 16, the Tide beat Owensboro Catholic 67-62. Walker also hit for double figures with 11.

Thompson scored 27 points, including 10 in the final quarter, to help lift the Tide to a 62-61 win over visiting Muhlenberg Central. The Spartans were in front 49-47 heading into the last eight minutes, but the Tide, with Thompson and Johnson accounting for all 15 fourth-quarter points, managed to come back and get the win. Johnson had 13 points, with Lake adding 12.

Joe Pentecost had 18 and Denny Slinker 14 for the Spartans.

In the last regular-season game, Owensboro, getting 19 points each from Bobby Woodward and John Harralson, posted an 86-75 victory in the Sportscenter to snap the Tide's five-game winning streak. Lake had 17 for the Tide, Johnson and Thompson 15 each, Walker 12 and Gary 10.

The district tourney opener was a slow-down affair, with the Tide getting past Graham 40-35. Walker paced the winners with 11 points. Thompson added 10.

Facing Greenville for the fourth time, having dropped two of the first three, the Tide, trailing 50-42 going into the final quarter, got a big lift from an unlikely source—Eddie Devine—and came back to beat the Blackhawks 62-60. Devine, a sophomore, scored eight points in the last stanza, a total matched by Thompson, while the Tide defense limited Greenville to just two field goals during those crucial eight minutes.

Thompson led the winners with 19 points, while Lake added 14.

Melvin Van Hooser had 18 and Gary McDonald 16 for the Blackhawks.

Round three against Muhlenberg Central proved to be even more of a thriller than the first two match-ups. The Tide led until the final seconds when the Spartans tied the score at 49-49 and sent the game into overtime; the first of two overtimes, to be precise. The first OT ended with the two clubs knotted at 57-57. When those next three minutes were over, the Tide had claimed the district title with a 60-59 victory,

Free throws were the difference. MC had seven more field goals (28-21), but the Tide made good on 18 of 29 free tosses while the Spartans hit three of 10.

Lake paced the winners with 20 points. Thompson finished with 16 and Gary 11.

Mike Withrow had 14, Denny Slinker 13 and Ronnie Maddox 10 for the Spartans.

The Tide's stay in the regional tournament was brief thanks to a powerful Caneyville team that won the regional tourney and then advanced to the semifinals of the Sweet 16. With Jerry Tilford scoring 22 points and Eddie Majors adding 19, Caneyville rolled to an easy 84-58 victory.

Lake had a big game for the Tide, scoring 24 points in his final outing. Johnson, also a senior, finished with 16.

The loss left the Tide with a final 20-14 record. But if Tide fans thought this was a mediocre season, they had no clue of the horrors that lay ahead. Coming up was the longest, darkest season in Golden Tide history.

Chapter 32

1962-63

The 1962-63 team bares the stigma of being the all-time worst in Central City's long and proud basketball tradition. This was the team with the fewest wins (eight) and the most losses (24). This was a club that suffered several humiliating defeats, including three to hated archrival Greenville by a combined total of 74 points.

At no time did this team win more than two consecutive games. While there were a handful of superb individual efforts along the way, the overall depth and talent was seldom a match for opposing teams. Another contributing factor to this team's sufferings was the absence of sophomore Joe Bowen, one of the Tide's premier inside players. Bowen was injured against Hopkinsville and missed 13 games.

If there was a bright side to this dismal season, it was the emergence of several young players who would go on to bring back glory days for Tide fans. Bowen and fellow sophomore Lee Stone had their moments, but it was two freshmen—David James and Rodney Kirtley—who offered signs that the future was going to be OK. James, in particular, became a big scoring threat during the latter third of the season, while Kirtley proved to be a steady scorer and rebounder.

Others on this club were Eddie Devine, Jimmy Davis, Gary Noffsinger, Larry Joe Higgs, David Moore, William "B.O." Keown, Tommy Wallace, Billy Gentry, Mike Gray, Charles Frank Winkler and Bobby "Noonie" Foster.

The problem was, while the Tide had players of average ability, the foes they faced were loaded with top-flight talent. There was Barry Jarvis, Tookie Nelson, David Decker and Jerry Jarvis at Bremen; Melvin Van Hooser, Gary McDonald and Mike Roll at Greenville; Bruce Penrod and Timmy Harrison at Drakesboro; Ronnie Maddox, Mike

Withrow and Joe Pentecost at Muhlenberg Central; Harold Hardison at Hughes-Kirk; Tommy Stovall at Graham; John Drake and John Elliott at Drakesboro Community.

And that's only the Muhlenberg County opponents. Outsiders included Christian County's Tommy Porter, Hopkinsville's Herb Covington, Daviess County's Wayne Chapman and Alan Powers, Madisonville's Willie Nisbett, Butler County's Billy Warren, Owensboro's Charles Taylor, George Moore and Jim Howes, and Hancock County's Don Snyder.

That was simply too much talent for this Tide team to overcome, despite some sterling individual efforts from Bowen, Devine, Kirtley and James.

After opening the season with losses to Bremen 71-51, Drakesboro Community 61-43 and Muhlenberg Central 68-45, the Tide finally put one in the win column by beating South Hopkins 65-46. In that win, Devine had 20 points, Bowen and Moore 11 each. Bowen was the Tide's leading scorer in the first two games, ringing up 19 points in each outing. Noffsinger had 10 in the loss to MC.

Five consecutive losses followed, courtesy of Christian County 72-52, Drakesboro 59-53, Hughes-Kirk 61-49, Beaver Dam 71-47 and Hopkinsville 76-52, the game that saw Bowen go down with his injury.

Several Tide players performed well during this bad stretch. Bowen had 24 against Christian County and 17 against Hughes-Kirk; Devine had 14 against Drakesboro and 11 against Beaver Dam; Moore had 17 and Kirtley 15 against Hopkinsville; and James hit double figures for the first time in his career with 10 against Beaver Dam.

Devine scored 14 and Kirtley 12 as the Tide beat Sacramento 51-42, then Devine had 15, James and Kirtley 10 each in a 54-40 win over Graham.

What followed was a six-game losing skid, beginning with losses in the Central City Invitational to Bremen 42-39 and Hughes-Kirk 51-47. Devine had 10 points against Bremen, which was led by David Decker with 15 points and Barry Jarvis with 10. In the consolation game, Moore had 16, Kirtley 13 and Devine 10 for the Tide, while Harold Hardison had 20 points and Eldon Hardison and Ray Newman 13 each for the Tigers.

Other losses came at the hands of Beaver Dam 58-44, Hartford 41-35, Bremen 60-52 and Greenville 84-50.

The only bright efforts in that horrid stretch came against Bremen, when Devine had 17 points, Kirtley 15 and Stone 10.

After Devine scored 14 and Stone 10 in a 52-37 win over Sacramento, Daviess County, behind 19 points from Alan Powers and 17 from Wayne Chapman, demolished the Tide 75-33. Next, Graham edged the Tide 52-50 despite a 19-point performance from James.

Tommy Stovall took game-high honors with 21.

James gunned in 24 points, Kirtley and Moore each added 11 as the Tide beat Hughes-Kirk 63-53. James came back with an 18-point effort but it wasn't enough to derail Madisonville, which claimed a 67-53 win. Devine also had a nice game, ending with 17 points.

Billy Warren scored 33 points to lead Butler County past the Tide 71-41, then the trio of Melvin Van Hooser, Gary McDonald and Mike Roll combined for 65 points as Greenville stormed to a 90-73 victory. Van Hooser had 23 points, McDonald 22 and Roll 20 for the Blackhawks.

James and Devine led the Tide with 16 each against Greenville. Bowen had 15 and Kirtley 14 in that loss.

James racked up 15 points, Kirtley 14 and Devine 13 as the Tide edged Drakesboro 60-59 despite a 32-point performance from Timmy Harrison. Then James hit for 22, Bowen 20 and Devine 11 in a 67-56 win over Owensboro Catholic.

The final three games of the regular season ended in losses to Calloway County 71-57, Muhlenberg Central 87-75 and Owensboro 85-36. James had 15 against Calloway County, Kirtley 19 against Muhlenberg Central and Devine 10 against Owensboro, which was led by Charles Taylor with 24 points.

The Tide caught a huge break by drawing a first-round bye in the district tournament, meaning they only needed one win to advance to the regional. That mission was accomplished with a 65-51 win over Drakesboro Community. Kirtley paced the Tide with 16 points. Bowen had 14, Moore 13 and Devine 11.

John Drake's 16 points were tops for Drakesboro Community.

The title battle was no match, with Greenville once again flexing its muscles in a 75-52 win. Gary McDonald had 20 points and Melvin Van Hooser 18 for the Blackhawks.

James led the Tide with 18 points, while Devine and Kirtley, both of whom were named to the all-district squad, finished with 14 and 11, respectively.

For the second straight year, the Tide's stay in the regional tournament lasted about as long as a Hollywood marriage. This trip ended with a 74-41 loss to Hancock County, the eventual regional champs. The game was fairly close for three quarters, but in the final frame the Hornets outscored the Tide 24-5 to win easily.

Don Snyder had 20 points for the winners.

Bowen was the only Tide player to hit double digits with 13.

Mercifully, this long nightmare season was finally laid to rest. Next season's club, with many familiar faces, wouldn't be a great one but it did make positive strides forward. And more important, it would lay the groundwork for a six-year span that ranks among the best in Golden Tide history.

Chapter 33

1963-64

If this season was anything it was a forerunner of great things to come. Although this club finished with a mediocre 17-16 record, it contained the seeds for future success. Juniors Joe Bowen and Lee Stone were back. So were sophomores David James and Rodney Kirtley. And later in the season, after a roster shake-up, sophomore James "Sonny" Alexander and freshmen Ralph Mayes and Mike Venerable joined the team.

What this meant, of course, was that this roster contained the eventual starting five on the 1965-66 team that many consider the school's all-time best—James, Kirtley, Alexander, Mayes and Venerable.

But when the Tide opened the season with a 70-53 win over Drakesboro Community, the starting five consisted of Jimmy Davis, Stone, Kirtley, Bowen and James. Others on the squad included Eddie Devine, Robert Lee Hunter, William Keown, Larry Joe Higgs, Tommy Wallace, Billy Gentry, Charles Frank Winkler, Mike Gray and Bobby Foster.

Bowen had 21 points and James 13 in the opening-game win. Hunter knocked in a fourth-quarter bucket to become the first black player to score for the Golden Tide.

A seven-point second quarter proved to be the Tide's downfall in a 75-64 loss at South Hopkins. Devine came off the bench to register 23 points, while Bowen added 18 and Stone 11.

James scored 18 points, including eight in the two overtime periods, to help lift the Tide past a strong Bremen team 75-73. The score was tied 61-61 at the end of regulation and 66-66 after the first OT before the Tide edged away for the win.

Bowen also had 18 points for the winners, with Davis, Stone and Kirtley all hitting for 11 points each.

Bremen's Barry Jarvis led all scorers with 26 points. Jerry Jarvis had 16, David Decker 12 and Tookie Nelson 11.

Christian County got 30 points from Tommy Porter en route to a 69-60 victory at Central City. The Tide had one more bucket than the visitors (21-20), but the Colonels connected on 29 free tosses (14 by Porter) to 18 by the Tide.

Bowen had 18 points in a losing cause, with Stone accounting for 14 and Kirtley 11.

Kirtley hit for 22 points, Bowen 20 and Devine 16 as the Tide topped home-standing Drakesboro 79-73 after trailing 60-53 heading into the final quarter. Kirtley and Devine sparked the comeback, totaling 14 points in those last eight minutes.

Bruce Penrod had 22 points for the Cardinals.

Kirtley stayed hot, hitting for 24 points in an 82-68 win over Hughes-Kirk. Devine finished with 17 points, Bowen 15, 13 coming at the charity stripe, and James 11. It was in this game that Mayes, the Tide's future all-state performer, scored his first two varsity points.

Eldon Hardison matched Kirtley's 24-point effort for game-high honors.

After posting back-to-back wins, the Tide dropped their next two games, losing thrillers at home to Daviess County 65-63 and Beaver Dam 67-66. In the first of those two losses, the Tide battled back from a 38-32 halftime deficit but could never get a nose in front. Against Beaver Dam, the situation was reversed; the Tide led 50-47 after three quarters, then squandered the lead.

Bowen was the top scorer in both games, getting 25 against Daviess County and 20 against Beaver Dam. James finished with 12 in the first game, 13 in the second.

Danny Barker led Daviess County with 22 points. Joe Mac Hill topped Beaver Dam with 25.

The Tide began a three-game winning streak with an easy 60-40 win at Sacramento. Bowen scored 18 points and Kirtley 17 in this victory. James turned in a break-out 33-point performance to lead the Tide past Graham 102-84. James received plenty of support from Bowen with 22 points, Kirtley with 13, Stone 11 and Higgs 10.

Tommy Stovall led the Nighthawks with 29 points.

Seven free throws in overtime were enough to lift the Tide past Muhlenberg Central 66-63. Those seven free tosses were all the Tide could manage during the OT. Bowen, the game's leading scorer with 23 points, accounted for four of those free throws, while Gentry hit two and James one. Stone and Kirtley each had 12 points in this win, with James adding 10.

Tommy Davis paced the Spartans with 18.

Failing to sustain their momentum, the Tide immediately dropped both games in the Central City Invitational, losing to Hughes-Kirk 69-66 and Greenville 68-62. Kirtley had 25 and Devine 19 against Hughes-Kirk, which rallied from a 52-51 deficit to earn the win. In the loss to Greenville, Kirtley scored 20, Bowen 16 and Devine 13.

Greenville's John Elliot led all scorers with 24.

A big fourth quarter, sparked by eight points from Davis, helped the Tide get past Hartford 57-40. Davis ended the game with 10 points, a total matched by Kirtley. Bowen led the winners with 17 points.

Sixteen points from Wayne Jernigan, 15 from John Drake and 14 each from Eddie Rose and John Elliott were enough to carry Greenville to a 71-59 win over the Tide. Devine and Kirtley had 14 apiece in a losing cause, with Bowen ringing up 13 and James 10.

Another big performance by Eldon Hardison (25 points) was enough to give Hughes-Kirk its second win in three tries against the Tide, a 78-65 victory at Beechmont. The winners also got 24 points from Steve Wood.

James had 18 for the Tide. Bowen chipped in with 17 and Stone 10.

Kirtley scored 18 points, Bowen 17 and Mayes 13 as the Tide ran past Sacramento 75-46. Kirtley followed that with a 27-point effort in an 83-56 win at Graham. Four other Tide players hit double figures, including Stone and Bowen with 14 each, Devine 11 and James 10.

Tommy Stovall again led Graham with 20 points.

A road trip to Trigg County and Calloway County resulted in a split, with the Tide dropping the first game 87-72, then winning the second game 99-56. Bowen had 22 points, James 13, Kirtley 12 and Devine 11 against Trigg County, which was led by Buddy Sivills' 27 points.

In the win over Calloway County, Bowen led with 25, while James had 18, Devine 12, Kirtley 11 and Davis 10.

Once again failure to hang on to a late lead resulted in a disappointing 78-76 loss at Beaver Dam. The Tide owned a 61-57 advantage heading into the last quarter, only to watch Joe Mac Hill account for 11 of his 25 points to lead Beaver Dam to victory.

Bowen scored 25 and Devine 21 for the Tide.

Giving a solid performance, the Tide easily disposed of Madisonville 81-67, thanks to 25 points from Bowen, 18 from Devine and 17 from Kirtley.

Greenville built a 52-32 halftime lead, then held on for an 88-76 win. Eddie Rose led the winners with 27 points, with John Elliott and Wayne Jernigan each contributing 19.

Bowen had 15, Devine 14 and Stone 13 for the Tide.

In a pair of strong performances, the Tide romped past Drakesboro 93-54 and Owensboro Catholic 73-46. Against the Cardinals, Kirtley scored 21 points, Bowen 20, James and Mayes 13 each and Devine 10. In the win over the Aces in the Sportscenter, Kirtley had 24 points, Devine 17 and James 12.

The Tide's final four regular-season games ended with a single win against three losses. This stretch began with a 67-57 setback against visiting Muhlenberg Central followed by a 79-67 win over Centertown. Devine and Bowen each had 16 points against the Spartans, with Bowen scoring 21, Davis 16, Kirtley and Mayes 10 apiece against Centertown.

With Barry Jarvis and Tookie Nelson combining for 57 points, Bremen pounded the Tide 102-71 at home. Jarvis finished with 32 points, Nelson 25 for the winners, who also got 17 points from David Decker and 10 from Jerry Jarvis.

Bowen led the Tide with 20 points. Devine had 12, James and Gray 10 each.

Owensboro, paced by Bill Heffelfinger's 23 points, stormed to a convincing 82-66 victory at the Sportscenter in the last regular-season game.

Bowen had 22 points and Devine 16 for the Tide.

With a record of 15-14, the Tide's chances of getting through the district tournament were iffy at best. They got a favorable first-round draw, getting a Graham club they had twice defeated in easy fashion. But looming ahead as a potential semifinal opponent was Hughes-Kirk, which owned two wins over the Tide in three tries.

The Tide did as expected in the opener, dispatching Graham 67-53 behind 20 points from Bowen and 14 from James. A big 25-13 second-quarter advantage was the difference in this game. In that decisive quarter, James had nine points and Bowen had seven.

Tommy Stovall led the Nighthawks with 17.

Getting big numbers from Bowen, Davis and Kirtley, the Tide advanced to the championship game by beating Hughes-Kirk 69-55. Bowen topped the winners with 17 points, while Davis and Kirtley had 16 and 14, respectively.

Defense was also instrumental in this win. The Tide limited high-scoring Eldon Hardison to three field goals and 13 points overall.

In a tense title-game battle, Greenville claimed the district crown by beating the Tide 62-56. This win gave the Blackhawks a four-game season sweep. John Elliott had 15 points for the winners, who also got 14 each from guards Don Cary and Wayne Jernigan, and 12 points from Eddie Rose.

Bowen scored 20 points and James 11 for the Tide.

Giving a less-than-sparkling performance against Hartford in the regional tournament opener resulted in a 51-43 loss. The Tide, who finished with a 17-16 record, could only manage 16 first-half points, putting them at a disadvantage that proved to be insurmountable. For the game, the Tide had two more field goals than Hartford (17-15), but the Mustangs made good on 21 free throws to the Tide's nine.

Davis, in his final game, led the Tide with 16 points. Bowen, a junior, finished with 11.

Hartford's James Henry had a game-best 20 points.

The past four seasons, especially the last two, were nowhere close to meeting the high standards set by earlier Central City teams. This was all about to change. For in the next six years, the Golden Tide would reclaim the missing magic and put on the court some of the mightiest teams in school history.

Chapter 34

1964-65

Of all the winningest Central City teams, the 1964-65 club just might be the best. It is certainly the most overlooked and under-appreciated. This team fashioned a 30-5 won-loss record. This team lost a one-point decision in the finals of the regional tournament to the team that went on to capture the state championship. More important, this is the team that brought renewed energy to a slumping program, the team that kicked off a remarkable six-year run in which the Golden Tide's record was 168-35, a winning percentage of 82.8.

This team had a lot working in its favor. There were battle-hardened veterans (Joe Bowen, Lee Stone, Rodney Kirtley, David James, Larry Joe Higgs), talented, emerging younger players (Ralph Mayes, Sonny Alexander, Mike Venerable, Kenny Lindsey, Billy Chris Pendley, Billy Kirkpatrick) and solid role players (Charles Frank Winkler, Mike Gray). It was a team with excellent size, strong rebounders, deadly shooters and hard-working defenders.

In every way this was a strong and powerful Golden Tide team.

For the opener, a 92-71 victory over South Hopkins, the starting line-up featured Mayes, Stone, Kirtley, James and Bowen. This would change as the season progressed, with the 6'6" Alexander taking over for Stone, who then became a valuable sixth man.

Bowen led the scoring with 22 points in that opening win. Kirtley had 18, Mayes 17, James 14 and Alexander 10 for the winners.

In their second outing at Bremen, the Tide built a 39-31 halftime advantage, then fell apart in the second half, dropping a 75-69 decision. The Eagles seized control in the third quarter, outscoring the visitors 21-10.

Kirtley paced the Tide with 19 points, while Bowen and James added 15 and 13, respectively.

David Decker led all scorers with 32 points, with teammate Tookie Nelson adding 25.

The Tide rebounded from that setback by rolling to three easy wins, beating Hughes-Kirk 105-70, Drakesboro 83-58 and Christian County 90-58. Mayes had 24 points, Kirtley 15 and Bowen 10 in the win over Hughes-Kirk, then James and Kirtley each had 15, Gray 13, Alexander 12, Mayes 11 and Bowen 10 against Drakesboro. In the win over Christian County, Bowen had 22, James 21, Mayes 17 and Kirtley 16.

Daviess County got 32 points from Paul Truitt, including six in overtime, to lead the Panthers past the Tide 82-80. Trailing by 11 heading into the final quarter, the Tide battled back to send the game into the extra frame, only to come up a bucket short.

James had 23 points to lead the Tide. Bowen finished with 15 and Mayes 13 in a losing effort.

Now sporting a 4-2 record, the Tide kicked it up a notch, winning their next 13 games, many in easy fashion. This impressive streak began with six players hitting for double figures in a 116-99 win at Beaver Dam. James led the way with 22 points. Others in double figures included Kirtley with 18, Mayes with 17, Bowen, Alexander and Stone all with 16 apiece.

Kirtley scored 21, James had 15 and Venerable 12 as the Tide routed Graham 90-45 prior to participating in back-to-back tournaments, beginning with an easy run through the Trigg County Invitational. To claim that title, the Tide beat Calloway County 83-62, Dawson Springs 91-77 and host Trigg County 80-56. James scored 21 and Bowen 18 in the opener, then Kirtley had 19, Bowen 17 and James 16 in the semifinal win over Dawson Springs. James and Bowen were the top guns in the title game, registering 24 and 23 points, respectively.

Returning home to host the Central City Invitational, the Tide captured more first-place hardware by beating Muhlenberg Central 82-61 and pesky Centertown 82-68. Mayes and James each had 17, Kirtley 16 and Alexander 15 against the Spartans, who were led by Wendell Goff with 14 points. Bowen came through with 23 points, James and Mayes each had 11 and Alexander 10 in the title-game win over Centertown.

Danny Decker and Barry Barnes led Centertown with 17 points apiece.

Facing Muhlenberg Central for the second time in a week, the Tide, getting 24 points from James and 15 from Mayes, beat the Spartans 73-62. Cletus Cosby and Dwight Wells each had 16 for MC.

The Tide pushed their winning streak to nine with a hard-earned 63-56 win over Greenville. The Tide forged a 31-24 halftime advantage, then played the visiting Blackhawks on even terms during the final 16 minutes to earn the victory. Mayes topped the winners with 19 points. Bowen and James each had 13.

Mayes and Kirtley scored 17 points apiece, James had 15 and Stone added 10 as the Tide got past Hughes-Kirk 81-65. Next, the Tide had to overcome a 33-25 halftime deficit in order to get past home-standing Madisonville 69-65. James was huge in this win, accounting for 16 of his game-high 20 points after intermission. Bowen had 17 and Kirtley 15 in this tough win.

LIT, Manual and Another Basketbrawl

Heading into a home game against Graham, the Tide had accepted a bid to participate in the Louisville Invitational Tournament for the first time since 1959. Before heading to Louisville, the Tide easily dispatched Graham 82-59 behind 22 points from Kirtley, 19 from James, 16 from Bowen and 11 from Mayes.

The Tide's first-round LIT foe was Manual, and for much of the game it appeared as if the trip to Louisville would be little more than a one-night stand. With Charles Turner seemingly scoring at will (he finished with 34 points), Manual jumped on top 23-13 after one quarter. Manual led 39-31 at the break, and was still in front 57-52 heading into the final frame.

The Tide caught up at 57-57 before Venerable dropped in a pair of free tosses to give his club the lead for the first time since the opening minutes. With the Tide still clinging to a 68-67 lead, Mayes sank two freebies to make it 70-67 with 1:53 remaining. But the Tide's hopes for a victory dimmed considerably when Turner racked up four unanswered points to put Manual in front 71-70 with 14 ticks left.

Following a time-out, Mayes in-bounded the ball to a wide-open Bowen, who laid in the game-winner with five seconds left. Manual failed to get off a shot in those finals seconds, and when Mayes batted down a long pass, that's when the real fireworks began.

"They throw the ball to midcourt, one of their guys catches it, throws it up and (Ralph) Mayes knocks it down," David James said. "Next thing you know, they're fighting. The horn sounds, Manual players are heading to the dressing room, when Stone and Gray lead the charge. That's when the fists really started flying. Stone came to the dressing room looking like a boxer. He had a cut over his eye."

Bowen's last-second bucket gave him 25 points for the night. James had 17 and Mayes 10 in this win.

One day later, the Tide's 13-game winning streak ended when DeSales pulled away late to claim an 82-71 victory. Kirtley paced the Tide with 23 points. Alexander finished with 15 and James with 14.

The Tide again rebounded from a loss by flexing their muscles, this time running off six consecutive wins, beginning with a hard-earned 73-67 victory over Beaver Dam, thanks to a 24-point effort from James. Kirtley had 14, Mayes and Alexander 13 each in this win.

Facing an excellent Greenville team, the Tide notched a 71-64 road victory. Mayes led the winners with 19 points. James finished with 16, Kirtley 12 and Alexander 11.

John Drake topped the Blackhawks with 18, while Wayne Jernigan added 16.

Overcoming a 30-point performance from Charles Davis, the Tide defeated Drakesboro 77-68 for their second straight road win. James led the winners with 25 points. Mayes had 17, with Kirtley and Alexander each tossing in 13.

In a game that saw 10 players dent the scoring column, the Tide pounded Sacramento 91-37. Mayes led the attack with 22 points. James had 17, Bowen 16, Kirtley 10, Higgs eight, Stone, Gray Lindsey and Venerable four each and Kirkpatrick two.

Playing a second straight game without Alexander, the Tide had little trouble beating Owensboro Catholic 85-51 behind 24 points from Mayes and 22 from James. Bowen and Stone also hit for double digits with 14 and 10, respectively.

Twenty-one points from Mayes and 17 from Alexander were enough to propel the Tide past Muhlenberg Central 81-65. Bowen had 13 and Stone 12 in this win.

Cletus Cosby led the Spartans with 23 points.

A dreadful fourth quarter in which the Tide were outscored 25-9 resulted in a 75-65 loss to Centertown. Barry Barnes did the most damage, scoring 13 of his 26 points in the final stanza. Kirtley paced the Tide with 21 points, while Bowen had 11, Alexander and Stone 10 each.

This would be the Tide's last loss until the regional tourney final.

The Tide closed out the regular season by posting hard-earned wins over Bremen 69-65 and Owensboro 60-58. Against Bremen, the Tide, sparked by James, came back from a six-point third-quarter deficit to earn their revenge win. James led all scorers with 23 points, 10 coming in the last frame. Mayes had 17, Kirtley 15 and Bowen 10 for the winners.

David Decker led the Golden Eagles with 22 points.

With Kirtley tossing in 17 points, Alexander 16 and Mayes 11, the Tide managed to sneak past visiting Owensboro by that two-point margin. The win gave the Tide a final regular-season record of 25-4 heading into the district tournament.

A Strong Finish, a Heart-Wrenching Loss

In the district tourney opener, the Tide had to overcome a 37-34 half-time deficit to put away the Spartans 81-65. James led the comeback, scoring 28 points, 17 after intermission. Mayes also played well, ending with 19 points, while Kirtley had 14 and Bowen 11.

Cletus Cosby matched James with 28 points to share high-scoring honors.

A big second half in which the Tide outscored Hughes-Kirk 44-21 was enough to earn an 81-57 semifinal win. Kirtley had 24 points, James 21 and Alexander 13 for the Tide.

Behind two free tosses by Bowen and six unanswered points from James, the Tide raced to an 8-0 lead en route to a 72-62 title-game win over Greenville. The Blackhawks managed to slice the lead to a single point on numerous occasions, but clutch play enabled the Tide to repel each charge.

James again paced the Tide, finishing with 22 points. Mayes had 17, Kirtley 16 and Bowen 11 for the winners.

John Elliott led the Blackhawks with 18.

The regional tourney's opening foe was Centertown, a club that owned a win over the Tide. And were it not for Alexander's late-game heroics, the Demons would have registered a second win, one that ended the Tide's season. With his team trailing, Alexander wrapped a pair of field goals around one by Centertown's Barry Barnes to lift the Tide to a 64-62 victory.

For the Tide, who led by as many as 18 points in the second quarter, James had 17 points, Alexander 14, Mayes and Kirtley a dozen each.

Danny Decker had 23 to lead all scorers.

After escaping that heart-stopper, the Tide stormed into the championship game by blasting Edmonson County 97-55 in semifinal action. This game was never close, with the Tide racing to a 46-20 half-time lead and never looking back.

The red-hot James led the attack with 22 points, giving him 110 in the past five outings. Kirtley chipped in with 19 points, while Alexander had 14, Mayes and Stone 13 each.

The title game meant a tussle with Breckinridge County and Butch Beard, who ranks among the greatest opponents Central City teams have encountered. One season earlier, Beard led the Bearcats to a runner-up finish in the state tournament.

This game was a defensive struggle from the opening tip-off to the final buzzer. Each club managed to pull in front by six points along the way, but neither team could build on that advantage.

The Tide led 25-23 at intermission, but trailed 40-38 heading in the final frame. In the decisive fourth quarter, the Tide, sparked by 10 points from Bowen, fought back to take a 52-49 lead with just over two minutes remaining. But in those crucial final moments, Beard accounted for five points and Jay Harrington hit a lone free throw to offset a late Kirtley bucket and give the Bearcats a 55-54 victory.

Poor free throw shooting killed any hope of victory for the Tide. During the last quarter, the Tide missed all five free throw attempts.

Beard, who would lead his team to the state title a week later, ended with 26 points.

Mayes led the Tide with 15 points, while Alexander and Bowen each had 10. The high-scoring James was limited to four points.

This had been a magnificent season, and with four starters returning, the outlook for 1965-66 was especially bright. And the returning players did not disappoint.

Chapter 35

1965-66

Many long-time Golden Tide fans will argue that the 1965-66 team is the best in school history. It's an argument that is difficult to refute. This team had everything required for greatness—experience, talent, shooters, rebounders, defenders, a strong bench. And you can toss in hunger as an added element. After all, this is essentially the same group of players who came within a whisker of beating eventual state champion Breckinridge County in last year's regional final.

In every way this was a powerful team, one that would finish with a 33-3 record while advancing to the semifinals of the state tournament. So dominant was this team that, not counting the three losses, only six opponents managed to stay within eight points.

But danger lurked, primarily due to the unknown factor. Remember, this was the year when regional re-alignment went into effect. Originally, it was reported that Central City and Greenville would be moved from the fourth region to the second region and placed in the eighth district along with Todd County and Fort Campbell. This move would have put the Tide and Blackhawks in with teams like Madisonville, Christian County and Hopkinsville.

That arrangement was quickly shut down by the powers that be. In the end, Central City, Greenville, Drakesboro, Muhlenberg Central, Graham and Hughes-Kirk were given a permanent home in the third region. In a mystery even Einstein couldn't solve, Bremen, a Muhlenberg County school, had long been located in the Owensboro (third) region.

"I knew we had the best team in the region that year," Tide coach Jackie Day said. "But I also knew it was going to be difficult for us. We would probably have to meet Owensboro somewhere down the road, and beating them in the Sportscenter wasn't going to be easy."

Four familiar faces returned to the 1965-66 starting quintet—seniors Sonny Alexander, Rodney Kirtley and David James, and junior Ralph Mayes. Joining them was cat-quick guard, junior Mike Venerable. Back-ups included Kenny Lindsey, Jeff Jones, Billy Chris Pendley, Billy Kirkpatrick, Jimmy Burney, Rocky Todd and Mack Dykes.

With James scoring 23 points, Mayes 20, Venerable 18 and Kirtley 17, the Tide opened the season by thumping home-standing South Hopkins 80-68. Game two resulted in an 85-52 win over Bremen, with Mayes hitting for 21 points, James 20 and Kirtley 16.

Those two victories were the start of a 10-game winning streak. Others victims included Hughes-Kirk 93-56, Drakesboro 92-72, Graham 122-61, Daviess County 90-77, Graham 91-58 and Muhlenberg Central 90-48. Then came a pair of wins in the Central City Invitational—86-51 over Hughes-Kirk and 72-71 over Earlington.

The win over Earlington was one in which the Tide blew a 10-point advantage heading into final frame, then had to hang on for the win. James led the Tide with 19 points, while Mayes had 17, Kirtley 15, Alexander 11 and Venerable 10.

During this streak several Tide players posted big numbers, particularly Mayes, who had 33 against Hughes-Kirk, 26 against Drakesboro, 32 against Graham and 22 against Muhlenberg Central. Alexander scored 23 against both Daviess County and Graham, while Venerable hit for 20 against Graham, James had 21 against Daviess County and Lindsey 16 against Graham.

A handful of opponents played well in a losing cause, including Hughes-Kirk's Larry Johnson (24 points), Drakesboro's Donnie Key (20 points), Graham's Bill Loney (19 points) and Earlington's Jim Hicks (20 points).

Caverna ended the Tide's unbeaten season by posting a come-from-behind 63-60 victory in the Trinity Invitational. The Tide owned a 39-26 lead at intermission, but Caverna won the third quarter 19-7 to tie it at 46-46 going into the final frame. In those eight minutes, Caverna was able to eek out the upset win.

Venerable paced the Tide with 16 points. Alexander finished with 13, Mayes and Kirtley 11 each.

James tossed in 19 points, Alexander 18, Venerable and Mayes 14 apiece in a 76-56 win at Greenville, which was led by Wayne Jernigan with 19 points.

Mayes Gets Hot, Another LIT Bid

In the Tide's next five games, all wins, Mayes was the top scorer. The gifted junior had 24 in a 91-60 win over Louisville DeSales, 22 in an 82-58 win over Madisonville, 22 in a 69-64 win over a strong Ohio County team, 17 in a 79-51 romp past Sacramento and 32 in a 100-78 win over Calhoun.

But Mayes wasn't alone in dishing out punishment. James had 20 against Ohio County and 28 against Calhoun; Alexander had 18 against Greenville and 17 against DeSales; Venerable had 17 against Calhoun and 15 against DeSales; and Jones had 13 against Sacramento.

Another change that occurred this season was the formation of Ohio County High School, which came about with the closing of Beaver Dam, Hartford and Centertown. Consolidating those three schools, all with a terrific basketball history, meant the formation of a single school that was an immediate regional contender. Owensboro and Ohio County were the biggest roadblocks standing between the Tide and a regional championship.

Beating Ohio County was accomplished without the services of Kirtley, who was sidelined for three games by an illness. Lindsey filled in admirably, scoring five points in that 69-64 victory. He came back to score 15 against Sacramento and seven against Calhoun.

Having accepted a bid to the Louisville Invitational Tournament, the Tide opened with a less-than-exceptional 53-45 victory over Atherton. James topped the Tide with 16 points. Mayes and Kirtley chipped in with 14 and 11, respectively.

This was not the Tide's last encounter with Atherton—the two teams would meet three times before the decade ended—and the next three went from bad to worse.

In quarterfinal action, Louisville Central used a huge third-quarter advantage (24-12) to bump the Tide out of the tournament by escaping with a 71-68 win. The Tide led 28-19 at intermission, but that third quarter proved to be the difference.

Although Lature Coleman had 19 points to lead Central, it was Ben Watkins' 15 second-half points that enabled his team to survive.

Mayes led the Tide with 17 points. Kirtley had 16, James 14 and Alexander 12 in a losing effort. This would be the Tide's last loss until the Sweet 16.

The first post-LIT outing was a tough one, a 69-63 win over visiting Greenville. The count was knotted 52-52 after three quarters, but the Tide, behind seven points from Mayes and six from James, managed to avoid the upset. All five Tide starters hit for double figures, paced by James with 20. Others included Mayes (14), Kirtley (13), Alexander (12) and Venerable (10).

Larry Elliott and Wayne Jernigan led Greenville with 24 and 22 points, respectively.

Blowing Folks Away

Following that close encounter with Greenville, the Tide reeled off six consecutive devastating victories, beating Drakesboro 94-69, Pine Knot 93-65, Monticello 89-79, Muhlenberg Central 110-69, Christian County 75-49 and Bremen 95-58.

In those six wins, either Mayes or James was the Tide's top scorer. Mayes racked up 30 against Drakesboro, 26 against Pine Knot, 31 against MC and 22 against Bremen. James scored 26 against Monticello, 31 against MC, 21 against Christian County and 22 against Bremen.

Other big efforts in this streak included Venerable with 18 against Pine Knot and MC, Alexander 16 against Christian County, and Kirtley 16 against Monticello.

Only the game at Monticello was a challenge. The host school was within three points (62-59) going into the final quarter, thanks to 27 points from Kermit Perkins and 20 from David Upchurch. But with the game on the line, James and Kirtley each tallied eight fourth-quarter points and Venerable added seven to help the Tide hang on for the win.

Traditionally, the Tide closed out the regular season with a game against Owensboro. In the past, those games were strictly important from a won-loss standpoint. This time, however, now that the two schools were in the same region, the game took on an entirely different meaning. This was a recon mission, with each team scoping out the other on the off-chance that they might collide again later on down the road.

The road to Louisville.

This game, like a second one if it materialized, would take place in the Sportscenter, home court for the Red Devils. For much of this game, it appeared as if Owensboro was going to stake its claim as the region's best team. After three quarters, the Red Devils owned a 48-

46 advantage. They led 35-30 at the break, but the Tide, getting seven third-quarter points from James and five from Kirtley, closed to within a bucket going into the last stanza.

Gutsy play down the stretch by Venerable, Mayes and James proved to be enough for the Tide to land a knockout blow, getting away with a 67-57 victory. James led the charge with 25 points, while Mayes had 13, Alexander 12 and Venerable 10, seven coming in that decisive fourth quarter.

All Eyes on the Sweet 16

With a sterling record of 25-2, the Tide opened post-season play by smashing Hughes-Kirk 96-63 in district action despite 34 points from the Tigers' Rudy Cundiff. Mayes had 28 to lead the winners, who also got 22 points from Alexander and 15 from James.

James knocked in 24 points, Mayes had 21, Alexander 13, Venerable and Lindsey 10 each in a 90-36 semifinal cakewalk past Graham. The Tide led this one 56-12 at the half.

The title game against Drakesboro wasn't so easy. After building a 68-53 lead through three quarters, the Tide were forced to hang on for an 80-78 win. In this one, the Cardinals outscored the Tide 25-12 in the last quarter.

"We had this game won," David James said, "and then we just stopped playing hard. When we did that, we let Drakesboro get back in it."

Mayes and Alexander paced the winners with 21 points apiece. Kirtley finished with 13 and James 10.

Bobby Ewing led the Cardinals with 20 points, while Ralph Dillihay and Donnie Key each contributed 17.

As things turned out, these two teams drew each other in the regional tournament opener. Also, in what was a huge break for the Tide, Owensboro and Ohio County were in the opposite bracket, meaning those two clubs would meet in the semifinal round.

In the regional opener, the Tide raced to a 33-26 halftime lead, then went on to register a more comfortable 80-64 win over the Cardinals. A balanced attack was the key, with all five Tide starters hitting for double figures, led by James with 18 points. Venerable and Alexander each had 16, Mayes 15 and Kirtley 10 for the Tide.

Ralph Dillihay paced the Cardinals with 18 points.

The Tide's semifinal encounter with Livermore turned out to be anything but easy. The Yellow Jackets battled hard before finally succumbing to the superior Tide 85-74. Mayes burned Livermore for 25 points, with Alexander and James each scoring 16, Kirtley and Venerable 14 apiece.

Ronnie Brown and Melvin Thomasson had 24 and 22, respectively, for Livermore, with Leslie "Chico" Burden adding 19.

In the other semifinal game, Owensboro edged Ohio County 74-70.

With a trip to the state tournament at stake, the Tide rode the hot outside shooting by James to a hard-fought 67-64 title-game victory. James blistered the Sportscenter nets for 20 points, all coming on long-range jumpers. He received solid support from Alexander with 16, Mayes and Kirtley a dozen each.

The score was tied 62-62 when James dropped in a bomb to put the Tide on top by a bucket. A free throw each by Kirtley and Mayes pushed the Tide's advantage to 66-62 with under a minute remaining.

P.T. Nichols scored for the Red Devils and drew a foul on Kirtley. His club trailing 66-64, Owensboro coach Bobby Watson quickly called a timeout. His instructions for Nichols were simple: intentionally miss the free toss in such a manner that a Red Devil teammate might snare the rebound.

Watson's plan proved to be only half successful. Nichols missed but it was a Tide player who got the rebound. The ball found its way into Venerable's hands, and he immediately drew a foul. Venerable sank the freebie to account for the final score, giving the third region crown and a Sweet 16 trip to the Tide.

Owensboro's Bill Heffelfinger led all scorers with 23 points.

Mayes, James and Alexander were named to the all-tournament squad.

A Superb Sweet 16 Effort

Making their first state tournament appearance since 1959, the Tide opened with a solid 87-75 victory over a Carlisle County team that owned a 29-4 record. After a tight opening quarter, the Tide, getting strong efforts from Alexander, Mayes and James, forged a 41-29 lead at intermission. The final 16 minutes were played on even terms.

James and Alexander each had 22 points for the Tide, with Mayes adding 21 and Kirtley 17.

The 1958-59 team, front row (l-r): Tommy Barnett, Frankie Mercer, Lance Gish, Lewis Chaney, Ben Mac Wolfe, Terrill Mayes. Back row (l-r): Jack Day, Carl White, Gene Dillingham, Sonny Stone, Eddie Vincent, Jackie Simpson, Jerry Mayes, Rogers Williams (manager).

Lewis Chaney (30), Frankie Mercer (34) and Lance Gish (31) look on as a Manual player grabs a rebound during 1959 state tournament action. Manual won 77-65.

Carl White and Jerry Mayes point to battle scars sustained by Jimmy Lynch and Jackie Welborn.

Golden Tide cheerleaders in 1962 were Sharon Casebier, Diane Stringer, Martha Henry, Gay Nell Martin and Deborah Withrow.

The 1962-63 team, front row (l-r): Gary Nofsinger, David Moore, Eddie Devine, Jimmy Davis, Joe Bowen, Larry Joe Higgs. Middle row (l-r): Larry Dale Erwin (manager), Tommy Wallace, William "B.O." Keown, Rodney Kirtley, Bobby Foster, Lee Stone, David James. Back row: Jackie Day and Ralph Evitts.

Corky in his St. Louis Cardinals uniform, 1963.

Greenville's great Roger Newman

The school's first integrated team, 1963-64, (l-r), Jack Day, Billy Gentry, William "B.O." Keown, David James, Mike Gray, Lee Stone, Jimmy Davis, Bobby Foster, Rodney Kirtley, Eddie Devine, Charles Frank Winkler, Joe Bowen, Tommy Wallace, Robert Lee Hunter, Larry Joe Higgs, Ralph Evitts.

The 1964 all district team include, kneeling (l-r), Joe Bowen (CCHS), Billy Mike Pendley, (Muhlenberg Central), Leon Goins (Drakesboro Community), Eldon Hardison (Hughes-Kirk), Wayne Jernigan (Greenville). Standing (l-r), John Elliott (Greenville), Tommy Stovall (Graham), Bruce Penrod (Drakesboro), Eddie Rose (Greenville), David James (CCHS), Mickey Dickerson (Drakesboro Community). Steve Wood (Hughes-Kirk) was absent.

The 1964-65 team, front row (l-r), David James, Joe Bowen, Lee Stone, Sonny Alexander, Rodney Kirtley, Ralph Mayes, Larry Joe Higgs. Back row (l-r), Jackie Day, Mike Oates, manager, Kenny Lindsey, Charles Frank Winkler, Mike Gray, Billy Kirkpatrick, Mike Venerable, Buddy Collier (manager), Wayne Divine.

Delmas Gish, Jack Day and George Taylor, a trio of super successful Golden Tide coaches, display some of the hardware their teams won.

Wayne Divine (left) in 1965, his first year as Jack Day's assistant coach.

Billy Chris Pendley lets one go from long range.

Mike Venerable goes up for a bucket in the Sportscenter.

Sonny Alexander gets squeezed by two Hughes-Kirk defenders.

The 1965-66 team, front row (l-r): Mike Venerable, Ralph Mayes, Rodney Kirtley, Sonny Alexander, David James. Middle row (l-r): Kenny Lindsey, Billy Kirkpatrick, Jeff Jones, Billy Chris Pendley, Jimmy Burney. Back row (l-r): Jack Day, Rocky Todd, Mack Arthur Dykes, Buddy Collier (manager), Wayne Divine.

Coaches reach into the hat to draw for the district tournament. The coaches (l-r) include Jerry Shanks (Greenville), Winfred Thompson (Muhlenberg Central), Allen Miller (Graham), Jack Day (Central City), Randy Swann (Bremen), Robie Harper (Drakesboro) and Gene Pardue (Hughes-Kirk).

Early 1960s JV cheerleaders included Marsha Bums, Beverly Pendley, Mary Jane Moss, Margaret Williams, Barbara Lile and Sheila Lacefield.

Jackie Day barks instructions during the 1966 regional tournament final against Owensboro. The Golden Tide won 67-64.

The 1966-67 team, front row (l-r), Ricky Smith, Billy Kirkpatrick, Rocky Todd, Mike Johnson, Duward Thomas, Lonnie Turley. Back row (l-r), Jackie Day, Billy Chris Pendley, Kenny Lindsey, Larry Pendleton, Ralph Mayes, Jeff Jones, Mike Venerable, Richard Shaver (manager).

Ralph Mayes (22) attempts to block a shot by Greenville's Tom Lewis as teammates Jeff Jones and Mike Venerable look on.

A group of dejected Golden Tide players after losing to Owensboro in the 1967 regional finals. From left, Billy Chris Pendley, Lonnie Turley, Ralph Mayes, Billy Kirkpatrick, Mike Johnson, Duward Thomas, Larry Pendleton, Rocky Todd, Mike Venerable, Ricky Smith and Kenny Lindsey.

The 1967-68 team, front row (l-r), Jimmy Casebier (manager), Ricky Smith, Steve "Bosco" Reynolds, Joe Stone, Rocky Todd, Ricky Turley, Taylor Sparks, Mark Eades, Richard Shaver, manager. Back row (l-r), Jackie Day, Freddie Mayes, Bobby Campbell, Mike Dossett, Jerry Humphrey, Jewell Hampton, Lucian "Boat' Taylor, Wayne Divine.

Cheerleaders Pat Moss, Mary Jane Withrow, Sherry Carroll, Julie Tucker, Pam Milligan and Sylvia Day hold up paintings of Tide seniors Freddie Mayes, Taylor Sparks, Mark Eades, Joe Stone, Mike Dossett, Lucian "Boat" Taylor and Steve "Bosco" Reynolds.

Freddie Mayes fires a short jumper against Ohio County.

Taylor Sparks shoots over an Owensboro defender as teammates Ricky Turley, Mark Eades and Freddie Mayes look on.

Ricky Turley launches a jumper against Hughes-Kirk. Turley ranks as one of the deadliest Golden Tide marksmen.

Mark Eades lays in an easy two points.

The 1968-69 team, front row (l-r), Eddie Renfrow (manager), Donald Sallee, Jimmy Talbott, Donald Morris, Freddie Mayes, Brad Todd, Lucian Taylor, Richard Shaver, manager. Back row (l-r), Jackie Day, Mark Eades, Taylor Sparks, Steve Reynolds, Joe Stone, Ricky Turley, Mike Dossett, Wayne Divine.

The 1969-70 team, front row, Richard Shaver (manager). Middle row (l-r), Tommy Hamilton, Donald Sallee, Jimmy Talbott, Jerry Taylor, John Taylor. Back row (l-r), Wayne Divine, Lucian Taylor, Mike Dossett, Taylor Sparks, Steve Reynolds, Joe Stone, Mark Eades, Freddie Mayes, Jackie Day.

Former Louisville Cardinals coaches Peck Hickman, John Dromo and Denny Crum.

Two Central City giants. Robert Walker and George Taylor, the men who transformed the band and basketball programs into something special.

The 1971-72 team, front row (l-r), Jerry Taylor, Tommy Eades, Rusty Dossett, Kenny Raley, Sammy Sparks, Tony Hopper, Carlos "T.T." Hampton. Back row (l-r), Terry Talbott, David Hunter, Ricky Sallee, Frank Sherrod, Terry Huddleston, Phil Goldston, Toby Stevenson.

Jerry Taylor and Tony Hopper display the spoils of victory after winning the 1972 district tournament. They are flanked by Carlos "T.T." Hampton and assistant coach Wayne Divine.

Tony Hopper, Wayne Divine and Jerry Taylor at the 1972 athletic banquet.

The 1972-73 team, kneeling, Richard Deavers and Philip Whitmer (managers). First row (l-r), Sammy Sparks, Terry Huddleston, Terry Talbott, Tommy Eades, Phil Goldston, Carlos Hampton, David Hunter. Back row (l-r), Bill Loney, Ricky Sallee, Steve Dukes, Eddie Gray, Rocky Watkins, Mike Shrewsberry, Wayne Divine.

Award winners at the 1973 banquet include Tommy Eades, Sammy Sparks, Carlos Hampton and Terry Talbott.

Bill Loney took over as Golden Tide coach in 1973.

The 1974-75 team, front row (l-r), Mike Shrewsberry, Steve Dukes, John Toll, Rocky Watkins, Rick Brothers, Mike Jenkins. Middle row (l-r), William Hamilton, Ronnie Stewart, Bobby Joe Gott, Steve Sparks, Dennis Laycock, Kerry Holden, Tommy Kirkpatrick. Back row (l-r), Bill Loney, Paul Wilcox, Marty Garrett, Bobby Wilcox, Chuck Childress, Jerry Young.

The 1981-82 team, front row (l-r), John Soderling, Penrod Eades, Charles Johnson, Jeff Sparks, Tommy Tinsley, Troy Crist, Darren Peveler. Second row (l-r), Rodney Burch, Dwight Gamble, Ben Lutz, Jeff Brothers, Terry Nofsinger. Back row (l-r), Robert Cheatham (manager), Jerry Young.

Penrod Eades, Wallace Ray Martin, Stanley Taylor and Jon Moore did some clowning after practice.

Greg Franklin, left, was named Muhlenberg County Player of the Year in 1989. He also won the award in 1988.

Curtis Shelton applies defensive pressure on an opponent during tournament action.

The 1988-89 team, front row (l-r), Tony Hopper, Maurice Summers, Claude Hampton, Greg Franklin, Steve Divine, Curtis Shelton, Mark Eades. Middle row (l-r), Jim Wilcox, Chris Cary, Jeremy Divine, Tyrone Saulsbemy, Paul Kirtley, Richard Deavers, Steve Sparks. Back row (1-r), Steve Newman, Kenny Alward, Jerry Gordon, Therron Cunningham, Brad Divine, John Kirtley, Nace Creager.

Maurice Summers, first on bottom row, Claude Hampton (50), Steve Divine (20) and Greg Franklin (34) made the all-regional squad after leading the Tide to the 1989 Sweet 16.

Tony Hopper led the Golden Tide to their 17th and final Sweet 16 appearance in 1989.

Central City's last team in 1989-90 included, sitting (l-r), Tony Hopper, Jeremy Divine, Therron Cunningham, Kelley Blair, Todd Pollard, Todd Hayes, Curtis Shelton, Mark Eades. Back row (l-r), Nace Creager (manager), Steve Sparks, Mark Smith, Richie Cook, Lamont Mitchell, Brad Divine, Mike Smith, Steve Newman, Richard Deavers (scorekeeper), John Kirtley (manager).

Two master musicians. Sir James Galway, left, shares a light moment with ex-Golden Tide player Jim Walker.

Author Tom Wallace with his boyhood hero Corky Withrow. These two ex-Golden Tide players combined for 3,144 career points. (Corky scored 3,136.)

Cliff Hagan and Corky Withrow, Kentucky Basketball Hall of Fame members.

Corky Withrow and King Kelly Coleman, 2014.

Corky Withrow and King Kelly Coleman, 2014.

Pictured from left: King Kelly Coleman, Howie Crittenden, Freddie Maggard and Corky Withrow.

Next up for the Tide was Glasgow, an 87-68 winner over Newport Catholic and future Boston Celtics great Dave Cowens in its opener. The Scotties, coached by future WKU head man Jim Richards, came into the quarterfinal round with a 31-1 record.

It was expected to be a white-knuckler. It wasn't. Giving one of their finest efforts of the season, especially in the second half, the Tide rolled to a surprisingly easy 79-54 victory. The Tide sat on a 31-22 lead at the half, but it was in those final 16 minutes, in which they outscored the Scotties 48-32, that the game turned into a runaway.

Mayes gave a monster effort, finishing with 32 points on 11 field goals and 10 of 13 from the charity stripe. Alexander and James also hit double digits with 18 and 10, respectively.

Glasgow's Johnny Vance, a future WKU quarterback, led his club with 22 points.

Big and powerful Louisville Male, led by all-state performers Eugene Smith and Ted Rose, ended the Tide's title hopes by notching an 81-68 semifinal win. Smith finished with 25 points and Rose had 17 for the Bulldogs.

The Tide only led once, 10-9 after a Kirtley free throw with 1:57 remaining in a first quarter that ended with Male on top 15-12. The second quarter was the difference. In those eight minutes, Male, getting 10 points from Willie Woods and seven from Rose, outscored the Tide 25-12 for a 40-24 lead at the half.

The two clubs played on relatively even terms in the third frame, which ended with Male sitting on a 57-40 lead. That advantage swelled to 73-49 with just over four minutes remaining. The Tide fought back, outscoring Male 19-8 to get within that final 13-point margin.

Smith was the Bulldog who kept his team in front, scoring 10 of his 25 points in the final quarter.

Mayes led the Tide with 22 points, earning all-tournament team recognition for his efforts. In his three state tourney games, Mayes scored 75 points, surpassing Corky Withrow's 72 for the most ever by a Golden Tide player.

Kirtley had 14 against Male, with James hitting for 13 and Alexander 11.

Male, expected to win it all, was stunned by Mike Casey and Shelby County in the championship game. The question then begs: How would the Tide have fared against Shelby County had they managed to get past Male?

"We certainly matched up a lot better against Shelby County than we did against Male," David James said. "Whether we could have beaten them, well, I don't know. Mike Casey was awfully good."

So was this Central City team, which ended with a sparkling 33-3 record. But with James, Kirtley and Alexander all departing, next season's club had some huge holes to fill. And it would, thanks to the trio of Mayes, Venerable and Lindsey.

Chapter 36

1966-67

When you lose players the caliber of David James, Rodney Kirtley and Sonny Alexander, it's only natural to expect a down turn in terms of success. After all, during the past two seasons that threesome was at the heart of Golden Tide teams that posted a 63-8 record and advanced to the state tournament semifinal round.

Replacing them wasn't going to be easy. James ranks as one of the deadliest shooters in school history. Kirtley was a steady scorer and rebounder, and Alexander was a maturing player with unlimited potential. Also, Alexander was 6'6" and Kirtley 6'4", meaning next year's club was going to be much smaller than its immediate predecessor.

Given the loss of so much offensive firepower, size, experience and rebounding, a down turn was not only expected, it was highly probable.

But it didn't happen. And that's because a returning player just happened to be one of the three or four greatest players in Golden Tide history—Ralph Mayes. Led by him, this bunch of courageous runts finished with an outstanding 27-7 record while coming within one victory of earning another trip to the Sweet 16.

Although Mayes was the catalyst, this team could not have succeeded had others not stepped up in a big way. And they did, particularly Kenny Lindsey and Mike Venerable. Along with Mayes, they were the only players on this squad with much real-game experience. Venerable had been a starter the previous season while Lindsey had been a valuable sixth man. For this team to win, those two would have to up their game several notches, which is exactly what they did.

Mayes would average 21.5 points per game, Lindsey 20.3, Venerable 14.1. This would be the only time in Central City history that two players averaged 20 points in the same season.

Joining those three in the starting lineup were Jeff Jones and Billy Chris Pendley. Other team members included Billy Kirkpatrick, Rocky Todd, Ricky Smith, Lonnie Turley, Larry Pendleton, Duward Thomas, Mike Johnson and Ricky Turley.

"We were a really small team," Lindsey noted. "Ralph was six-three, but he was a natural guard. Jones was six-two if you really stretched him out. Mike, Billy Chris and I were all about five-nine. So for us to win, we had to shoot well, play strong defense and not get wiped out on the boards. The key for us was the press. We pressed all the time, and since we were in such great physical shape, we won a lot of games in the fourth quarter."

The season began with Mayes giving a preview of coming attractions, hitting for 32 points in a 92-62 win over Webster County. Lindsey had 17 points, Venerable 13, Jones 12, Pendley six, Kirkpatrick and Pendleton four each, Todd and Johnson a bucket apiece.

Mayes followed the season opener with a 33-point effort as the Tide ripped Bremen 98-67. Lindsey finished with 26, Pendley 13 and Venerable 10 for the winners. Next, in a 102-49 pasting of Graham, Lindsey scored 23, Jones and Mayes 20 each, Venerable 19 and Pendley 14.

Terry Chaney paced Graham with 18, while future Tide coach Bill Loney added 13.

Easy victories continued to build up as the Tide dispatched Drakesboro 87-54, Graham 90-67, Daviess County 74-58, Hopkinsville 109-84 and Muhlenberg Central 97-68 before participating in the Central City Invitational.

There was no shortage of high-scoring performances during this streak, the highlight being 44 points from Mayes against Hopkinsville, thus making him the first Tide player since Corky Withrow and Lance Gish to crack the 40-point barrier.

In this impressive winning streak, Mayes also had 32 against MC, 27 against Graham and 24 against Drakesboro; Lindsey scored 28 against Hoptown, 27 against Graham and 25 against Drakesboro; Venerable had 20 against Daviess County and 18 against Drakesboro.

In the CCIT opener, Venerable rammed in 26 points, Lindsey 24, Mayes 20 and Jones 13 as the Tide advanced to the championship game by beating Bremen 92-73. The Eagles stayed close for a half, but a big 24-12 third-quarter advantage by the Tide broke the game open.

Joe Nelson led the Eagles with 23 points, while Carl White added 20.

In the title game, Earlington, led by Justin Sharp's 23 points, raced to a 27-14 first-quarter lead and then went on to claim the crown with a 75-65 victory. Tyrone Hopson finished with 19 points and Greg Martin 14 for Earlington, which would go on to win the state championship in March.

Venerable topped the Tide's scoring with 23 points. Lindsey had 20 and Jones 13, while Mayes, who fouled out, was held to nine.

The Tide hit the road to participate in the Owensboro Invitational, notching an opening-round 86-60 win over Owensboro Catholic. Lindsey hit for 24 points, Mayes 23 and Jones 15 in this easy victory. The only negative came when Lindsey missed a free throw, his first misfire after connecting on 32 in succession.

With Felix Thruston tossing in 24 points, third-region powerhouse Owensboro handed the Tide an 80-68 defeat in the first of three meetings between these two clubs. Thruston got plenty of help from George Crowe and Jerry Davenport, both of whom had 15 points.

For the Tide, Mayes had 19, Lindsey 17, Jones 16 and Venerable 12.

In a relatively low-scoring affair, the Tide brushed off home-standing Hughes-Kirk 64-46. Mayes finished with 17 points, Venerable 15, Lindsey 13 and Pendley 11. Next, the Tide manhandled Greenville 99-58 thanks to a 27-point performance from Lindsey. Mayes and Venerable also posted big numbers, hitting for 21 and 18 points, respectively.

Larry Elliott led the Blackhawks with 15 points.

The Tide split their next four games, sandwiching losses to DeSales 81-78 and Ohio County 85-67 around wins over Leitchfield 91-62 and Madisonville 91-68. Several Tide players put up impressive numbers during this stretch, headed by Mayes with 32 against Leitchfield and Lindsey with 31 against Madisonville. Venerable scored 17 against both DeSales and Ohio County.

A four-game winning streak began with Lindsey hitting for 30 points and Mayes adding 21 in a tough 84-73 victory over stubborn

Livermore. Venerable chipped in with 16 points in this first of four brushes with disaster.

Facing a second straight McLean County foe, the Tide managed to hang on for a 73-71 win at Calhoun. The Tide led 55-47 after three quarters, but the Bulldogs fought back to make it interesting. Mayes scored 23, Lindsey 22 and Venerable 16 for the winners.

The same scenario played out at Greenville, with the Tide holding a 53-44 advantage after three quarters, then having to hold on for a 73-72 victory. Mayes finished with 25 points, Lindsey 17, Jones 14 and Venerable 13 for the Tide.

Larry Elliott had 19 for Greenville.

Staying on the road, the Tide, getting 25 points from Mayes and 22 from Lindsey, got past Drakesboro 72-66. Jones had 11 points and Venerable 10 in that win.

Drakesboro's Tommy Warman led all scorers with 26.

The Tide's four-game winning streak ended with a 61-58 setback at Webster County. Lindsey led the Tide with 22 points. Mayes had 16 and Jones 12.

A huge 31-point fourth quarter, fueled by 10 points from Pendley, lifted the Tide to an 86-61 win at Livermore. Pendley finished with 14 points as all five Tide starters cracked double figures. Lindsey had 21, Mayes 20, Venerable 13 and Jones 11.

With Mayes scoring 26 points, the Tide crushed Monticello 86-69. Pendley and Lindsey each accounted for 16 points, with Venerable adding 12 in this impressive win. Mayes came back to put in 30 points as the Tide ripped Muhlenberg Central 115-68 at MC. Lindsey added 20 points, Venerable 14, Pendley 12 and Jones 11 as the Tide upped their season record to 21-5.

It took a big fourth quarter for the Tide to slip past Bremen 60-58 at home. The Tide trailed 44-39 heading into those final eight minutes. Jones came up big during crunch time, scoring seven of his team-best 16 points in the last stanza. Venerable and Mayes each had 13 points for the Tide, who played this game without Lindsey.

Joe Nelson had 21 points for the Golden Eagles.

In the season finale, the Tide pulled off a stunning upset, beating powerful Owensboro 58-50. By controlling the pace and getting a monster fourth quarter effort from Lindsey, the Tide managed to earn their biggest win of the season. The Tide led 26-23 at intermission, extended their advantage to 38-28 after three quarters, and then with Lindsey scoring 13 of his 19 points in the final quarter, they held off the Red Devils to get the victory.

Mayes had 15 points and Pendley 10 in this win. For the game, the Tide shot 57.1 percent from the field while becoming the first team to out-rebound the Red Devils (22-21). Mayes and Jones each had eight rebounds for the winners.

Ronnie Jackson paced Owensboro with 15 points. Felix Thruston, the Red Devils' first-team all-state performer was held to a single field goal and seven points overall.

District play began with the Tide beating Bremen 72-54 in a game that was closer than the final score indicates. After three quarters, the Tide held a slim 48-43 advantage. In the last stanza, the Tide got nine points from Venerable and eight from Mayes to pull away for a comfortable win. Lindsey led the Tide with 20 points, while Mayes had 18, Venerable 14 and Jones 13.

Carl White topped Bremen with 21 points.

Semifinal action against Hughes-Kirk turned out to be no contest, with the Tide easily winning 82-39. In this win, Lindsey had 21 points, Venerable 19, Mayes 16 and Pendley 15.

Looming ahead in the championship game was Greenville, a club the Tide had twice defeated during the regular season, once by a 41-point margin. But with the title riding on the outcome, the Blackhawks broke open a close game by dominating the second half en route to a 75-61 victory.

Larry Elliott had 22 points, Tom Cornette 19 and Doug Cornette 16 for the champs.

Venerable's 23 points paced the Tide. Mayes ended the night with 17 points, while Jones added 10.

In what turned out to be a most uneven performance, the Tide opened regional tourney play by beating Leitchfield 77-65. The Tide were red hot in the first half, building a 51-18 lead at the break. That huge advantage proved to be necessary. Over the final two quarters, Leitchfield outscored the Tide 47-26, at one stage cutting the difference to 10 points.

Lindsey led the winners with 24 points, all on field goals. Mayes scored 14, Venerable 12 and Jones 11 for the Tide.

On deck was Ohio County, which owned an 85-67 regular-season victory over the Tide. And for three quarters it looked as though the

Eagles would be the ones advancing to the championship game against Owensboro. The Eagles were in front 21-16 at the half and 34-33 after three quarters.

But the fourth quarter belonged to the Tide, who outscored Ohio County 19-14 for a 52-48 win. Lindsey paced the Tide with 15 points, while Mayes had 13 and Pendley 10, including six in that crucial fourth-quarter comeback.

Lowell Tarrants topped Ohio County with 14 points.

Going into the championship game against Owensboro, no one had any doubts about the Tide's game plan. Slow the pace, keep possession as long as possible and make every shot opportunity count, preferably going for easy layups rather than jump shots. And most of all don't get murdered on the boards.

For a half the Tide's plan worked to perfection. At the break the score was knotted at 21-21. Outscored nine to four in the third stanza, and now having to pick up the pace in order to catch up, the Tide were no match for the Red Devils, who captured the crown with a 52-33 win.

Felix Thruston, held in check in the previous encounter, led Owensboro with 22 points.

Mayes, in his final game, had 10 points for the Tide. He would later be named a first-team all-state selection.

This small, gutsy, courageous team finished the season with a fine 27-7 record. It ranks among the great overachievers in Golden Tide history. And Mayes, who scored 2,076 career points and later starred at Vanderbilt, surely ranks among the top three or four Golden Tide players ever.

Lindsey, along with averaging 20.3 points per game, connected on 81.3 percent of his free throws, ranking him among the top for charity stripe accuracy.

But this team was heavy on seniors, with all five starters graduating at the end of the year. This meant the 1967-68 club was going to have plenty of new faces. Fortunately, there was no shortage of basketball talent to go along with those new guys who were set to take over.

Chapter 37

1967-68

Given the absence of names like Mayes, Lindsey and Venerable, not many people had high hopes for the 1967-68 team. This was certain to be a young and inexperienced club, and as history normally shows us, youth and lack of experience can be a lethal combination in the world of sports.

And yet this team ended up surprising virtually everyone, finishing with a 22-11 record. And while youth and inexperience did factor in on several occasions, this young group claimed wins over such foes as Louisville Durrett, Ohio County, Madisonville and Christian County.

Rocky Todd was the only returning player with any game experience at all, and he would acquit himself well all season. But what no one expected was the consistently high level of play by the four newcomers—junior Ricky Turley, and a trio of gifted sophomores, Steve "Bosco" Reynolds, Mark Eades and Joe Stone. That foursome was instrumental in helping this young team become big overachievers.

Joining them were Freddie Mayes, Rick Smith, Bobby Campbell, Taylor Sparks, Mike Dossett, Jewel Hampton, Jerry Humphrey and Lucian "Boat" Taylor.

This was a team that had good size (Stone was 6'4", Turley and Reynolds 6'3") and some deadly shooters (Turley, Reynolds, Eades and Sparks). As with any young team, success or failure depended on playing solid defense and minimizing turnovers.

The Tide opened the season with a come-from-behind 65-62 win over Bremen. Trailing 51-47 after three quarters, the Tide got seven fourth-quarter points from Reynolds, six from Turley and five from Todd to earn the victory. Reynolds paced the winners with 20 points, while Turley had 16 and Stone 11.

Don Richey had 19 for Bremen.

Turley hit for 25 points, Reynolds had 18 and Eades 14 as the Tide rolled past Graham 76-45 in their next outing.

The first loss came against Drakesboro, which easily beat the Tide 69-45. Jolly Jernigan led the Cardinals with 18 points, while Tommy Warman added 17.

Turley paced the Tide with 14 points.

The Tide rebounded from that loss to claim back-to-back easy wins, beating Muhlenberg Central 84-60 and Graham 88-59. Turley scored 25 points, Stone 18, Eades 17 and Reynolds 12 in the win over MC, then Stone came through with 24, Reynolds 16, Turley 15 and Todd 14 against Graham.

Playing at Hopkinsville, the Tide fell behind early and were never able to catch up, eventually dropping a 64-61 decision. Eades led the Tide with 20 points, while Reynolds finished with 18 and Todd 10.

In a tune-up for the Central City Invitational, Turley knocked in 22 points, Stone 21 and Eades 17 in an impressive 75-67 win over Daviess County. In the CCIT opener, Reynolds had 18 points and Turley 14 as the Tide slipped past Muhlenberg Central 56-55.

In the title game, Drakesboro, getting 24 points from Tommy Warman and 15 from Jolly Jernigan, took home the big trophy by posting a 66-64 victory. The Tide did manage to make things interesting after trailing 50-39 heading into the final quarter. Eades, Stone and Turley each had 14 points and Reynolds 12 for the Tide.

The Tide split their next two games, beating Louisville Durrett 81-74 and then losing to Greenville 54-52 in the first of three close struggles between those two ancient rivals. Against Durrett, Turley topped the scoring with 22 points. Reynolds contributed 18, Eades 17 and Stone 15 in that win.

Greenville built a 43-33 lead after three quarters, then had to hang on late to escape with the win. Tom Cornette led the Blackhawks with a game-high 19 points.

Stone had 17 and Turley 13 in a losing effort.

After Turley dumped in 29 points and Stone 21 in a 73-66 win over Hughes-Kirk, Stone tallied 44 points in wins over Ohio County 68-46 and Livermore 65-60. Stone accounted for 24 points in the first win, 20 in the second.

A trip to Western Kentucky ended in a split decision, with the Tide losing 73-72 to Trigg County, then coming back one night later to beat Lone Oak 85-64. Stone continued to post big numbers, hitting for 24 against Trigg County. In that win, Turley had 19 and Reynolds 15. Against Lone Oak Turley led with 25 points, Reynolds had 19, Stone 13, Todd 12 and Eades 10.

That 25-point performance by Turley was the first in what proved to be a record-setting run by the red-headed "Rocket." In the Tide's next three games, Turley scored 91 points, getting 30 each in victories over Webster County 78-68 and Madisonville 66-65, and 31 in an 85-67 win over Leitchfield.

With those efforts, Turley became the first Golden Tide player since Corky Withrow to score 30 or more points in three successive games.

Several fellow Tide players performed well during this stretch, including Eades with 18 against Webster County and 15 against Madisonville, and Smith, who had 14 against Leitchfield while filling in for the injured Stone.

Greenville, getting 24 points from Tom Cornette, snapped the Tide's winning streak by pulling off a 74-71 victory in enemy territory. Cornetter got help from Rice Eaves with 18 points and Steve Peterson with 14.

Todd had 17 to lead the Tide, with Turley adding 16, Eades 15 and Stone 13.

Behind 22 points from Stone and 18 each from Reynolds and Turley, the Tide bounced back to beat dangerous Drakesboro 77-71. That win was followed by a narrow 69-67 victory over Owensboro Catholic. Turley paced the winners with 21 points. Others in double figures included Reynolds with 17, Stone 16 and Eades 11.

Playing less-than-inspired basketball, the Tide dropped two of their next three games, beginning with an 83-71 setback at Livermore. They managed to sneak past Hughes-Kirk 71-68 in their next outing before falling to Muhlenberg Central 65-63 at home.

Stone, Reynolds and Turley each had 20 points in the loss to Livermore. Against Hughes-Kirk, Turley had 17, Eades, Stone and Reynolds 16 apiece. Stone led with 23 against MC.

Getting 26 points from Turley and 20 from Eades, the Tide captured the first of two road wins by beating Christian County 76-73. Then Reynolds hit for 20 points, Stone 18, Eades 17 and Turley 10 as the Tide ripped home-standing Bremen 76-60.

Terrell Nelson paced Bremen with 21 points.

A third straight road game ended with a 64-55 loss to Owensboro in the Sportscenter. The Red Devils, led by George Crowe, took command early and never were seriously threatened. Crowe had 23 points for the winners.

Turley was the game's top point producer with 28.

Taking a 20-9 record into post-season play the Tide faced Graham in the district opener. In what proved to be a hard-fought battle, the Tide, behind 21 points from Reynolds, 13 from Stone and 12 from Turley, pulled out a 63-54 victory.

Russell Oates had 21 points for the Nighthawks.

Semifinal action against Hughes-Kirk turned out to be another struggle. The Tide owned a slim 42-40 lead after three quarters before going on to post a 61-52 win despite missing seven fourth-quarter free throws.

Turley and Reynolds led the winners with 22 and 15 points, respectively.

Tim Porter scored 15 for the Tigers.

In the championship game, clutch play by Tom Cornette and Steve Peterson inside the final minutes was enough to lift Greenville to a 72-70 victory. This was the Blackhawks' third win over the Tide this season, with those three games decided by a total of seven points.

Greenville was sitting on a 62-57 lead with 3:11 remaining when four unanswered points by Reynolds pulled the Tide to within a single point at 62-61. Cornette connected on a bucket and a pair of free throws to push the Blackhawks' advantage to 66-61. After Stone and Peterson exchanged two points each to make it 68-63, Turley hit a pair of freebies and Reynolds knocked in a field goal to close the gap to 68-67 with 1:10 left.

Cornette canned two more free throws before Stone hit one for the Tide to make it 70-68 with 14 ticks remaining. In those waning seconds, Peterson hit a pair of free tosses and Stone put in a field goal to account for the final score.

Cornette led all scorers with 24 points, while Peterson added 18.

Reynolds had 20 for the Tide, including 10 in the final stanza. Turley finished with 18 points and Stone 17 in a losing effort. Those three players were named to the all-district squad.

Thanks to Bob Embry, the Tide's stay in the regional tournament was short-lived. Embry banged in 37 points to lead Caneyville to an easy 93-61 first-round win. Caneyville would go on to capture the regional crown and then advance to the semifinals of the state tournament.

Stone and Reynolds were the only Tide players in double figures, ending with 15 and 10 points, respectively.

The best thing about sophomores is they eventually become juniors and seniors. This sophomore class, led by the trio of Reynolds, Stone and Eades, also included Mayes, Sparks, Dossett and Taylor. It would be this group that led the Tide to a 56-9 record over the next two seasons.

Chapter 38

1968-69

Seldom in Central City's long basketball history has a team welcomed the return of so much proven offensive firepower. Ricky Turley, now a senior, was back, along with juniors Steve Reynolds, Mark Eades and Joe Stone. All four of those players averaged in double figures the previous season.

That talented quartet would be joined by junior Freddie Mayes, a clever, heady player whose primary goal was to run the offense from his point-guard position, and Taylor Sparks, a super shooter.

Joining those six were Mike Dossett, Lucian Taylor, Jimmy Talbott, Donald Sallee and Brad Todd.

This club would win its first 18 games, crack the 100-point barrier seven times, beat Tom Payne and highly ranked Louisville Shawnee in a classic thriller and finish with a 26-5 won-loss record. Yet, despite those accomplishments, this season ranks among the most disappointing in Golden Tide history.

The Tide opened with a pair of top-the-century-mark wins—101-72 over Bremen and 101-35 over Graham. In the opener, Turley and Eades each had 26 points, Reynolds and Mayes 16 apiece. Against Graham, six players hit for double figures, headed by Eades with 20. Others included Stone and Reynolds with 15 each, Sparks with 13, Mayes and Turley with a dozen apiece.

A very good Drakesboro team offered a serious challenge before finally dropping a 75-65 decision, thus becoming the first of only seven conquered foes to stay within 10 points of the Tide. Mayes did the big damage against the Cardinals, hitting for 20 points. Reynolds had 14, Stone 13, Turley and Eades 10 each.

Billy Warford led Drakesboro with 18 points.

The Tide continued to roll, beating Muhlenberg Central 102-56, Graham 87-40, Hopkinsville 77-64, Glasgow 69-59 and Allen County 67-61, improving to 8-0 heading into the Central City Invitational.

Stone scored 27, Reynolds 24 and Eades 17 against MC, then Reynolds had 24 and Stone 21 in the win over Graham. Against Hoptown, Turley paced the scoring with 22 points, while Eades had 17, Stone 13 and Mayes 12. On the road trip to Glasgow and Allen County, Reynolds had 21 in the first game, Mayes had 17, Turley and Eades 16 each in the second outing.

The CCIT was expected to feature a championship battle between the Tide and Drakesboro. But that game never materialized. While the Tide crushed Muhlenberg Central 110-56 in the opener, Drakesboro was bumped off by Hughes-Kirk 51-49. In the romp past MC, Reynolds had 22 points, Turley 20, Mayes 16, Eades 14 and Stone 10.

MC's Bobby Perry led all scorers with 29 points.

One night later, the Tide took home the big trophy by beating Hughes-Kirk 82-64 behind 24 points from Reynolds, 19 from Turley, 14 from Eades and 11 from Stone.

Steve Foster finished with 27 points for the Tigers.

The Tide collected more hardware by beating Owensboro Catholic 91-66 and Hancock County 77-61 to win the Owensboro Invitational Tournament. Stone burned the Aces for 23 points in the opener, with Reynolds adding 18, Eades and Turley 15 each. In the title game, Reynolds and Turley had 18 points apiece, Mayes 12 and Stone 11.

Stone came through with 24 points, Turley 22, Eades and Reynolds 18 each as the Tide handled a solid Greenville club 100-72. In this impressive victory, the Tide connected on 44 field goals.

Greenville's Steve Peterson led all scorers with 29.

Home-standing Hughes-Kirk slowed the pace, hoping to pull off the big upset. The plan didn't work—the Tide escaped with a 62-49 victory. Reynolds topped the winners with 17 points, while Stone had 12 and Mayes 10.

In what was one of their best efforts of the season, the Tide remained unbeaten by posting a 96-86 win at Madisonville. Turley had 28 points, Eades 22, Reynolds 20, Stone and Mayes 12 each in this hard-earned win.

With a Louisville Invitational Tournament bid secured, the Tide rolled into that event with an unblemished 18-0 record by scoring road wins at Ohio County 73-60, Leitchfield 102-72 and Webster County 78-60.

At Ohio County, Turley had 19 points, Eades and Turley 13 each. Against Leitchfield, Turley scored 21, Eades 16, Stone 15, Reynolds, Mayes and Sparks 12 apiece. Reynolds was the top gun against Webster County, torching the nets for 28 points.

The win at Ohio County was especially impressive. Two months later, the Eagles would finish as runner-up to Louisville Central in the state tournament.

Now ranked third in the state behind Louisville Central and Louisville Male, the Tide were set to meet Atherton in the LIT opener. This was a game the Tide were expected to win with ease. However, two days before leaving for Louisville, Turley and Stone were hit hard by the flu bug.

"Joe and I were really sick," Turley remembers. "We had a high fever and we were throwing up. When we got to Louisville, Coach Day put us in a room together, away from the other guys. Essentially, he quarantined us. We both played against Atherton but neither of us played particularly well. Even with that, there is no way we should have lost that game. They just outplayed us, that's all you can say."

Atherton, a team that finished with a 13-15 record, pulled off a shocking 53-52 upset. This would be the first of three improbable Atherton wins over powerful Golden Tide team during a span of two seasons.

Led by 19 points each from Gary Byrd and Skip Wiegand, Atherton led 39-33 after three quarters, then held on in the closing seconds to secure the victory.

Reynolds had 20 for the Tide, with Turley adding 11 and Mayes 10. Stone was limited to six points and Sparks added five, while Eades, who went into the game averaging in double figures, was shut out.

The Atherton setback proved to be a turning point for this Golden Tide team. After winning their first 18 games, the Tide would lose five of their final 13.

"After the Atherton game, I think we only had one really good game," Turley said. "We played very well in the win over Louisville Shawnee. But I don't think we were ever the same team after the LIT."

Eades, after going scoreless against Atherton, came back to put in 29 points in a 90-79 win at Greenville. Stone had 23 in that victory, with Reynolds adding 18 and Turley 14.

Steve Peterson led Greenville with 24 points.

At Drakesboro, the Cardinals, thanks to seven fourth-quarter points from Jolly Jernigan, edged the Tide 55-54. Billy Warford led the winners with 16 points. Jernigan finished with 13.

Eades again topped the Tide with 18 points, while Turley and Reynolds added 15 and 12, respectively.

Following that loss the Tide got back on track by reeling off four straight impressive victories, beating Louisville Durrett 77-74, Sacramento 121-57, Hughes-Kirk 70-46 and Muhlenberg Central 86-53.

Turley did the most damage during this run, hitting for 23 against Durrett, 29 against Sacramento and 25 against MC. Eades scored 22 against Durrett, Reynolds had 21 and Stone 20 against Sacramento, while Mayes tallied 20 against Hughes-Kirk.

Next up was one of the most-memorable games in Golden Tide history, one that ranks alongside the Central City-Wayland classic in which Corky Withrow and "King" Kelly Coleman each scored 40 points. This encounter was against Louisville Shawnee and its towering 7'1" all-state standout Thomas Payne.

"The gym was absolutely packed," Turley said. "There were so many people sitting on the floor that you couldn't see the out-of-bounds lines. It was a wild night."

And a wild game the Tide won 91-90 despite Payne's 41-point performance. The score was tied 46-46 at intermission, then Shawnee took a 68-64 lead after three quarters. Late in the game, Shawnee was on top 86-85 when Mayes hit a jumper to give the Tide an 87-86 advantage. A bucket by Payne nosed the visitors ahead 88-87, but Mayes again came through with a basket to put the Tide in front for good at 89-88.

With four seconds remaining Sparks snared a missed shot and got the ball to Eades, who was immediately fouled. Eades dropped in both freebies to make it 91-88. An uncontested Shawnee basket at the buzzer accounted for the final 91-90 score.

Reynolds led a balanced Tide scoring attack with 21 points. Turley had 19, Mayes 18, Eades 14, Stone 13 and Sparks six.

Next, Reynolds burned Bremen for 27 points in an easy 96-67 win. Sparks, starting for the absent Turley, knocked in 17, Eades had 15, Mayes 12 and Stone 10.

Based on the Tide's last six games, it appeared as if the high-powered team seen during the early part of the season had returned. But that wasn't the case. The Tide would end the season by dropping three of their final four games, beginning with an 80-73 setback at Daviess County. Wilson Chapman led the winners with 20 points.

Reynolds matched Chapman's 20 points to share game-high honors.

The Tide closed out the regular season with an 88-85 overtime loss to Owensboro at home. Jerry Thruston paced the winners with 20 points.

Eades had 24 for the Tide, with Turley scoring 21, Reynolds 12, Stone 11 and Sparks 10.

Dragging back-to-back losses with them, the once-mighty Tide limped into district tournament action, facing Hughes-Kirk in the opener. After struggling for three quarters, the Tide were able to break away from a 43-43 deadlock and escape with a 57-53 victory.

This was a costly win, however. Mayes sustained a sprained ankle in the first quarter, an injury that had a profound impact on the Tide's chances of righting what was clearly a sinking ship.

Sparks led the Tide with 16 points, while Reynolds had 14 and Turley 12.

Hughes-Kirk's Tim Porter was the game's top scorer with 21.

Two nights later, Greenville, behind 22 points each from Steve Peterson and Rice Eaves, sent the Tide packing by notching a 75-68 semi-final victory. The game was close for three quarters, but the Blackhawks were the better team down the stretch, outscoring the Tide 24-18 in the final eight minutes.

Turley had 20 points in his last game. Stone finished with 16, Reynolds 13 and Eades 11.

This season has to fall into that "what-if?" category. What if Mayes hadn't been injured? How would the Tide have performed against Greenville if Mayes, the team leader, had been at full strength? Would his presence have made a difference, or was this a team on a fast track downhill?

Either way it had to be frustrating for the players, knowing they had beaten Ohio County, which finished as runner-up to Louisville Central in the state tournament, and Louisville Shawnee, the only team to beat Louisville Central all season, and then failed to even make it out of the district tournament.

Despite the disappointment, next season's outlook couldn't have been brighter. Four starters—Reynolds, Eades, Stone, Mayes—were set to return, along with Sparks, who would fill that fifth spot.

But next season, superb as it turned out to be, would have an ending eerily similar to this one.

Chapter 39

1969-70

Rarely in Central City's rich basketball history have back-to-back seasons followed the same pattern as the previous season and this one. Check it out: Last year's club had a 26-5 record; this one went 30-4. Last year's team won its first 18 games; this one won its first 19. Last year's club dropped its first game to Atherton in the Louisville Invitational Tournament; same thing happened to this team. Last year's team cracked the century mark seven times; same for this team. Last year's team beat Louisville Shawnee 91-90; this team beat Shawnee 102-101.

In the end, however, this was the more dominant team, scoring 80 or more points 25 times while only three defeated opponents managed to stay within 10 points of the Tide. Having said that, this team for all its terrific attributes would follow last year's club into that "what-if?" category. Why? Because this team would play more than half its games minus point guard Freddie Mayes, who went down with a leg injury (torn cartilage) in game 13.

Mayes was part of a talent-rich senior class that included Steve Reynolds, Mark Eades, Joe Stone, Taylor Sparks, Lucian Taylor and Mike Dossett. Also on the roster were Jimmy Talbott, Donald Sallee, Jerry Taylor, John Thomas Taylor, Tommy Hamilton and Tommy Eades.

The Tide opened the season with an NBA-type 129-102 win over Bremen in a game that saw seven players score 20 or more points. For the Tide, Reynolds had 29, Stone 25, Sparks and Eades 20 each. Mayes and Dossett also hit for double figures with 17 and 13, respectively.

For Bremen, Lanny Walker had 27, Roger Nelson 23 and Daniel Jones 22.

With 10 players scoring, six in double figures, the Tide swept past Graham 130-54. Reynolds led the charge with 24 points, followed by

Stone and Mayes with 22 each, Eades with 16, Sparks 13 and Lucian Taylor 12.

Dangerous Drakesboro was the Tide's next victim, losing 92-74. Reynolds finished with 25 points, Eades 22, Stone 16 and Sparks 13 in this win.

Earl Williams led Drakesboro with 23.

The Tide continued to roll, pounding Muhlenberg Central 71-35, Graham 131-50, Hopkinsville 91-78, Glasgow 99-58, Allen County 102-70 and Hughes-Kirk 91-68. Sparks and Reynolds each scored 14 in the win over MC, Stone had 21, Reynolds 19, Eades 18, Mayes 14, Sparks and Dossett 12 apiece against Graham. It was in the Graham game that freshman Tommy Eades scored the first eight of his 2,238 career points.

Reynolds hit for 32 against Hopkinsville, which was led by Bird Averitt's 38 points. Reynolds came back with 25 in the win over Glasgow, getting strong support from Sparks and Stone with 15 each, Eades and Mayes with 14 apiece. Mayes and Reynolds each had 19 against Allen County, with Eades tossing in 18, Stone 17, Sparks 14 and Dossett 10. Eades ended with 27, Mayes 22 and Reynolds 20 in the win over Hughes-Kirk.

The Central City Invitational resulted in two more easy wins—91-73 over Sacramento and 72-55 over Louisville Valley. Stone and Reynolds each had 21 points, Mayes 18, Sparks 14 and Eades 13 against Sacramento, then Reynolds erupted for 30, Eades added 15, Mayes 11 and Stone 10 against Valley.

Greenville battled the Tide hard for three quarters before falling 87-63. Reynolds had 26 points for the winners, Mayes 17, Eades 14 and Stone 11.

It was in the Tide's next win, 93-73 over Trigg County in the Hopkinsville Invitational that Mayes went down with his injury. His only appearances for the remainder of the season were brief stints in the first two regional tournament games. With Mayes sidelined, Dossett and Lucian Taylor filled in the fifth starting position.

Stone had a giant game against Trigg County, racking up a career-best 34 points on 15 field goals and four free throws. Reynolds finished with 27 and Eades 12 in this win. One night later, Reynolds hit for 23 points, Eades 15, Stone and Sparks 12 each as the Tide advanced to the finals by beating Todd County 74-67 in their first real test of the season.

In the championship game, Stone and Reynolds each tallied 26 points and Sparks added 14 to lift the Tide past Bowling Green 80-70. The Purples led 60-56 after three quarters, making this the first time all season that the Tide trailed heading into the final eight minutes.

Another tough opponent was on deck when the Tide returned home from their championship run. Ohio County made things interesting for a half, but with Reynolds scoring 30 points, Eades 19, Stone 15 and Sparks 14, the Tide pulled away for an 86-73 victory.

Against a solid Bremen club, it was Sparks who held the hot hand, scoring 28 points to lead his team to an 89-78 win. Reynolds chipped in with 22, Stone had 15 and Eades 11.

Lanny Walker hit for 20 to lead Bremen.

Behind huge performances by Reynolds, the Tide prepped for the Louisville Invitational Tournament by easily dismissing Leitchfield 76-59 and Webster County 107-84. Reynolds scored 28 in the first of those two outings, then came back to hit for 35 against Webster County.

Stone and Eades also put up big numbers in the win over Webster County, finishing with 20 and 19 points, respectively.

For the second straight year, the powerful and undefeated Tide were pitted against Atherton in the LIT opener, and for the second straight year, no one gave the Rebels a chance at pulling off the upset. And yet, it happened. Trailing 45-40 after three quarters, Atherton, which ended with a final record of 12-15, limited the Tide to nine fourth-quarter points while scoring 16, enough to walk away with a 56-54 victory.

Gary Byrd led the Rebels with 29 points. For the Tide, Eades had 19, Stone 16 and Sparks 11, while the high-scoring Reynolds was held to eight.

This would not be the last time these two teams squared off against each other this season.

Rebounding from that setback, the Tide came back to beat Greenville 100-82 in the first of five consecutive runaway wins. Against Greenville, Eades had 29 points, Sparks 19, Stone 17, Dossett 16 and Reynolds 11.

Greenville's Rick Newman led all scorers with 34.

After beating Greenville, the Tide ripped Drakesboro 86-56, Sacramento 81-64, Hughes-Kirk 81-51 and Muhlenberg Central 87-61. Points were evenly spread around during this stretch. Reynolds had 28 against Drakesboro, Stone had 27 against Sacramento and 26 against

MC, with Sparks hitting for 24 against the Spartans and Eades 19 in the win over Drakesboro.

Given the results and the similarity to past games against the same opponents, the Tide's two-game trip to Louisville might as well have been a journey to *The Twilight Zone*. First, there was a wild 102-101 win over Shawnee followed by a 64-62 loss to Atherton. This was Atherton's third consecutive victory over the Tide, with the difference in those three games a total of five points.

In a game where defense was a no-show, Eades turned in a career-best 38-point performance to lead the Tide past a Shawnee squad that battled back from an 81-68 third-quarter deficit to make things interesting. Eades finished with 13 field goals and 12 of 15 from the charity stripe. Reynolds ended the high-scoring affair with 26 points, while Stone added 25.

Shawnee's Marvin Travis led his team with 35 points.

Once again proving it had the Tide's number Atherton took a 28-22 halftime lead and then held on for the big win. Atherton's Gary Byrd led the winners with 19 points, 14 coming after intermission.

Stone and Eades each had 16 for the Tide, while Reynolds had 14 and Sparks 13.

Giving a poor performance against Christian County resulted in the Tide suffering an embarrassing 86-61 home-court spanking. The outcome of this one was decided early, with the Colonels grabbing a commanding 22-6 lead after the first quarter.

Gary Durham led the Colonels with 22 points. Reynolds and Lucian Taylor each had 13 for the Tide.

Coming off back-to-back losses, the Tide ended the regular season by beating Daviess County 88-75. Sparks topped a balanced scoring attack with 25 points. Stone accounted for 20, Reynolds and Eades 17 each in the final home game for this group of seniors.

After drawing a first-round bye, the Tide easily took care of Muhlenberg Central 77-48 in semifinal action. Eades had 20 points for the winners despite missing six of eight free throw attempts. He received strong support from Sparks with 18 points, Stone with 17 and Reynolds with 14.

Facing Greenville in the title game, the Tide ended their arch-rival's three-year hold on the championship hardware by rolling to a convincing 86-64 victory behind 25 points from Sparks, 18 from Eades, 17 from Reynolds and 16 from Stone.

Kenneth Drake led Greenville with 19 points.

Reynolds made sure the Tide's regional opener against Hancock County turned out to be no contest, scoring 28 points in a 92-44 romp. The talented Reynolds scored 16 points during the opening half, in which the Tide built a 39-14 advantage.

Sparks continued to play well, finishing with 18 points. Stone and Eades had 17 and 12, respectively.

Semifinal action against Edmonson County proved to be another laugher. With Eades and Stone each tossing in 20 points, the Tide stormed into the championship game with an 82-65 victory. Sparks had 17 points in this win, while Lucian Taylor added 11. Mayes, making a brief appearance, scored the final four points of his injury-prone career.

In the regional final, with a trip to the state tournament on the line, the Tide faced Owensboro for the only time all season. The Red Devils took control early, forging a 21-15 lead after one quarter. They upped their advantage to 39-28 at the half, and were still in front 54-45 after three quarters.

That's when the Tide, led by Sparks, Lucian Taylor and Dossett, began to climb back into the hunt. With Sparks and Taylor each scoring seven points and Dossett four, the Tide made a final charge, only to come up on the short end of a 73-69 score.

Sparks was brilliant, leading all scorers with 24 points. Stone, Reynolds and Eades all contributed 11 points apiece.

Roy Thruston and Geary Taylor each tallied 20 points for Owensboro.

Sparks, Stone, Eades and Reynolds were voted onto the all-tournament team. Reynolds would later be named a third-team all-state selection.

All five Tide starters scored in double figures for the year, led by Reynolds with a 21.9 average. Others included Stone (16.9), Eades (16.6), Sparks (14.3) and Mayes (13.8).

This concluded a mixed-bag decade that had some of Central City's all-time greatest teams and its absolute worst. Coming up was an even wilder decade, one that featured two coaching changes, a top-notch left-handed sharpshooter, several very strong teams and for the first time in school history, back-to-back losing seasons.

Chapter 40

1960s Sideline Shots

The Music Man

It's difficult to believe that any former Golden Tide player has rubbed shoulders with more famous people than Jimmy Walker. As one of the premier flutist in the world, Jim has met, collaborated with and befriended such iconic figures as John Williams, Paul McCartney, Leonard Bernstein, James Galway and Jean-Pierre Rampal, the granddaddy of modern classical flutists, who called Jim "his favorite jazz flute player."

But for Jim, who appeared on *The Tonight Show* and *The Today Show*, and who, as the founding member of the jazz quartet Free Flight, had a number one record, his love for music was matched by his desire to play basketball.

"I was a basketball nut," Jim said. "I would chew pencils during Central City versus Greenville games back when it was Corky (Withrow) against Roger (Newman). Playing basketball was something I always wanted to do."

Until he was in the eighth grade Jim attended Greenville High School. That year he transferred to Central City, where his father, Robert Walker, was band director. The elder Walker was to the Central City band what George Taylor had been to the basketball program—the founding father.

Despite a lower back problem that prevented him from playing for a couple of years, Jim joined the junior varsity team as a sophomore. Then as he became more serious about his music, he "retired" and sat out his junior year.

"My junior year the team was loaded with talented guards who were better than me," Jim said. "I wouldn't have seen much action that year if

I had remained on the team. Because of that, and because of the music thing, I chose to sit out."

But Golden Tide coach Jackie Day had other ideas. Knowing that most of those guards would be graduating, and knowing the 1961-62 roster was thin on back-court talent, Day, always a big Walker fan, sought out the senior to be.

"At the start of my senior year, Coach Day and I had a single conversation," Jim remembers. "He asked me if I would like to rejoin the team. I immediately said yes."

Shaking off the rust, Walker had a good year as a senior, hitting for double figures on nine occasions. His best efforts included 19 points against Beaver Dam, 17 against Drakesboro, 15 against Hopkinsville and 14 against Christian County.

"Basically, I was a slightly overweight guard who fouled too much," Jim said. "But being a member of the Golden Tide was one of the enduring wonderful memories of my days in Kentucky."

Since leaving Kentucky, Jim's accomplishments are nothing short of staggering. He has played in venues ranging from Carnegie Hall to Hollywood. He has been the Principal Flutist for the Pittsburgh Symphony and the Los Angeles Philharmonic. The New York Philharmonic borrowed him for a 1982 South American tour. His expressive playing can be heard on dozens of movie soundtracks and commercial recordings.

These days Jim spends at least 20 hours a week teaching young flutists in such places as Duquesne University, Carnegie-Mellon, University of Pittsburgh and Arizona State University, just to name a few.

Little wonder, then, that Jim is considered the "renaissance man of the flute."

LIT, Manual and Basketbrawl #2

If the 1956 brawl between Central City and Butler County is the most infamous, then surely the runner-up spot goes to the Golden Tide club that scrapped with Manual in the 1965 Louisville Invitational Tournament. The Tide won 72-71, but not without a fight.

A *real* fight.

"I was assigned to guard a guy named Charles Turner," David James remembers. "He was very quick, and he was scoring a bunch of points. Anyway, we went down on the floor and he hit me. I swung at him with a backhand. He said, 'I want you' and when I went after him, he went up in the bleachers.

"Well, after things calmed down, it's late in the game and we're taking the ball out under our basket. Coach sets up a box play for Joe (Bowen). Joe scores, putting us one point ahead. They throw the ball to midcourt, one of their guys catches it, throws it up and (Ralph) Mayes knocks it down. Next thing you know, they're fighting. The horn sounds, Manual heads to the dressing room, when (Lee) Stone and (Mike) Gray lead the charge. That's when the fists really started flying. Stone came to the dressing room looking like a boxer. He had a cut over his eye."

According to David, there was a moment when it appeared as if the two combatants might square off again.

"We were staying at the Kentucky Hotel," David said. "We went out to eat and who do we see coming toward us? The Manual players. I'm thinking we're going to have to fight them again. But those guys just walked up to us, shook our hands and told us we'd played a great game."

Lindsey Gets Frozen Out

Unselfishness is an idea that has forever been instilled in Golden Tide players. Who scores doesn't really matter. Putting points on the scoreboard is all that counts. Get more points than the other team, you win. It's that simple.

But occasionally, being magnanimous can be more of an ideal that an actual reality. Just ask Kenny Lindsey, who filled in admirably for Rodney Kirtley in the 1965-66 team's 69-64 victory over a very good Ohio County team.

In fact, Kenny just might have been more effective than he bargained for.

"In the first minute of that game I came down and nailed two straight baskets," Kenny said. "Heading down the court I was feeling pretty good about myself. That's when I saw (David) James and (Ralph) Mayes look at each other, shake their head and frown, like they were thinking 'what's this all about?' Well, I can tell you what it was about. I never touched the ball again that night."

And did David and Ralph really freeze out their teammate?

"Kenny has been saying that for years now," David said. "I don't know if we did or not, but he sure believes we did."

"I had one free throw the rest of the game," Kenny said, laughing. "So, yeah, they made sure I didn't do *too* much."

Dealing with a Giant

Throughout the years Golden Tide teams have gone up against some big guys, many standing 6'7" or 6'8". But without the question, the giant among giants was Louisville Shawnee's 7'1" Thomas Payne, who scored 41 points in his team's 91-90 loss to the Tide during the 1968-69 season.

"I played against some big guys before but none nearly as big as Payne," Ricky Turley said. "He was a monster, and his wingspan was enormous. Joe (Stone) was assigned to guard Payne, and I can still see Joe hanging on to Payne's trunks. Of course, no one was going to stop him; we just hoped to keep him from scoring a hundred points against us."

Rick had a good game against Shawnee, scoring 19 points. According to him, he was able to put up points because he figured something out early in the game.

"Payne's goal was to block every shot," Rick said. "He wanted to swat everything away. I also realized he was susceptible to being faked out. I would beat my defender, drive along the baseline, and then fake like I was going up to shoot. Payne would go up to block it, and when he did, I would slip to the other side of the bucket and put up the shot. His hand would be above the rim on the opposite side of the basket, which really left me wide open on the other side. By using his desire to block every shot, I was able to score a bunch of points."

Payne would, of course, go on to become the first black to play for the University of Kentucky.

The 1970s

Won – 194

Lost – 118

Winning Pct. – 62.2

Player of the Decade

Tommy Eades

Other Notable Players

Keith Briggs
Mike Brothers
Rick Brothers
Steve Dukes
Bobby Joe Gott
Calvin Gott
Nathan Gott
Eddie Gray
Carlos (T.T.) Hampton
Tony Hopper
Terry Huddleston
David Hunter
Mike Jenkins
Billy Knight
Bill Perkins
Tommy Phillips
Donald Sallee
Ricky Sallee
Mike Shrewsberry
Sammy Sparks
Steve Sparks
Jimmy Talbott
Terry Talbott
Jerry Taylor
John Taylor
Rocky Watkins
Robin Wolfe

Chapter 41

1970-71

This decade began with another transitional team, one that featured a roster filled with new and unfamiliar faces. Gone were formidable talents like Steve Reynolds, Mark Eades, Joe Stone, Freddie Mayes, Taylor Sparks, Lucian Taylor and Mike Dossett. Coming on to replace those guys was a host of rookies, players yet to prove what they could do once the ball was in play. And like previous untested clubs of similar construction, this team would lack consistency, playing superb basketball one night and then struggling the next night.

This youthful team finished with a 15-13 record. What stands out about this season was a dreadful finish in which the Tide dropped their final four games.

Starters for the opening game against Bremen—a 94-85 loss—were Jimmy Talbott, Tommy Hamilton, Tommy Eades, Brad Todd and John Taylor. Others on the roster included Donald Sallee, Phil Goldston, Sammy Sparks, Kenny Raley, Jerry Taylor, Carlos "T.T." Hampton, Donald Morris, Terry Talbott, Terry Huddleston and Ricky Sallee.

In that opener, the Tide led 71-66 after three quarters, only to watch Bremen take command in the final eight minutes, outscoring the visitors 28-14 to claim the victory. John Taylor led the Tide with 26 points, while Jimmy Talbott added 24.

Roger Nelson paced the Golden Eagles with 25 points.

Bouncing back from that disappointing defeat, the Tide reeled off five straight victories, beating Graham 88-52, a strong Drakesboro team 92-86, Muhlenberg Central 84-52, Graham 99-75 and Calhoun 70-67.

It was during this stretch that Eades, a 6'2" sophomore southpaw, began to flash the shooting accuracy that would eventually place him among the three or four deadliest marksmen in Golden Tide history. Eades scored 20 and 26 in the wins over Graham, and 24 against Drakesboro.

But Eades wasn't the lone Tide player posting big numbers. Taylor had 29 in the win over Drakesboro, Talbott had 25 against Calhoun and 21 against M.C., Hamilton accounted for 22 against Graham, with Sallee hitting for 19 against Calhoun.

The win over a Drakesboro squad that featured Reggie Warford, Dale Todd and Earl Williams was particularly impressive. The Tide led 65-59 heading into the final quarter, then had to fight off a sustained challenge by the Cardinals, sparked by 12 fourth quarter points from Todd, to get away with the win. Williams led the Cardinals with 27 points, while Warford had 22 and Todd 20.

Taylor had 29 for the Tide, including 10 in the final quarter. Eades ended with 24 and Sallee, now a starter, added 16.

But the good times failed to last. After winning those five games, the youthful Tide lost their next three, beginning with a 71-63 home-court loss to Hopkinsville. In this game, the Tide simply did not play well, especially in the second half. At the break they were in front 36-34.

Talbott and Eades led the Tide with 19 points each.

Next up was a road trip that saw the Tide lose to Glasgow 75-68 and Allen County 85-74. Eades had 15 points, Talbott 13 and Taylor 11 against Glasgow, then Sallee had 19, Eades 18 and Taylor 16 in the loss to Allen County.

Dismal free throw shooting was a key factor in those three losses (as it would be the entire season). During this stretch the Tide missed 27 free throws.

Overcoming a 38-point performance from Ricky Gibson, the visiting Tide topped Hughes-Kirk 87-80. Eades paced the winners with 28 points, with Taylor adding 22, Talbott 19 and Sallee 12.

Two nights later, the Tide faced off against Hughes-Kirk again, this time in the Central City Invitational opener. With Talbott, Hamilton and Eades each accounting for 21 points and Taylor adding 16, the Tide scored a convincing 103-77 victory.

Ricky Gibson again led the Tigers with 23 points.

In the title game, Drakesboro got 27 points from Dale Todd and 26 from Reggie Warford en route to a comfortable 84-72 win. This game was not as close as the final score indicates—the Cardinals led 65-42 after three quarters.

Eades had 28 to lead the Tide.

The Drakesboro game turned out to be the last one for Hamilton, who left the team (and school) to join the military. His absence was felt, especially inside, where his size and strength were needed for defense and rebounding. With Hamilton gone, Jerry Taylor moved into the starting lineup.

In the first post-Hamilton outing, Eades came through with 27 points as the Tide slapped Greenville 101-63. Jimmy Talbott had 21, John Taylor 15 and Terry Talbott 12 in this win.

After losing to Madisonville 86-71 despite 24 points from John Taylor, the Tide won their next three games by a total of five points, edging Butler County 73-71, Bremen 82-81 and Leitchfield 67-65. Against Butler County, John Taylor was the top point-getter with 23 points. Eades knocked in 20, Talbott 16 and Sallee 11.

In the win over Bremen, Talbott scored 26, Sallee 21 and Eades 15. Their combined effort was just enough to offset huge performances from Ronnie Cartwright and Roger Nelson, who finished with 29 and 28 points, respectively.

Eades scored 22, Sallee 18 and Talbott 11 in the 67-65 win at Leitchfield.

The Tide dropped an 86-70 decision at Webster County, then bounced back to defeat Ohio County 81-74 and Greenville 86-84. Against Webster County, John Taylor led the way with 25 points, while Eades added 20. At Ohio County, John Taylor finished with 23 points, Talbott 21, Jerry Taylor 12, Sallee 11 and Eades 10.

In the win over Greenville, Talbott had 22, Eades 21 and John Taylor 20, but it was the inspired play by Sparks that lifted the Tide to victory. Sparks, a sophomore guard, came off the bench to score 14 points, including 12 in the second half.

For the second straight time, Drakesboro proved to be too much for the Tide, winning 90-78 despite the absence of Dale Todd. Reggie Warford led the Cardinals with 23 points.

Eades had 28 for the visiting Tide, followed by John Taylor with 14, Sparks with 12 and Talbott with 10.

Returning home the Tide suffered a humiliating 64-57 loss to Sacramento. Leading 38-37 after three quarters, the Tide fell apart in the final eight minutes, being outscored 27-19. John Taylor was the lone bright spot for the Tide, finishing with 21 points.

With five players hitting for double figures, the Tide easily beat a Hughes-Kirk team minus Ricky Gibson 82-52. For the Tide, Sallee had 18 points, John Taylor 15, Talbott 14, Sparks 13 and Eades 10.

Eades snapped out of a minor scoring slump by tossing in 27 points in a 92-55 romp past Muhlenberg Central. John Taylor had 20 points in this win, with Talbott adding 18 and Sparks 10.

Now sporting a 15-9 record, the Tide headed down the home stretch, hoping to ride the momentum from the last two wins into post-season play. But that momentum quickly melted away. As things turned out, those 15 wins were all this team was going to get.

The final three regular-season games all resulted in losses, beginning with a 94-82 setback at Christian County. This was another game in which the final score was no indication of how dominant the Colonels were. They led 76-58 after three quarters. Maxie Stamps and Mike Fort led the winners with 23 points apiece.

For the Tide, Talbott had 24 points, John Taylor 19, Eades 18 and Sallee 13.

The final two regular-season games—both played in Owensboro—ended with losses to Daviess County 72-65 and Owensboro 68-46. Eades was the Tide's leading scorer in both games, hitting for 25 against Daviess County and 19 against Owensboro.

In the district tournament opener, the Tide blew an early lead before falling to Bremen 55-48. After Bremen battled back to knot the score at 35-35 heading into the final stanza, Roger Nelson took charge, scoring eight of his 11 points in that deciding quarter. Also, Eddie Majors made good on all six free tosses in the last frame.

Gary Lewis led the Golden Eagles with 22 points. Ronnie Cartwright also hit double figures with 14.

Talbott paced the Tide with 18 points, while Eades added 17.

The loss left the Tide with that final 15-13 record. But with several key players returning, the Tide's future looked bright. Those players would be joined by a new face, and with him as one of the leaders, the 1971-72 Golden Tide team turned out to be one of the school's best and most-exciting.

Chapter 42

1971-72

Throughout its basketball history, Central City has had several players who only joined the team for their senior year. H.L. "Hub" Hope transferred from Drakesboro and helped the 1953-54 team go unbeaten. Pat Franklin and Jimmy Simmons came aboard for the 1959-60 campaign, bringing size, strength and talent to that club. And Jimmy Walker's presence was a big lift for the 1961-62 team.

But without question, the senior "walk-on" who made the biggest impact was Tony Hopper. Too small to have a chance at earning playing time, a frustrated Hopper left the JV team during his sophomore year. Soon thereafter, Mother Nature blessed him with a big growth spurt. Over the next few months Hopper grew "five or six inches." By the end of his junior year, he was almost 6'0" and still growing. Big enough to not only play, but also talented enough to win a starting position on a Golden Tide team that rates as one of the school's all-time best.

While this was to be Hopper's first and only season as a Golden Tide player, it also turned out to be Jackie Day's final season as head coach. He would call it quits, take the principal's job and hand the coaching reins to his long-time assistant Wayne Divine.

Day's final club centered around Tommy Eades, now a 6'2" junior, and Sammy Sparks, a smart, heady guard who could put points on the board. Jerry Taylor was also back, along with Kenny Raley, Carlos "T.T." Hampton, David Hunter, Terry Talbott, Phillip Goldston, Terry Huddleston, Ricky Sallee, Frank Sherrod, Toby Stevenson and Rusty Dossett.

This club would finish with a 29-6 record against one of the most-challenging schedules any Golden Tide team ever faced. In Muhlenberg County alone, the competition was fierce, with no fewer than four teams (Central City, Drakesboro, Bremen and Greenville) all with 20-plus victories. And against that trio of foes, the Tide beat each one three times.

This was also the year that Eades exploded as a scorer, racking up 899 points for a 25.7 scoring average. Along the way, the deadly lefty connected on close to 65 percent of his field-goal attempts.

Eades, Sparks, Hopper, Raley and Taylor were the starters in the Tide's 79-67 opening-game win over Bremen. Taylor led the winners with 20 points, Eades had 18, Hopper 12, Stevenson 11 and Sparks 10.

Roger Nelson had 18 for the Golden Eagles.

Eades hit for 25 points and Hopper added 20 as the Tide rolled past Graham 90-51. Raley and Sparks contributed 13 and 10 points, respectively in this easy win.

Game three at Drakesboro was a different story. Behind 37 points from Dale Todd and 21 from Reggie Warford, the Cardinals clipped the visitors 90-85 in the first of four epic battles between these two squads. Eades paced the Tide with 33 points. Stevenson finished with 13, while Hopper, Sparks and Hampton each had 10.

After that setback the Tide reeled off 10 consecutive wins, beginning with a 112-57 smashing of Muhlenberg Central. In this win, Eades finished with 25 points, Taylor 17, Raley 16, Hopper, Stevenson and Sparks with 11 each, and Hampton with 10.

Calhoun proved to be a pesky opponent but with Eades hitting for 27 points and Hopper 24, the Tide won a tough road game 95-86. Sparks chipped in with 18 points and Taylor added 14 for the winners.

This game turned out to be the last one for Raley, who suffered a hand injury that curtailed his season. With Raley sidelined, Hampton moved into the starting lineup. It was a change that altered this club's style of play. Replacing Raley, a rough and tough bruiser, with the much-quicker Hampton transformed this team into one with tremendous speed and agility, which it used to great advantage, both offensively and defensively. This was now a no-nonsense fast-breaking team that also successfully utilized the full-court press on defense.

Behind 32 points from Eades and 20 from Hopper, the Tide claimed a second straight tough road win by topping Hopkinsville 88-82. Taylor and Sparks also hit for double digits, finishing with 15 and 11 points, respectively.

Keith Tandy had 34 points for Hoptown.

Prior to the Central City Invitational the Tide notched three more wins, beating Glasgow 80-65, Allen County 95-55 and Hughes-Kirk 106-62. Sparks led the way against Glasgow, ending the night with 22 points. Eades had 21, Hopper 16 and Hampton 13 against the Scotties.

Hopper was the big gun in the win over Allen County, tossing in 31 points. Sparks had 21, Taylor 17 and Eades 12 in this victory. Against Hughes-Kirk, Eades and Sparks combined for 50 points, with Eades scoring 28 and Sparks 22. Others in double figures included Taylor with 13, Hampton and Hopper 10 apiece.

Jeff Arnold led the Tigers with 32 points.

The CCIT opener resulted in an easy 93-53 win over Russellville. Eades scored 26 points, with Hopper and Sparks each tossing in 20. Taylor also hit doube figures with a dozen.

In the title game, the Tide overcame a six-point halftime deficit to slip past Drakesboro 80-78. Still trailing 63-61 after three quarters, the Tide got eight fourth-quarter points from Hopper and six from Eades to pull out the win. Eades finished with 22, Sparks 18, Hopper 15 and Hampton 12 for the Tide.

Drakesboro's all-state performer Reggie Warford led all scorers with 32.

At Greenville, Eades torched the Blackhawks for 29 points to lead the Tide to an 80-68 win. Sparks had 18 points, Hopper 17 and Taylor 12 in this win over the Tide's oldest arch-rival.

In the first of back-to-back games against Leitchfield, Eades scored 26 points as the Tide held on for a tough 71-64 home-court win. Sparks offered solid support with 16 points, while Hampton added 15.

Leitchfield was the Tide's opening-round foe in the Owensboro Catholic Invitational, and this outing had a different outcome. This time it was Leitchfield that held on for a 73-67 win. With the score knotted 52-52 heading into the fourth quarter, Leitchfield's Barry Barnes took over, accounting for 12 of his game-high 26 points in those final eight minutes to lead his club to the win.

Eades led the Tide with 21 points. Sparks had 14, Taylor and Hopper 11 each, and Hampton had 10.

Behind 26 points from Eades and 24 from Sparks, the Tide claimed third place by beating Ohio County 90-81 in the consolation game. Hopper and Taylor knocked in 19 and 13 points, respectively.

Playing in a treacherous environment against a very good team, Eades erupted for 40 points to lead the visiting Tide past Bremen 79-71. The Tide grabbed an early lead, then held off repeated charges from the Eagles to get away with the win. Eades hit for 18 field goals and four of six free throw attempts to account for his 40-point total.

Sparks had 17 points for the Tide. Ronnie Cartwright led Bremen with 23.

Hopper had the hot hand in the Tide's next outing, hitting for 27 points in an 89-68 victory over Ohio County. Eades came through with 20 points, Sparks 16 and Taylor 13 in a win that improved the Tide's record to 15-2.

That record quickly dropped to 15-4 following back-to-back losses at Madisonville 76-67 and Paducah 81-72. Eades was the Tide's top scorer in both games, hitting for 19 against Madisonville and 24 at Paducah. Hampton finished with 17 in the first game, Sparks had 17 against the Tornado.

Those two losses were followed by a second 10-game winning streak, starting with Eades tossing in 23 points as the Tide beat Trigg County 69-52. Taylor and Hopper each had 12 points and Sparks 10 in this road win.

Thanks to nine fourth-quarter points from Hampton, the Tide managed to get past Greenville 87-84 at home. The Tide held a 53-39 lead at the half, then had to fight for their lives down the stretch to sneak away with the victory. Eades led the winners with 28 points, while Hampton had 21. Sparks also had a good game, finishing with 18 points.

Jamie Gregory paced Greenville with 29 points, while Ed McCarraher added 22.

With all five starters hitting for double figures, led by Eades with 33 points, the Tide notched a 94-80 win over Drakesboro. Hopper ended the game with 20 points, followed by Taylor with 16, Sparks 15 and Hampton 10.

Dale Todd had 25 for Drakesboro.

In quick succession, and fueled by a red-hot Eades, the Tide ran off wins over Sacramento 91-45, Hughes-Kirk 84-70, Butler County 77-69 and Muhlenberg Central 93-55. Eades racked up 104 points in those four wins, scoring 24 in each of the first two games, 31 against Butler County and 25 against MC.

Several other Tide players posted big numbers during this run. Sparks and Hampton had 20 and 19 points, respectively, against Sacramento, while Hopper had 20 against MC.

But if Eades had been hot in those four games, he was downright sizzling in a 108-63 pasting of Graham, hitting for 44 points on 21 field goals and a pair of free tosses. His 21 buckets was one shy of Graham's total of 22.

Hopper had 19 points in this easy win, with Sparks adding 14 and Taylor 10.

It took a more balanced scoring attack for the Tide to earn their next win, an 84-83 thriller over Christian County. It also didn't hurt that the visiting Colonels misfired on 10 free throws. Eades paced the winners with 25 points. Sparks had 16, Hampton 15, Taylor 14 and Hopper 12 for the Tide.

David Major led the Colonels with a game-high 31 points.

Sparks and Eades each tossed in 23 points and Hopper added 15 as the Tide beat visiting Daviess County 80-76 in another tense encounter. Then in the regular season's final game, powerful Owensboro, led by Jerry Thruston's 27 points, ripped the Tide 78-57. This Red Devil squad would go on to capture the state championship.

Eades had 22 points and Sparks 14 for the Tide.

When the district tournament pairings were announced it was clear that there would be no easy stops along the way for this Golden Tide team. Bremen, always dangerous, was the Tide's opening-round opponent. Looming in the crucial semifinal round—provided the Tide survived Bremen—was Drakesboro, arguably the county's most-talented team. To earn a trip to the regional tournament, the Tide would have to successfully navigate in deadly waters.

The opener against Bremen followed the expected script—a thriller that went down to the wire. Overcoming a magnificent 34-point effort from Bremen's Ronnie Cartwright, the Tide fought their way to a narrow 80-76 victory. To get this win, the Tide received a big boost from little-used Terry Talbott, who came off the bench to score 11 points. Hopper paced the winners with 22 points, while Eades had 19, Sparks 14 and Taylor 10.

An outstanding second half, in which the Tide outscored Drakesboro 47-27, resulted in a 77-60 semifinal win. The Tide trailed 33-30 at the break, then dominated the final two quarters to get their ticket punched for the regional. Eades scored 16 of his game-high 28 points after intermission. Hampton gunned in 16 points, Hopper 13 and Sparks 12 for the Tide.

Reggie Warford, in his final game, accounted for 27 points. Warford would, of course, go on to play for the University of Kentucky.

Eades hit for 28 points, Sparks 25 and Hopper 20 as the Tide took home the big trophy by easily handling Greenville 90-75.

Jamie Gregory had 31 points to lead Greenville.

Facing Owensboro Catholic in the regional tourney opener, the Tide broke away from a 50-50 deadlock after three quarters to pull out a narrow 68-65 win. Hopper and Sparks were the heroes in this victory. Hopper scored 10 points and Sparks hit four straight crucial free throws in the final quarter to enable the Tide to escape. Eades led the winners with 25 points, while Hopper had 22 and Sparks 13.

Next up was Leitchfield, which had split a pair of regular-season games with the Tide. Those two encounters had both been close; this one would be even closer. And the outcome wasn't what Tide fans were hoping for.

With Barry Barnes and Kendall Clemons each scoring 26 points, Leitchfield edged the Tide 75-72 in overtime. Five missed free throws in the fourth quarter, along with Hopper's early exit via the foul route, proved to be the Tide's undoing in this disappointing loss.

Eades led the Tide with 23 points, while Hampton had 19 and Sparks 10.

After leading this club to a 29-6 record, Jackie Day stepped down as head coach. During his 14 seasons at the helm, his teams had a 333-135 record for a 71.2 winning percentage. He guided the 1959 and 1966 teams to the Sweet 16, with that '66 club advancing to the semifinals. His teams captured the district title six times, and four of his players—Lance Gish, Ralph Mayes, Steve Reynolds and Tommy Eades—earned all-state recognition.

Day's successor would be his trusted assistant Wayne Divine. And Day wasn't leaving Divine with an empty hand to play with, not with Eades, Sparks and Hampton all set to return for their final season. The incoming coach had some serious weapony at his disposal.

Chapter 43

1972-73

Wayne Divine had been a standout player at Bremen in the late 1950s and early 1960s. After graduating, he attended WKU, where he earned his degree in 1965. At the same time, Ralph Evitts resigned as Jackie Day's assistant coach. Divine applied for the position, was quickly hired and became one of the school's best and longest-serving assistant coaches.

At the end of the 1972 school year, George Taylor stepped down as superintendent. Delmas Gish, the long-time principal, moved up to take Taylor's old job. When Day opted to become principal, he handed the coaching job to Divine. Bill Loney, the former Graham star, was hired as Divine's assistant.

Divine was fortunate to inherit three superb players from the previous season's standout club—Tommy Eades, Sammy Sparks and Carlos "T.T." Hampton. With that trio leading the way, Divine guided the Tide to a 24-8 record in what turned out to be his only year as head coach.

Eades, Sparks and Hampton were joined in the starting quintet by Terry Talbott and David Hunter. Other team members included Phillip Goldston, Ricky Sallee, Frank Sherrod, Terry Huddleston, Rocky Watkins and Steve Dukes.

Divine's tenure got off to a rocky start, an 87-70 loss to his old Bremen alma mater. Divine had Ronnie Cartwright and Danny Creager to thank for this loss. Cartwright burned the Tide for 40 points, with Creager adding 20.

Eades led the Tide with 26 points, while Sparks had 23 and Talbott 12.

Sparks had to step up big in the Tide's next two outings, wins over Drakesboro 94-66 and Muhlenberg Central 72-68 that were achieved without Eades, who was sideline with a sprained ankle. Sparks tossed in 31 in the win over Drakesboro and 23 against MC. Hampton had 21 against the Cardinals, while Hunter had 11 points in each win.

With Eades back in the lineup, and with five players hitting for double figures in the next three games, the Tide cracked the century mark with wins over Graham 111-83, McLean County 105-63 and Hopkinsville 115-89. Against Graham, Eades scored 28 points, Sparks 23, Hampton 19, Hunter 18 and Goldston 10. In beating McLean County, Hampton and Eades each had 23 points, Talbott 19, Hunter 18 and Sparks 11. Eades hit for 35 against Hoptown, with Talbott getting 24, Sparks 21, Hunter 18 and Hampton 10.

The Tide's next two victories came courtesy of last-second shots by Eades and Sparks. Eades knocked in a five-foot jump shot with four seconds remaining to lift the Tide to a 70-69 win over Glasgow. One night later, Sparks nailed a 25-footer at the buzzer to give his club a 72-70 victory over Allen County.

Eades finished with 32 points in the win over Glasgow and 25 against Allen County. Talbott and Sparks had 14 apiece in the first of those two wins, with Hunter hitting for 18 and Hampton a dozen against Allen County.

Eades rammed in 30 points, Sparks had 17 and Hampton 11 as the Tide claimed a 68-62 win over Hughes-Kirk in the first of yet another pair of tough struggles. Next was an 89-85 victory over Greenville, with Eades scoring 36 points, Sparks 27 and Hampton 10.

Ed McCarraher paced Greenville with 25 points.

Eades turned in a monster effort (34 points, 21 rebounds) in the Tide's 94-80 win over Trigg County in the Central City Invitational opener. Sparks finished with 22 points, while Hunter and Hampton had 16 and 13, respectively.

Thanks to a defense that limited Eades to 10 points and big games from Tim Tudor and Randy McCarty, Greenville walked away with the big trophy by posting a 79-74 win. Tudor led the winners with 23 points, while McCarty had 21.

Hampton paced the Tide with 20 points. Hunter chipped in 18 and Sparks 14.

Eades shook off his lowest scoring effort of the season by pouring in 69 points in wins over Leitchfield 75-53 and eighth-ranked Madisonville 84-82. Eades had 30 points against Leitchfield and 39 against the Maroons. Sparks finished with 25 points in that Leitchfield win.

In the Ohio County Invitational, Sparks scored 25 points, Eades 23, Hunter and Talbott 15 each in an easy 99-70 victory over McLean County. Then, for the second straight tournament, Greenville was the Tide's foe in the title game. And for the second time, the Blackhawks came out on top, overcoming a 71-63 deficit heading into the final quarter to escape with an 80-78 win courtesy of a game-deciding bucket by Stuart Oberg.

Randy McCarty led the champs with 25 points. For the Tide, Hunter had 19, Eades 18, Sparks 17 and Hampton 12.

Shaking off that loss, the Tide won their next four games, beginning with a 76-68 revenge win over Bremen. Eades had 29 points, Sparks 16 and Hunter 14 for the Tide.

Danny Creager topped Bremen with 22 points.

The Tide's next two wins didn't come easily—79-76 over Henderson County and 65-58 over Ohio County. Those were followed by a less-harrowing 125-77 romp past Drakesboro. Each of those wins featured a different leading scorer for the Tide. Hampton had 22 against Henderson, Eades 24 against Ohio County and Sparks 24 in the win over Drakesboro.

In match-up number four against Greenville, the Tide fell for the third straight time, losing 81-69 despite 27 points from Eades and 18 from Hampton.

Randy McCarty led the Blackhawks with 19 points.

Eades pitched in 35 points and Talbott 18 as the Tide beat Hughes-Kirk 80-64 in the first of five games without Sparks, who was sidelined with pneumonia. Eades was even hotter in the Tide's next game, blistering Apollo for 41 points in a 101-84 win. Hampton also had a big night against the Eagles, scoring 26 points.

Butler County came to town and pulled off a 57-55 upset in a game that saw the Tide only attempt two free throws. Eades led the Tide with 26 points, while Huddleston chipped in with 12.

With Sparks still recuperating, the Tide stormed to easy wins over Muhlenberg Central 89-60 and Graham 78-55 to improve their record to 21-5. Eades scored 27 in the win over MC and 36 against Graham. Huddleston continued to play well filling in for Sparks, racking up 26 points in those two games, while Sallee had 11 against MC.

Sparks's return to the lineup did not translate into success. The Tide dropped their next two games, losing to Christian County 71-65 and Daviess County 77-56 in what was easily the team's poorest effort of the campaign. Eades had 25 points in the loss to Christian County, then was held to a season-low six points in that Daviess County debacle. Against Daviess County, Sparks had 20, Hampton 12 and Talbott 10.

The Tide finished on a strong note by beating McLean County 73-56 before knocking off defending state champion Owensboro 69-60. In the win over McLean County, Eades finished with 24 points, Talbott 16, Sparks 14 and Hampton 10.

Against the Red Devils, Sparks paced the Tide with 20 points, while Hampton had 18, Eades 15 and Talbott 11.

Kenny Higgs and Greg Webster each had 15 points for Owensboro.

For the second straight year, the district tournament pairings placed the Tide in a power-heavy bracket. First up was Greenville, a club that owned three regular-season wins over the Tide. Survive that and Bremen, a team the Tide split regular-season games with, was on deck. This bracket was no place for the weak at heart.

In the opener, Greenville raced to a 34-24 advantage at the half, sending the message that a fourth win over the Tide was almost inevitable. But late in the third quarter and on into the last frame, the Tide went on a 22-2 rampage to seize control of the game. When the final horn sounded, the Tide, riding a 39-point effort from Eades, had survived by posting a 65-60 win.

Randy McCarty's 24 points paced the Blackhawks.

The critical semifinal game against Bremen was the exact opposite of the opener against Greenville. In this one the Tide led at the end of each of the first three quarters, only to fall apart in the last frame.

Final: Bremen 67, Golden Tide 58.

It was a tough loss, one made even more disappointing because Eades and Hampton were both suffering from a stomach virus. Despite being ill, Eades ended his great career with a 16-point effort. Sparks and Talbott each tallied 14 points in a losing cause.

Danny Creager led Bremen with 21 points, with Ronnie Cartwright adding 16.

Eades and Sparks were named to the all-district squad. Later, Eades was voted Muhlenberg County Player of the Year.

As a senior, Eades scored 802 points for a 26.7 average, good enough to earn second-team all-state recognition. For his career, he finished with 2,238 points, second only to Corky Withrow on the Golden Tide's all-time scoring list.

From 1925 through 1972, only three men held the coaching position at Central City—George Taylor, Delmas Gish and Jackie Day. Obviously, coaching changes were rare occurences. When Wayne Divine became the fourth man to fill the coaching seat, it was assumed that the job would be his for many years. But things didn't turn out that way, and for the second time in two short years a new coach would occupy the hot seat.

Bill Loney.

Chapter 44

1973-74

After only one year as an assistant, Bill Loney, the ex-Graham standout, became the fifth Golden Tide coach since 1925. Although highly intelligent and a sound teacher of fundamentals, Loney's tenure had a very up-and-down series of results. While he did have several solid teams—two of his clubs had 24-win seasons—there were also some less-than-satisfying campaigns. Only once in the basketball program's long history have Golden Tide teams suffered back-to-back losing seasons, and those came about while Loney was the head coach.

Unlike his predecessor, Wayne Divine, Loney didn't inherit an experienced, talent-rich team. He took over a club that relied heavily on sophomores. In fact, one reason—and it's a critical one—that no Loney-helmed team ranks among the school's all-time best is that he never had the luxury of coaching a genuine superstar. He had several tough, talented guys, but none that even remotely approached the level of a Corky Withrow, Lance Gish, Ralph Mayes, Steve Reynolds or Tommy Eades. Loney never had a player he could count on night after night to go out and score 25 or 30 points.

Without a superstar to build around, life in the world of sports can be difficult and uncompromising. Given that, Loney's record might need to be viewed in a more positive light.

Starters in Loney's first game were senior David Hunter, junior Rocky Watkins and sophomores Mike Shrewsberry, Steve Dukes and Eddie Gray. Other team members included Ricky Sallee, Rick Brothers, John Toll, Ricky Holland and Tommy Kirkpatrick.

In the opener, a 58-44 win over Bremen, Shrewsberry had 16 points, Hunter and Watkins 12 each.

Loney's first team, which ended with a 16-12 record, got off to a fast start, following the win over Bremen with victories over Muhlenberg Central 90-78, Drakesboro 64-54, Graham 80-61 and Leitchfield 59-56.

Watkins was the leading scorer in two of those wins, hitting for 21 against MC and 19 against Graham. Hunter led the way with 17 in the win over Drakesboro, while Shrewsberry had a game-best 16 against Leitchfield.

What hurt this youthful team was its inability to come out on top in close games. Of the team's 12 losses, nine came in games decided by nine points or less.

The Tide's unblemished mark ended with an 87-70 loss to Hopkinsville. In that game, Hunter had 21 points, Gray 14, Dukes 12 and Shrewsberry 10. In yet another down-to-the wire thriller, Dukes hit for 20 points to lift the Tide past Allen County 80-78.

Prepping for the annual Central City Invitational, the Tide split a pair of games, losing to Greenville 60-57, then edging past Hughes-Kirk 53-51 in overtime. Hunter was the top scorer in each of those games, getting 18 against Greenville and 19 against the Tigers.

Watkins knocked in 16 points, Shrewsberry had 14 and Sallee 11 as the Tide topped Ohio County 80-66 in the CCIT opener. One night later, Hunter tallied 17 points and Gray added 16 as the Tide claimed the trophy by beating Hughes-Kirk 64-49.

It was at this stage, sporting a 9-2 record, that the Tide's season began to unravel. Of their next nine games, they would lose seven, beginning with a 109-79 smackdown at Paducah. Shrewsberry was the lone bright spot in this debacle, finishing with 26 points.

After Apollo nipped the Tide 60-58 despite 17 points from Watkins, Hunter came through with 18 points and Dukes 17 in a 70-69 overtime win over Ohio County. Despite continued strong play by Hunter, the Tide fell to Henderson County 74-71 and Trigg County 69-61. Hunter accounted for 37 points in those two losses.

Hunter came back with a career-best 30 points to help the Tide beat Drakesboro 85-72. In this victory, Shrewsberry had 19 points, Gray 12 and Watkins 10.

A tip-in by Pat Segers just ahead of the final horn was the difference in Greenville's 56-55 win over the Tide. Watkins led the Tide with 14 points in the the first of three straight losses. In rapid succession, the

Tide lost to Hughes-Kirk 62-58 and eighth-ranked Butler County 84-77. Dukes had 24 in the Hughes-Kirk loss, a total matched by Hunter against Butler County.

With Dukes again hitting for 24 points, the Tide snapped out of their funk by beating Graham 93-79 despite a 33-point effort from the Nighthawks' Freddy Drury. This was the first of four consecutive wins by the Tide.

Next, it was Watkins who tossed in 24 points to lead his club to a 78-73 win over Muhlenberg Central. Then the rapidly improving Dukes rammed in another 24 points in a 76-73 win over Daviess County. Dukes had plenty of support as five Tide players hit for double figures, including Hunter with 13,Watkins 12, Sallee 11 and Shrewsberry 10.

In another strong outing, the Tide, again with five players cracking double digits, disposed of Bremen 74-60. Hunter finished with 17 points, Watkins 14, Gray, Dukes and Sallee 10 apiece.

Danny Creager led Bremen with 23.

Closing out the regular season, the Tide dropped two of their final three games, sandwiching losses to Christian County 74-68 and third-ranked Owensboro 107-69 around an 80-74 win over McLean County.

Hunter had 20 points against Christian County, then Watkins led with 22 in the win over McLean County and 16 against an Owensboro team that got 35 points Kenny Higgs and 25 from Greg Webster.

The Tide's post-season appearance was brief, thanks to a 70-69 loss to Greenville. In this poor effort, the Tide fell behind early and never could catch up, thanks to strong performances from Blackhawks Pat Segers (25 points) and Stuart Oberg (20 points).

Watkins paced the Tide with 17, while Hunter and Sallee added 13 and 11, respectively.

Thus ended Loney's first season at the helm, a campaign featuring plenty of close games, some of which went the Tide's way and nine that didn't. But Loney now had that solid group of sophomores coming back, along with senior-to-be Watkins. And it would be this group that provided Loney—and Tide fans—with back-to-back strong seasons.

Chapter 45

1974-75

Considering the youth and inexperience, Bill Loney's first team performed fairly well. His second team would do even better. Led by a solid junior class, the 1974-75 club won 11 of its first 12 games, topped some very strong opponents, then went on to finish with a 22-9 record.

This record likely would have been even more impressive had junior Eddie Gray remained with the team throughout the season. But the burly Gray left at midseason for personal reasons, and his absence impacted this year's team and next year's as well.

Rick Brothers and Steve Dukes were the two primary go-to guys on this team. Brothers was a superb shooter, while Dukes rates among the best Tide players ever who could maneuver and score down low. Early on, Rocky Watkins played well, but his output tapered off drastically during the latter half of the season. Mike Shrewsberry was solid, Mike Jenkins had some big moments, and Steve Sparks proved to be an excellent scorer once he moved into the starting quintet.

Others on this club included Dennis Laycock, John Toll, Ronnie Stewart, Johnny Dale Elieff, Bobby Joe Gott, William Hamilton, Tommy Kirkpatrick, Kerry Holden and Chuck Childress.

The Tide opened the campaign by splitting their first two games, beating Bremen 64-58 in a come-from-behind victory, and then losing 85-83 in overtime to a superb Drakesboro club. In the opener, Brothers rang up 17 points, Dukes 15 and Watkins 11. Against the Cardinals, Watkins had 24 points, Brothers 19 and Dukes 15.

Doug Jernigan scored 27 for Drakesboro, while teammate Eddie Rhodes had 21.

Dukes and Brothers each tallied 20 points and Gray added 14 as the Tide beat Muhlenberg Central 76-62 to kick off a long winning streak. Victims in this run included Graham 115-67, Hughes-Kirk 82-62, 13th-ranked Bowling Green 78-62, Hopkinsville 80-75, Greenville 76-66, Drakesboro 65-61 in OT and McLean County 71-63.

Dukes was especially effective during this streak, torching Bowling Green for 36 points, Hoptown for 24, Greenville for 25 and McLean County for 24. Brothers scored 24 against Hughes-Kirk and Shrewsberry had 24 in that revenge win over Drakesboro.

Despite a career-best 24 points from Toll, the Tide's run ended with a 62-61 loss to Madisonville. Dukes hit for 18 points, Jenkins and Shrewsberry 15 each as the Tide responded by beating Apollo 84-68, then a Dukes free throw with four ticks remaining lifted the Tide to a 63-62 victory over Trigg County. Watkins had 14 points and Brothers 13 in that win.

Beginning with a 64-58 setback against Henderson County, the Tide dropped three of their next four games. Against the Colonels, the Tide had more field goals (29-24), but they only attempted two free throws, missing both. The charity stripe was the difference. Dukes paced the Tide with 20 points.

After Dukes scored 27 points and Brothers 21 in a 78-68 win over Ohio County, the Tide lost to district foes Drakesboro 66-63 and Hughes-Kirk 79-69. Sparks led the Tide with 22 points against Drakesboro and 17 against a Hughes-Kirk team fueled by 27 points from Ricky Minton.

Once again the Tide responded well, racking up wins over Butler County 71-57, Muhlenberg Central 75-68, Graham 77-75 and Christian County 67-65 despite being down 57-51 after three quarters. Dukes was the top scorer in three of those four wins, hitting for 24 against Butler County, 17 against Graham and 23 against Christian Couny. Jenkins led the way with 17 in the win over MC.

The Tide's regular season did not end well, with two losses in their final three games, beginning with a 68-61 defeat at Daviess County. In this one, the Tide led 49-46 after three quarters, but could not hold on for the win. Brothers and Jenkins led the Tide with 22 and 15 points, respectively.

Shrewsberry blistered the nets for 24 points to help the Tide storm past Bremen 93-54. Then in the season's final game, the Tide fell to Owensboro 62-60 in the Sportscenter. Trailing 49-38 heading into the last quarter, the Tide, getting 11 points from Brothers and six from

Sparks, battled back to make things interesting, only to come up a bucket short.

Brothers paced the Tide with 19 points, Dukes had 18 and Sparks 14 in this loss.

The district tournament draw was a mixed blessing for the Tide. They got a first-round bye, but their semifinal opponent would be Drakesboro, which had won two of three regular-season battles. At stake in this struggle was a spot in the title game and a trip to the regional tournament.

The opening half belonged to the Tide, who held a 31-23 lead at the break. But the Cardinals, sparked by Doug Jernigan, fought back to tie it at 43-43 heading into the final frame. Those eight minutes belonged to Jenkins and Dukes, who combined for 17 fourth-quarter points, enough to help lift the Tide to a 67-57 victory. Dukes led all scorers with 27 points, while Jenkins finished with 16 and Brothers 11.

Jernigan paced Drakesboro with 17.

The title game against Muhlenberg Central was close, but with Brothers scoring 22 points, Dukes 16 and Jenkins 10, the Tide took home the big trophy with a 67-59 victory.

Dukes made sure the regional tournament opener against Cloverport was never in doubt, scoring 27 points in a convincing 71-56 Tide victory. Sparks also hit double figures with 13.

In semifinal action, the Tide were no match for Owensboro, which blew the game open early, then went on to post an easy 74-53 victory behind 19 points from Joe Thruston.

Jenkins led the Tide with 16 points, Shrewsberry had 13, Sparks 11 and Brothers 10, while Dukes, the team's leading scorer, was limited to a single first-quarter bucket before fouling out.

This had been a solid campaign, and with Dukes, Brothers, Jenkins, Shrewsberry and Sparks all set to return, the outlook for next season was bright indeed.

Chapter 46

1975-76

Although this veteran team acquitted itself well, going 24-13 and putting itself in position to earn a Sweet 16 berth, it can also be argued that in some ways this was disappointing season. Before the season began, few would have guessed that this club would lose 13 games. But it did. And the chief reason was lack of depth. Primarily, six players did most of the heavy lifting.

This was a club that finished dead last in its own Christmas tournament, then turned around and won the tougher, more prestigious Owensboro Invitational Tournament. This was a team that beat the likes of Bryan Station, Owensboro and Ohio County, yet lost six games by fewer than four points.

(Incredibly, both scorebooks for this season are missing, and newspaper reports leave out eight games, six wins and two losses.)

Seniors Steve Dukes, Rick Brothers, Mike Shrewsberry, Mike Jenkins and juniors Steve Sparks and Dennis Laycock are the ones who garnered virtually all playing time. Fellow team members included Bobby Joe Gott, Ronnie Stewart, William Hamilton, Johnny Dale Elieff and Kerry Holden.

Once again, Eddie Gray's absence played a huge role in this team's fortunes.

After Brothers scored 24 points, Sparks 18 and Dukes 17 in a season-opening 87-55 win over Bremen, the Tide followed up by beating Muhlenberg Central. Next up was Drakesboro, the district's most-talented team, and the Cardinals, led by Doug Jernigan's 25 points, spanked the Tide 85-65. Dukes had 20 for the Tide.

Dukes hit for 22 points and Jenkins 20 in an 82-66 victory over Graham, then the Tide dropped three straight games, including two in the CCIT. First, Hughes-Kirk edged the Tide 62-60 on a 17-foot jump shot by Jeff Kirtley with six seconds remaining. In the annual CCIT, the Tide lost to Hopkinsville 71-70 on a last-second bucket by Paul Day, then lost again to Drakesboro 71-68. Dukes was the leading scorer in the first two games, getting 28 against Hughes-Kirk and 17 against Hoptown. Jenkins and Brothers had 22 and 20, respectively, in the loss to Drakesboro.

Still bleeding from those losses, the Tide entered the Owensboro Invitational with low expectations for success. To make matters worse, they faced the powerful host school in the opening round. But with Dukes scoring 21 points and Jenkins adding a dozen, the Tide fought back from a halftime deficit to upset the previously undefeated Red Devils 54-52.

On the following afternoon, the Tide again overcame an early deficit to top Owensboro Catholic 61-49 to advance to the title game. Against the Aces, Dukes had 21 points, Jenkins 13 and Sparks 12. Later that night, the Tide claimed the title when Sparks knocked in a 10-footer that lifted the Tide past heavily favored Lexington Bryan Station 66-64. Dukes paced the champs with 30 points, while Brothers had 14 and Shrewsberry 12.

In the Tide's next three outings, two ended in defeat. A lone 72-68 win over Greenville was sandwiched between losses to Madisonville 81-69 and Apollo 83-77. The Apollo game was dominated by 6'11" Tom Wendt, who finished with 29 points and 23 rebounds.

Behind 24 points from Dukes, 23 from Shrewsberry and 20 from Brothers, the Tide began an impressive four-game winning streak by topping Henderson County 85-80. That was followed by wins over Trigg County 80-68, regional contender Ohio County 78-67 and Drakesboro 71-54. A different player was the Tide's top scorer in each game, with Dukes putting in 22 against Trigg County, Brothers 23 in the Ohio County win and Jenkins 19 against Drakesboro.

Greenville, getting 25 points from Nat Nofsinger, handed the Tide a disappointing 73-57 home-court loss that snapped the winning streak. Brothers led the Tide with 17 points. The Tide split a pair of squeakers in their next two games, edging Hughes-Kirk 64-63 and then losing to Butler County 67-65. Jenkins topped the scoring with 16 points in the win, while Brothers had 23 in the loss.

Sparks rang up 24 points as the Tide went on a modest three-game winning streak by pouncing Graham 80-64. Brothers put in 25 points and

Shrewsberry 20 in an 80-68 win over Muhlenberg Central, then Dukes accounted for 24 and Brothers 22 as the Tide ripped Jeffersontown 91-75.

But once again the good times didn't last very long. Playing back-to-back home games, the Tide fell to Christian County 74-64 and Daviess County 76-72 despite leading by 12 points in the third quarter. Brothers led the scoring with 19 points against Christian County, Dukes had 30 in the Daviess County loss.

After dispensing with Bremen, the Tide entertained Owensboro, and for the second time, they pulled off the big upset, winning 58-56 on a Sparks basket inside the final seconds. To get this win, the Tide had to rally from a 41-26 deficit midway through the third quarter. Sparks led the Tide with 21 points, followed by Dukes with 13 and Brothers with 10.

In the district tourney opener the Tide blasted Bremen 85-49. One night later, behind 17 points from Shrewsberry, the Tide advanced to the title game by smashing Graham 73-43. In that win, Sparks had 14 points, Jenkins 11 and Dukes 10.

But the big news came in the other semifinal game, when Greenville stunned Drakesboro 84-67. The Cardinals entered the tourney with a district-best 24-4 record.

The final game was close until Greenville went stone cold in the final quarter, going nearly five minutes without scoring. That lengthy drought was all the Tide needed to claim the championship with a 67-48 victory. Shrewsberry led a balanced attack with 17 points. Jenkins finished with 15, Brothers 14 and Dukes 10.

This would be the Tide's last district championship for eight years.

The regional tournament was missing a familiar face—Owensboro. The Red Devils had been eliminated by Apollo in the district opener, which made this regional tourney a wide-open affair. Apollo, Central City and Ohio County were regarded as the teams to beat.

Senior forwards Dukes and Brothers made sure the Tide didn't suffer an upset at the hands of Hancock County in the tourney opener. Dukes scored 24 points and Brothers added 23 in this easy romp. Shrewsberry also cracked double figures with 16.

The Tide's 63-62 semifinal loss to Apollo will always rate among the most-thrilling, most-heartbreaking games in Golden Tide history. The outcome of this struggle wasn't decided until the final second of the game, when a free throw by Laycock rimmed out.

Although Laycock, a 5'7" junior guard, didn't enter the game until there was only 1:43 left to play, twice inside the final six seconds he had a heavy burden laid on his shoulders. Here's how the drama unfolded.

Apollo took a 63-61 lead on a Jeff Jones bucket, his only one that night. With six seconds remaining, Laycock drew a foul, went to the line and missed the front end of the bonus. On the ensuing rebound, Dukes fouled Apollo's Tom Wendt, who missed the critical freebie.

The Tide rebounded, and with a single tick remaining, Laycock was fouled, sending him to the charity stripe for a one-plus-one. In a tension-filled Sportscenter, Laycock knocked in the first freebie to cut the Apollo lead to one point. But when Laycock's second free toss rimmed out, Apollo had its one-point victory.

Dukes had 18 points in his final game, while Sparks and Shrewsberry each contributed 15.

Apollo captured the title with a 10-point win over Ohio County, a club the Tide defeated by 11 during the regular season.

Losing Dukes, Brothers, Jenkins and Shrewberry to graduation all but ensured a tough road ahead next season. And that's precisely what happened. The Tide was about to enter what one long-time knowledgable Golden Tide observer correctly called "the dark years."

Chapter 47

1976-78

From 1926, George Taylor's first full season as head coach, through 1976, Central City only had one losing record. That's half-a-century's worth of sustained excellence. That was about to change in a most dramatic fashion.

Over the next two seasons, Golden Tide teams had records of 9-21 and 12-16. Overall, that computes to 21 wins and 37 losses. Little wonder, then, that these have been called "the dark years."

It's not as if coaches Bill Loney and Jerry Young laid down on the job, or that the players failed to put forth maximum effort. That didn't happen. Everyone from top to bottom did their best. But talent is what separates winners from losers, and during this particular stretch, the Tide's talent level simply wasn't what it normally was.

If Steve Sparks had not been in uniform, it's doubtful that the 1976-77 team would have won nine games. Sparks, the third of George Taylor's grandsons to wear the black and gold, following older brothers Taylor and Sammy, had a superb senior season. He scored 633 points for an average of 21.1, which ranks among the top 10 in Golden Tide history. (See the Miscellaneous Records section for the complete list.)

Joining Sparks on this club were Bobby Joe Gott, Mike Brothers, Kerry Holden, Bill Perkins, Johnny Dale Elieff, Robin Wolfe, Calvin Gott, Chuck Childress, Tim Tucker, Charlie House and Keith Briggs.

This team struggled from the first game, a 68-65 loss to Bremen, thru to the district tourney opener, a 57-56 loss to Hughes-Kirk. There were six losses by 25 points or more, including an 85-58 home-court drubbing at the hands of Graham.

What about bright spots? Well, an 83-81 win over Hopkinsville, a 76-66 win over Ohio County and a 63-61 upset of Daviess County are about all you're going to find.

Sparks was consistently superb, hitting for 20 or more points on 16 occasions, with highs of 37 against Hoptown, 36 against Providence and 32 against Pleasure Ridge Park.

Bobby Joe Gott also had some big nights, hitting for 27 and 22 in two wins over Muhlenberg Central and 23 against Bremen.

Only two other Tide players led the team in scoring. Holden had 20 and 18 in two games against Graham, while Elieff led with 17 in a 72-64 win over McLean County.

Although the 1977-78 club ended up with a losing record (12-16), this bunch showed big improvement over the previous season. The reason was better balance. Unlike last year's club, which was led by Steve Sparks, this team had several players capable of putting points on the board. In all, six different players took high-scoring honors during the season.

Members of this team included Calvin Gott, Keith Briggs, Wallace Martin, Robin Wolfe, Nathan Gott, Mike Brothers, Bill Perkins, Jon Moore, Tim Tucker, Billy Knight and Kevin McCracken.

Despite the improvement, this team was no match for district foes Drakesboro, led by Eddie Rhodes, Barton Johnson and Doug McCoy, or Bremen, which had the superb trio of Ray Harper, Leon Harrison and Bobby Campbell.

The Tide began this season with losses to both of those teams. Bremen, getting 28 points from Harper and 19 from Campbell, ripped the Tide 89-69. Then with Rhodes scoring 23 points and Johnson 22, Drakesboro easily dismissed the Tide 85-72.

Along the way there were some impressive Golden Tide victories. They beat Grayson County 64-54, Allen County 64-60, Ohio County 72-71, Trigg County 89-79, Muhlenberg Central three times and Hughes-Kirk twice.

There were also several strong individual performances as well, especially from Perkins and Brothers. Perkins had big nights against Allen County (29 points), Hughes-Kirk (26) and Muhlenberg Central (22). Brothers hit for 26 against McLean County, 25 against Trigg County and Bremen, 23 against Ohio County and 22 against Greenville.

Wolfe had 24 in a loss to Hopkinsville, Briggs had 20 against McLean County and 19 in a win over MC, Calvin Gott led with 15 against Graham, and Tucker was the top gun with 14 against MC.

Another sign of improvement over the previous season was a better post-season showing. This team drew a first-round bye, then bumped off Muhlenberg Central 65-56 in overtime to earn a spot in the district tourney championship game and a berth in the regional tournament.

With the game tied at 51-51 at the end of regulation, the Tide took command in the extra frame, outscoring the Spartans 14-5 to get the victory. Perkins and Brothers each had 16 points for the Tide, while Briggs chipped in 12.

Drakesboro pushed its season mark to 25-0 by thrashing the Tide 74-49 in the title game. The brilliant Eddie Rhodes led the Cardinals with 26 points.

Brothers paced the Tide with 15 points.

This second straight long season ended with a 68-61 loss to Hancock County in the regional opener. Perkins led the Tide with 16 points, followed by Briggs with 11 and Gott with 10.

Golden Tide fans had endured two long, cold winters in the form of back-to-back losing seasons. But with a host of players set to return, the outlook appeared to offer some hope.

Maybe "the dark years" were in the past.

Chapter 48

1978-79

After consecutive dismal seasons, this team, which carved out a 19-12 record, finally brought some sunshine back to the program. This was a young club whose only seniors were Calvin Gott, Robin Wolfe and Tim Tucker. The real strength came from a strong group of underclassmen, headed by Keith Briggs, Wallace Martin, Billy Knight, Tommy Phillips and Jon Moore.

Other members of the squad were Nathan Gott, Kevin McCracken, David Higgs, Danny Vincent, Darren Ray, Andy Dennis and Clarence Brewer.

Briggs hit for 24 points, Gott had 13, Moore 11 and Wolfe 10 in a season-opening 72-57 win over Dawson Springs. That victory was followed by a 91-74 loss to a very strong Bremen team that would go on to finish as runner-up to Owensboro in the regional tournament later in the season. Gott led the Tide with 17 points, while the Golden Eagles were paced by David Decker and Gary Hardison with 21 apiece.

Behind 22 points from Briggs and 20 from Gott, the Tide slipped past Drakesboro 88-82 to kick off a three-game winning streak. The Tide beat Muhlenberg Central 58-55 and Graham 62-56 to improve their record to 4-1. Briggs was the top scorer in both games, getting 19 against MC and 15 against Graham.

Briggs stayed hot in the Tide's next two games, scoring 20 in a 92-71 loss to Warren Central and 24 in a 105-69 win over Hughes-Kirk. In that game, six Tide players cracked double figures. Gott had 17, Wolfe 15, Martin 12, Knight and Phillips 10 each.

Facing Drakesboro in the Central City Invitational opener, Briggs knocked in 23 points, Phillips had 13, Wolfe 12 and Martin 10 in a 70-62 victory. But Bremen, with Ray Harper tossing in 23 points, took home the big hardware by posting a 66-58 come-from-behind victory. The Tide led 46-45 after three quarters, but Harper was the difference, scoring 11 of his points in those final eight minutes. Gott and Briggs paced the Tide with 24 and 22 points, respectively.

Balanced scoring was the key in wins over Grayson County 84-54 and Trigg County 58-54. Against Grayson County, Wolfe had 17 points, Martin and Briggs 15 each, and Gott 12. In the win at Trigg County, Briggs led the way with 16, followed by Gott and Knight with 15 and 12, respectively.

An appearance in the Todd County Invitational resulted in a third-place finish. After a first-round 68-52 loss to Warren East, the Tide came back to beat Russellville 79-55 in the consolation game. Briggs had 19 points in each game to lead the Tide. Gott scored 15 and Moore 14 in the win over Russellville.

After getting drilled 79-53 by Apollo, the Tide responded by getting past McLean County 75-70 and Greenville 71-69. Briggs led with 20 in the Apollo loss, Gott had 18 against McLean County and Wolfe came off the bench to score 16 against the Blackhawks.

A similar scenario followed in the Tide's next trio of games—a 68-66 loss to Ohio County followed by wins over Breckinridge County 99-64 and Drakesboro 70-61. Gott had 20 points in the loss, Briggs 25 in the win over Breckinridge County and Martin rattled in 24 against Drakesboro.

Martin continued to post big numbers in the Tide's next two outings, scoring 24 in a 78-74 loss at Greenville and 21 in a 68-66 win at Hughes-Kirk. Briggs also played well against the Tigers, finishing with 20 points.

In one of their most-impressive performances of the campaign, the Tide rolled past Butler County 97-80. Gott paced the Tide with 26 points, Briggs had 23, Martin 14, Knight and Moore 10 each in this victory. Then with Briggs tossing in 20 points and Martin adding 17, the Tide made it two wins in a row by edging past Muhlenberg Central 65-62.

That modest winning streak came to a crashing halt, courtesy of back-to-back road losses—a decisive 94-57 pasting at Christian County and a 74-61 setback at Daviess County. Martin had 15 points against the Colonels, who would finish as runner-up in the state tournament, while Briggs 20 had against the Panthers.

Once again the Tide responded in a positive way, bouncing back to register their biggest win of the season, a 57-54 upset of heavily favored Bremen. After falling behind 17-8, the Tide fought back to within a single point (44-43) heading into the last quarter. In that frame, the Tide outscored the visitors 14-10 to claim the victory.

Knight, Martin and Briggs each had a dozen points for the winners. Bremen's Ray Harper led all scorers with 22.

Facing powerful Owensboro in the Sportscenter, the Tide almost pulled off a second straight upset before finally falling 60-52 in two overtimes. The score was tied 49-49 at the end of regulation, then neither club scored in the first extra period. But the Red Devils nudged ahead early in the second frame and never looked back.

Briggs led the Tide with 22 points.

In something of a bizarre district tourney opener, the Tide held cold-shooting Greenville scoreless until the second quarter, then went on to rout the Blackhawks 72-53. The score was 14-0 after the first quarter, and Greenville didn't score until Kelly Bard put in a free throw with 7:01 remaining in the second period.

Briggs paced the Tide with 21 points, while Knight had 16 and Wolfe 11.

Behind 43 points from Briggs and Gott the Tide stromed into the finals by ripping Drakesboro 74-59. Briggs finished with 22 points, Gott had 21.

The title game was no contest, with Bremen jumping to an early lead and then racing to an easy 76-57 victory. The winners were led by their backcourt duo of Ray Harper and Bobby Campbell, who scored 25 and 21 points, respectively.

Knight and Gott each had 12 points for the Tide, while Moore added 10. Briggs, the Tide's leading scorer, was limited to a season-low two points.

The Tide's season came to an end with a disappointing 69-68 loss to Ohio County in the regional tourney opener. That setback left the club with a final record of 19-12. It had been a solid season, and with most of the key players set to return, Golden Tide fans had big hopes that next season would be even better.

Chapter 49

1979-80

The last team of the 1970s turned out to be a good one, finishing with a 24-8 record, the best during Bill Loney's tenure as head coach. The saving grace for this team, which lacked real size, was a roster loaded with veterans who were hard-nose, competitive, smart players. This was a group that always gave maximum effort.

Keith Briggs, Billy Knight, Wallace Martin, Tommy Phillips and Jon Moore had all been starters at some point during the previous season. Nathan Gott would step in and fill the spot left vacant when older brother Calvin graduated. Kevin McCracken was another returning veteran. New faces included Darren Ray, Charles Johnson, Andy Dennis, Danny Vincent, Tommy Tinsley and Trent Gott.

Although this team fashioned a solid record, ultimately this season ended in disappointment, a first-round loss to Bremen in the district tournament.

The Tide opened the campaign by winning eight of their first nine games, beginning with an 87-79 victory at Dawson Springs. Briggs led the winners with 25 points, followed by Knight with 16, Moore 14 and Gott 11.

The lone loss came at home against Bremen. Led by 25 points from Eddie Heltsley and 16 from Ray Harper, the visitors edged the Tide 64-62. Briggs again led all scorers with 26 points.

Knight racked up 26 points and Briggs added 19 as the Tide began their seven-game winning streak by topping Drakesboro 85-56. Other foes to fall included Muhlenberg Central 90-73, Graham 62-56, Scott County 52-50 and Hughes-Kirk 87-64.

Briggs was the scoring leader in four of those wins, putting in 27 against MC, 17 against Graham, 20 against Scott County and 24 against

Hughes-Kirk. In the win over Hughes-Kirk, Moore had 21 points and Martin had 20. Phillips had a big game in the win over Graham, coming through with 13 points.

Huge performances from Briggs and Knight were enough to lead the Tide to a pair of easy wins in the Central City Invitational. Briggs had 28 points in a 109-86 win over Drakesboro, then Knight poured in 29 in a title-game 91-69 win over Hughes-Kirk. In the opener, Briggs received support from Knight with 19 points, Moore with 16 and Martin with 14. In the championship game, Phillips finished with 18.

The good times ended with a disappointing 67-63 loss at Grayson County. Despite 27 points from Knight, the Tide, who led 51-49 after three quarters, failed to hold on for the victory.

With four players hitting for double figures, paced by Briggs with 21 points and Martin with 20, the Tide rebounded by easily defeating Trigg County 85-60 prior to participating in the Owensboro Invitational. Against Trigg County, Knight and Phillips had 16 and 12 points, respectively.

Briggs scored 28 and Knight added 19 as the Tide opened OIT play with a 72-63 win over Owensboro Catholic. In semifinal action, the Tide, despite leading after three quarters, fell to Ohio County 70-65. Briggs led the Tide with 21 points, while Martin had 20.

Giving arguably their finest performance of the season, the Tide, behind a 31-point outburst by Knight, completely demolished Bremen 94-75 to claim third place. Knight had 10 field goals and made good on 11 of 12 free throws to account for his total. Briggs finished with 18 points, Martin had 13, Phillips 12 and Gott 11.

Bremen's Ray Harper led all scorers with 33.

In the Tide's next four games the best they could do was break even. They defeated Graham 67-61 and Breckinridge County 62-53, and fell to Apollo 73-54 and Greenville 69-68. During this stretch, several Tide players gave solid efforts. Ray came off the bench to score 11 points in the win over Graham, then Briggs had 24 points in the Apollo loss and 21 against Greenville. Martin scored 15 points against Breckinridge County, while Phillips matched that number in the loss to Greenville.

Turning in another superb performance, the Tide avenged an earlier loss by bumping off Ohio County 80-77. Gutsy free throw shooting down the stretch was the difference in this big come-from-behind win. In the final quarter, Knight connected on four freebies, Martin three and Phillips two. For the game, the Tide made good on 26 of 32 attempts. Briggs paced the winners with 23 points, while Knight had 19 and Moore 11.

That victory was the first of an eight-game winning streak in which the Tide dispatched Christian County 64-62, Drakesboro 67-49, Hughes-Kirk 72-62, Muhlenberg Central 82-71, McLean County 77-74, Butler County 76-64 and Crittenden County 70-59.

Briggs and Knight led the scoring in each of those wins. Briggs had his best outings against McLean County (27 points) and Christian County (25), while Knight's best efforts came against Butler County (22) and Crittenden County (21). Martin had 20 in the win over MC and Moore pitched in 14 against Butler County.

Sparked by hot-shooting Thomas Stokes, Greenville came to town and handed the Tide a sound 72-58 homecourt loss. Stokes was brilliant in the final quarter, accounting for 14 of his game-best 28 points.

Phillips paced the Tide with 12 points, while Martin and McCracken each contributed 10.

In the regular-season finale, the Tide battled powerful Owensboro before dropping a 72-62 decision. The Red Devils, who would go on to capture the state tourney title, were led by Dwight Higgs with 26 points.

Briggs paced the Tide with 17 points, with Phillips and Knight each scoring 12.

The district tourney opener pitted the Tide against Bremen in a showdown between two of the region's top teams. This marked the fourth time the two squads had squared off this season, with the Tide winning two of three.

But this game belonged to Bremen's great guard Ray Harper, who scored 34 points to lead his team to a 69-61 victory. Harper had 16 points in the final quarter, including making good on all 10 free throw attempts. For the game he went 14 for 14 from the stripe.

Briggs topped the Tide with 17 points, while Martin had 14 and Knight 13 in a losing effort.

Although the season ended on a sour note, overall this had been a solid campaign. But if Golden Tide fans were hoping things would improve, they were in for a big shock. Coming up was the Tide's fifth—and final—losing season.

The 1980s

Won – 208

Lost – 112

Winning Pct. – 65.0

Player of the Decade

Greg Franklin

Other Notable Players

Joe Byerly

Shannon Coombs

Troy Crist

Brad Divine

Steve Divine

Penrod Eades

Todd Franklin

Dwight Gamble

Claude Hampton

Dennis Hoskins

Charles Johnson

Ben Lutz

DeWayne Maddox

Wallace Martin

Robby Millard

Terry Nofsinger

Darren Peveler

Curtis Shelton

John Soderling

Maurice Summers

Tommy Tinsley

Chapter 50

1980-81

Central City's final decade in existence began in a most inglorious way—a season in which the Tide won 10 games and lost 19. This club, which featured several returning veterans, lacked the overall size and talent to compete against bigger, stronger, better-equipped opponents. The result was inevitable—another long, dark year.

The roster included Wallace Martin, Jon Moore, Darren Ray, Kevin McCracken, Troy Crist, John Soderling, Tommy Tinsley, Trent Gott, Jeff Sparks and Charles Johnson, who would emerge as this club's lone standout performer.

Only during the last month of the season did this team offer any hint of success. This came in the form of a four-game winning streak, the longest stretch during the campaign.

After losing to Apollo 63-48 and Ohio County 55-53, the Tide's record stood at 6-17. The winning streak began when Martin pitched in 20 points, Johnson 13, Moore 12 and Ray 10 in a 70-57 victory over Muhlenberg Central.

In their next outing, the Tide, behind a 25-point effort from Johnson, battled to a 69-62 win over McLean County. Martin added 13 points in this victory, while Ray had 12 and Moore 11.

Thanks to 32 points from Johnson, the Tide made it three wins in a row by blasting home-standing Butler County 84-52. The Tide led this game 42-14 at intermission. Moore finished with 13 points, Ray had 11 and Crist added 10.

To keep the streak alive, the Tide had to overcome a 44-point performance from John Worth to edge past Daviess County 78-76 in another impressive road win. Ray was outstanding for the winners, finishing with 24 points. Johnson and Martin had 18 and 12 points, respectively.

Owensboro, the eventual regional champs, ended the Tide's run by posting a 76-66 win in the Sportscenter. The Tide trailed by a single point (31-30) early in the second half, but the powerful Red Devils manage to pull away for the win.

Johnson led all scorers with 23 points, while McCracken and Martin each finished with 12.

The Tide's appearance at the post-season party was brief and uneventful. There would be no magic moments for this club. Facing Drakesboro in the district tourney opener, the Tide were handed a 61-56 setback, bringing a merciful end to a dismal campaign.

Johnson topped the Tide with 21 points, with McCracken adding 10.

Drakesboro's Duncan Cain led all scorers with 26.

For the season, the Tide did have a trio of players who averaged in double figures, headed by Johnson's 15.1 scoring clip. Martin finished with a 13.3 average and Moore put in 10.8 points per game.

Fortunately, for Tide fans, Johnson would be back for his senior season in 1981-82. And he would be surrounded by a gritty group of smart young players who knew how to win. Their efforts would help lead the Tide to another 20-win season.

Chapter 51

1981-82

Bill Loney's last season as head coach turned out to be a good one. With a team built around senior Charles Johnson, Loney guided the Golden Tide to a 20-11 record that included wins over traditionally strong foes like Apollo, Breckinridge County, Daviess County, Ohio County and Christian County.

What's so remarkable about this team's success is the number of new faces who showed up. Traditionally, teams with an influx of new and unproven players tend to struggle. This club didn't. While it won't rank as one of Central City's all-time great squads, it is one that performed with surprising consistency given its youth and inexperience.

This was a team in which the sum was superior to the individual parts. There was no genuine superstar, although there was one—sophomore Penrod Eades—waiting in the wings. Johnson, Eades, Darren Peveler, John Soderling, Tommy Tinsley and Troy Crist did the majority of work for this team. Backing them up were Trent Gott, Jeff Sparks, Rodney Burch, Dwight Gamble, Jeff Brothers, Randall Martin, Ben Lutz, Terry Nofsinger and Todd Franklin (another future superstar).

The Tide opened this season with a 67-58 defeat at Hughes-Kirk. This would be the first of three Golden Tide losses to the district's best team. Shan Baggett led the Tigers with 20 points. Johnson had 13 for the Tide, with Soderling and Crist adding 10 apiece.

Twenty points from Johnson and 19 from Peveler were enough to lift the Tide past Bremen 67-65. Then Soderling turned in a 24-point performance to lead his club to an easy 95-52 win at Drakesboro. In that game, Johnson finished with 22 points, Tinsley had 14, Peveler 13 and Gott 12. It was in this game that Eades scored the first four of his 1,633 career points.

After Johnson hit for 28 points in a 67-57 win over Muhlenberg Central, the Tide stalled, dropping two of their next three games. Graham, coached by ex-Tide standout Taylor Sparks, got 20 points from Greg Uzzle in a 59-58 victory. Guards Soderling and Crist paced the Tide with 22 and 18 points, respectively.

Peveler scored 16 as the Tide topped Butler County 60-55, then Hughes-Kirk, getting 34 points from Shan Baggett, claimed a convincing 72-56 win at Central City. Baggett would finish his career with 2,148 points, 10th best all-time in Muhlenberg County history.

Johnson provided the antidote to that loss by tossing in 25 points in a 92-66 win over Drakesboro and 22 in a 71-64 win at Hopkinsville. Johnson stayed hot in the Tide's next outing, hitting for 24 points against Ohio County. But his efforts weren't enough—Ohio County won it 64-62.

With five players hitting for double figures, led by Peveler with 19, the Tide easily dismissed Drakesboro 80-60 in the Central City Invitational opener. Johnson had 16 in this win, followed by Eades with 14, Crist 12 and Tinsley 10.

But for the third time in less than a month, Hughes-Kirk notched another win over the Tide, taking home the big trophy with a 71-56 victory. Eades, with 18 points, was the lone bright spot for the Tide. Ronnie Mallory led the Tigers with 28 points.

There would be a final reckoning between these two teams in March.

A 78-66 thumping of Muhlenberg Central in the Graham Invitational was the start of a seven-game Golden Tide winning streak. Soderling led the Tide with 26 points. In the title game, Eades had 24 points, Johnson 17 and Crist 12 as the Tide took the crown by defeating Graham 62-56.

Eades pitched in 22 points and Johnson 20 as the Tide made it two straight over Graham, winning this one 72-67. Facing Apollo in the Sportscenter, the Tide came away with a 59-47 win. Soderling topped the winners with 16 points, while Tinsley had 15, Johnson 13 and Eades 11.

Keith Withrow, Corky's son, led the Eagles with 12 points.

In rapid succession, the Tide beat Breckinridge County 62-58, South Hopkins 90-65 and Ohio County 63-57. A balanced scoring attack was the key in that trio of victories. Against Breckinridge County, Johnson had 18 points, Eades 17, Soderling 14 and Tinsley 10. Johnson scored

21, Eades and Soderling 19 each, and Tinsley 15 in the win over South Hopkins. Eades had 22, Soderling 15, Tinsley 13 and Johnson 12 in that difficult revenge win over Ohio County.

Just as things were going good the Tide once again stalled, managing only a single victory in their next three games. That win came against Christian County 85-65, with Johnson scoring 28 points, Eades 22 and Soderling 18.

The two losses were administered by Greenville 63-61 and Bremen 65-60. Johnson was the big gun in each of those games, ending with 23 against Greenville and 16 against Bremen.

Taking on archrival Greenville for the second time in two weeks, the Tide earned a measure of revenge by walking away with a 62-57 win. Johnson keyed the win with 18 points, while Eades had 14, Tinsley 13 and Soderling 10.

The Tide continued to roll, beating Muhlenberg Central 64-56, Butler County 74-61 and Daviess County 47-46. Eades had 20 points and Soderling 18 against MC, then Johnson scored 22 and Eades 21 in the win at Butler County. Against Daviess County, Johnson led the charge with 22 points.

With the season grinding down and tournament play around the corner, the Tide went into a sudden tailspin, losing their final three games, beginning with a 62-60 loss at McLean County. That was followed by a 69-55 loss at Hancock County and an 80-65 home-court loss to Owensboro.

This was not exactly a confidence booster with post-season play coming up.

Johnson did his best to keep the Tide afloat, hitting for 22 against McLean County, 20 against Hancock County and 20 in the Owensboro loss.

The Tide's 20th victory came in a most-dramatic fashion against a most-unlikely opponent. Facing Hughes-Kirk, a team they had lost to three times, the Tide pulled off a shocking 52-50 overtime win when Soderling ventured into heavy traffic and flipped in the game-winning bucket with four seconds remaining.

Soderling almost won the game in regulation with a desperation heave at the buzzer that rimmed out. After trailing 41-34 heading into the final quarter, the Tide battled back to take a 50-49 lead. Hughes-Kirk's Shan Baggett connected on one of two free tosses to even the count at 50-50. Peveler then missed a shot with two seconds left and the ball went out of bounds. Soderling stole the inbounds pass and launch his shot, which barely missed.

The Tigers missed a shot early in the OT, then the Tide held the ball until Soderling hit the big bucket.

Johnson led the Tide with 18 points, while Soderling had 13 and Eades 12.

Baggett, who scored all nine of his team's fourth-quarter points, topped all scorers with 25.

But the Tide's magic didn't last. In semifinal action, Bremen, getting 18 points from Eddie Heltsley, handed the Tide a 55-47 loss.

Johnson had 20 points and Eades 13 for the Tide.

At the end of the school year, Loney resigned as head coach and accepted the top job at Henderson County. Suddenly, Central City school officials were in need of a replacement, and only one name was on their list. The call went out to an ex-Tide player who quickly agreed to become the school's sixth coach since 1925.

Tony Hopper.

Chapter 52

1982-83

Like Delmas Gish and Jackie Day, Tony Hopper is a native-born Central City product. They are the only three Golden Tide coaches whose blood is as much black and gold as it is crimson. All three were raised in Central City, attended school there and wore the Golden Tide uniform. These facts mark them as uniquely different from the other men who guided this successful basketball program.

Hopper played on Day's final team in 1971-72. He possessed superb talent and a deep understanding of the game. Hopper was a coach-on-the-floor type, so it was only natural that he would eventually get into the coaching business. When Bill Loney left to take the top position at Henderson County, Hopper was the logical choice to take over the Golden Tide program. He got the call, and quickly said yes.

Hopper brought new energy to a program that had gone 30-30 over the past two seasons. His first team, led by junior Penrod Eades, finished with a 22-12 record. Over the next eight years, until the school closed its doors in 1990, his teams had a 178-82 record for a 68.5 winning percentage. Two of his teams won 30 games, and his 1988-89 club made the last of Central City's 17 state tournament appearances.

Along with Eades, starters in Hopper's first game were Darren Peveler, Ben Lutz, John Soderling and Troy Crist. Other team members included Dwight Gamble, Randall Martin, Rodney Burch, Jeff Brothers, Todd Franklin, Terry Nofsinger, Shannon Coombs, Robby Millard and Terry Sweatt.

Hopper's first game, played at home, ended in a 64-63 loss to Hughes-Kirk. Nine missed free throws killed the Tide's chances of getting Hopper's tenure off to a rousing start. Gamble came off the bench to lead the Tide with 16 points. Soderling and Eades each finished with 10.

Gamble bailed the Tide out in a low-scoring 44-42 win at Bremen, once again coming through with 16 points. In a much more comfortable 95-62 win over Drakesboro, Eades snapped out of his scoring slump by tossing in 24 points. Soderling added 18, Martin 14 and Gamble 12 in this win over the Cardinals.

A trip to Christian County to participate in the Druther's Classic resulted in losses to Union County 78-76 (despite leading 68-58 after three quarters) and Warren Central 88-64. Soderling was the leading scorer in the opener, hitting for 23 points. Eades had 25 against Warren Central, which was paced by Craig Eversoll's 30-point effort.

Fifteen points each from Eades and Gamble, 14 from Lutz and 11 from Soderling helped the Tide kick off a four-game winning streak by blasting Muhlenberg Central 81-56. Eades and Peveler each racked up 25 points, Soderling had 23 and Lutz 16 in an impressive 93-82 win at Butler County. In the Tide's next two wins—63-56 over Hughes-Kirk and 52-39 over Drakesboro—Eades topped the scoring in each game, hitting for 20 and 19 points, respectively.

After winning four straight road games the Tide came home and failed to defend their own turf, losing back-to-back thrillers to Hopkinsville 69-68 and Ohio County 47-46. The Ohio County loss was especially disappointing, given that the Tide, leading 42-34 after three quarters, could only manage four points in the final frame.

Eades had 22 against Hoptown, with Soderling and Peveler adding 18 and 16, respectively. Eades led with 16 points against Ohio County.

Next, the Tide claimed another Central City Invitational title by beating Drakesboro 66-51 and Greenville 97-55. Against Drakesboro, Eades and Peveler each had 14 points. In the win over Greenville, Eades had 22, Peveler 20, Soderling 15, Gamble 14 and Nofsinger 10.

Despite 27 points from Eades and 16 from Lutz, the Tide fell to Owensboro 72-65. That loss was followed by wins over Graham 66-52, a game in which Franklin led the way with 23 points, and Apollo 59-56 in overtime. Gamble had 16 against Apollo.

The next stretch proved to be disastrous, resulting in losses to Breckinridge County 87-74, Owensboro 74-54 and South Hopkins 67-65 in overtime. The lone bright spot in this dark period was a 67-60 win over Greenville. Eades and Peveler were the big guns in these four games. Eades had 24 against Breckinridge County and 23 against Owensboro, while Peveler scored 17 against both Greenville and South Hopkins.

With a record of 11-9, and reeling from a trio of recent setbacks, the outlook for this team's future was shaky at best. Even a winning season was no guarantee. What this club needed was for someone to step up and take charge. And that's precisely what happened. With Eades and Peveler leading the way, this team rattled off nine consecutive victories, beginning with a 68-53 win at Christian County. In this win, Eades had 22 points, Soderling 20 and Peveler 18.

Over the next seven games—all wins—either Eades or Peveler was the top scorer. Those wins came against Bremen 61-49, Greenville 74-60, Graham 59-55, Ohio County 81-63, Muhlenberg Central 76-65, McLean County 69-62 and Butler County 75-68. During this run, Eades accounted for 167 points, with a high of 34 against Butler County and 28 against MC. Peveler had 24 against MC and 23 against McLean County.

The Tide saw its winning streak come to a halt at Daviess County in the regular-season finale. The Panthers limited Eades to seven points en route to a 62-52 win. Peveler paced the Tide with 16 points, while Lutz chipped in 11.

In the district tournament opener, Eades had 18 points, Lutz 16 and Peveler 10 as the Tide pounded out a 69-52 win over Muhlenberg Central. Those 69 points turned out to be more than the Tide and Bremen combined to score in semifinal action. With Bremen slowing the game to a snail's pace, and despite making just nine field goals, the Tide slipped past the Eagles 33-32 in overtime. Lutz paced the winners with 13 points, 11 coming at the charity stripe.

The championship foe was Greenville, a team the Tide had defeated three times, once by a whopping 42 points. Although a huge underdog, the Blackhawks, getting 26 points from Bryan Wells, bumped off the Tide 69-66 in double overtime to take home the big trophy. The score was knotted 60-60 at the end of regulation and 62-62 after the first overtime.

Gamble led the Tide with 16 points. Eades had 14, Lutz 13 and Soderling 11.

Eades and Soderling made sure the Tide got off to a good start in regional action, hitting for 26 and 21 points, respectively, in an 81-66 win over McLean County. This was a solid all-around effort, with all five starters cracking double figures. Lutz contributed 13, Peveler 11 and Gamble 10 in this win.

Two nights later the Tide's season ended with a 65-61 semifinal loss to Owensboro Catholic. The Tide owned a 29-27 halftime lead, but the Aces, fueled by James McNary and Scott Warren, grabbed the upper hand in the third quarter and never relinquished it. McNary had 19 points, while Warren added 18, 11 coming in the final frame.

Peveler and Eades each had 16 for the Tide, with Soderling adding 12 and Lutz 11.

Hopper's first season at the helm turned out to be a success. But his next season would be even better. With Eades, Gamble and Lutz set to return, Hopper's second club would be the first Golden Tide team in 14 years to have a 30-win season.

Chapter 53

1983-84

Two huge breaks—one good, one bad—were key factors in this team's final 30-9 won-loss record. With seniors Penrod Eades, Dwight Gamble and Ben Lutz back for their final season, along with juniors Todd Franklin and Terry Nofsinger, most experts figured this would be a formidable team. And as the record shows, it certainly was.

The good break: While attending the 1983 state tournament, Eades and Lutz befriended DeWayne Maddox, who was a junior at Ohio County. Whatever the two Tide players said must have made a strong impression, because during the summer Maddox chose to transfer to Central City. At 6'3", his presence in the lineup provided a relatively small team with a strong inside player who could score, rebound and defend.

The bad break: In late December Lutz suffered a serious knee injury that sidelined him for six weeks. At the time the Tide had a 14-0 record. In the 14 games he missed, the Tide went 9-5.

This was an extremely balanced team—no fewer than six players led the team in scoring. It was also a tested club, one that appeared in four regular-season tournaments.

Along with the five players mentioned above (and Maddox), other team members included Randall Martin, Shannon Coombs, Robby Millard, Terry Sweatt, Todd Crist, David Everly and Gary Leggs.

Maddox made an immediate impression, racking up 21 points in a season-opening 83-48 romp past Bremen. In this win, Lutz contributed 14 points, Eades, Franklin and Martin 10 apiece.

The Tide's next two wins were almost identical—75-54 over Drakesboro and 77-54 over Hughes-Kirk. Eades accounted for 22 points against the Cardinals, while Gamble led the way with 15 against Hughes-Kirk.

In a real scheduling quirk, the Tide faced those same two opponents in the Graham Invitational, which turned out to be a showcase for Maddox, who registered 24 points in a 106-56 pasting of Drakesboro and 20 points in a 96-51 romp past Hughes-Kirk. Lutz had 23 points and Eades 20 in that opening-round win over the Cardinals.

Six straight victories followed, leading up to appearances in the Central City Invitational and the Owensboro Invitational. Here are those scores and the Tide's leading scorers in each outing: 75-65 over Muhlenberg Central (Eades 25), 90-72 over Butler County (Eades 29), 97-60 over Hughes-Kirk (Maddox 26), Drakesboro 41-39 (Lutz 15, Franklin 11), Hopkinsville 86-81 (Maddox 25, Eades 18) and Greenville 86-68 (Franklin 33, Maddox 23).

Lutz dropped in 24 points and Maddox added 18 as the Tide beat Russellville 78-66 in the CCIT opener. In the title tilt, facing Drakesboro for the fourth time, the Tide battled to a hard-fought 61-58 overtime victory, thanks to three key OT points from Franklin.

In the OIT opener against the host school, the Tide, getting eight fourth-quarter points from Eades and five from Nofsinger, overcame a 51-45 deficit to edge the Red Devils 64-62. Maddox and Franklin paced the winners with 16 points each, while Eades added a dozen. Nofsinger finished with nine points, all coming in the second half.

It was in the final quarter of this game that Lutz went down with his knee injury.

Fighting off 20-point efforts from Rex Chapman and Greg Baughn, and playing their first game minus Lutz, the Tide advanced to the title game by beating Apollo 75-59. Eades led all scorers with 24 points, while Maddox and Franklin added 16 and 14, respectively.

The championship game against Henderson County, now coached by Bill Loney, wasn't close. Loney's Colonels ended the Tide's run at perfection by posting a convincing 74-52 win. Franklin led the Tide with 16 points.

Now a much smaller team, with Martin filling in for Lutz, the Tide bounced back to claim back-to-back road wins, beating Graham 62-45 and Apollo 68-50 in the Sportscenter. Eades was the team's leading scorer in each game, hitting for 21 against Graham and 22 against Apollo.

Rex Chapman led Apollo with 16 points.

Now sporting a 17-1 record, this club suddenly went into a mysterious dive, losing four of its next six games. Those setbacks began with a 61-58 double overtime loss to Breckinridge County despite 23 points from Eades, 16 from Maddox and 10 from Martin. Against Owensboro, the Tide blew a 50-42 lead after three quarters and fell 71-65. Nofsinger was the Tide's leading scorer with 18 points.

The four-game Madisonville Invitational began with a 52-49 loss to Daviess County and ended with a 65-54 loss to the host team. Sandwiched in between were wins over Symsonia 88-75 and Daviess County 65-55. Eades was the Tide's leading scorer in all four games, racking up 22, 25, 27 and 21, respectively.

If Eades was dynamite in those four games, then Maddox was TNT during the Tide's next three games, hitting for 31 in a 67-55 win over Christian County, 26 in an 83-58 blasting of Bremen and 32 in a 100-86 win over Greenville. Against the Blackhawks, Franklin had 25 points, including 16 in the second quarter, and Eades added 21.

Eades scored 19 points and Franklin 17 as the Tide managed to overcome a 33-point effort from Ricky Courtney to edge Graham 71-67. Then Eades hit for 24, Franklin 18 and Maddox 16 as the Tide made it five wins in a row by beating Muhlenberg Central 77-65.

Despite welcoming Lutz back into the lineup, the Tide saw their winning streak snapped at McLean County, losing 73-57. Maddox and Eades each had 17 points for the Tide, while Lutz scored four points in his return to action.

Prior to taking a trip to Louisville, the Tide, with five players hitting double figures, ripped Butler County 88-53. Eades led with 20 points, followed by Maddox with 19, Franklin and Martin 14 each and Lutz with 13.

In the first of two games in Louisville, the Tide, getting 20 points each from Franklin and Eades, 18 from Maddox, 16 from Lutz and 10 from Coombs, easily handled Ninth & O 109-68. One night later Fern Creek established an early lead and then went on to beat the Tide 63-53. Franklin led the Tide with 15 points.

The final two regular season games ended in a split—a 57-53 win over Daviess County and a 45-39 loss to Madisonville. Maddox had 18 points against the Panthers, while Eades had 13 and Lutz 11 in the loss to the Maroons.

Although none of the games were easy, the Tide managed to claim another district championship by beating Bremen 58-49, Hughes-Kirk

59-45 and Drakesboro 71-64. Eades tossed in 19 points and Franklin 18 in the opener, then Eades came back with 19 against Hughes-Kirk. In the title game, Franklin and Eades each tallied 17, Maddox 14 and Gamble 11.

Facing Owensboro in the regional tourney opener, the Tide trailed 49-36 heading into the final quarter. But with Franklin knocking in 10 fourth-quarter points, they battled back to make it interesting, only to drop a tough 57-55 decision. Franklin led the Tide with 18 points, while seniors Eades and Maddox finished with 14 and 12, respectively.

With its 30 wins this team ranks as one of the school's most successful. Eades led the scoring with a 17.8 average, followed by Maddox at 16.5 and Franklin at 13.7. But with Eades, Maddox, Lutz, Gamble and Martin all graduating, the outlook for next season was dicey. It would be a very small team, one that would depend heavily on the backcourt duo of Franklin and Nofsinger.

Chapter 54

1984-85

This club surely must rank among the smallest in Golden Tide history, so small in fact that Todd Franklin, a natural guard, was forced to handle a forward position. The usual starting quintet consisted of Franklin (6'2"), Terry Nofsinger (5'9"), Shannon Coombs (5'8"), Robby Millard (6'1") and Todd Crist (6'0"). Other team members included Terry Sweatt, Chris Mayhugh, David Everly, Gary Leggs, Joe Byerly, Chris Bumps, Jeff Mitchell and Rusty Lile.

Despite its lack of size, this team carved out a 20-11 record and took home another district tournament championship trophy. For this bunch to succeed, Franklin and Nofsinger would have to put up big numbers, and both did, especially Franklin, who averaged 22.6 points per game. Nofsinger scored at a 14.8 clip.

The Tide opened the campaign with back-to-back wins over Drakesboro 63-50 and Hughes-Kirk 68-58. In the opener, Franklin scored 21 points, Nofsinger 16, Millard 12 and Coombs 11. Against the Tigers, Franklin led the way with 26 points.

With Franklin watching from the sidelines, the Tide fell to Muhlenberg Central 70-58. Nofsinger paced the Tide with 25 points, while Millard had 21. For MC, Joey Wells scored 22 and Duane Harvey 19.

After that loss the Tide reeled off three straight wins, beating Graham 62-52, Hughes-Kirk 68-66 in overtime and Drakesboro 92-72 prior to participating in the Franklin-Simpson Invitational. The Tide had a different leading scorer in each of those three wins. Nofsinger had 18 against Graham, Millard had 18 against Hughes-Kirk and Franklin had 29 against Drakesboro. In that win over the Cardinals, Nofsinger finished with 27 and Coombs 21.

Franklin racked up 31 points to help the Tide top Todd County Central 58-46 in the FSIT. In semifinal action, the Tide got 29 points from Franklin and 18 from Nofsinger, but it wasn't enough to get past Bowling Green. The Purples won 54-51, coming from five points down after three quarters. Facing the host school in the consolation game, the Tide, despite 34 points from Franklin, dropped an 81-80 decision. Millard and Nofsinger each had 15 points in this disappointing loss.

Back in friendly territory, the Tide took the Central City Invitational crown by beating Graham 55-50 and Muhlenberg Central 53-50. Franklin was the top scorer in both games, notching 19 against Graham and 24 against MC.

Twenty-two points from Nofsinger, 20 apiece from Millard and Franklin and a dozen from Coombs were enough to lift the Tide past Greenville 79-64. Franklin came back with 30 points as the Tide handled Breckinridge County 61-54 to improve their record to 10-3. Coombs had 15 points in this win, with Millard adding 10.

Then hard times hit in the form of three consecutive blowout losses. Apollo, with Rex Chapman tossing in 22 points, began the Tide's downward slide with a 73-56 win. Next, the Tide were soundly thrashed by Owensboro 87-63 and Hopkinsville 74-48. Nofsinger had 25 points against Apollo and 17 against Owensboro. Franklin was the top gun with 23 in the Hoptown loss.

A 29-point effort from Franklin helped the Tide snap out of their funk by beating Bremen 68-57. But the good times didn't hang around very long. Blowing a 10-point halftime lead, the Tide lost at Greenville 62-59 primarily because they couldn't stop Doug Thompson, who scored 30 points, 20 coming after intermission.

Nofsinger led the Tide with 25 points.

The come-from-behind situation reversed itself in the opening round of the All "A" Classic. In this outing the Tide trailed 39-33 after three quarters, then roared back to claim a 52-47 victory over Gallatin County. Franklin paced the winners with 22 points.

Second-round action against Bardstown Bethlehem was essentially a shoot-out between Nofsinger and Chris Dickerson. Dickerson had 34 points and Nofsinger 30. The final, though, wasn't as close as their individual duel. Dickerson's club won easily 69-49.

Franklin hit for 24 points as the Tide edged past McLean County 55-53, then Franklin came through with 25, Coombs 13, Millard 12, Byerly 11 and Nofsinger 10 in an easy 82-49 win over Louisville Ninth & O.

Despite having six more field goals than Graham, the Tide dropped a 78-77 home-court decision. The Nighthawks made good on 28 of 40 free throw attempts to come away with the win. Franklin led all scorers with 37 points. Bryan Baggett and Jamie Kinkade paced Graham with 21 and 20 points, respectively.

The Tide bounced back to claim a pair of narrow wins, beating Muhlenberg Central 49-48 and Daviess County 59-54. Franklin scored 21 against MC and 26 against the Panthers.

Ending the regular season on a sour note, the Tide lost at home to Madisonville 57-44. The game was close for three quarters, but with Shane Belcher scoring 10 of his 21 points in the final frame, the Maroons pulled away for the win.

Franklin had 14 points for the Tide.

In the district tourney opener, Millard had his best game of the season, accounting for 26 points in an 82-61 win over Hughes-Kirk. Franklin finished with 20 points, Nofsinger 14 and Coombs 11 in this victory.

The semifinal game against Greenville was a thriller that saw the Tide come from behind to escape with a 58-56 win. Millard again played well, scoring seven of his 15 points in the crucial fourth quarter. Franklin led the winners with 26 points.

To claim the title, the Tide would have to get past Muhlenberg Central, a club they had faced three times, winning two and losing one. Those were close; this one was even closer. Overcoming a 46-41 third-quarter deficit and then surviving in overtime, the Tide nipped MC 62-60. Franklin had 20 points for the Tide, followed by Millard with 14, Nofsinger 11 and Coombs 10.

After a slow start, the Tide, behind 20 points each from Nofsinger and Franklin and 19 from Millard, managed to pull away for a 69-53 victory over Whitesville Trinity in the regional tournament opener. The Tide actually trailed after the first quarter, and only owned six-point advantage at the half.

In semifinal action, Owensboro proved to be too big and strong for the Tide to handle, advancing to the finals with a 61-44 win. Playing in their final game, Franklin had 17 points and Nofsinger 13 for the Tide.

Avery Taylor led the Red Devils with 18.

This small band of warriors gave the Golden Tide another 20-win season. And Franklin, who finished his career with 1,299 points, became the latest Tide standout to be named Muhlenberg County Player of the Year.

Losing Franklin, Nofsinger and Coombs virtually assured that next year's club would struggle. And it did, managing to barely escape with a winning record.

Chapter 55

1985-86

Given the size of the school, it's been something of a miracle that Central City has sustained such a consistently high level of success on the basketball court. Unlike larger schools, where the talent pool is almost always deep, Central City seldom had that luxury. Many times there were classes with only three or four potential players, and in some instances, those players were of limited ability. A Corky Withrow or a Ralph Mayes or a Tommy Eades doesn't come around very often.

So the fact that when Central City closed its doors it was the winningest program in the state is an incredible accomplishment. What it means is that more often than not, those players who did wear the black and gold uniform often achieved beyond their talent level.

This was certainly the case with the 1985-86 club. A team of limited size and ability managed to have a winning season, finishing 17-16. Along the way, this team won the Central City Invitational, the Ohio County Invitational and advanced to the regional tournament. Yes, there were some dark times—a six-game losing skid—but for the most part, this club acquitted itself in good fashion.

There wasn't a superstar on the club, although there was one waiting in the wings. Greg Franklin, only a freshman, had a superb year, averaging just under 10 points per game. Franklin would go on to become the third most prolific scorer in Central City history, trailing only Withrow and Eades. He would become a first-team all-state selection, and would twice be named Muhlenberg County Player of the Year.

But the leading scorer on this team was senior Robby Millard. In 15 of the team's 33 games, Millard was the leading scorer, 10 times hitting for more than 20 points in a game. His best efforts were 28 points in an 81-50 rout of Graham and 27 in a 54-47 win over Daviess County.

For the opener, a 74-51 pasting of Drakesboro, Millard was joined in the starting lineup by Joe Byerly, Gary Leggs, Chris Bumps and Rusty Lile. This quintet was not set in stone. At various times, Franklin, Chris Mayhugh, Dennis Hoskins and Steve Divine, another freshman who would make a name for himself, were starters.

Other team members included Todd Crist, David Everly, Jeff Mitchell, Maurice Summers and Paul Kirtley.

In that opening win Millard led with 22 points, followed by Byerly with 15, Bumps and Lile 10 each.

Balanced scoring was a plus for this club. Along with Millard, at various times Lile, Byerly, Leggs, Franklin and Hoskins took home high-scoring honors. Byerly had several strong efforts, hitting for 26 against Graham, and 23 against both Todd County Central and Fern Creek. Lile's best performance was a 20-point outing against Muhlenberg Central, while Leggs led the way with 16 points in a 48-28 win over Bremen in the title game of the CCIT. One night earlier, with Byerly scoring 20 points, Lile 13 and Millard 12, the Tide whipped Graham 61-55.

The Tide captured the Ohio County Invitational crown with a pair of wins by a combined total of four points. Behind 26 points from Millard, the Tide advanced to the title game by edging Owensboro Catholic 58-55 in double overtime. Millard hit for 18, Franklin 14 and Leggs 11 as the Tide slipped past Ohio County 71-70 to get the big trophy.

By this stage of the season, Franklin had moved into the starting lineup. And like most freshman, Franklin's play was often inconsistent. But there was no question that this young southpaw was poised to be something special. Though only a youngster, when his game was on, he could light it up in a hurry, which he demonstrated by leading the team in scoring on six occasions, with a high of 22 against Owensboro.

It took a 40-39 victory at Ohio County in the final regular-season game to give the Tide a winning 15-14 record heading into the district tournament. Byerly accounted for 14 points and Millard 10 in this low-scoring affair.

The Tide opened district play by beating Hughes-Kirk 45-36 in another game that was something less than racehorse basketball. Millard led the winners with 12 points, while Byerly and Leggs each contributed 10.

In the crucial semifinal game, the Tide, getting 22 points from Byerly and 16 each from Millard and Franklin rolled to a convincing 76-59 victory. The win assured the Tide a trip to the regional tournament and a winning season.

Facing Muhlenberg Central in the championship game, the Tide found no answer for Joey Wells, who pitched in 30 points to lead the Spartans to a 68-65 win. Millard paced the Tide with 21 points, while Lile added 20.

A miserable fourth quarter assured the Tide that their stay in the regional tournament would be brief. Trailing Breckinridge County by a single point (33-32) heading into the fourth quarter, the Tide managed just five points in that final frame. The result was a 48-37 loss.

Millard and Lile were the only two in double figures, finishing with 14 and 11 points, respectively.

This had been a long, tough season, one that had been a struggle from start to finish. While this club won't go down as one of the school's finest, it is a team that can proudly hold its head high. This bunch got just about everything it could from the talent on hand. And that's no small accomplishment.

Chapter 56

1986-87

With Greg Franklin and Joe Byerly returning, it was a given that this club would be much improved. That duo provided plenty of firepower, while Steve Divine, a classic point guard with a pass-first mentality, made sure the scorers got the ball. It would be this trio that was at the core of this team's success, which resulted in a 19-10 record.

Rounding out the roster were Chris Bumps, Dennis Hoskins, Gary Leggs, Maurice Summers, Paul Kirtley, Claude Hampton, Jerry Gordon, Jarrod Dickinson and Curtis Shelton, who, three years down the road, would have the best single season by a Golden Tide player since Corky Withrow.

While Franklin did everything expected of him, the big surprise was Byerly, who emerged as a consistent big-time scorer. In fact, it was Byerly and not Franklin who led this club in scoring. For the season, Byerly had 521 points for an 18.0 average, while Franklin's numbers were 501 and 17.3.

High expectations for this club failed to translate into a fast start. In the first three games, a lone 76-48 win over Whitesville Trinity was sandwiched between losses to Drakesboro 67-65 and Hughes-Kirk 62-56. Franklin was the leading scorer in all three games, hitting for 27 against the Cardinals, 23 against Trinity and 16 against Hughes-Kirk.

Byerly took over in the Tide's next three outings, scoring 27 in a 71-67 win over Muhlenberg Central, 25 in a 66-45 win over Graham and 22 in a 74-59 revenge win over Drakesboro. At Drakesboro, Franklin had 20 points and Hoskins 15.

Byerly continued his rampage, tossing in 23 points as the Tide ripped Webster County 87-56 in the Central City Invitational opener. Franklin finished with 20 points, while Hoskins added 16.

In the low-scoring title game, Divine came through with 15 points to lift the Tide past Hughes-Kirk 48-44.

A terrible performance resulted in a 52-43 loss to Owensboro Catholic in the Owensboro Invitational. The Tide fell behind early and were never able to catch up. Hoskins led the Tide with 15 points.

Byerly, Franklin and Hoskins provided the big numbers in wins over Ohio County 69-67, Breckinridge County 62-55 and Bremen 78-31. Byerly had 25 points, Franklin 21 and Hoskins 17 against Ohio County, then Franklin scored 21 and Hoskins 19 in the win over Breckinridge County. In the Bremen laugher, Byerly had 24, Franklin 16 and Hoskins 13.

A 93-54 blowout loss to Owensboro was the first of five setbacks—including three at home—in the Tide's next eight games. With 25 points, Byerly was the lone standout against Owensboro.

The other four losses during this stretch were administered by Apollo 60-49, Hughes-Kirk 58-53, Todd County Central 54-44 and Ohio County 57-55. The trio of wins came against Graham 65-57, Greenville 90-69 and Muhlenberg Central 67-56.

There were some nice individual performances along the way, topped by Franklin's 33-point effort against Greenville. He also scored 26 in the loss to Ohio County. Byerly had 26 against MC, Hoskins 20 against Graham and Divine 14 against Hughes-Kirk.

That Ohio County loss would be the last time the Tide was on the short end of the score during the rest of the regular campaign. They would come out on top in their final five games, beginning with a 65-45 win at McLean County. Franklin and Hoskins each accounted for 16 points in this win, while Summers and Byerly had 15 apiece.

In rapid succession the Tide rolled into post-season action with wins over Bremen 60-46, Greenville 58-52, Christian County 48-45 and Daviess County 66-50. Franklin scored 16 against Bremen and 24 against Daviess County, while Byerly tossed in a season-best 32 in the win over Greenville and 20 against Christian County.

Sporting a 17-8 record heading into district tourney play, the Tide faced Graham in the opener. After jumping to a 16-10 first-quarter lead, the Tide, behind 21 points from Hoskins and 17 from Franklin, went on to post a comfortable 67-43 victory.

With Byerly scoring 21 points and Franklin adding 16, the Tide put away Muhlenberg Central 56-49 in semifinal action. MC had four more field goals (22-18), but the Tide won it at the charity stripe, making good on 20 of 25 attempts.

Hughes-Kirk had been something of a nemesis for the Tide, taking two of three regular-season encounters. In the championship game, the Tigers made it three out of four by riding Jason Hardison's 22-point performance to a 66-63 win. Hardison accounted for 20 of his points in the second half.

Franklin paced the Tide with 26 points, while Byerly and Divine had 16 and 15, respectively.

For the second straight year, the Tide's visit to the regional tournament was brief, and in a tip of the hat to déjà vu, once against it was Breckinridge County that spoiled the party, winning this one 63-60 in triple overtime. The score was knotted 48-48 after regulation play, then 51-51 and 56-56 before Breckinridge County managed to ease away for the win.

Free throws were the difference in this heart-stopper. The Tide had a field goal advantage (24-19) but the winners connected on 25 of 34 free tosses to survive.

Franklin led the Tide with 17 points.

This had been an excellent season, and with Franklin, Divine, Hoskins and Summers all coming back, along with the introduction of the three-point bucket, the 1987-88 campaign should be even better.

And it was.

Chapter 57

1987-88

For small teams, those susceptible to being battered in the paint area, the three-point shot was seen as the great equalizer. If coaches opted to pack their defense in tight, that would leave the three-point shooters open. Of course, for this to work, having guys capable of scoring from long range was essential.

And this Golden Tide team was blessed with a trio of players who could do just that. Juniors Greg Franklin and Steve Divine, and sophomore Curtis Shelton were born for the three-point shot. And vice versa. For the next three years, this trio of long-distance bombers would lead Central City to its final 70 victories, its last 30-win season and its 17th Sweet 16 appearance.

With Franklin having a monster year (721 points, a 22.5 average), the 1987-88 club put together a 23-9 record. He was joined in a very small starting lineup by Divine, Shelton, Dennis Hoskins and Maurice Summers. Others on this club included Claude Hampton, Paul Kirtley, Tyrone Saulsberry, Jerry Gordon, Jeremy Divine, Therron Cunningham, Brad Divine and Chris Cary.

Franklin registered the first trey in Golden Tide history en route to a 27-point performance against Drakesboro. Divine added 23 points and Shelton 11, but for the second straight year the Cardinals claimed the season opener, winning 78-70.

The Tide reeled off four straight wins prior to participating in a pair of holiday tournaments, beating Hughes-Kirk 63-53, Muhlenberg Central 67-64, Graham 88-68 and Drakesboro 76-61. Franklin was the leading scorer in all four wins, hitting for 20, 20, 23 and 27, respectively.

Those wins came despite some huge efforts by opposing players. Jason Hardison had 30 for Hughes-Kirk, Terry Nunley 34 for MC and Jamie Kinkaid 29 for Graham.

Opening against Hughes-Kirk in the Central City Invitational, Franklin hit for 23 points and Divine 18 as the Tide eased to a 70-62 victory. In the championship game, after leading deep into the final quarter, the Tide sputtered late, eventually losing to Union County 66-63. Franklin had 21 points, Divine 16 and Summers 15 in this loss.

Before taking part in the Owensboro Invitational, the Tide traveled to Louisville to square off against Atherton, a team that had dominated past encounters between the two schools. This one proved to be no different. Despite 34 points from Franklin, the Tide fell 85-74. If any one school can be said to have the Tide's number, surely it has to be Atherton.

In the OIT, the Tide quickly moved into the title game by beating Ohio County 50-49 and Greenville 59-52. Franklin scored 19 points and Hoskins 17 in the opener, then Franklin knocked in 18 and Shelton and Divine 13 apiece in the win over Greenville. Behind 21 points each from Hoskins and Franklin and 19 from Divine, the Tide took the title with a 77-66 win over host Owensboro.

The Tide's next two games resulted in a split, a 92-65 win over Ohio County followed by a 66-63 loss to Breckinridge County. Franklin had 29 points and Hoskins 18 against the Eagles, then Hoskins came through with 21, Franklin 17 and Divine 16 at Breckinridge County.

Four straight wins followed—two were easy (Bremen 73-44, Graham 79-44) and two were narrow escapes (Owensboro 82-79 in OT, Logan County 50-49). Franklin and Hoskins had 19 and 17 points, respectively, against Bremen, then all five starters hit for double digits against Owensboro, topped by Franklin's 33-point performance. In that impressive win, Divine had 15, Hoskins 13, Summers 11 and Shelton 10.

Franklin was to leading scorer against Graham with 22 points, while Hoskins led the way with 17 against Logan County.

After losing 64-63 to Christian County despite 28 points from Franklin, the Tide came back to win road games at Greenville 65-49 and Hughes-Kirk 73-71. Franklin topped the scoring against Greenville with 18 points. To beat Hughes-Kirk, the Tide had to overcome a six-point deficit heading into the last quarter. Leading the comeback was Franklin, who tallied 14 of his 29 points in that final frame. Divine finished with 14 points and Summers 13 for the winners.

Jason Hardison led all scorers with 30 points.

Facing Apollo in the Sportscenter, the Tide got smacked 67-51 despite leading at intermission. Franklin's 20 points were the only bright spot in this disappointing setback.

A 75-69 win over Muhlenberg Central was the first of three straight over district foes. After clipping MC, the Tide beat Bremen 69-49 and Greenville 67-65. Hoskins and Divine each had 17 against MC, then Franklin had 26 against Bremen and 23 against Greenville.

Franklin put in 27 points—hitting for five treys—and Hoskins added 19, but the Tide were upended by McLean County 74-67 in overtime.

With Franklin scoring 25 points in each of his club's final two regular-season games, the Tide ended on a positive note, beating Daviess County 72-50 and University Heights 65-54.

The district tournament opener against Muhlenberg Central was a battle from beginning to end, with the Tide finally coming out on top 68-61. The score was even at 46-46 after three quarters, but the Tide, getting 14 fourth-quarter points from Franklin, eased away for the win. Franklin finished the night with 26 points. Hoskins and Divine had 15 and 12, respectively.

Divine hit for 17 points, Hoskins 14, Franklin 13 and Shelton 11 as the Tide claimed a 71-60 semifinal win over Graham. But one night later, it would be Drakesboro that walked away holding the championship trophy, thanks to a 63-62 title-game victory. Nate Gadson led the Cardinals with 21, while teammate Emichael Jones added 16. Franklin had 23 for the Tide, followed by Divine with 13 and Hoskins with 12.

In the first round of the regional tournament, Divine knocked in 22 points, Franklin 20 and Hoskins 14 as the Tide ripped McLean County 75-40, a club they had lost to two weeks earlier.

The semifinal game turned out to be the exact opposite. Owensboro, a team the Tide defeated twice during the regular campaign, advanced to the finals by posting a 63-54 victory, courtesy of a 29-point performance by Orlando Stewart.

Franklin paced the Tide with 17 points, while Divine added 14.

This small team, which featured three guards and two forwards, ended with a 23-9 record. And the three-point shot was a big reason why this club succeeded. For the year, Franklin hit for 45 treys and Divine 15. In all, the Tide made good on 67 three-pointers.

With Franklin, Divine, Summers and Shelton all coming back, the outlook for the 1988-89 season was brighter than the sun. And this group delivered, giving Central City fans one of the greatest rides in school history.

Chapter 58

1988-89

By 1988 consolidation was the beast knocking at the door. Although few Muhlenberg County residents were in favor of the change, it was as inevitable as the sun rising in the East. The powers that be had spoken, and nothing was going to change their tune. For most of the 20th Century, high schools and their athletic teams had been the heart and soul of so many small communities. That was all about to end.

Golden Tide, Blackhawks, Cardinals, Nighthawks, Spartans, Golden Eagles and Tigers were familiar team monikers that were all soon to fall victim to changing times. Were those changes for the better? Doesn't really matter, does it? They happened, and that's the end of the story.

But with consolidation still two years away, Golden Tide fans had plenty to be excited about. Tony Hopper returned a veteran club, headed by high scoring senior lefty Greg Franklin. Joining him in a strong starting quintet were Steve Divine, Curtis Shelton, Maurice Summers and Claude Hampton. Back-ups included Jerry Gordon, Paul Kirtley, Tyrone Saulsberry, Chris Cary, Jeremy Divine, Therron Cunningham and Brad Divine.

This powerful group gave Tide fans something special, winning 30 games against a tough schedule, capturing the All "A" Classic, and, of course, earning Central City its 17th and final Sweet 16 appearance.

Not surprisingly, this team got off to a quick start, winning its first six games prior to participating in the King of the Bluegrass Holiday Classic. The Tide beat Hughes-Kirk 73-58, Muhlenberg Central 58-55, Graham 93-59, Jeffersontown 74-70, Drakesboro 101-68 and Christian County 69-66.

Balanced scoring was a key to this club's success. In the opener against Hughes-Kirk, Franklin scored 25 points and Hampton had 23. After

Franklin hit for 35 against MC, Divine led the way with 23 in the win over Graham. Franklin tossed in 20 against J-town and Christian County, then Shelton came through with 24 against Drakesboro. Summers finished with 17 points against Christian County and 16 against Drakesboro.

The King of the Bluegrass in Louisville resulted in the Tide earning a split, beating Bourbon County 80-64 and Eastern 79-63, and losing to Madisonville 71-51 and Fairdale 79-59 after falling behind 17-0. Franklin had 25 points and Hampton 20 against Bourbon County, then Franklin scored 16 in the Madisonville loss. In the final two games, Franklin had 22 against Eastern and Shelton 16 against Fairdale.

If the King of the Bluegrass was a hit-and-miss effort, the All "A" Classic left no doubt who was the class of the tournament. Led by Franklin, the tourney MVP, the Tide claimed the crown by topping McDowell 75-55, Dilce Combs 76-48, South Hopkins 68-57 and Holy Cross 76-62. Hampton had 18 in the opener, then Franklin scored 26 against Dilce Combs and 28 against South Hopkins. In the title game, Shelton finished with 20, Franklin 18, Divine 16 and Summers 14.

The Tide extended their winning streak to seven straight by besting Drakesboro 100-57, Breckinridge County 65-54 and Bremen 64-30. Summers led with 24 in the win over Drakesboro, then Franklin pitched in 22 against both Breckinridge County and Bremen.

Owensboro ended the Tide's run, pulling out a 61-60 win in the Sportscenter. Franklin led the Tide with 23 points, while Divine added 12.

A final appearance in the Louisville Invitational Tournament was spoiled by Valley 77-66 in the opening round. Poor free throw shooting killed any hopes the Tide had of advancing. For the game, the Tide hit just 15 of 26 free tosses, missing the front end of six bonus opportunities. Franklin had 17 points and Hampton 16 in this loss.

Those back-to-back setbacks awakened the killer instinct in this Tide team, because they soon went on a scorched-earth rampage, closing out the regular season by running off 10 straight victories with an average winning margin of almost 24 points per game. This surely must rank as one of the most dominating runs in Golden Tide history.

The fallen foes included Graham 84-52, Christian County 84-73, Hughes-Kirk 79-58, Apollo 78-59, Muhlenberg Central 65-46, McLean County 73-48, Bremen 89-61, Greenville 74-58, Daviess County 80-58 and University Heights 81-53.

Only the game at Christian County was competitive. To earn this win, the Tide had to stage a big second-half rally after trailing 44-34 at intermission. In those final two quarters, the Tide connected on 17 of 24 field goal attempts for a sizzling 71 percent. Franklin had 24 points in this win, followed by Summers and Shelton with 15 apiece, Hampton with 14 and Divine 13.

Among the top point-getters in this stretch were Franklin (27 against Apollo, 25 against Greenville), Divine (26 against MC, 24 against Hughes-Kirk), Summers (21 against McLean County), Hampton and Shelton (20 each against Bremen).

Heading into a district tournament they were expected to win easily, the Tide quickly advanced to the finals by beating Graham 89-44 and Hughes-Kirk 81-62. In the opener, Franklin had 18 points, Hampton 17, Summers 14 and Divine 10. Against the Tigers, Divine pitched in 22 points, Summers 21, Shelton 18 and Hampton 12.

Someone neglected to inform Muhlenberg Central—and Chris Knight, in particular—that this was supposed to be the Tide's tournament to win, Behind a huge 16-point, 19-rebound performance from Knight, the Spartans, after trailing throughout, came back in the final quarter to post a 68-65 upset. Knight got strong support from Terry Nunley and Steve Casey with 16 and 15 points, respectively.

Franklin led the Tide with 21 points, while Divine had 20 and Summers 14.

Franklin, Divine, Shelton and Summers were named to the all-tournament squad.

Summers made the big noise in the Tide's regional tourney opening-round 70-49 win over Hancock County, ending the night with 20 points. Divine followed with 14, Hampton 12 and Franklin 11 in this easy romp.

In semifinal action, the Tide, getting 26 points from Franklin, 22 from Summers and 20 from Shelton, bombed Ohio County 91-68 to advance to the championship game for the first time since 1970. The game was close for a half—the Tide led 37-34 at the break—but 81-percent third quarter shooting proved to be the difference.

Owensboro, a club that owned a 61-60 regular-season win, was all that stood between the Tide and a 17th state tournament appearance. This battle, with everything at stake, was equally tight. But in this one the Tide made the crucial plays in crunch time, knocking down big buckets, hitting free throws and coming up with big steals, all of which resulted in a 77-69 victory.

The Tide were on top 44-43 at the half and 60-58 heading into the final quarter. Still clinging to a 67-64 advantage with 4:10 remaining, a Franklin jumper was followed by a rebound bucket and free throw by Hampton that increased the lead to 72-64. The Red Devils scored on their next possession, then forced the Tide into a turnover. But when Divine intercepted a pass and went in for a layup that made it 74-66, it was all over.

The Tide had prevailed.

Franklin had 28 points to lead the champs. Summers scored 17, Hampton 15 and Divine 12 in this huge victory.

Franklin, Divine, Hampton and Summers were voted onto the all-regional team.

Ranked fifth among Sweet 16 teams, the Tide squared off against fourth-ranked Bryan Station in the opening round. After falling behind 45-33 midway through the third quarter, the Tide roared back to slice the difference to 47-46 late in the third frame.

Following a pair of Divine free throws that tied the score at 54-54 with 5:40 remaining, the Defenders' all-state performer Mike Allen took charge, accounting for 14 of his game-high 27 points to push his club to a 71-68 win.

Once again horrible free throw shooting cost the Tide a chance at victory. In the third quarter alone, the Tide missed nine free tosses. For the game they were 16 of 28.

Franklin closed out his brilliant career with a 19-point effort. The Tide's other three senior starters also played well in their final game. Hampton finished with 16 points, Divine 15 and Summers 11.

Losing those four seniors meant Central City's next—and final—team would be young and inexperienced. Few expected it to be very successful. But what no one could have imagined was the monumental season a 5'10" senior guard would have. Thanks to him, the Tide's last campaign was rather quite remarkable.

Chapter 59

1989-90

Were it not for Curtis Shelton, Central City's final season would be judged as average. A 17-9 record doesn't rank among the school's best, nor is it among the worst. In truth, given the number of new, inexperienced players, this club's achievements were higher than anticipated. And much of the success has to be credited to Shelton.

Now a senior, no longer laboring in the giant shadow cast by Greg Franklin, Shelton, a 5'10" guard, exploded as a scorer, putting up points in flurries. Consider this: his 28.6 scoring average is third best in Golden Tide history, trailing only the legendary Corky Withrow. Twelve times he hit for more than 30 points in a game, with a high of 44. Like Withrow, Shelton is the only Tide player to score 30 or more points in four consecutive games. Remarkable numbers, any way you slice it.

"One of the smartest players I ever coached," Tony Hopper said. "Curtis had a great knack for reading screens, for getting open. He could get his shots. And when he did, he knocked them down."

Another key component to this team was sophomore point guard Brad Divine. Like former Tide standouts Tommy Eades and Greg Franklin, Divine was a southpaw. And like his brother Steve, Divine was a natural leader, one of those players who understands all there is to know about the game of basketball. Divine provided solid support for Shelton, handing out plenty of assists while scoring 14 points per game.

Those two were joined in the starting lineup by Therron Cunningham, Todd Pollard, and Mike Smith. Also on Central City's final roster were Kelley Blair, Jeremy Divine, Todd Hayes, Richie Cook, Lamont

Mitchell, Steve Newman, Mark Smith, James Saulsberry, Troy Hampton, Kevin Reed and Darren Thomas.

With Shelton racking up 64 points, the Tide opened their last season by beating Hughes-Kirk 68-50 and Muhlenberg Central 75-62. Shelton accounted for 36 points in the opener and 28 against MC. In the MC game, Divine, hitting for six three-pointers, finished with 21 points.

(This team proved to be prolific from three-point range, connecting on 133 treys for the season.)

Six more victories extended the Tide's record to a surprising 8-0. Victims included Graham 67-34, Drakesboro 88-49, Christian County 80-74, Greenville 64-62, MC 63-59 and McLean County 89-74 in the opening round of the Owensboro Invitational. Although Shelton was the leading scorer in each of those games, with highs of 36 against McLean County, 34 against Christian County and 30 in the win over MC, several of his teammates also had big nights. Cunningham had 20 against McLean County, Divine scored 22 against MC and Pollard registered 14 against Drakesboro.

In the OIT semifinal round, Divine pitched in 23 points, Shelton 20 and Cunningham 19 but it wasn't enough as the Tide lost to Owensboro Catholic 67-66. Trailing 52-41 heading into the last quarter, the Tide rallied only to come up short.

It was during the next four games—two wins, two losses—that Shelton went on his record-tying rampage, scoring 30 in a 64-48 win over Drakesboro, 31 in a 72-71 loss to Breckinridge County, 39 in a 77-69 overtime win against Bremen and 44 in an 80-71 loss to Owensboro.

Cunningham was the big gun in a 102-45 pasting of Graham, putting in 24 points, including 15 in the opening stanza. Divine and Shelton each had 18 points, Mike Smith 15 and Blair 14.

After Shelton tossed in 22 points and Divine 17 in a 61-57 win over Providence, the Tide dropped back-to-back squeakers, losing 79-76 to Christian County and 67-65 in OT to Apollo. Shelton led the way with 29 against Christian County, then Divine and Shelton each had 24 in the Apollo loss.

With Mitchell now in the starting quintet, the Tide won their next two games, beating Hughes-Kirk 75-57 and Providence 82-57. Against Hughes-Kirk, Shelton scored 23 points, Mitchell 19, Cunningham 14 and Divine 12. In the win over Providence, Shelton hit for 30 and Cunningham had 16.

Those two victories were immediately followed by a pair of road losses—72-65 at Ohio County and 67-62 at Bremen. Shelton had 31 and 33 points, respectively, in those setbacks.

On Feb. 16, 1990, after more than half a century of heated battles, the Tide faced off for the final time against their oldest and most-bitter rival—Greenville. It is impossible to imagine Muhlenberg County hoops without the many hotly contested tribal wars between the Golden Tide and the Blackhawks. Their intense dislike for each other (and their mutual respect, if only grudgingly given), was older than Yankees-Red Sox, Celtics-Lakers, UK hoops against just about everybody. Remember, their rivalry dates back to the 1920s, before Adolph Rupp took over at UK and long before the Celtics and Lakers even existed.

In this final encounter, Shelton rang up 33 points, Divine had 20 and Mitchell 12 as the Tide won it 73-67 at Greenville. To account for his total, Shelton made good on 14 of 15 free throws.

It would be in the Tide's next outing that little-used Steve Newman etched his name into the trivia book by scoring the last two points—on free throws—in the final game played in Central City's gym. The Tide beat Daviess County 88-61, getting 29 points from Shelton, 19 from Divine, 13 from Cunningham and 10 from Mitchell. Newman, who scored four points, closed it out with those two freebies during the waning seconds.

Despite 33 points from Shelton, the Tide lost a 73-68 double-overtime thriller to University Heights in the final regular-season game, giving them a 16-8 record heading into district tourney action.

Thanks to 10 three-point buckets, the Tide rolled past Drakesboro 77-32 in the opener. In all, 10 Tide players scored, topped by Shelton with 25 and Cunningham with 12.

This would be the last of Central City's 1,578 victories.

In the semifinal round, Muhlenberg Central built a big advantage and then held on down the stretch to edge the Tide 50-48. Shelton led the comeback effort, scoring 12 of his game-best 23 points in that final frame.

When the season's final whistle blew, the era of Muhlenberg County basketball came to an end. The Golden Tide would wage no more battles against the Blackhawks, Cardinals, Nighthawks, Golden Eagles, Spartans or Tigers. Those days now belonged to the past. All that remained were the glorious memories.

Chapter 60

1970s/80s Sideline Shots

Tony Hopper—From Runt to Standout Performer

As a youngster growing up in Central City, Tony Hopper had a love for basketball and a dream of playing for the Golden Tide. He desperately wanted to wear the black and gold uniform. But Mother Nature and genetics wouldn't cooperate. Tony was simply too small to be a basketball player.

"I was a little-bitty thing," Tony remembers. "One of the smallest in our class. I was on the JV team, but I realized that I was never going to play. So I made the decision to drop out."

Then a funny thing happened—over the next 12 months or so, Tony grew about six inches, putting him close to the six-foot mark. "I was a 17-year-old senior, which is never a good thing," Tony says. "I continued to grow all through my senior year and into my first year of college.

But after sitting out for a year and a half, would he even be allowed to try out for the team? Only one way to find out—ask the coach.

"In the spring of my junior year, Coach Day had one of those meetings for anyone who wanted to try out," Tony said. "And I showed up. Coach Day tells the story that he told me if I was good enough to be a starter, he would let me join the team. I don't remember it exactly that way, but I'm sure he's correct. After all, he wouldn't want a senior to come out only to take up a spot on the bench."

Tony was given the green light but the question remained: After sitting out for so long, would he be up to the task of earning a starting spot?

"That summer I worked by tail off," Tony said. "Coach would have the varsity guys in three days a week and the JV guys for the other two days. I went all five days. When I was done there, I would go down to

Marion Tinsley's house and spend hours shooting on his goal. Then at night, I would go off and try to find some pick-up games to play in."

Well, Tony not only started, he became an integral part of a team that remains one of the school's most exciting. That 1971-72 club finished with a 29-6 record. Tony scored 531 points for an average of 15.6. He hit for 20 or more points 11 times, with a career-high 31-point effort against Allen County.

Not bad for a kid who only a few months earlier had been the runt of his class.

Tony went on to play some college ball, then decided to get into the coaching ranks He eventually ended up as the head guy at his alma mater, where he led the Golden Tide to a 178-82 record for a 68.5 winning percentage. Two of his teams won 30 games in a season, and his 1988-89 club was the school's last one to play in the state tournament. It was Tony who coached the final game in Central City's glorious basketball history.

Unselfishness and a Standing O for Eades

That 1971-72 team remains one of the most exciting in Golden Tide history. But what made this bunch such a fun team to watch?

"Well, it didn't hurt that we had Tommy (Eades) on our team," Tony Hopper said. "He was incredible that season, shooting close to 65 percent from the field. There were times when he was so hot you were almost shocked when he missed a shot.

"We all loved to play, we were a quick, fast-break, full-court pressing type team," Tony added. "We had a great press. Plus, we were all unselfish. We shared the ball really well. Losing to Leitchfield in the regional tournament semifinal game was disappointing. We should have beat them."

Tony recalls a game the Tide played at Bremen, during which he made a decision that turned out to have positive results.

"I had a minor hand injury and couldn't really shoot that well," Tony said. "So I decided to do nothing but feed the ball to Tommy. And that's what I did. When the game was over, Tommy had 40 points. We got on the bus and all the JVguys stood up and applauded him. It was quite a moment."

These days, Tommy seldom gets any standing ovations. More often than not, he's catching grief from a coach who isn't pleased with the way things are going. That's only natural, given that Tommy swapped his unform for the stripped shirt worn by basketball game officials.

While those unhappy coaches might complain, the fact is, Tommy has distinguished him as one of the finest officals in all of college hoops. He has officiated games in virtually all top conferences, including the SEC, the Big 10 and the ACC.

And, of course, topping it all, Tommy has also officiated in the Final Four.

Here's a wager only a fool would bet against: Regardless of what teams are playing, and no matter how many All-Americans are in action, it says here that Tommy Eades is the best shooter on the court.

Penrod Eades, Ben Lutz...Ace Recruiters

Over the years, opponents have accused Central City of being a "recruiting" school. According to those foes, when the Tide needed a player, they simply go out and get him. And yet, the records don't back up those accusations. Yes, there have been a few players who transferred to Central City, among them H.L. "Hub" Hope and Oscar Perry, both of whom came from Drakesboro. Probably, there were a handful of others throughout the decades, but even if there were, that doesn't exactly make Central City a recruiting school.

However, there was one instance when a couple of Golden Tide players did engage in a bit of recruiting. This happened during the 1983 state tournament, when Penrod Eades and Ben Lutz crossed paths with DeWayne Maddox.

"We only knew him from playing Ohio County," Ben remembered. "We ran into him at the Hyatt, where we were all staying. For three days we all hung out together, watched a lot of games and talked a lot about basketball. Penrod and I told him how good Central City could be if he joined us. Ohio County had been down for several years, and the thought of possibly getting to the state tournament made the talk turn serious. We convinced him he was the missing piece, that if he came and played with us, we could make it to the Sweet 16."

And did the Eades/Lutz sales pitch work?

"By the time we all went home, DeWayne had already spoken to his parents about transferring," Ben said. "They moved to Central City that summer and he joined us in the fall. I can't say he was necessarily unhappy at Ohio County, but the thought of making it as far as we thought we could go was something he really wanted."

Maddox performed well in his only year with the Tide, averaging 16.5 points per game.

As recruiters, Penrod and Ben did well.

Soderling Wades into Heavy Traffic

Only a handful of players are lucky enough to know the feeling that comes from hitting a last second game-winning bucket. Without question, the most memorable of all is Billy Duvall's miraculous shot that beat Hartford in the 1955 regional tournament championship game.

John Soderling is another Tide player who knows how it feels to be the big hero. His moment of glory came in a 52-50 overtime upset of powerful Hughes-Kirk in the 1982 district tournament.

"Yeah, I went in among the tall trees to make that shot," John said. "I went between two defenders, then made the shot over Shan Baggett, who was a big guy. There were four seconds remaining."

Along with his own heroics, John offered high praise to coach Bill Loney and teammates Penrod Eades and Tommy Tinsley for their contributions to this win.

"We got behind early, then Coach Loney had us spread out and kind of four-corner them," John said. "That worked in our favor. Then Penrod got hot and we were able to get back in the game. But the real hero might have been Tinsley. In the second half we went to a triangle-and-two defense. Tinsley guarded Ronnie Mallory and completely shut him down. Mallory had 12 points, all in the first half. Tommy really smothered him."

Always the unselfish point guard, John is still handing out assists to his teammates.

Epilogue

"Hail to the Black and Gold, hail to you,
Hail alma mater, ever so true,
We love no other, so let our motto be
Victory Central High, varsity."

If those of us who graduated from Central City had a dollar for every time we sang that school song, we would all be very wealthy individuals. Even now, when former students gather for a school reunion or a class reunion, that song will be sung. And while we're singing it, we stand a little taller. Pride has a way of making you feel bigger than normal.

When Central City High School closed its doors in 1990, the heart and soul of our community was ripped out. Same goes for Greenville, Drakesboro, Graham, Bremen, Beechmont, Powderly and Dunmor. Each of those communities suffered a loss that could not be overcome. They were never the same once those schools shut down.

There are those who say it's a mistake to make too much out the exploits of high school activities. They argue that a basketball game or a band competition don't really count. They couldn't be more wrong.

True, Central City versus Greenville was only a basketball game played by a bunch of high-octane teen-agers. But it mattered.

When the Central City band took part in competitions, it was just a bunch of kids playing musical instruments and marching in step. But it mattered.

When Title IX put girls on equal footing with boys, and when Central City took on Greenville, it was just a bunch of young ladies competing in a basketball game. But it mattered.

When the Golden Tide cheerleaders were exhorting the fans to wake up and support their team, it was just a bunch of pretty young ladies yelling, screaming and cheering. But it mattered.

It mattered for Central City fans just like it mattered for fans of our fellow Muhlenberg County schools. Why did it matter? Because what those kids achieved gave their community its identity, its energy and its sense of pride.

Take away pride and you leave a huge hole that can't be filled.

Perhaps consolidation was inevitable. After all, there are always those in high places—the *best and brightest*—who maintain that bigger is better. Maybe they are right. Maybe not. If past experiences have taught us anything, it's that the so-called best are seldom as good as they think they are, and the brightest are rarely all that smart.

Initially, after consolidating, there were two Muhlenberg County schools rather than seven... Muhlenberg North and Muhlenberg South. Their rivalry would be intense, but never did it rise to the level of the hundreds of fierce battles waged for decades between those small schools all located within 10 miles of each other.

Then, a few years down the road, those two schools would merge, leaving only a single Muhlenberg County school. Their teams would be called the Mustangs. Football would be added to the list of activities, and facilities for the athletic teams and the band would be first-class in every regard. And although support for those students who participate, and the level of energy they put forth, is outstanding, there is simply no denying the fact that it is not the same as it once was.

Something is missing, and that is tradition.

Progress? Perhaps. But progress at what cost?

Miscellaneous Records

Year-by-Year Record

Year		
1921-22	13-3	(Tim Meinschein)
1922-23	8-2	
1923-24	12-4	(R.H. Carlson)
1924-25	9-8	(Arthur G. Bacon)
1925-26	6-11	(George Taylor)
1926-27	20-5	
1927-28	23-7	
1928-29	29-5	
1929-30	30-4	
1930-31	34-4	
1931-32	24-9	
1932-33	24-4	
1933-34	31-3	
1934-35	28-7	
1935-36	32-4	
1936-37	28-3	
1937-38	31-5	
1938-39	20-13	
1939-40	26-8	
1940-41	20-10	
1941-42	32-3	
1942-43	21-6	(Delmas Gish)
1943-44	22-10	
1944-45	37-4	
1945-46	23-6	
1946-47	34-4	
1947-48	25-6	
1948-49	20-8	
1949-50	29-5	
1950-51	20-9	

1951-52	19-13	
1952-53	24-9	
1953-54	35-1	
1954-55	30-6	
1955-56	30-4	
1956-57	20-15	
1957-58	18-14	
1958-59	32-5	(Jack Day)
1959-60	23-10	
1960-61	21-12	
1961-62	20-14	
1962-63	8-24	
1963-64	17-16	
1964-65	30-5	
1965-66	33-3	
1966-67	27-7	
1967-68	22-11	
1968-69	26-5	
1969-70	30-4	
1970-71	15-13	
1971-72	29-6	
1972-73	24-8	(Wayne Divine)
1973-74	16-12	(Bill Loney)
1974-75	22-9	
1975-76	24-13	
1976-77	9-21	
1977-78	12-16	
1978-79	19-12	
1979-80	24-8	
1980-81	10-19	
1981-82	20-11	
1982-83	22-12	(Tony Hopper)
1983-84	30-9	
1984-85	20-11	
1985-86	17-16	
1986-87	19-10	
1987-88	23-9	
1988-89	30-6	
1989-90	17-9	

All-Time Coaching Records

Coach	Years	Won	Lost	Pct.
Tim Meinschein	1921-23	21	5	80.8
R.H. Carlson	1923-24	12	4	75.0
Arthur G. Bacon	1924-25	9	8	52.9
George Taylor	1925-42	438	105	80.1
Delmas Gish	1942-58	407	120	77.2
Jack Day	1958-72	333	135	71.2
Wayne Divine	1972-73	24	8	75.0
Bill Loney	1973-82	156	121	56.3
Tony Hopper	1982-90	178	82	68.5
Totals	**69 Years**	**1,578**	**588**	**72.9**

Won-Loss Record by Decade

Years	Won	Lost	Pct.
1921-30	150	49	75.4
1931-40	278	60	82.2
1941-50	263	62	81.0
1951-60	251	86	74.5
1961-70	234	101	69.9
1971-80	194	118	62.2
1981-90	208	112	65.0
Totals	**1,578**	**588**	**72.9**

Golden Tide 1,000-Point Club

PLAYER	POINTS
Corky Withrow (1956)	3,136
Tommy Eades (1973)	2,238
Greg Franklin (1989)	2,233
Ralph Mayes (1967)	2,076
Lance Gish (1959)	1,817
David James (1966)	1,817
Steve (Bosco) Reynolds (1970)	1,726
Penrod Eades (1984)	1,633
Lewis Chaney (1959)	1,610
Steve Dukes (1976)	1,584
Rodney Kirtley (1966)	1,568
Joe Stone (1970)	1,433
Mark Eades (1970)	1,406
Keith Briggs (1980)	1,331
Todd Franklin (1985)	1,299
Joe Mac Howard (1951)	1,296
W.C. Mobberly (1947)	1,284
Steve Sparks (1977)	1,220
Joe Bowen (1965)	1,196
Sammy Sparks (1973)	1,158
Curtis Shelton (1990)	1,154
Ricky Turley (1969)	1,114
Steve Divine (1989)	1,044
Rick Brothers (1976)	1,043

All-Time Highest Season Scoring Averages

PLAYER	GAMES	POINTS	AVERAGE
Corky Withrow (1955-56)	34	1,052	30.9
Corky Withrow (1954-55)	36	1,086	30.2
Curtis Shelton (1989-90)	26	743	28.6
Tommy Eades (1972-73)	30	802	26.7
Tommy Eades (1971-72)	35	899	25.7
Lance Gish (1958-59)	37	893	24.1
Todd Franklin (1984-85)	30	677	22.6
Greg Franklin (1987-88)	32	721	22.5
Ralph Mayes (1966-67)	34	731	21.5
Steve Reynolds (1969-70)	34	722	21.2
Steve Sparks (1976-77)	30	633	21.1
Ralph Mayes (1965-66)	36	755	21.0
Kenny Lindsey (1966-67)	34	690	20.3
Greg Franklin (1988-89)	34	689	20.3

State Tournament Results

1928—St. Xavier 53, Central City 14
1929—Central City 30, Henderson 27
Heath 22, Central City 15
1930—Kavanaugh 24, Central City 18
1931—Central City 30, Benham 19
Manual 16, Central City 15
1932—Paris 44, Central City 16
1934—Danville 18, Central City 16 (OT)
1935—Inez 20, Central City 15
1938—St. Xavier 31, Central City 13
1945—Central City 54, Rineyville 37
Central City 32, Madison 28
Central City 34, Harlan 30
Male 54, Central City 42
1947—Clark County 53, Central City 43
1950—Central City 60, Tompkinsville 51
Central City 45, Campbellsville 41
Clark County 59, Central City 55
Corbin 71, Central City 69
1954—Inez 72, Central City 57
1955—Pikeville 78, Central City 74
1956—Carr Creek 70, Central City 68 (OT)
1959—Manual 77, Central City 65
1966—Central City 87, Carlisle County 75
Central City 79, Glasgow 54
Male 81, Central City 68
1989—Bryan Station 71, Central City 68

All-State Tournament Selections

Bernard "Peck" Hickman (1929, 1931)
Bobby Watkins (1945)
W.C. Mobberly (1945)
Gilbert Teague (1945)
Joe Mac Howard (1950)
Corky Withrow (1955, 1956)
Lance Gish (1959)
Ralph Mayes (1966)

Louisville Courier-Journal All-State Selections

Bobby Watkins (1945*)
W.C. Mobberly (1945, 1947*)
Joe Mac Howard (1950, 1951)
Corky Withrow (1954, 1955*, 1956*)
Lance Gish (1959)
Ralph Mayes (1966, 1967*)
Steve "Bosco" Reynolds (1969, 1970)
Tommy Eades (1973)
Greg Franklin (1989*)
(Denotes First Team)*

All-Louisville Invitational Selections

Tommy Gray (1948)
Marion Tinsley (1948)
Corky Withrow (1955, 1956)
Winfred Thompson (1956)
Lance Gish (1959)

Muhlenberg County Most Valuable Player (Award Began in 1962)

Ralph Mayes (1966, 1967)
Steve Reynolds (1969, 1970)
Tommy Eades (1973)
Penrod Eades (1984)
Todd Franklin (1985)
Greg Franklin (1988, 1989)
Curtis Shelton (1990)

Kentucky-Indiana All-Star Game Participants

Joe Mac Howard (1951)
Corky Withrow (1956)
Ralph Mayes (1967)

Miscellaneous

Most State Tournament Appearances –(4, Peck Hickman)
Most State Tournament Games Played – (6, Peck Hickman)
Most Points State Tournament Total – (75, Ralph Mayes)
Most Points State Tournament Game – (34, Corky Withrow vs. Carr Creek, 1956)
Most Points Career – (3,136, Corky Withrow, 1952-56)
Most Points Single Game – (53, Corky Withrow vs. Bremen, 1956)
First Player to Score 1,000 Points Career – (1,284, W.C. Mobberly, 1943-47)
First Player to Score 500 Points in a Season – (564, W.C. Mobberly, 1947)
First Players to Score 20 Points in a Game – (27, Jim Rice, 20, Arvall Eades vs. Dawson Springs, 1923)
First Player to Score 30 Points in a Game – (30, W.C. Mobberly vs. St. Xavier, 1946)
First Player to Score 40 Points in a Game – (40, Corky Withrow vs. Dunmor, 1954)
Only Players to Score 30 Points in Three Consecutive Games – (Corky Withrow, 1954-55, 1955-56, Ricky Turley, 1967-68, Tommy Eades, 1972-73, Curtis Shelton, 1989-90)
Only Players to Average 20 Points per Game in Same Season – (1966-67, Ralph Mayes, 21.5, Kenny Lindsey, 20.3)
Most Points Scored by an Opponent – (53, Jimmy Harper, Hughes-Kirk, 1958)
Players with Most Career Wins – (119, Corky Withrow, 1952-56, 116, Peck Hickman 1927-31, W.C. Mobberly 1943-47)
Biggest Winning Margin – (94 points, Central City 99, Dunmor 5, 1935)
Most Wins in a Season – (37, 1944-45)
Best Winning Percentage Season – (97.2, 35-1, 1953-54)

All-Time Greatest Opponents

Mike Allen (Bryan Station)
William "Bird" Averitt (Hopkinsville)
Steve Barker (Apollo)
Butch Beard (Breckinridge County)
Ralph Beard (Male)
Bill Bibb (Owensboro)
Jerry Bird (Corbin)
Bobby Bland (Leitchfield)
Jimmy Brown (Beaver Dam)
Bill Ray Cassady (Inez)
Jerry Claiborne (Hopkinsville)
Lynn Cole (Paducah)
Kelly Coleman (Wayland)
E.A. Couch (Carr Creek)
Rex Chapman (Apollo)
Wayne Chapman (Daviess County)
Don Crosley (Daviess County)
Rod Drake (Owensboro)
Randy Embry (Owensboro)
Jimmy Feix (Henderson)
Travis Ford (Madisonville)
Bobo Foster (Owensboro)
Ralph Gilliam (Pikeville)
J.M. Gipe (Owensboro)
Logan Gipe (Owensboro)
Cecil Goff (Hartford)
Robert "Snake" Grace (Christian County)
Charley Hadden (Lafayette)
Cliff Hagan (Owensboro)
Radean Hammers (Butler County)
Dwight Higgs (Owensboro)
Kenny Higgs (Owensboro)

Butch Hill (Beaver Dam)
Jim Hutchens (Lafayette)
Wally Johnson (Butler County)
Jeff Jones (Apollo)
Wallace "Wah Wah" Jones (Harlan)
Roy Kidd (Corbin)
Kenny Kuhn (Male)
Freddie Maggard (Carr Creek)
Don Mills (Berea)
Jim Mitchell (Madisonville)
Ed Mudd (Male)
Tom Payne (Shawnee)
Billy Puckett (Clark County)
Linville Puckett (Clark County)
Frank Ramsey (Madisonville)
Terry Randall (Adair County)
Bobby Rascoe (Daviess County)
Gene Rhodes (Male)
Bobby Joe Rickard (Sacramento)
Ted Rose (Male)
Curt Selvy (Corbin)
Frank Selvy (Corbin)
Bobby Shepherd (Carr Creek)
Ralph Shearer (Adair County)
Kenny Sidwell (Caverna)
Lewis Snowden (Clark County)
Everett Stallworth (Male)
Charles Taylor (Owensboro)
Barry Teague (Madisonville)
Felix Thruston (Owensboro)
Jerry Thruston (Owensboro)
Jerry Tilford (Caneyville)
Harry Todd (Earlington)
Herbie Triplett (Inez)
John Turner (Newport Public)
Charlie Tyra (Atherton)
Bobby Watson (Owensboro)
John Worth (Daviess County)

All-Time Greatest Muhlenberg County Opponents

Kenny Arbuckle (Greenville)
Shan Baggett (Hughes-Kirk)
Bobby Campbell (Bremen)
Ronnie Cartwright (Bremen)
Larry Cary (Muhlenberg Central)
Billy Carver (Hughes-Kirk)
Carl Carver (Hughes-Kirk)
Danny Creager (Bremen)
David Decker (Bremen)
Joe Robert Divine (Bremen)
Wayne Divine (Bremen)
John Drake (Greenville)
Jimmy Eades (Bremen)
John Elliott (Greenville)
Larry Elliott (Greenville)
Bob Gillespie (Graham)
Rip Gish (Bremen)
Tommy Gross (Greenville)
Eldon Hardison (Hughes-Kirk)
Harold Hardison (Hughes-Kirk)
Jason Hardison (Hughes-Kirk)
Jimmy Harper (Hughes-Kirk)
Ray Harper (Bremen)
Robie Harper (Hughes-Kirk)
Leon Harrison (Bremen)
Lamar Holland (Hughes-Kirk)
Nookie Hope (Drakesboro)
Barry Jarvis (Bremen)
Jerry Jarvis (Bremen)

R.T. Jarvis (Bremen)
Doug Jernigan (Drakesboro)
Wayne Jernigan (Greenville)
Barton Johnson (Drakesboro)
Dwain Jones (Muhlenberg Central)
Wallace Ray Martin (Drakesboro Community)
Gary McDonald (Greenville)
R.C. McElwain (Dunmor/Hughes-Kirk)
Ricky Minton (Hughes-Kirk)
Jimmy Mitchell (Drakesboro)
Glen Mohon (Dunmor)
T. Morgan (Hughes-Kirk)
Roger Nelson (Bremen)
Rondal "Tookie" Nelson (Bremen)
Roger Newman (Greenville)
T.R. Newman (Greenville)
Nat Nofsinger (Greenville)
Steve Peterson (Greenville)
Shelby Pogue (Hughes-Kirk)
Don Raymer (Muhlenberg Central)
Eddie Rhodes (Drakesboro)
Joe Richardson (Hughes-Kirk)
Johnny Roark (Graham)
Mike Roll (Greenville)
Joe Roop (Drakesboro)
Jerry Shanks (Muhlenberg Central)
Curtis Shelton (Drakesboro Community)
Larry Sparks (Greenville)
Thomas Stokes (Greenville)
Dale Todd (Drakesboro)
Reggie Warford (Drakesboro)
Tommy Warman (Drakesboro)
Denny Wester (Drakesboro)
Jim Williams (Graham)
Leroy "Kilroy" Willis (Drakesboro Community)

About the Author

Central City native Tom Wallace is the award-winning author of five mysteries featuring Lexington, Kentucky Detective Jack Dantzler, including his most recent, *The Fire of Heaven*. Other Dantzler mysteries include *The List, Gnosis, The Devil's Racket* and *What Matters Blood*. He also wrote the thriller, *Heirs of Cain*.

In 2010, Tom's novel, *Gnosis*, won the prestigious Claymore Award at the Killer Nashville Writers' Conference. *Gnosis* would go on to become one of the most downloaded e-books on Amazon in 2013. In 2007, *The Devil's Racket* also took home a top prize, capturing the Mystery Novel Award.

A graduate of Western Kentucky University's outstanding Journalism Department, Tom spent many years as a successful sportswriter in his native Kentucky. From 1983-86, he served as sports editor for the *Gleaner* in Henderson, where he twice was honored by the Kentucky Press Association for writing the best sports story in the state.

From 1986 until 1993, Tom worked for the legendary broadcaster, Cawood Ledford, serving as editor for *Cawood on Kentucky*, a weekly publication covering UK basketball and football. During that time, Tom also wrote many of Cawood's TV and radio commentaries. He also helped put together and write *Cawood's Comments*.

As a free-lance writer, Tom has authored eight sports-related books, among them the highly popular *Kentucky Basketball Encyclopedia*, an in-depth history of the University of Kentucky's legendary hoops program. He has also written books with former Wildcats Travis Ford and Jeff Sheppard. In addition to those books, Tom and the late John McGill wrote *Embracing the Legend* with former UCLA coach Jim Harrick.

Tom, a Vietnam vet, is an active member of Mystery Writers of America and the Author's Guild. He and his wife, Marilyn, live in Lexington. His website is www.tomwallacenovels.com.

Index

D

I

J

K

S

T

KENTUCKY BASKETBALL BOOKS
by Acclaim Press

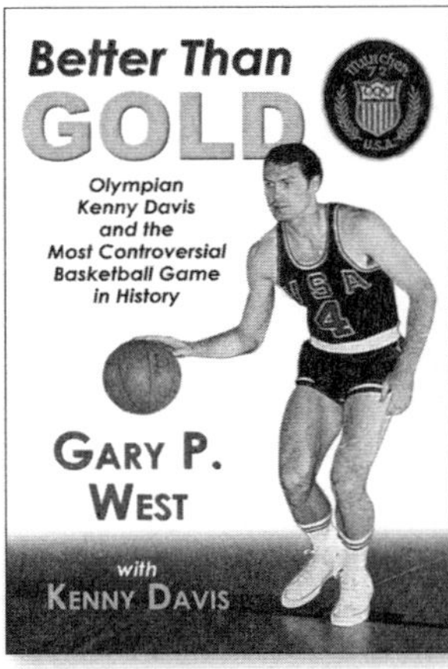

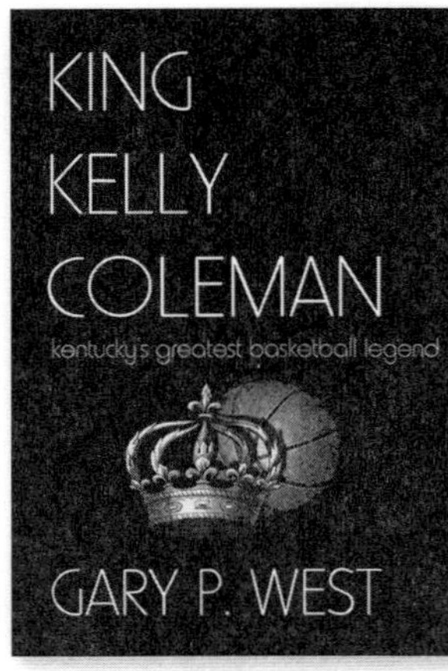

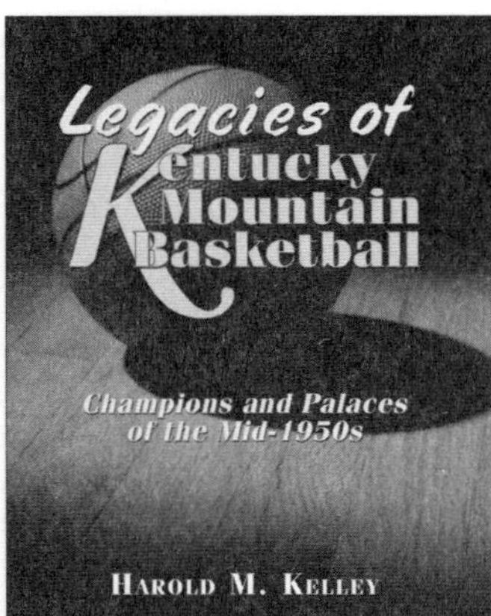

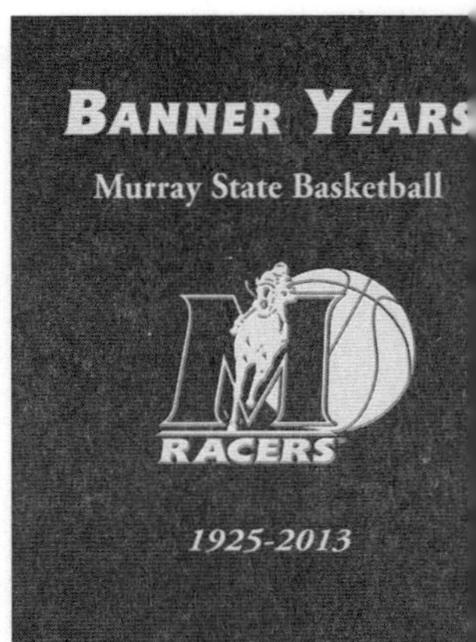